JACK WOOD
One Life

From Barnsley then through the war to the
Palestine Police Force and after

First Published in Great Britain in 2006 by Tucann Books
Text © Jack Wood
All rights reserved
Design © TUCANN*design&print*

ISBN Nº 1 873257 66 X

Produced by: TUCANN*design&print*, 19 High Street, Heighington Lincoln LN4 1RG
Tel & Fax: 01522 790009
www.tucann.co.uk

Chapter 1

There is a beautiful village called "Ash-vale", it nestles at the foot of a range of hills known as the "Hogs Back" and these hills run through part of the county of Surrey. Many years ago this village was very different indeed. There were very few houses, and no purpose built roads, only well trodden cart tracks.

There was one particular stone built cottage at the end of what could be called the main street. It had large gardens on three sides, at the front was a small garden with a gate which opened out onto this street and all the outside walls of the cottage were painted white, it being aptly named "White Cottage", and very distinguished looking it was too. And so in the early hours of the morning of the 11th day of March in the year 1922 I opened my eyes for the first time upon this great big wonderfully mysterious World. The family who lived there were very close friends of my Mother's. She had gone to see them intending to pay them a visit and then return home to my Father in Pirbright but she hadn't reckoned with my impatience to put in an appearance. My Mother was born in the county of Norfolk, but spent most of her working life in Surrey. She worked as a fully qualified childrens' nurse: a Nanny. Having employment with a number of the landed gentry, and consequently lived in some very glamorous households. She was elegant, well educated, very reserved, and spoke softly and correctly. She was one of five children. Her maiden name was Jessie Lillian Hipkin. In 1921 she met and married my Father.

Jessie Lillian (Jack's mum) At Ruffwood College in Farnham near Gilford after recovering from rheumatic fever 1917

He was born in a coal mining village in the county of Yorkshire, some three miles outside the market town of Barnsley. He was also part of a large family, being one of six children, with four brothers and one sister. His name was Benjamin Wood. He was well educated, commencing and completing his education at the school in the village of Worsbrough. He left school at the age of twelve, and started work straight away at Barrow Colliery where he took a job working underground driving a pit pony pulling tubs through the workings. At sometime

3

during the next six years, he progressed to the job of digging out the coal, which was very hard work indeed. One day he asked permission from his parents to join the Police Force but they weren't overjoyed at the idea so when he reached the age of eighteen he joined the Army and went into the 2nd Battalion of the Coldstream Guards. It was while he was serving with them, stationed at Pirbright in Surrey, that he met my Mother. He enjoyed his time in the Guards and talked about it a lot, especially doing the duties at Buckingham Palace, marching between the two sentry boxes outside the Palace gates. He was tall and very smart and always carried himself well. Being brought up in Yorkshire he could have been expected to speak in the local dialect but he didn't. Probably his time in the Army helped him to speak correctly. It is said as a rule that ex-Army men are very strict with their families and I was to find out over the years that he was certainly no exception to the rule. He had signed on for three years and when his time was up, I would have been about two months old. He took Mother and I to live with his parents in the village known as Worsbrough Bridge.

Their cottage type house was in a terrace of four, it being the end one and numbered one Beaumont Terrace. It was stone built and surrounded with gardens belonging to each of the houses. It was situated on the outskirts of the village and on the edge of some beautiful countryside. To reach the terrace you had to leave the main road and turn into a small well used dirt track about 15 yards in length which led to a five barred gate. The occupants of the other houses were, at number two, Dad's elder brother George, his wife Jane, and their daughter May (who would have been about seven years of age at the time). At number three, lived the local policeman, a giant of a man with a large black Walrus moustache. He took his job very seriously and carried it out to the letter. His name was Backhouse, affectionately called "Bobby Backhouse" by the village locals. When I was about eight, he and I had a difference of opinion on one particular subject, but more about that later. At number four, the other end house, lived a dear old lady. I will always remember when I was a little older and able to get about a bit on my own, paying her many visits when she made me feel welcome and provided me with cups of tea, drinks of fizzy lemonade, cakes and biscuits. The thing I remember most of all, were the Cream Crackers, she would smother them in butter, and never seemed to mind the mess I made. I have fond memories of those visits to that lovely lady (Mrs. Coop was her name).

The inside of my Grandparents house was beautifully decorated, spotlessly clean and nicely furnished. Downstairs there was a large living room with two steps leading down into a spacious kitchen. From this kitchen a door opened out onto a small stone-flagged area, from which there was a footpath about one hundred yards long stretching to the end of the back garden. The kitchen appeared to be the focal point of the whole house. In those days the housewife had to work very hard doing all the things necessary to keep

Elijah and Elizabeth with their children John and Annie Wood taken at the Lodge Worsborough Village 1921.

4

the home running on an even keel without the labour saving gadgets we have at the present time.

Most of the people did their own baking and on the days upon which Grandma did her baking, which was usually three days each week, a large part of the kitchen was taken up by large earthenware receptacles. At varying stages all manner of breads, cakes and tarts would be mixed and prepared for the oven. It was a very hot and time consuming job and because of the large number of loaves and oven bottom cakes needed to feed such a large family the kitchen was a hive of activity for quite a few hours. Whilst all this was going on the normal everyday meals also had to be prepared.

In order for all this cooking and baking to be done there was a coal fired cooking range. A truly magnificent piece of equipment which dominated almost the whole of one side of the kitchen. Anyone who might venture too close would soon feel the tremendous amount of heat it produced. The majority of the large amounts of hot water needed each day came from an object known as a "Set Pot" which was unobtrusively positioned in a corner. It had it's own coal fire situated underneath a large round cast iron bowl with a heavy lid and water was retrieved from it by using a ladle. Many gallons of water were also heated on the Yorkshire Range in big cast iron pans.

The floors in both the living room and kitchen were made of stone and were covered with heavy carpets. To clean these carpets they had to be taken outside into the garden and draped over a very thick rope which was suspended between two stout wooden posts, then beaten vigorously with a piece of wood, not unlike a baseball bat in appearance. When as much of the dust as possible had been removed each carpet was given a wash and scrubbed vigorously to remove any stains. After all the carpets had been dealt with a good soak in a hot relaxing bath would have been most welcome but there was no bathroom in the house.

There was a large galvanised bath which had two carrying handles, one at each end, and it would usually be placed in front of the kitchen fire. It would be filled with hot water from the "set-pot" ready to have a good soak. There was no privacy whatsoever, and as this bath was taken in the kitchen it was usually taken at night when everyone else was in bed. Once you had taken the bath that wasn't the end of the problems by any means because the water had to be emptied. This meant using a large ladle to remove it from the bath and pour it down the shallow stone sink, a very slow and tedious process.

As there was no bathroom in the house, there was no toilet either. Provision of a kind was made in the bedrooms by making use of a "Chamber Pot". The toilets were situated in a stone-built building at the end of the dirt road in front of, and to the side of, the terrace.

Another chore which took place about twice a week was the washing. This was another time when the kitchen would be turned upside down. The "Set-Pot" would be going full blast heating the many gallons of water which were going to be needed. There were five main pieces of equipment required, these were two galvanised tubs, a Posse, a rubbing board and a mangle.

One of the Peggy Tubs would be filled with almost boiling water, some washing powder added and the clothes put inside it. The Posse would then be placed inside the tub and by using the handle in a backwards and forwards motion, pull and push fashion, it would swirl the clothes around in the tub. This was extremely hard work. When this had been done many times the Rubbing Board was placed in the tub half in and half out, and an article of clothing from the tub brought up to it and the article in question given a liberal going over with a bar of carbolic soap and rubbed with great vigour up and down the corrugated sheet. It would then be dropped into the other Peggy Tub which had been filled with warm clean water and rinsed thoroughly before being fed through the Mangle rollers. The large cast iron wheel was turned, and water squeezed out of it. One pass through wasn't sufficient. The grub screw would be turned several times making the gap between the rollers smaller every time, and after each turn the article of clothing would be passed through again until all the excess water had been removed.

The next stage would be to hang all the washed clothes somewhere to get dry, in fine weather this was no problem as they would be taken out into the garden and pegged onto long washing lines, but when it was raining they were hung up inside the kitchen. There were some lengths of rope attached to pulleys in the ceiling and when these ropes were manipulated two long timber frames would be lowered. They were about ten feet long and the clothes were draped over these. When all the lengths were full the ropes were manipulated again and the frames returned to their hiding place at the ceiling with the clothes hanging down.

There was very little in the way of entertainment but there was a public house called the Red Lion Hotel just across the road and so the menfolk had no difficulty being entertained during its opening hours. My uncle George, his wife Jane and their daughter May came round very often from next door and sometimes they would take part in an impromptu sing song. Everyone would be seated comfortably in the living room, a song suggested, and it would begin. My aunt Annie, had a nice but powerful voice and during these musical interludes would put it to very good use. She could be heard above them all.

Music was obtained from a Gheisha Gramophone. The records were made of bakelite, very heavy, and 78 revolutions per minute. It was quite a performance preparing things so that we could have some music. The Gramophone itself was a wooden box with a hinged lid, when this lid was lifted it had a turntable underneath. At one side of the box was a handle, this had to be turned in order to wind up the clockwork mechanism which provided the power to turn the turntable. Above the turntable was an arm containing the "Voice Box" which had a small steel needle inserted into it which was held in place with a small retaining screw. The needles had a fairly thick point and would probably play between fifteen and twenty records before having to be replaced. When everything was ready with the mechanism fully wound up and a record put in place, a small lever just inside the box near the arm had to be moved forwards and then the turntable would start to spin. Then was the time to place the needle on the outside edge of the record. The sound came out of two small doors at the front and a large copper trumpet which was attached to the top of the box. It was possible to swivel this trumpet in any direction to project the sound into any part of the room. The music tone side of it wasn't too bad but it sounded a bit "Squawky".

My Father started work at the colliery with his Father and brothers. It must have given Mother quite a shock when she saw them return for the first time after completing their shift, utterly filthy from head to toe with their black faces, and only the whites of their eyes showing through the coal dust. In those days there were no bathing facilities at the pit head and at shift change over times the streets were full of these figures in filthy clothes with their "clogs" making an awful sound as they clanked over the cobblestoned streets and footpaths. These men looked awesome and not a little frightening.

Almost all the area surrounding the village of Worsbrough Bridge was made up of beautiful countryside with fields, hedges, and hundreds of magnificent trees of all shapes and sizes. Beyond the hedge at the bottom of Grandmother's garden there was a field leading up to a small farm which was also a Water Mill. With all these open spaces you could be forgiven for reaching the conclusion that this must have been a healthy place in which to live, how wrong you would be! The fresh air was overpowered by the obnoxious smell coming from the collieries. Each one of them was surrounded by mountainous black "heaps". These were made by the collieries and were known as "slag heaps" (a pile of dirt and particles of coal dust). It was transported from the pit head in large metal buckets which travelled along cables suspended in the air up to a conveyor belt that directed it onto the top of one of these existing heaps. As time progressed the inside of these heaps became so hot they were actually on fire on the inside. This heated up the outsides and this produced an awful smell. It also made a distinct haze which surrounded the area and it wasn't only the immediate area that was affected, it engulfed places many miles away. I did part of my growing up here and it seemed to me as if it was "dusk" all the time.

With all the things going on in the household which must have been entirely foreign to my Mother I do wonder what she must have been thinking during our stay there. It must have been very hard to come to a strange place in which everything was so much out of character to what she had been used to. How she did come to terms with all those hard and difficult situations I shall never know but come to terms with them she did. I never once heard her complain about being brought to this most unhealthy grimy place. My Grandfather brought my Grandmother to this place many years before and I am sure she must have had the same feelings and had to cope with things very similar to those my Mother was experiencing. Of one thing I am certain, she would have helped her in many ways.

Dad's parents were married in a place called Darley Bridge in the county of Derbyshire, on the 19th of October 1889. Grandmother was born in Derbyshire and her Christian names were, Elizabeth Ann. She had been in service from a very early age, the majority of her time was spent doing the duties of Cook. She was a wonderful person, and although she had to work hard bringing up her family she was always pleasant and cheerful and spoke quietly, and correctly. She was well educated and had knowledge of a great many things. If anything at all was proving difficult for any member of the family it was to Grandma they would turn and it was usually solved to everyone's satisfaction. Her pantry was always full of excellent food, most of it home made. They were all marvellous, but the most wonderful things that stay in my memory were the large and so beautifully decorated Christmas Cakes. She would stand them in the middle of the table looking so resplendent with the mince pies, jam tarts, pork pies and all manor of goodies that go towards making a wonderful Christmas party. It was extremely difficult to take my eyes off them

My Grandfather came from the county of Yorkshire. His name was Elijah Wood. He worked in the coal mines all the working days of his life and was a typical Yorkshireman and most definitely a rough and ready type of person. He was tall, well built and always carried himself well. He had a large black moustache and the clothes he wore were nearly always dark in colour along with the traditional peaked cap. To me he was awesome. I never got to know him very well as I would only have been about seven when he died, but I got the distinct impression on the few occasions I found myself in his company that he only just "tolerated"

7

me. Maybe I am being a little unfair to him because we never had enough time to really get to know one another, he would join in all the games and sing-songs but didn't appear to show a great deal of enthusiasm so there is no way I could have known what he was thinking.

The first child born to my Grandparents was a boy they named George Frederick, on the 24th of July 1891. I always got on very well with him even when I was very young and he gave me a nickname which caused quite a bit of amusement, he would tap me gently on the head and call me "Georgie Bud". I believe he had a rough life although his wife, my Aunt Jane, took very good care of him after they were married but he did have many traumatic experiences during the Great War (World War One), he was in the army and was sent to France where he saw action in the trenches. He spent the majority of his life working underground in the coal mines. After him came John Bonsal, he was born on the 30th of April 1896 and he and I had some good times together especially after he got married, which was quite late on in his life. He was also in the army during the war. Then came Charles Henry, born on the 13th of August 1899, I regret to say I never knew him as he died in his early teens. Then my Father arrived, named simply Benjamin. He was born on the 24th of July 1901. Then for a change a girl arrived named Annie Elizabeth, she was born on June the 13th 1903. And finally on the 24th of March, 1905, William was born, and once again I wasn't to have the pleasure of knowing him as he also died in his early teens. My Aunt Annie was inclined to be a bit hard, and gave the impression she was always looking for faults in people. She had her own strong opinions about almost everything and I found it hard to relax in her presence. She was a very hard worker and learned everything she could from her Mother and became almost as proficient in all subjects.

And now to my Mother's family. I am not in possession of any of the dates upon which her family was born I do know however that Mum was born on the 6th of March. Her Father was practically brought up in the Army and he served many years in the Royal Norfolk Regiment achieving the prestigious rank of Regimental Sergeant Major. He was obviously a strict disciplinarian. I never spent much time with him but the little I did made me very impressed with everything about him. He did have an air of authority stamped all over him. My Mum's Mother, was apparently very similar to her in a great many aspects, she was elegant, well educated, reserved, and well spoken, but I never saw her as she died when Mum was very young. Mother's eldest sister was called Gladys. She met and married a British soldier named Ernest and they emigrated to Canada where they built up a large beef cattle farm. They had a family of one girl, Sheila, and one boy, Raymond. What exactly happened after many years out there I am not sure but it appears they were doing very well until one year there was a long continuous period when everything around them was snowed under, they were unable to get supplies of fodder to the thousands of cattle that were spread out over an extremely large area, and consequently the majority did not survive. Absolutely overcome with the tragedy they returned to England in 1936 and started a completely new life in Norwich. After Gladys came the eldest boy in the family he was called Arthur, but went mostly by the name of Sonny, he was a very pleasant person but inclined to keep himself very much to himself. All Mother's family lived in or around Norwich and I didn't have many opportunities to go so far afield during my early years, which was a great pity really. Her younger brother Edward, nicknamed Ted, was someone very special to me. Both he and Sonny spent many years in the same army regiment as their Father, and served many years abroad (most of them in India). Last but not least the baby of the family was Eileen. She was a very nice unassuming lady.

It should be quite plain to you that life was very different indeed, even attending school had its drawbacks. Before the advent of a "free" primary school education the Wesleyan Day School, affectionately known as the "Tin School", situated at the rear of St. James Church in Worsbrough Bridge, was one where all the children had to pay one penny for the privilege of attending for one week.

To go from one place to another people walked, but there were services offered by horse drawn wagonette, and in 1902 the Barnsley and District Electric Traction Company Ltd was inaugurated. They began to run a tramway service from Barnsley to Worsbrough Bridge or to Worsbrough Dale and there were twelve trams serving these two routes.

Ernest and Gladys Wright, Jack's mum's sister

Jack's mum's brother Ted. Herbert Edward Hipkin, Norwich and Norfolk Regiment taken in India

Herbert Reginald, Sergeant Major Hipkin, Jack's mum's dad

Chapter 2

My parents and I stayed at Beaumont Terrace for almost two years. Then we moved to a council house in a village called Ward Green, and it was about one mile away from my Grand-parent's home. The house itself was almost new, standing in a road known as Napier Mount with a number of other semi-detached houses. It had a small front garden and a reasonable sized one at the rear. The living room had a coal fireplace, the kitchen a gas cooker, and there were two bedrooms with a coal fireplace in each. The lighting was by gas and there were brass fittings in all the rooms, and in these fittings were gas mantles. The toilet was built into the house, but the door to it was on the outside so to get to it you had to go out of the back door, turn right and it was on the corner. The cooking and baking would be much easier; just a turn of a knob and the heat was there; the bathing facilities were the same but the water could be heated on the cooker and poured into the bath in its position in front of the fire. The Lighting for the road outside was taken care of by the council, they employed a man who would come round every evening before it got dark to light the lamps. These lamps were almost as high as the ones we have nowadays. The effect wasn't brilliant but at least it was much better than having to find your way round in total darkness. Every morning, very early, the Lamplighter would come back and turn them off.

It was only a short walk to Grandmother's house and we went there quite often. When the weather was nice we would go for walks around the area. Usually we were accompanied by other members of the family, my aunts and uncles, and when May wasn't at school she would come along too. I particularly liked the walks through the park, it was so peaceful and pretty with the large expanse of grass, and the large trees. We would walk up one field and when we arrived at the top we would climb over a style and go into the village of Worsbrough. The menfolk in our party would then call at the Edmunds Arms, public house. The ladies in our party would stroll around until the menfolk had quenched their thirst and then we would start the return journey home over the style and down through the park. When I was about three I had a very nice navy "Sailor Suit" of which I was very proud, complete with hat and the navy blue and white collar that draped over the back of my shoulders. I was told that on one such walk we were coming back down this field when someone thought it would be a good idea to let me have a run on my own. Up to that point in time I did have to be holding someone's hand when we were out on these jaunts. For the first time I was free! I took off, with cousin May trying to keep up behind me. Then my front boot landed at the beginning of a sloppy cow pat . It slid through it at the same time my rear end hit the floor. From the heels of my boots to the back of my hat I was no longer a nice shiny navy blue and white only a smelly mixture of slimy brown and green. When things had settled down one of my hands was somewhat gingerly grasped with arms outstretched, the other members of the party keeping a respectful distance, and we made our way back home. We had many lovely walks to various parts of the surrounding countryside but until I became much older it was always a case of, "Hold my hand, or we will go straight back home, cow pats, or no cow pats!".

I would have been nearly four when my aunt Annie married a young man named Harold Roebuck. He was a farm labourer and when my aunt used to take me to see him at his place of work I did really enjoy myself. He was employed at the farm owned by the colliery where Dad worked and I was fascinated with the animals, of which there were many. Horses, Cows, dogs, and even cats. I was never in a hurry to leave there and spent hours climbing the hay and straw barns. I was to become very much involved with uncle Harold and we became close friends. He had a powerful "Bass" voice and he, along with Annie, became active members of the local church choir. He was also a welcome addition to the sing-songs whenever they took place.

We were all having a really nice time in our council house, with Dad working regularly we had quite a good standard of living and everything seemed set for us to settle down here. It was not to be, because in 1926, just two years after we had moved in, came the General Strike. Everyone stopped working and no-one knew how long this state of affairs would continue. We had no money coming in from anywhere and the amount of food we had stored would soon run out. After a few weeks the whole house became extremely cold as our supply of coal had run out. So, very early one morning, Dad got a hessian sack, a strong shopping bag, a small copper shovel, and with me dressed in a warm coat, a couple of cardigans and some gloves, he and I set off down the road. He told me we were going to a slag heap near the mine where he worked to pick some coal.

The outside covering of the heap was so thin that anyone walking on it would be in great danger of falling through into the fire itself. Everyone knew it was unsafe and punishable but very few took any notice. With the strike being on many people found themselves in the same predicament, so when we arrived it was a hive of activity. We started from the bottom working our way up selecting pieces of coal, the bigger the piece the better and these were put into the sack but it was a slow process.

I had been very firmly instructed not to stray too far away from Dad so that he could grab me if I got into any difficulty. The smell was awful but gradually the sack began to fill. Dad wasn't carrying it anymore, just dragging it behind him. Very soon he stopped and tied the neck of the sack tightly. He hadn't filled it to the top as it would have been much too heavy to carry if he had done, he then took the shovel and used it to put some of the black dust which was all around into the shopping bag. Then we were off back down the heap. For me it wasn't before time either as the smell had started to make me feel sick. All my pockets were full of decent sized pieces and as I was only tiny I began to feel very tired on the way back. It would have been almost three miles. When we eventually reached home the sack was emptied into the coal house, a fire lit in the living room, and soon the house began to feel warm.

Some of the dust from the shopping bag was put into a bucket and a few hands full of cement were added to the bucket with enough water to make a paste when the dust and cement were mixed together. A handful of this paste was picked up and rolled into a ball. As each one was rolled it was placed on newspaper in front of the fire to dry and when they were they could then be used in place of coal. They kept the fire going and gave out a reasonable amount of heat but they were no good at all for lighting it, coal had to be used for that. Wood for lighting the fire was also in short supply. A way of getting round this was to collect some newspapers and fold them in a certain way. During the following months quite a few trips were made to the heap enabling us to have fires.

Things were pretty bad all over the country in so far as food was concerned and they became so bad that the government arranged for "soup kitchens" to be set up. They were operated in small establishments in villages. The one in Ward Green was in a fish and chip shop and when it was "soup" day all three of us went to this shop and joined the queue. I had been given three of our aluminium pudding basins to take with me and when we eventually reached the counter I handed over these basins and a ladle of soup was poured into each one. I was given one chunk of bread for each of them. The allocation was one bowl of soup and one chunk of bread for each member of the household, that is why we all had to attend to show how many we were. Dad was far from pleased at what he called, "going out with a begging bowl" but he knew how necessary it was to obtain all three portions so he suffered. Many years later when this subject was being discussed I found out that I had been given almost all of the soup and a large amount of the bread. I know that all three portions put together didn't amount to much but I am sure I should not have been given all of them. Things all round got very much worse so Dad decided he had better do something about it. He heard there were some jobs going at the post office, he arranged an interview and got the job. He started work at once in the small town of Wombwell about six miles from Barnsley and about the same distance from Ward Green. To get there, and back, he had to walk through fields, along the canal bank, under and over railway bridges, then along about one mile of roadways when he reached the outskirts of the town. It wouldn't have been an easy journey at any time and considering the early start he had to make travelling all that way in the dark more often than not it would have been hazardous to say the least. After two weeks we had money once again and very soon things were back to normal.

He made those journeys for a few months until one day he came home with the good news that he had managed to find somewhere for us to live in Wombwell. We were going to be sorry at having to leave our council house because apart from those awful times during the strike we had been very happy there.

We took up residence in our new home, and all the time we seemed to be comparing it to the one we had been forced to leave. It was certainly different and at first sight, not for the better either. We would have to make the best of it. The house itself was one in a terrace of five and situated in a street which was a cul-de-sac with a very high wall at the end of it. There were houses both sides of the street and it wasn't very wide. It had no gardens and the front door opened out onto the street with two steps down to the pavement. At the rear was an asphalted yard about twenty yards in depth and forty yards wide, the width stretching the full length of the five houses. Across this yard were the toilets, which were shared between the houses. Sharing a toilet wasn't very nice at all. In most other aspects it was very similar to the council house with two rooms downstairs, kitchen and living room, and two bedrooms upstairs, but they were all smaller.

The town was very spread out with pockets of streets and houses all around. The actual shopping area was quite small with a high street containing a number of shops and one street leading off it with a few more larger stores on one side. A market was held in an area behind the shops, it was well attended and it could be said it was the focal point of the town. All in all it didn't appear to be a bad place in which to live.

We were now quite a long way from my grandparents home. There were two ways available for us to go there, we could either walk, or take a double decker tram. These trams, ran on two metal lines which were embedded in the middle of the road, and were powered by a pole attached to the top of the tram which was spring loaded enabling it to push up to an electric cable fixed above the lines. They didn't roll along the road they jerked their way along. I suppose they were fitted with some kind of springs to make the ride comfortable, but this was certainly not evident when you were riding on them as the seats were not well padded. On a short journey it felt as if you had acquired more than your fair share of bumps and bruises by the time you came to get off. The trip from Wombwell to Worsbrough Bridge meant having to travel six miles to Barnsley then change trams to catch one to Worsbrough Bridge which could see you waiting again for that one. We didn't use this option very much; only if the weather was unkind, and besides it cost money.

Even though it was a good six miles for us to walk we did this more often than not. There were two ways we could go and they were both very pleasant routes. One of them meant staying on the roads all the time, we would leave the house and walk about one mile before arriving at the beginning of Wombwell Wood, it had a road running through it and after travelling for another mile along this road we would leave it and turn right over a railway crossing, usually having a word or two with the crossing keeper who would stick his head out of the signal box window, then go down a tree lined lane which was a very steep slope where there was a railway bridge over the road, this slope levelled off after about one hundred yards and then began to rise sharply as it went over another level crossing and then still going uphill it went over a canal bridge, and having passed that the lane widened out into a decent road with houses on both sides and a footpath. At the beginning of this road on the left hand side was a farm. The road then took us to the Tram terminus at the bottom of Worsbrough Dale. We would then turn left and take the road which after about a mile would bring us out only a couple of hundred yards from the entrance to Beaumont Terrace, our destination. It was an interesting journey with plenty of unusual things to look out for most of the way and I never once got bored during any one of those walks. There was very little traffic on the roads except for maybe a farmer's horse and cart, or a pony and trap, and it was a long way, but if I became too tired Dad would give me a "piggy back" ride. Mum wasn't all that robust and I don't think walking was her favourite pastime but she managed very well. Dad of course was in his element. He would say, "Pick your feet up they will put themselves down".

When the weather was exceptionally nice, instead of walking along the road when we reached the beginning of the wood we would branch off and walk through it. This was always fascinating for me with Dad telling me the names of most of the trees and showing me which berries were suitable to eat, like the wild raspberries and the purple bilberries. He knew the names of a great many of the birds we saw and pointed them out to me as they flew around. I had a special liking for the linnet with it's haunting song and the way it made it tail off at the end as if it was flying away out of sight when in actual fact it could be seen sitting in a tree or bush quite close by. We would push our way through the shrubbery taking care not to make contact with the brambles. There were times when we disturbed a pheasant or a partridge and heard their cries of alarm echoing through the trees as they flew into the air. There were many squirrels and they always seemed so busy all the time, but they were very timid and would always scurry away and seek refuge in some tall tree if they thought we were getting a little too close. Sometimes we would see a weasel or a stoat, but it was only a fleeting glimpse as they disappeared into the undergrowth.

The route to my grandparents' house that I favoured most was where we took the shortest route to Worsbrough Bridge through all the fields. We would leave the house and go past the small park at the top of the street which contained a couple of swings, a see-saw, a nice long slide, and a roundabout. After passing the park we crossed a road and entered the first of the many fields we were to negotiate during the next hour or so, going under a small bridge and under an exceptionally long and high viaduct. Plenty of wildlife was to be seen in these fields, there were rabbits, hares, mice and voles. I shall always remember the first mole I saw. It looked so small and harmless but it was to prove that looks can be deceptive because when I managed to catch it and was holding it in one hand, intending to stroke it, it wriggled so much that I ended up holding it only by it's tale, it immediately swivelled it's tiny head round, sank it's very sharp teeth in, and took a firm grip of the end of my little finger. The little blighter hung on and didn't half take some dislodging. On the odd occasion we had a glimpse of a Fox as it ran across a field. The mice, moles, and voles, had to be aware of everything around them, and not only on the ground as the air was a place where danger could be upon them like a flash of lightning. I refer to the hawk. It would glide gracefully around, appearing to be unconcerned with all that was going on but when it's exceptional vision spotted some movement below it would remain perfectly still except for the beating of it's wings, until suddenly it would swoop down, it's long sharp claws grasping at some unsuspecting little animal and fly away to a tree branch where it could enjoy an undisturbed meal.

After we had negotiated the fields and the fences, we would come out underneath the bank of the canal and scramble up onto the tow path (the footpath at the edge of the water). There were many different specimens of fish in the canal and it sometimes took ages waiting for one particular type to show itself so that it's identifying marks could be pointed out. I found it hard to believe there could be so many different types in one stretch of water, but I had an advantage over the children of today because the canals and waterways were so much cleaner. On a fine day the bottom was clearly visible and the fish could easily be seen even when they were a long way down. Sometimes we would have to move off the towpath to allow it to be used for the purpose for which it was made, that is, "towing a barge". A man would be walking with a strong looking horse and it had a number of chains and ropes attached to it's harness. These were fastened somewhere at the front of the barge. Both horse and man appeared to be taking a leisurely stroll along the path, but there were occasions when the horse could be seen to "dig it's toes in " and strain a bit. These barges looked to be very heavy as they were low down in the water, laden with such things as coal, corn, timber, and other goods suitable for them to carry. The canal widened out into what was known as the "Basin" and came to an end only about one hundred yards from the five barred gate at the entrance to my Grandparents home where I was ready for a rest!

I quickly realised there were quite a few children living in and around our street and a lot of them played in the yard behind our house. At this stage I had been told I could go into the yard but I must not venture any farther afield as I was still only four years of age. I had only been allowed to go into the back garden of the council house but as there had been no other

14

children around I had been on my own all the time so I had no knowledge of the kind of games children played in a group. I had to learn how to mix and join in. I soon got the hang of 'Hide and Seek' and 'Kick Can'. These were good fun, extremely noisy, but good fun all the same. "Rounders" was a game even the adults used to play, and when they did we children were expected to keep well away from the yard when it was progress. Of course there were the games in which I could not take part until I had acquired the items which were necessary in order to compete. Nearly all my playmates had little string bags which contained anything up to fifty glass "marbles", some of these were very attractive with lines running through the middle of them and each line of a different colour. There were many ways to play a game with them and all very competitive. The one that was played the most was carried out between the edge of the footpath and the road, the "gutter". The first player would roll his marble along the gutter in any way he chose and then the second player would roll his and try to make contact with it. If he was fortunate enough to do so then that marble became his, but the second player could not roll his marble as he chose it had to be "Filliped". In order to perform this the marble had to be placed on the nail of the thumb which was resting on the bent forefinger between the first and second joints, then slightly easing the thumb backwards and immediately pushing the nail into the finger and flick upwards, this would then cause the marble to be propelled forwards (hopefully), and if the aim and speed were correct a hit could be expected. I couldn't play until I had wheedled a few pennies from Mum to buy a bag and a reasonable number of marbles.

Another terrific game was with "cigarette cards". They came in the packets of certain brands of cigarette, one in each pack. They were colourful and depicted all kinds of sport, or birds, animals, and flowers, and each subject had a collectable number. I cannot remember all the different types but there were many. If you knew someone who smoked then it was quite easy to obtain them but my Dad smoked a pipe so no cigarette cards would be coming my way from that quarter and Mum didn't smoke. However some newsagents sold packs of cards. When I became aware of this it only took a very short while for me to convince my Mum that it would be an unthinkable state of affairs, if, for the sake of only a few pennies, I was going to be the odd one out every time a game of cigarette cards was played! She was very understanding and saw the logic in my explanation and decided to help me out. Suitably armed I went into the yard and enquired about the rules of the game. Apparently it could be played in various ways and having first tried a few I found the one I liked the best. For this, it meant one player would stand one of his cards up against a wall with the bottom resting on the ground and the top leaning against it at an angle, each of the participants would stand behind a line drawn on the floor about six feet away from the wall, and taking it in turns, would hold one of his cards between his first and second fingers and skim it towards the one standing up in an attempt to knock it over. When someone was successful and managed to skittle it he would then collect all the cards that were on the floor from all the previous unsuccessful attempts. It wasn't easy and there could be quite a lot of cards on the floor when success was achieved so It was also possible to lose a lot at this game which made it very competitive.

On school days I was the only child left in the street so I made good use of the opportunity to get some practice in at these games. I became so engrossed in these activities that I was reluctant to wash and change in order to accompany Mum on shopping expeditions, even though I did like going round the shops when on most days I would get a few sweets. One shop I always looked forward to visiting was called "Liptons", it was very clean and bright with a refreshing smell of dairy produce. I had found a way to amuse myself while Mum was waiting to be served. The shop floor was made up of small shiny tiles and to prevent people slipping it was always covered with clean sawdust. I would go to the door, take a run, and slide towards the bottom counter taking most of the sawdust with me causing it to pile up at this counter. On a good day I could get quite a few nice slides in before I was "politely requested" to "Pack It In". After leaving the shop I was always admonished by Mum, but I considered it to be worth it.

When the boys and girls came home from school and had had their tea, we would all meet up in the yard. When it got dark early they would all move out into the street where there were lights, but I wasn't allowed to go into the street. It was almost six months before I was allowed to go into the street so until then there was nothing I could do but to conform and wait.

CHAPTER 3

There was very little to do at home during the long winter evenings, we would have tea and a couple of hours later I was shipped off to bed but sometimes during those two hours if we began to feel a little peckish Mum would cut a few slices from a loaf of bread and we would toast them in front of the fire, and about twice a week a chap would call selling "pikelets" (the original crumpets), and these were given the same treatment. The coal fire would be raked and worked on so that it had all the glowing embers at the front to give out plenty of heat and no smoke which would turn the slices of bread and the pikelets into a nice golden brown, and when a nob of butter had been applied they tasted smashing.

When Mum was indulging in her favourite hobby, knitting, I would spend a lot of time looking out of the front window or having a go at copying out some letters of the alphabet she had written down for me. I much preferred scribbling on the sheet of paper or using a colouring book but I was informed that learning to make nice pictures had its uses but knowing how to write was really more important.

We all had cardigans, pullovers, gloves, bobble hats, and socks, which Mum had knitted and they were very welcome, especially during the winter. When these socks developed a hole in them they were not discarded; in those days they were darned, using a special mushroom shaped piece of wood and some of the same colour wool. I had a swimming costume for over twenty five years that Mum made for me when I was about eleven, and as it was made of wool it stretched as I grew. She was an excellent knitter but there were also many articles she made from crochet work.

I liked sweets, although I didn't have them often as our financial circumstances didn't allow it, but there was a little shop at the corner of our street where for a hapenny I could get two ounces of chocolate chewing nuts, and for another hapenny a gobstopper of reasonable sized proportions which could last a long time if it was sucked slowly. One particular type of sweet was very popular not only was it a nice tasting bar of toffee, it had another attraction. It was double wrapped and care had to be taken removing these wrappers because slotted in between them was a small square piece of paper which had a letter of the alphabet printed on one side of it and on the other side it was gummed like a postage stamp. These letters were feverishly collected and exchanged. The reason for all this was that the letters in the wrappers had to be used to make up the names of football teams, but there were only a certain number of teams eligible, these were printed on a leaflet you could get in the sweet shop along with a strip of cardboard which had a square for each letter to be stuck on. Exactly how many squares were on the strip I am not sure but I know there were at least five as one of the teams was Leeds, and sometimes this could be difficult to obtain as the letter "E" seemed to be one the manufacturer kept in reserve and only released it on the odd occasion. Collecting these letters was exciting and once you had obtained the full name of a team and stuck it onto the strip you would walk to the shop with your completed card, present it joyfully to the shopkeeper, who would hand over one bar of toffee, with another letter inside, without you having to pay. This was really something.

It could get very depressing in winter when it was extremely cold and snowed hard for long periods, sometimes there would be drifts as high as ten feet in and around the towns and the roads and footpaths could have a deep covering, but we very rarely had the difficulties most people experience today because the local councils were organised. If it looked as if there could be problems they would send for gangs of men to deal with it and they would clear the footpaths and some roads, then apply salt and grit even while the snow was still falling. Anyone who was unemployed, able and receiving unemployment payments knew that if their services were required to clear snow or any other task needing to be done urgently they had to make themselves available in order for them to continue receiving unemployment benefit. I believe they received some kind of payment when they were called out, in addition to the normal benefit.

The frosts were hard and prolonged causing plenty of burst water pipes but it wasn't all doom and gloom as one type of entertainment came into it's own at these times. The frosts penetrated deep into the rivers and canals forming a thick covering of ice which proved very suitable for varying sports, especially Ice Skating. Dad had a pair of skates which he fastened to his boots with leather straps. He would come home from work one afternoon, have his dinner, and ask Mum to dress me in warm clothes, hang the skates over his shoulder, and together we would walk the half mile or so to the canal. When we arrived at the canal he would sit on the bank and put the skates on, then step out onto the ice and "glide" off. He was a very good skater and it wasn't long before he was out of sight round a bend in the canal and until he returned I amused myself by sliding around in my boots. However, there was one time when things didn't go according to plan. I hadn't been feeling very well for a few days so to help keep the bitterly cold winds at bay Mum had fortified me with an extra large bowl of very hot bread and milk before we left home, as well as the dreaded cod liver oil and malt earlier in the day. When Dad was struggling to put his skates on I was standing just behind him, looking over his shoulder but this time I wasn't feeling very well at all and I really couldn't help it when suddenly the contents of my stomache came up and out all over him, on his jacket, down the back of his head and neck, and inside his shirt. He exclaimed something (which I don't care to remember). He had just managed to fasten the skates on so he stood up, stepped out onto the ice, and set off along the canal like a madman. He was gone a long time but he had got it all out of his system because he was exceptionally calm when he did get back.

Yorkshire has always been noted for it's Working Mens' Club entertainments and there was something going off in at least one of them in our area every night, singers, dancers, comedians etc; they also had afternoon parties for families which we attended sometimes. I always looked forward to going when I was told there was one on, but I do have a vivid recollection of one such party that I didn't enjoy one little bit. There were a lot of people present including children of all ages. Everyone sat down at long dining tables loaded with food. There were buns, cakes, sandwiches, plates of boiled ham, eggs, tomatoes, in fact everything needed to provide a very good feed. It was a case of help yourself from each of the plates as they passed by on their way to another part of the table. I put a number of things on my plate and started to eat when someone, I don't know who, put a round red thing about the size of an egg on my plate. I had no idea what it was but eventually I decided to try it, I cut a reasonably sized piece off it, put it in my mouth, tasted it, and immediately spat it out onto my plate, it had tasted horrible. Now, table manners and etiquette were the hallmark of meal times at home and if I ever transgressed in any way I was made aware of it quickly and in no uncertain terms. I knew as soon as I had forcibly removed that piece of whatever it was from my mouth that I was in trouble. The tirade I expected from Dad didn't come, even though he was sitting straight across from me, instead he leaned over towards me and put another three of the red objects on my plate and, together with the one I had already started on, he cut them all into thin round slices explaining as he did so that this was called "beetroot" and that it was healthy food and good for me. Then he handed me a slice of bread and butter and said "Eat". The way he said it told me that I was going to have to eat it whether I liked it or not, so I took my fork and picked up one thin circle, put it in my mouth, took a bite of bread, chewed for as short a time as possible, and swallowed, then repeated the process. It took time but eventually it was all gone. I was feeling awful and took no further part in any of the festivities and when we arrived home I received a strong reprimand. Since that day I have never touched the stuff!

It wasn't Christmas and it wasn't my birthday but one day I received a wonderful present, a little dog. I was told it was a Yorkshire Terrier about six months old and I was invited to give him a name of my choice. Many suggestions were forthcoming from my parents, I studied them all, and named him, "Mick". He was only small, with two tiny ears, a short stubby tail, and a sharp pointed face, and with him being nearly all white with brown and black patches he looked very attractive. The first time he gave his lungs an airing by barking it was so loud for such a small dog that it frightened the life out of all of us bit it meant he would certainly let us know if there was anyone around. We soon got on well together, a nice collar and a long lead were purchased but I was too small to hold him on my own because he was very strong and when I had been allowed to try it if one of my parents hadn't been there to grab the lead he would have dragged me along the ground behind him!

About this time it was decided we would have a daily newspaper delivered, it was called the "Daily Herald" a paper which was said to support the working class and the Labour Party, and Dad was a staunch Labour man. It was arranged that on the first Friday evening after the deliveries had been made for one week the newsagent would call for payment, he duly arrived and was promptly greeted by Mick. A very noisy greeting, but once the man was in the house and the door closed, Mick stopped barking after Dad had told him to "shut op". A short conversation ensued, the payment was made, and the man moved towards the door when Mick started his noise again and began darting in and out, snarling and snapping at his ankles and grabbing his trouser bottoms. Despite all our efforts to calm things down Mick wasn't having any until the man took a sweet bag from his pocket and from inside he took two or three small round brown things and dropped them on the floor at his feet whereupon Mick investigated and promptly gobbled them up. The man explained that they were "aniseed balls", he liked them and always carried some around with him as he had heard that animals, especially dogs, liked them as well. It had done the trick as Mick had eaten them and was now stretched out in front of the fireplace. The paper man left after receiving profound apologies from Mum and Dad, and that he could come into the house every Friday evening, no problems, but he couldn't leave until he had donated some of those aniseed balls to his tormentor. A very small price to pay I suppose in order to ensure his ankles and trouser bottoms remained intact!

When the ban on playing in the street had been lifted after six months or so my life altered dramatically. I had a great time playing all the games and making many new friends which meant I was fully occupied in the evenings and weekends. When my little dog arrived I had plenty to do during the daytimes as well, becoming more and more involved with him. Mum helped a lot by making time to take him for walks with me almost every day and I was beginning to learn how to handle him and how to give him instructions. I was really enjoying myself and was quite prepared for it to carry on indefinitely but sadly that was all going to change. I had reached the age of five and my schooldays were about to begin. Preparations had been going on for quite a few weeks with a considerable amount of shopping having taken place. I had been kitted out with new shorts, cardigans, boots, knee length stockings, shirts, a warm coat, and of course a cap. It had been decided that I should stay at school for lunch so a small leather bag with a strap which went over my shoulder to carry it and another smaller one to fasten to keep it closed was going to hold sandwiches which Mum would prepare each day, along with a small bottle of milk. Both Dad and Mum had been expressing their delight at my inauguration into the world of learning and had tried their very best to impress me with their stories of how much I was going to like it and all the things I should be looking forward to doing; I wasn't so sure. With there being no "Nursery Schools" in those days, I wasn't going to have the benefit of a "panning in" period like the young children of today, I was going in at the "Deep End". Nevertheless, one morning I was dressed in all my finery and found myself walking through the gate into the school playground with Mum. We went into a room where I was handed over to a lady who said she was the headmistress. Mum spoke with her for a while and after giving me a hug and a kiss she left.

I do remember that part of the proceedings fairly well but everything else regarding my first introduction and what was to follow in the next week or so is rather vague. The Headmistress had taken me to a classroom that first day and left me in the charge of a lady teacher who directed me to a double desk with a wooden bench seat which I was to share with another pupil. The classroom seemed to be full of children and there was a blackboard and easel in front of the teacher's desk. As soon as I had settled down we were told to take a pencil and sheet of paper out of the desk and copy what was written on this blackboard, in white chalk were the letters of the alphabet. For the first few days everything was strange and new to me and I spent most of the time trying to keep up with all that was happening but when the blackboard showed the alphabet to be copied for the fourth time in four days I took a stroll to the cloakroom, collected my coat and lunch bag and walked out of the school gate. My departure had been brought about by those three lessons of copying the alphabet. I had copied it so many times at home under the watchful eye of Mum that I knew it all off by heart. Her duties taking care of children had also entailed teaching them to read and write so she knew exactly what was required.

When I went out of the gate I hadn't the faintest idea what I was going to do but at least I was out of that stuffy classroom and free to go wherever I wished. As I had a liking for the park at the top of our street I made my way there and played around on the swings. The slide was good but even that had it's drawbacks with the day being anything but warm. It's metal construction was very cold to my legs and rear end. Then I sat on a swing and ate my sandwiches and drank the milk, after that I walked about a bit in the park to keep warm and as I had no idea of the time I thought I had been here long enough so to make Mum happy I picked a few flowers and went home. I knocked on the door, Mum opened it, I presented her with the flowers and she seemed quite pleased although she did have a funny look on her face. It was half past eleven, and I was home, four and a half hours early. Anyway I had a drink and sat near the fire to restore my very cold limbs and was returned to school to be placed in the hands of a very puzzled teacher. I spent most of the afternoon wondering what Dad would have to say when he got home although I needn't have worried because he never said a word, so Mum must have decided to give me a second chance.

The next morning wasn't too bad we did quite a lot of fairly interesting things and I especially enjoyed the colouring lesson, I had lunch from my little bag but in the afternoon it was back to the alphabet so I took off. It was at this stage when I must have decided that because I had enjoyed my few hours of complete freedom so much I would repeat the performance on a regular basis and I did just that, some days Mum would drop me off in the playground and I would wait until she was out of sight and then make a move. I had sorted out the problem of knowing what time it was by looking through the window of a shop at the top of our street where there was a large clock just inside the door. After a while staying in the park and the two or three fields adjoining it got boring so I decided to take a look around the town. It was much more interesting and I spent a lot of time in the market. But there was something I wasn't aware of, the town was part of my Dad's daily delivery round. After those days I had chosen to abscond, my teacher always informed Mum but she never told Dad. Then one day he came across me looking in some shop window. When the furore calmed a bit he made me follow him around doing the last few deliveries and then took me to see the headmistress who told him of my constant truancy. He left and I stayed until Mum picked me up and I went home and faced the music. Suffice to say I didn't leave school until it was home time ever again. I had to come to terms with it and in the end began, grudgingly, to like it. I was later told that it had taken almost three months before my wanderings came to an abrupt halt.

School photo 1927 - Jack is on the middle row second in from the teacher

Later that same year our walks to my Grandparents' home were altered somewhat as my uncle Harold was promoted and became the manager of the farm where he worked. A house on the farm went with the job so he and my aunt Annie went to live there. We started going to see them fairly regularly as it was quite a bit nearer than going all the way to Worsbrough Bridge. We walked on the road through the wood but instead of turning and going over the railway crossing we had to go straight on up a very steep hill in an area known as Dove Cliff. When we did eventually arrive at the top, totally exhausted, the farm was just over the hill with a short walk down a lane. I always looked forward to going there as I was so interested in everything going on and seeing all the animals.

I have previously stated that I now attended school on a regular basis which is quite true but there were the times when I had no need to go: Like holiday times for instance. I did like the summer holiday and my small pal Mick enjoyed it as much as I did because he was taken for more walks when I was at home. There were other times when I had to be away from school when I was ill and I had all the usual illnesses, Chicken-Pox, Measles, Influenza, Yellow Jaundice, Mumps, and more than my fair share of colds and fevers. At these times I was made to stay in bed and if it was cold a fire would be lit in the bedroom. Occasionally Mum would use this fire to make some toffee as it helped to keep me interested and the end product was always welcome.

Apart from the illnesses and the holidays I was beginning to enjoy school but one evening I made a real mess of things. I was playing in the living room and during the course of one game I tried to knock a hole in the dining table leg with my forehead. I was well aware that I had a reputation of being a "Thick Head" at times but it wasn't "Thick" enough to come off best in an argument with solid timber. I was rushed off to a doctor's surgery with a gaping hole in the centre of my forehead. The doctor stemmed the flow of blood and even though there was a gash some two inches or so in length and the bone was clearly visible he informed my parents that it would be unwise to put any stitches in. When it closed after many weeks of walking about with a large white dressing wrapped around my head I was left with a scar more than an inch wide just below my hair line.

I had looked forward to being allowed out into the street during the daylight hours and eventually I was deemed to be safe enough to join in the games with my pals around our lamp post and for a time I lived up to the faith which was placed in me, but then in what would have been the last few weeks of my fifth year I blotted my copy book. A group of us were playing about in front of the shop at the end of our street. There was a small area where kids would congregate and at one side of this was a low wall around the garden of an adjoining house with iron railings fastened to it. These were about two feet high, patterned and had designs which came to a point at varying intervals, not an exceptionally sharp point but a point nevertheless. I don't have any vivid recollection of how it came about but during a game of climbing on this wall some poor woman had the unenviable task of lifting me bodily from one of these points. She was walking past, saw what had happened and acted on impulse to lift me clear of the point upon which I had impaled myself. I had somehow managed to get it stuck into my throat and because of her swift action had not done any further damage. Once again Mum had an alarming experience, I was carried home and then taken to the doctor's where all the necessary cleaning up operations were carried out. I believe a few stitches were inserted this time. Again there is a scar, a round one this time.

The following year I received a brand new fairy cycle from my parents for my sixth birthday. It was beautifully painted in bright colours with lots of shiny chromium plated parts and quite naturally I couldn't wait to jump on it and set the wheels in motion but there was a snag, I could only just reach the pedals. On the Sunday it was decided we would pay a visit to my Aunt and Uncle at the farm and when Dad said we would take the cycle along with us for me to get some practice in on the country roads I became very excited. It was a nice day, cold but fine, and we set off early so that we would have plenty of time at the farm. We had lunch at the farm and because it would get dark fairly early we started for home shortly afterwards. Every time we left the farm to return home it was the usual practice for my aunt and uncle to walk us to the top of the steep hill and then go back down the lane. This day we all set off together but then uncle and I got a short way in front of the rest as I was doing my cycle riding bit with him doing his best to keep me from sliding off the saddle as I wobbled from side to side in an effort to reach the pedals. We arrived at the top of the steep hill when the rest were still some way behind. Whatever prompted him to do what he did next I shall never know, but he gave me a very firm push. The drop in the road at that point was so sharp it wasn't necessary to push at all as it would have rolled on it's own. I picked up speed very quickly. At this stage in my cycling experience I had not been called upon to do anything when I wished to stop except ease off the saddle and plant my feet firmly on the floor as I was never moving very fast. I couldn't risk leaving the saddle, so my feet would be unable to reach the floor. The farther I went down the hill the faster I went. There were tall trees and bushes at both sides of the road and I saw them flashing past at one heck of a lick. Then I remembered what Dad had told me when he had explained the bits and pieces on the cycle and what they were for. He had said a small lever on the handlebars required pulling towards me if I ever needed to stop, and I surely needed to stop now. I kept hold of the handlebars and extended the fingers of my right hand which enabled me to grasp the lever and pull it hard towards me. The next thing I remembered was going over the handlebars and landing flat on my back, the bike dropping on top of me. Dad's explanation had not covered the fact that fairy cycles had only one brake and that was for the front wheel, if this wheel came to a sudden stop at speed it would stop but the rest of the bike and it's passenger would not. Fortunately I wasn't seriously hurt, just a large bump on my forehead, my knees were grazed, and my jacket was torn at the elbows with a little skin removed from one elbow, but there were a lot of tears. While Mum attended to my wounds Dad gave my uncle a lot of "advice"! I do remember almost everything that happened on that fateful afternoon even though I was only six years old at the time. There were very few motorised vehicles on the roads which made it reasonably safe for bicycle riding and I did eventually learn to ride mine properly and had many pleasant hours pedalling around all over the place.

When we first arrived in Wombwell my Mum was informed by Dad that she must make every effort to purchase as much of our weekly shopping as possible at the Co-operative stores as it was "said" that it was run by the people for the people. He was of the opinion that their goods were better and much cheaper and what was more important to him every year we would get some cash back through the Dividend scheme they operated. Anyone intending to shop at the Co-op would fill in some kind of application form to become a Co-operative Society member and be allocated a personal number which was then used every time they made a purchase from a store. The assistant would reckon up the total cost of the purchases and write it down on a carbon copying pad together with the customers personal number and hand them the top copy, a small pink slip. The dividend was announced in September of each year, usually about three pennies in the pound which meant a return of three pennies for every one pound spent. All the pink slips had been impaled on a piece of copper wire hung up on the inside of the kitchen door and when the dividend was declared they were removed from their resting place and placed on the kitchen table where each of the amounts spent were written down and totalled up. This could usually take an hour or so and there were many heated arguments because they were unable to agree over the totals.

Money was always tight and almost every outlay had to be hard thought out, but there was one instance when Mum took a huge gamble. We were not the proud possessors of either a radio or a gramophone as they were regarded by Dad as unnecessary luxuries, but Mum had seen a small Cossor radio for sale in one of the second hand shops. Apparently she had noticed it there for a few weeks but hadn't the courage to get it until the day she took me along with her and bought it. I do remember her saying "I hope your Dad won't be too angry, but it is cheap and I would like to be able to listen to some music, and hear what is going on in the world". I knew she was very worried as to just what his reaction would be, he could soon "Fly off the Handle" and when he did it wasn't very nice to be around. When we got home Dad was at work so Mum placed it on the sideboard and fastened the wires onto the accumulator (a kind of oblong glass receptacle which produced the power for the radio) and then inserted a piece of wire which the shopkeeper had given her to use as an aeriel and looped it over the top of a picture rail. She switched it on and fiddled a bit and we could hear music. It was not very loud or plain but at least it was working and if you sat almost on top of it then it wasn't too bad at all. Then Dad came home and I made myself scarce. I could hear them talking and it was very loud at first but then it calmed down so I went back downstairs. Dad was moving the aeriel around the room and telling Mum to turn the dial, there was music playing, and as he moved the aeriel around more it got louder and plainer until it sounded really nice. He fastened the ariel securely to the wall and then it was his turn to fiddle with the dials, eventually he found someone talking and said it was the News and just sat there and listened. I could see he was quite pleased and so Mum was happy and no doubt very relieved. From then on when he was at work she would have music on but when he came home it was a case of find the news, listen to it for a while, and then anything could be put on. We had that little radio for almost ten years; it was certainly money well spent.

One of the boys in the house next door was called Johnny and we were quite good friends, he was slightly older than me and we had some good fun together. One "Bit of Fun", though would have been regarded by our parents as not so much a bit of fun as downright naughty. We both received a little pocket money and the maximum I ever received was two pennies but he sometimes got more. Someone at school had told him that if we wanted to try having a "smoke" we should take one penny and put it into a slot machine and get out of it a small oblong packet containing two "Crayol" cigarettes and two red tipped matches from a shop in town that had one of these slot machines fixed on the wall outside. One evening after tea we armed ourselves with one penny each and set off in search of this shop. We found the slot machine and after first taking a good look round to see if anyone was watching, decided to have a go. I put my penny in and sure enough out popped an oblong packet which on being opened revealed the two cigarettes and the two red-tipped matches. We became very excited as neither of us had tried a smoke before and had no idea what it would be like. There weren't many people about as most of the shops were closed so we went round to the side of the shop and put a cigarette in each of our mouths. I took one of the matches, struck it on the wall, and the wind immediately blew it out! So I had another go but this time I cupped my hands around it to shield it from the wind, it did the same thing again. This was now tragic, we didn't have another match so there was only one thing for it and that was for Johnny to use his penny and get another packet and after again making sure no-one was watching, that is what he did. This time we were not going to take the risk of having the wind blow the match out again so we walked up the street and found a shop that had a long covered entrance and went right to the bottom of it and positioned ourselves close up against the shop door and with cigarettes once more in our mouths I struck another match and it stayed alight. In fact we had to blow it out after having lit both cigarettes. I suppose it could be said that we did have a smoke but in reality we didn't as we simply drew the smoke into our mouths and blew it out again straight away. On the way home Johnny said someone had told him that if he was going to try smoking he should make sure he took some spearmint chewing gum with him and eat some afterwards as smoking made your breath smell. He had remembered and we both had a piece. We still had two cigarettes and one match so they were put into one of the packets and I hid them in a safe place in my room when I got home. We arranged to go out again the following evening and I took the packet and we found a good spot out of the wind and had another puff or two. We didn't use the slot machine very often because I don't think either of us were too keen on smoking although we wouldn't admit it.

Jack and his crayon smoking pal - 1930

We had other ways of amusing ourselves which again wouldn't have had the approval of our parents. When it began to get dark early in the evenings a few of us would select a house that had a decent sized garden at the front or the rear with a hedge and a gate at the entrance to it and take along with us a bobbin of black cotton to which we had attached a fairly strong straight pin at the end and threaded through and tied a small shirt button to the cotton about one foot below the pin. The tallest one in the party would approach a downstairs window with extreme caution and push the pin into the top of the window frame, allowing the button to dangle in line with one of the panes of glass, and then as he returned quickly but quietly to where the rest of us were hiding behind the hedge he would let the cotton run out from the bobbin which he was holding in his hand. It was a job to stop the younger ones from giggling but it was very important we made no noise as it would have spoilt the fun. Once we had all settled down it was time for the game to commence and the one holding the bobbin would pull the cotton reasonably tight, not too much or it would pull the pin from the window frame, then slacken it so that the button rested on the window pane and by pulling and easing off a few times in quick succession the button would hit the window causing a tapping sound which could be heard inside the house. We would then keep everything still and wait for the response from the householder, this was usually by someone coming to the window and looking out or opening the door and coming out to have a look round. It was very rare any of them realised what was causing the sound but it was then best to wait a few minutes after they had either gone back into the house or closed the curtains before doing it again. We weren't too bad, after playing the trick on them no more than three times we would retrieve the pin and go in search of another victim.

There were certain times during those years I enjoyed very much. Easter, with it's beautifully decorated eggs, some small, others large, I do think I must have been exceptionally lucky because the ones I received from Mum, Dad, and relatives, were always on the very large side. The ones I got from home were usually demolished in quick time but I knew that when we went on one of our frequent visits to Grandma's or the farm there would be more waiting for me. Then there was Whitsuntide, which was a special time when all the younger children would have new clothes. Many businessmen would provide "Floats" (horse drawn drays or carts which were beautifully decorated) and some children were selected to ride on these as they toured the streets on Whit Monday, but the day for actually showing off their new clothes was on the Sunday. One form of entertainment for young and old in May was one in which I couldn't bring myself to indulge, although many found it to be highly delightful and that was dancing round the Maypole. It took place in the many recreation grounds in the area and the Maypole was provided and decorated by the local council. These holidays and times of festivity were great but although it was cold and the nights came in early I seemed to enjoy myself much more during the winter months. I have already mentioned the ice skating but there were other things equally as entertaining and one of these was Bonfire night. On the night a fire would be lit in the yard with coal and some small logs, all placed inside a not too large circle of stones. Stools and chairs were brought out and everyone sat around this circle keeping very hot at the front but unfortunately freezing at the rear. It was a communal fire and everyone chipped in; some would bring out the bonfire toffee, others brought Parkin. The largest potatoes would have been collected and saved during the previous few weeks and were placed inside the stones surrounding the fire, the skins got burnt almost to a cinder but they tasted wonderful especially when garnished with a smidgin of butter. Chestnuts would have been put in their places early, again inside the stone circle, to enable them to get cooked before it was time for all the children to go to bed. Care still had to be taken of their natural habit to suddenly "Fly". The menfolk would take the responsibility of lighting the fireworks making sure the small children deposited the burnt out sparklers inside the circle of stones before they had time to hold the end that was still very hot. There were some tears as could only be expected at a gathering of this kind but top priority was given to the task of ensuring that absolutely no-one received any burns and on most of these nights it was very successful. Spinning wheels were pinned to the toilet doors, Roman candles stood on the ground at a safe distance, Rockets placed in a precarious position inside an empty tin can or milk bottle and no-one could be absolutely certain at which angle they would eventually take off. Despite all these hazards we were taken care of.

Of course the most exciting time during any year was Christmas. The hours of searching in all the likely places for carefully concealed presents you put in during that period, and ears and eyes working overtime at the mere mention that someone had been out shopping. It all added up to that night you went to bed unable and unwilling to go to sleep. "Mum, I am thirsty, can I come down for a drink", was one of my ploys to enable me to have a last minute look round. My little friends had all kinds of stories to tell of how they would stay awake pretending to be fast asleep hoping to catch a glimpse of the man in the red coat and white beard and how they woke up to find the bedroom had been transformed and presents were scattered around. I received many wonderful presents but one in particular I shall always remember; a "Hornby" train set. The amount of pleasure I had from that toy was unbelievable and it also gave Mick some fun chasing the little engine and carriages round it's track.

For one week during the winter months the town came alive with music, screams, and laughter; the annual fair had arrived. The screams were coming from the heart stopping rides and the laughter from the various stalls that combined to form a type of enclosure for the whole proceedings. Everything was explained to me by my friends who had already been and it sounded very exciting, but I was unable to see for myself as it was deemed to be unsafe for me to walk around such a place unaccompanied. I was assured that, "I had no need to worry, someone would definitely take me before it went away". I did worry though as it had got to the last two days of the fair's presence and I still hadn't been. That same day Dad came home from work, had his dinner, gave me four pennies, and leaving Mum in the house we made our way towards the commotion coming from the fairground. My eyes must surely have been sparkling at the thought of what was in store. I would be able to have a go on the Dodgems, ride a cock horse on the Cocks and Hens, swoop through the air on the Flying Chairs, stagger along the violently jerking monstrosity known as the Cakewalk, and try my hand at winning a prize or two. We arrived, and my first choice the Dodgems was turned down flat as Dad mumbled something about "not wanting to have his brains scrabbled". Then in his opinion the Cocks and Hens picked up far too much speed for such a little boy as myself, and as for the Flying Chairs, "did I want to be sick all over the place"? The "Cakewalk" then? "Don't be daft". It was the same excuse for all the rides as something would have been detrimental to my health if I was to be allowed on them, but even though I was disappointed I wasn't downhearted as there were still the prizes to attack. So, arms bulging with the muscles I didn't have, we approached the coconut stall. I would knock them flying just wait, and wait I had to do till in the end it was decided I couldn't be expected to knock those small objects from their deep hiding place in the collars of their posts. "Just look at them, they are so far down it's a wonder the stall holder doesn't do himself an injury when he has to lean over to lift them out". "The floating ducks ?". " No, that's a little kid's game". "So, what am I ?". "Not that baby-ish, surely "?. The conversations between us were all very much in the same vein, I trying to convince, he putting the blockers on, and all interspersed with, "It's all a waste of money really, you will have to learn to take care of your money ". Those four pennies were burning a hole in my pocket and the way things were going they would be burning my pocket all the way back home, so you can imagine how taken aback I was when he stopped at a stall and said "have a go on this one". It was the famous Roll a Penny stall. I took one penny out, lined the little wooden ramp up so as to roll it to stop on the highest number on the board, let go, and we were in business, it was like waiting for one of the few buses to Barnsley as it rolled and swivelled so many times before it eventually dropped over flat and remained motionless. Yippee, it had dropped full in the centre of one of the numbers even though it was the lowest one on the board, number two. I had won and I would now have five pennies to roll down and would certainly win some more, but when the stall holder flicked the two pennies towards me I was getting ready to roll one of them again when a firm hand gripped mine and a voice said, "let's go now, you are winning, don't run the risk of losing it". We had a few more places to "look" at, then we went home!

Having read the above it is more than just possible that you may have formed the opinion that my Father had been very hard on me that particular afternoon and I must say that was what I thought at the time, but as things have turned out I am convinced he did me a great favour. The Wombwell fair arrived every year afterwards and when I was old enough I used to go, but only for a look round; the rides held no fascination for me and the games of "skill and chance" were something I looked upon with more than a certain amount of scepticism, taking into account the ludicrous rewards on offer. This attitude is in every way similar to my Father's.

Christmas didn't have the monopoly where presents were concerned Birthdays had a good say in the matter as well and again I considered myself to be very lucky having a Mum and Dad who appreciated having a little boy who did his very best to please and not annoy them in any way. I would be taken to Grandma's where there were aunts and uncles and to the farm to see uncle Harold and aunt Annie at some time close to my birthday when almost everyone had been given some idea of what I would like for that particular year. The presents were, more often than not, just what I had been hoping for. When we were here in this home with all the people I dearly loved it was impossible to remain annoyed at anything for very long.

CHAPTER 4

I was seven years of age when I moved from the infants to a junior school, still in Wombwell, which was slightly nearer to home and as far as I was concerned much better. Everything was doing nicely at home although Mum and Dad hadn't been going out much together, then one evening there was great activity, they were both trying on their best apparel and discussing their appearance. When I could get a straight answer from one of them it seemed as if Mum had found somewhere for them to go together to do a spot of dancing and the most amazing part about it was she had persuaded Dad to have a go. I was left in the capable hands of Johnnie's Mother and away they went. I enjoyed myself staying with the neighbour for eight or nine weeks while they tripped the light fantastic every Friday night but it was hectic during the hour they were getting ready because after that first night Mum acquired the appropriate dresses for the kind of dance they were going to. I won't forget seeing her for the first time in her outfit for the Charleston. That long ankle length tight fitting dress which made her appear to be so very tall, the queer looking object she wore on her head, a headband, with two or three long feathers standing up which had most probably been plucked from the tail of some poor unsuspecting pheasant, and the two strings of beads that stretched almost down to her knees. It was all a bit of a muchness for me and she looked so funny I could hardly stop myself from breaking out in fits of laughter but that would never have done as it would most certainly have invoked the wrath of the gentleman with the exceptionally white shirt and black dicky bow tie who was standing barely two feet away. There were two other dances they liked in particular, the Two-Step and the Shuffle Bottom, the mind boggles at how the latter was performed.

The area in which we were living was reasonable but people were having a hard time of it financially. If a pair of boots or shoes were wearing thin on the soles or heels it wasn't simply a matter of pop down to the shoe shop and replace them, nor was it feasible to take them to the cobblers (shoe repairers), as they couldn't afford to pay the prices they charged, it was a case of do the best you can with what you have. Most families had a "Hobbin-Foot", which to some people was known as a "Last". It was made of cast iron and had three particular shapes on it, two of them in the shape of a boot or shoe sole, (one ladies and one gents), and the third a heel. Each of these shapes were at the end of a short leg and whichever way it was stood on the floor one would be uppermost with the other two forming a very solid base upon which it could stand. The mode of operation was to decide which shape you were going to need then place it on the floor with the one you required at the top, then you would need to open the inside of the boot/shoe wide enough to enable you to slide it onto the shape from the toe end, keeping the tongue clear, the inner sole of the boot would then be resting firmly on the metal shape and in a position to enable you to carry out the repair. Some would cut a sole or heel from an old pair of which the uppers had seen better days and nail them on. The soles and heels could be repaired with leather or rubber whichever was available at the time as both were suitable for the job.

One outcome of being short of money, had a disturbing affect on my pal Johnnie and it came about when there were a lot of us in the yard one afternoon when his Dad just happened to mention that he would like Johnnie to have his hair cut but at present he couldn't afford it. My Dad had said he had a pair of shears and would be pleased to give him a trim. Now these particular shears were hand operated and although serviceable, were very much the worse for wear with several teeth missing which caused them to pull and tug rather than cut. I can testify to this as he always used them to cut my hair despite my protestations. Well, he got the shears and sat Johnnie on a stool in the yard, put a piece of cloth round his shoulders and tucked it into his neck, then set to work. I watched, along with the others, the shears went in, a little tug, a pull, and they were clear, but there were more tugs and pulls than actual cuts and every time Johnnie flinched so did I. This went on for a while with Johnnie flinching and shuffling about on the stool and Dad taking his usual grip on the top of his head then suddenly, with a cry of anguish, Johnnie turned to face Dad and said in a pitiful voice, "Oh mister, I am sure it wouldn't hurt so much if you pulled them out, one at a time". He was trying to get off the stool and remove the cloth from around his neck but Dad wasn't to be outdone by such a mere triviality as a few yanked out hairs and he managed to calm him down, replaced the cloth, and resumed normal service. Johnnie stopped squirming and with a look on his surly face as black as thunder endured the last few moments in silence. When it was all over Johnnie had gone back into their house, no doubt to shed a few tears probably more of relief that it was finally finished than from any actual pain he had suffered, Dad came out with the statement that he couldn't understand why people complained about his beloved shears and what all the fuss had been about. Shortly afterwards he was to have good reason to change his mind.

It came about one afternoon, he came home from work, had his dinner and then announced that he was fed up with his hair being too long and proceeded to cajole Mum into cutting it with those shears. She did state a preference for doing it with her scissors but he insisted she use the shears. He always had his usual army haircut, short back and sides, and kept it well under control, but this time it had grown exceptionally long at the back, and this was to be the cause of all the problems that were to follow. He sat on the stool in the kitchen with a cloth suitably placed around his neck and Mum was having a few practice runs with the shears, gingerly squeezing the handles in and out. After some words of encouragement from him like, "get on with it woman", she placed the front of the shears in the nape of his neck, and squeezing in and out she progressed up the back of his head. All was going well until she decided it was time to taper them outwards, then they jammed. They were locked into the thickest part of his hair and wouldn't move. He jumped up off the stool then realised that by standing up he was allowing the weight of the shears to pull his hair down which caused him to have even more discomfort so he promptly sat down again. Mum took hold of the shears and tried to wriggle them free. He was giving instructions that were not helpful to Mum in any way and she just became more agitated. Then, having taken all the instruction and abuse she was prepared to suffer she took her scissors and cut off all the offending trapped hair; the shears were now free and so was he. It had taken a good ten minutes and a painful ten minutes they must have been, not just for him though as Mum was in a state of shock. I on the other hand remained seated in the corner, ears flapping but mouth tightly closed. Eventually he ceased to rant and rave and declared he would go to the barber the very next day. Meanwhile he was sporting a large bald patch at the back of his head. He also decided to permanently retire his beloved shears much to the relief of all concerned.

We went to Grandma's one Saturday morning intending to stay overnight and as summer time had arrived it was a nice warm day so we walked through the fields. I was looking forward to a couple of nice days roaming around the park and exploring the wood at the end of the garden but after having dinner I decided to go across the road to see uncle George, aunt Jane, and May, in Beaumont Terrace. I only stayed for a short while and then took a stroll in to Grandma's old garden and went down the bank at the side of the little stream. Because it was such a hot day I took off my boots and socks and had a paddle in the shallow part. After a while I went in a little deeper until the water nearly reached the bottom of my shorts. I found that I was really enjoying myself and much to my surprise I wasn't afraid of the water as I had expected. I played around for quite some time and then went back across the road to the lodge. That paddle was to be the first of many, I went back the following day making some sort of excuse to get out of the house and couldn't wait for the next time we would be coming here. We did come for the odd day but I found it too difficult to get away on those brief visits, then shortly after Dad had a few days off and we came for one whole week and I managed to get away every day. The first time I went I did very much as before staying in the shallow end and larking about in general before I had to go back for dinner. For the first three days I was content to paddle and splash about and all the time trying to make my journeys to the stream appear as if I was somewhere in the wood. I had spent quite a lot of time building a house from tree branches and leaves, and even contrived to have my Mum and an aunt visit the place and showed it off. On the afternoon of the fourth day it was really warm and I had been getting braver and braver with my efforts to paddle, going in slightly deeper all the time so I decided to remove my shorts, vest, and underpants as they were in danger of getting soaked. I had now reached the stage where my feet at times were coming off the bottom as it was so deep, then it happened, I had been leaning backwards and the feet did leave the floor, both of them but I leaned forward pretty sharpish and they settled back on the bottom. I tried to repeat the process many times but it was proving difficult. I was still scared to go in too deep but I soon realised I would have to overcome that feeling if I wanted to float properly. We were going back home in three days time so I managed to go twice on each of the next two days and in an effort to overcome my fears I did go in deeper but keeping as close to the bank as I could just in case I needed to grab hold of something in a hurry. The last few attempts were encouraging, I kept leaning backwards getting my feet to come off the bottom and when I had got the hang of being able to lean forward quickly and put them down again I began to make real progress. With all the splashing about I was doing I found that I was moving, only backwards at first then I tried leaning all the way forward, and after nearly drowning myself a few times by the end of that second day I was moving backwards and forwards. The most exciting thing about it was knowing that I could stay up and not sinking all the time. I was wondering how to get away on the last day, but when I got up next morning it was raining. I had only one or two chances to practice after that on the odd weekend we went but then the weather put paid to my excursions. I never did go back as that year I started to go to the local swimming baths with the school. The first day I was doing a bit of everything, a kind of dog paddle, and an attempt at "speed" with arms flailing everywhere and puffing and blowing but I think I was the only one who could stay on top of the water without holding on grimly to the pipes. The teacher noticed my feeble attempts and showed me how to use arms and legs to their best effect but it took a few school visits before I was able to go across the pool in a fairly reasonable fashion. Dad had told me he would soon be taking me to learn to swim but when he heard I was going with the school once a week and that I could already do a bit he took me every week in the evenings. He was a very strong swimmer and with his instruction I came along in leaps and bounds, and after a few years swimming was something I became really good at. I shall be ever grateful to that tiny little stream as it had played a major part in helping me to overcome the fear of water.

I regarded the small wood as mine with it being almost part of the Lodge garden and I spent hours making a hideaway and there were plenty of places in which to hide as the whole area was overgrown. In the spring and summer there were snowdrops, bluebells, daffodils and buttercups etc all growing in or around the wood; it was a small boy's paradise and I spent many happy hours in there, even on my own it was enjoyable just pretending to be whoever I wanted to be.

An interesting pastime was to sit on a branch of one of the tall trees at the edge of the wood adjoining the park and watch the comings and goings of people and vehicles entering the park through the large gate and one day it gave me an idea. The road leading into the park rose sharply and the gate used to rise as it was being opened to clear the inclining surface and when it had reached the other side of the road it would forcefully clip itself on to a hook which was fastened on to a small two foot high concrete block. This hook had to be released before the gate could be closed but once it was released the gate would close itself, in fact it had to be held back very firmly or it would slam into the gatepost with one heck of a bang. It needed to be operated correctly and this is where I thought I could be of some help.

There were a number of people who came through the gate to enter the park, some in cars others with a pony and trap. Some came through merely to admire the scenery, others to reach their homes which were in the village at the other end of the park, and some to look at the beautiful building that was Worsbrough Hall. This Hall was built in the Elizabethan style of architecture with a centre and two wings and was very imposing indeed, in it's heyday it had wonderful gardens laid out in the front, and commanded spectacular views of the surrounding countryside, but unfortunately it was allowed to deteriorate. Most of the people had cars and had to stop to open the gate, drive through, stop again and close it. I had seen them doing this and I, being the kind and considerate person that I am, thought they might show their appreciation if I were to relieve them of this chore, so one Sunday morning I positioned myself at the front door of the Lodge and when a car approached I went to the gate and opened it. When they had gone through I closed it and almost all of them did show their appreciation by throwing a few coins in my direction. The pennies and half-pennies all added up and although Mum hadn't been keen to allow me to do the job initially I would keep some and give the rest to Mum. I had always looked forward to going to the Lodge at any time but now that I had a lucrative hobby it made our visits much better. For the following three or four months everything was fine then I got into the habit of riding on the gate when I was closing it. I would release the hook on the concrete block and jump on as it was closing and stop it from hitting the post too hard by dropping off and hold it back by sliding my feet on the road, but I did it once too often.

I was riding with my right foot on the bottom bar, it slipped off and was trapped between this bar and the road. It was pretty painful and my foot and ankle swelled out of all proportion, an examination was made and the diagnosis was, I had a badly sprained ankle and a bruised foot. I received a well deserved telling off and reminded that we had to walk the six miles home that evening, and how was I going to do it with a sprained ankle?. For obvious reasons I made no comment. Grandma had the answer to most problems and she got some long thick dark green leaves from the garden, I was told later it was called Cumphrey, added two large Dock leaves and put some brown sticky paste on them and wrapped and tied the whole lot tightly round my foot and ankle, I had to sit with my leg resting on a chair for what seemed ages. The time came for us to start getting ready to go home, the dressing was taken off my foot and ankle, I took a few hesitant steps and much to my surprise it wasn't too bad at all, a bit tender but we arrived home without too much trouble although I did have to rest a few times.

The journeys to the lodge seemed to become more frequent during the months leading up to wintertime. The time I spent in my hideaway in the wood got shorter as it was too cold and wet to sit and shiver on a pile of damp leaves. The tree climbing was nowhere near as interesting when there were no leaves on those trees to provide adequate cover from prying eyes and all in all it was pretty dull having to mooch around in the house. The brilliant idea I had come up with for earning a copper or two opening the gate was at it's lowest ebb at this time of the year as only the people who lived in the village needed to come through and I had found through past experience that they were the least likely ones to appreciate my efforts. A trip across the road to see uncle George, aunt Jane and May was always good especially if I called on the dear old lady Mrs. Coop and had a cream cracker or two but I soon got bored and needed something to liven things up a bit. My prayers were answered one Sunday afternoon. The usual headgear for this neck of the woods was the traditional peaked flat cap but in the early thirties the Bowler hat came into fashion. The cap stayed for work and every day use but the bowler was regarded as more "Classy" and if ever there was a need to dress up, especially at weekends it was put on and displayed with great aplomb. Dad only wore headgear at work, the post office regulation cap that was similar to the one known as a Pork Pie cap, round at the top with a small peak, it was compulsory for him to wear it and he would have been in serious trouble if he hadn't done so. However, Mum decided it was time he became fashionable and bought him a Bowler and despite all the reasons he put forward as to why he never intended to wear it she persuaded him to do just that and he wore it one Sunday morning when we went to the lodge. How I managed to keep my face straight every time I looked at him I don't know because he looked like someone who was going to explode any minute. When we arrived he was ribbed a bit by his father and brother's, but not uncle Harold as he was already the proud owner of a Bowler. Now it was usual for the men folk to go to the Red Lion for a drink at lunchtime on Sundays and this day was to be no exception. Grandma organised dinner so that it would be ready for just after closing time, two thirty, and when it was almost that time Mum and the rest of us went out and stood near the park gates and waited for them to return. It wasn't long before they appeared. The way they oozed out of the door it looked as if they had thoroughly enjoyed their drinks and plenty of them too. To Mother's surprise Dad appeared to be as tipsy as the others and she didn't look very pleased either, but what happened next made her absolutely speechless. As they were walking towards us, someone knocked the bowler from Dad's head, it dropped at the feet of the nearest person who, on seeing it on the floor took a whacking great kick at it. His aim wasn't brilliant, owing to his befuddled brain, but it did travel for a short distance along the footpath. Then they proceeded to use it as a football, dribbling and passing it to each other. By the time "it", and they, reached us, "it" was a Bowler no more. The round top and the sides had parted from the rim and it had disintegrated. No-one bothered to pick up the remnants, we just went in and had a somewhat sombre dinner and when we walked home that evening it wasn't the usual happy journey. Needless to say Dad never got another Bowler.

Then tragedy hit the family, at some time during that winter Granddad was taken ill and died shortly afterwards, he had been an excellent husband and Father and was going to be sorely missed. Maybe this is not the right time to narrate this little story about him but it was well known that he thought the world of my Grandmother and this will show his dry sense of humour and his readiness to play practical jokes. For some reason, of which I am not sure, he went away somewhere for a few days and just before he was expected to return my Grandmother received a letter from him saying he would be home on a certain day and that he had bought some pigs and would she prepare things. At the time she had a fairly large family to look after but she managed to clean out the building which had been used to keep pigs in before and whitewashed it, then covered the floor with suitable bedding, it must have been hard work for her on top of caring for all the family as well. He arrived home on the day and greeted her in the usual manner but said nothing about the transport that would be bringing the pigs, but after he had washed and changed and had a meal he said, "Oh I nearly forgot, look what I have brought for you", with that he took out of his pocket a small box and opened it to reveal three tiny pink pot pigs then he doubled up in fits of laughter. What Grandma said I don't know but what she was thinking would have probably been more to the point.

Round about 1929 Elijah and Elizabeth Wood taken at the Lodge Worsborough Village Barnsley (Grandma & Grandad Wood)

34

I have only a slight recollection of attending his funeral. I seem to remember it was snowing and the cemetery in Worsbrough village was covered in deep snow and that his grave was only just inside the gate. I never did get to know him very well as he never seemed to say much when I was around but if my Grandma loved him, as surely she did, then I am certain he was a very good man and his absence made the Lodge an extremely subdued place for a very long time.

There was great excitement when it was announced that the first Double Decker Bus would be coming through the town. It was well advertised and people lined the streets to catch a glimpse of it. I had heard about it from my friends in school and we had all taken up a good viewing position long before it arrived. When the cause of all the commotion did come past it was bedecked with bunting and there were some V.I.P.s on board, plus the driver who was sitting in what looked to be a definitely too small a position on the left hand side as we looked at it just behind an enormous bonnet and the steering wheel appeared to be much too big for him to handle. As it was trundling past it was possible to see some people sitting on the upper deck and a large majority of the onlookers were saying "You will never get me to ride on the top deck of that thing".

There was more excitement when an air show was put on just outside of town. I had somehow managed to be there and it was quite an experience as I had never seen an aeroplane before. This was 1929 and although there had been planes during the First World War there were never many seen in this neck of the woods. Here at the show there were bi-planes doing loop the loops, flying upside down, and swooping low over the field amid screams of sheer terror from everyone around; it was very thrilling and when they ceased doing their acrobatics they landed in the field and invited people to come up to them and take a closer look, with the pilots explaining things. I listened intently and I was fascinated by it all. Looking at the planes we have today those men who flew those bi-planes were very brave men indeed.

About two months later Dad was promoted and transferred to the general post office in Barnsley which was the start of a chain of events which were to have an affect upon all our lives in the not too distant future. This office was a good six miles away and he needed to be there very early in the morning so he bought a motor bike. It was a monster, and if my memory serves me well I believe it was an A.J.S. He worked at his new job for about a month and as it was summertime he decided it would be nice if he and Mum could go on the bike to visit her relatives in Norwich. They set off one morning to make the journey to Norwich and they reached their intended destination later that evening albeit having travelled most of the way by train owing to the monster breaking down less then half way there! They had a nice time and spent four days there before returning home, on the train. The bike didn't return until the following week after it had undergone extensive repairs. Ever since I became old enough to understand that Dad had been a soldier I made it known that I wanted to follow in his footsteps one day but that was a long way off, so instead I began to take an interest in those of the miniature kind; "Toy Soldiers". I had noticed that there were a few shops in Wombwell where it was possible to purchase these and Mum took it upon herself to buy me one or two on a fairly regular basis. It wasn't long before I had a reasonable collection. They were all made of solid lead, brightly coloured and painted in very fine detail. Apart from the soldiers themselves I obtained all the relevant equipment. I had guardsmen of all descriptions, Welsh, Irish, English, and the attractive looking Scottish with their kilts and bagpipes. I thought they were all marvellous but I did have a preference for the Scots. In the end I had so many different types that I was able to form them into groups containing the various regiments and all headed by their own marching band, and those of the fighting variety in their three different firing positions; standing, kneeling, or laying down, were placed in strategic places in accordance to the way my imagination was working at the time. The mounted columns with some black, some white, and other shades of horses were mainly the Lifeguards so resplendent in their silver or gold glistening helmets and breast plates, together with all kinds of tents, artillery, and horse drawn wagons. Everything combined to make it a really fascinating hobby but to buy all the things I had must have been expensive for my parents because none of them could be called cheap. On the Christmas before my eighth birthday I received a present which was to transform my activities in the war games and was to become a very important part of my collection. It was a "Fort" and was really wonderful camouflaged as it was in such fine detail. It was made of wood but paper mache' had been used to give a proper landscape effect making it appear as if the walls and surrounds were uneven as they probably would have been on the real thing, and all done in camouflage. It had ramparts, a moat, four turrets, a drawbridge, and an outstanding approach road leading up to the main entrance. This road was so wide it was possible to have horsemen riding four abreast. When it was not in use it could be packed away, inside itself, leaving only a square box shape which was easy to put away out of sight. All this, soldiers and all, were kept inside my bedroom. I collected all manner of things for this collection right up to my leaving school at the age of fourteen. I had been very careful when handling those tiny objects to avoid getting any scratches or chips in their paintwork and when the time eventually came for me to hand them over to someone else they were all in mint condition.

Jack on a day trip to Sunny Blackpool, 1930

Jack in sunny Blackpool on a donkey, 1930

Towards the latter part of that year, 1930, my Mother had been attending a hospital which was quite some distance away. She went nearly every week and always brought back at least one toy soldier, then at the beginning of February 1931 she went away for a few days and when she returned she was carrying a little bundle which turned out to be my baby sister. Her name had already been decided upon, it was Jacqueline Stephanie. Up to that time I had been given all the attention, but it changed over night although I was not put out in any way about the change in my status in fact I soon began to take advantage of it by being able to get out of the house much more and enjoy myself with all the new found freedom. Jacqueline progressed nicely, and later that same year we moved once again, this time to an area just on the outskirts of Barnsley much nearer to where Dad was working as one of his friends had found a house for us to rent. I don't think any one of us wanted to move because we were settled and very happy here but it was going to be easier for Dad not having to travel to work on that obnoxious motor bike. Of one thing I am absolutely certain, and that was that Mum had no idea what she was letting herself in for.

Even to narrate this next episode in our lives is extremely difficult because it could so easily have ended in tragedy. Mum and Dad went to inspect the house and found it to be extremely dirty so aunt Jane and her sister Ada were asked to give us a hand cleaning it which they said they would be pleased to do. It didn't alter the position, design, or any other aspects of the house, but it was clean, really clean, and it smelled lovely, of healthy Carbolic soap.

Jack's father Benjamin Wood 1931, with Jack and sister Jacquline in Wombwell Wood

37

Later that week, after I had wished all my friends at school and around home an almost tearful goodbye, we moved into the house.

It was a three storey building and two of the storeys were above the ground at the front with one downstairs window and one bedroom window and a front door which opened out onto a narrow footpath adjoining the main road. Looking at it from the front it appeared to be like any other normal house and it only became obvious that there was a third storey when it was seen from the rear where there were three windows, two of them on the same level as those at the front, one living room one bedroom, and the third was below these alongside a back door which opened out into a very small brick walled yard. To get to this room from inside the house, which was more like a cellar than a room, you had to traverse a long stone stepped stairway from the kitchen above. The tiny walled yard was about eight feet long, six feet wide, and two feet six inches high, with a wooden gate of about the same height as the wall. Beyond this small yard was a much bigger one, some thirty yards wide and sixty yards long with a very uneven asphalt surface and numerous pot holes. Across this one were some buildings, toilets and coal houses, with what appeared to be some small unfenced gardens which were not very well cultivated but contained a few flowers and bushes. There were four houses in the terrace, ours being the end one, and at the side of it was a slip road that lead down from the main road at the front of the houses, it was very steep indeed. It was about thirty yards long and eight yards wide stretching from the main road at the top and merging into the large yard at the bottom. It was level with the top of the small walled yard as it came down the side of the house, there was no fencing of any kind so if you were to step off the slip road at that point you would fall into our small yard. There was another row of houses next to ours which were separated only by the slip road which meant that where this road started it was enclosed on both sides by the gable ends of our house and the first house of this next row attached to which was a wall about seven feet high which extended all the way down that side of the slip road which meant that the back yards and gardens of the two rows were entirely separated by this wall. At the other end of our large yard was an enormous building with a heavy gauge timber fence around it about fifteen feet high with two strong looking solid gates of the same height, the building itself had a wide and very high door, it had no windows but from every nook and cranny steam was exuding from all around the walls. When I first saw it I had no idea what it was.

The facilities inside our house were minimal; the kitchen sink was the only place where a wash could be taken and the galvanised bath was prominently hung inside the inner kitchen door. The last time we moved we were undecided as to how it would turn out but this time we were all in no doubt about the outcome, it was going to be awful. We had been there about two days and I was inspecting our garden across the yard, Mum was doing some washing and Jacqueline was in her pram inside the small yard. It was quiet and very peaceful until suddenly this peace and quiet was shattered, an awful noise was coming from the top of the road at the side of the house. I looked up and saw a huge lorry with it's tail gate down out of which were jumping a number of cows, bellowing and snorting as they did so. There must have been about ten of them and they were obviously having difficulty negotiating the sloping tail gate, slipping and sliding all over the place. A man appeared from inside the lorry shouting loudly and swiping at the nearest cows with a big stick, most of them by now had managed to get off the tail gate and were milling about at the top of the road but he somehow got behind them and with all his stick waving and shouting and bawling the cows must have sensed he wanted them to head down the road towards the yard and they began to run down it, not in a straight line though they were turning and twisting and trying to go in any direction. The first cow had arrived at the bottom of the road when Mum must have looked out of the door just as it did so, she screamed and dragged Jacqueline and the pram inside the door and slammed it shut and at that precise moment a cow was passing across the top of the small wall where it was pushed sideways and immediately lost it's footing and dropped over into the small yard flat on it's back where after a lot of frenzied rolling around it regained it's feet and leapt over the little gate and went farther along the big yard towards the gates at the other end, then turned round and ran towards some of the others who were coming towards it causing them to scatter in all directions. While all this was happening I was crouched down alongside the toilet wall, I could see everything that was going on but as there were only a few small shrubs and a couple of even smaller bushes in front of me I won't say I felt safe. Then two men came out of the large gates at the end, which they left open, and attempted to get the cows to go through them. After a very long time all the cows were eventually manoeuvred through the gates and disappeared inside the building. Later that day I found out that the building was a privately owned "abattoir", a slaughterhouse. As soon as I knew it was safe I went inside the house to see Mum, she was carrying Jacqueline and was still very upset and frightened. Cows were not the most adorable creatures in Mum's life at the best of times but to see them running riot only a few feet away from her back door must have been absolutely terrifying.

When Dad came home from work he was told of the happenings of that morning. he was furious especially when he heard of the near miss with Jacqueline in the pram. It was too late to do anything that day but next morning he went to the council offices and told them of the problem. Apparently the abattoir had been the subject of closure for quite some time but the council had not been able to make it stick owing to some technicality or other. Now that our trouble had been brought to their attention they said they would push again to see if they could do any better than before. After leaving the offices Dad got in touch with the owner of the abattoir himself and demanded of him what he was going to do about the problem. The owner claimed he didn't know this sort of thing was happening and said the cows should not have been allowed to come down the road and into the yard, the truck driver had orders to reverse down the road and back up to the gates before opening the tail gate and he could only think why the driver hadn't done so was because the road was so steep. He did say however that he would make sure it never happened again, and it never did , not while we were there anyway. The house and the area were not nice but I had to go to school; I was a little pensive at having to go to a new one but I needn't have worried: it was good, the teachers were very interested in all we did and I seemed to be slightly more forward in the lessons we were doing than my new class mates therefore I was able to fit in reasonably well. It was only a very short walk from our house but it was much smaller than my previous school with only a small yard attached to it so playtimes were not excellent and there weren't any swimming lessons. One very sad thing came out of the move to Barnsley when my parents had to decide that my pal Mick would not be able to accompany us when we moved! At the time I was told that Dad did find a nice place for him on a farm and that he would be very happy there, but some years later I discovered he had been sent to the veterinary surgeon. Finding this out all those years after still made me rather angry but better to have told me the other story than the truth at the time as it would have been very difficult to come to terms with the truth at that stage in my life.

After only a few miserable months in that awful house we moved to a really nice one, it was on the same side of town but in a much better area and situated in a wide open tree lined street with houses on both sides, so wide apart the place looked very fresh and healthy. The one we moved to was in a terrace of four and elevated from the street having six steps down from the front door to the bottom of a small walled garden where there were three or four stone slabs leading to a small gate which gave access to the footpath and the road, it was a pleasing front entrance altogether with nice plants all around the top part near the door and the steps were wide and evenly spaced making it look very attractive. Just at the bottom of these steps fitted into the wall of the house was a round metal grill which the coal man opened enabling him to drop the required amount of coal into a small cellar, it was only a small place with just enough room for a few bags of coal and was reached by a stone stairway from the living room. At the rear of the house there was an extension, this was the kitchen, it stuck out from the main body of the building with the back door built into it, the next door neighbour had one of a similar shape and the two buildings formed a kind of square with a small area of flag stones leading to a wall that had four steps in it to reach a much bigger asphalted yard running on top of the wall to two small brick buildings at the far side. This yard would be about fifteen yards deep and thirty yards wide stretching the width of the four houses plus a small road that came in at one end, the other end was blocked off with a fairly high wall.

Our three neighbours had no gardens except for those near their front doors, but there was a decent sized piece of grassland at the side of the service road leading into the yard which came with ours. Dad dug it over in parts but he left a large space of grass in the centre and sometime later that year he bought a large bell tent, one that was big enough to sleep ten people, and he showed me how to put it up. This was pretty hard, especially when there were only two of us. It had a large heavy centre pole and a lot of guy ropes that needed to be attached to wooden pegs which were knocked into the ground to hold it secure, it was quite a job and he insisted on taking it down and putting it up so many times it made me wonder what the real reason was for all this hard work, but all he would say was we must have plenty of practice in order to get proficient as it might come in handy some day. I did like sleeping outside: It was very refreshing, a bit uncomfortable with all the trailing to and from the house but it was something different.

There weren't many children of my age in this area and with the school being so far away the ones from there were not allowed by their parents to come and play with me. So I decided to find some nearer and to this end I joined the Cub scouts at the church about a mile away from home. I had to attend the church as often as possible on the Sunday mornings. It got me out on Friday evenings and the Sundays and I did make one or two friends, albeit not the usual tearaway types I had been used to. I progressed to the Scouts and went on quite a few camping holidays with them in tents, the best one being to the Isle of Man, it was a gorgeous place and the weather was good, and I had a really nice holiday. I especially liked the boat trip across the sea to the port of Douglas, it was the first time I had been away on my own but I seemed to cope reasonably well. There were also short week-end camps at an established Scouting area in the countryside just out of town which were interesting and educational as we did the training for various proficiency badges. I took a great interest in these and managed to pass all those I went in for. During the summer after my eleventh birthday I went on a one week camping holiday with the school along with a few boys from our school and some from other schools in the area. It was meant to give us experience of life away from home but I didn't enjoy it one little bit. It was to a permanent camp on the shores of one of the large reservoirs in the countryside and we slept in wooden huts. I hated it so much that after receiving a rollicking for wandering off and being caught having a lone swim in the reservoir I decided I had done all I wished to do in that camp and I set off early on the fourth day and walked the twelve miles home. It was late evening and dark before I eventually arrived.

Boy Scouts Brigade Jack first on the left taken at Barnabus Street, Rockingham Street Barnsley 1931

One Sunday in the summer of 1933 Dad decided he would give us all a treat and take us to the seaside, he had borrowed a car from one of his workmates and we had a very comfortable and pleasant journey to Primrose Valley, a part of the east coast near Filey. It was a beautiful warm sunny day and we arrived about mid-day. There weren't many cars about in those days and car parks weren't readily available but there was an exceptionally large grass field at the top of a footpath which lead down to the sands. Dad decided to park at the top end of this field as it sloped rather sharply to the cliff edge where there was a steep drop to the beach some fifty feet below. When the car was safely locked and a couple of decent sized stones strategically placed in front of one front and one rear wheel we made the trip down the winding awkward path and found a nice spot on the sand and had our picnic lunch. I made a few sand castles and kept Jacqueline amused and then we made the short walk along the beach to the sea front at Filey. There we had a cup of tea and a bun plus some icecream and then took a steady walk back. When the sun started to get a bit low in the sky we walked back up the path and returned to the car. All was ready for the return journey to Barnsley, then the car refused to start. Dad nearly broke his arm when the starting handle kicked back on him, not once but a few times. Eventually he looked at the distance between the front of the car and the end of the field before deciding there was only one thing for it and that was to give it a bump start. There would be no need for anyone to push as it was on a slope. After four attempts it didn't start! The edge

41

of the cliff was getting ever nearer and the disturbing thing uppermost in all our minds was what came after that edge, namely the drop that went straight down to the beach. The most ridiculous thing was that Jacqueline and Mother were still seated in the back, and I still sitting in the front. Well he always said if at first you don't succeed have another go and that is what he did. He made one "Last" desperate effort as I sat watching the last few blades of grass disappearing underneath the car and it started. That is why I am able to write this now, instead of being splattered all over the beach at Primrose Valley on that delightfully pleasant, but very memorable day!

Where we were now living was a lot farther away from the lodge. We could catch a tram or if we were lucky one of the intermittent buses but as always if it was possible to walk, we did. It wasn't such a beautiful and pleasant walk as when we went through the woods and fields.

We were all happy with the house and the area in which we were living, it had some problems but nothing we couldn't handle with a little patience and tolerance, Dad was especially pleased as our nearest shop was a Cooperative store so Mum had no excuse for shopping elsewhere, and his place of work was only a brisk ten minute walk away. He had been promoted again and did most of his deliveries out in the country and in order to do this he had the use of a small van, the property of the Post Office.

I was nearly at the age when I would have to move to a more senior school and things were progressing nicely for all of us, Jacqueline was three and when the weather was good she used to spend a lot of time in the garden with Dad or myself, we had by this time made a wire netting run in which were ensconced about a half a dozen laying hens and a separate run for a few chicks that the hens had hatched themselves. Jacqueline spent many hours in the run with the hens although I don't think they appreciated all the attention she was giving them.

In the winter when we'd had a good snowfall there was a very nice place just made for sledging, it was exactly opposite our home at the end of a row of about six houses. It was a very long and bumpy field a good three hundred yards long and it ended by going up a banking and dropping over into the canal. I had a proper sledge, iron runners and all. With the canal being so near I had also been introduced to fishing.

I had been to school and one afternoon when I was coming home there was a great deal of smoke hanging about in the air and when I reached home I looked over towards the very large hillside opposite, it was just getting dark but the sky instead of being a dull grey was an orangy red with a glow that appeared to stretch for miles with smoke billowing up into the air all around. It would have been difficult for me not to have noticed the number of bonfires dotted about on this hillside; there were about half a dozen. I went into the house and Dad was at home so I told him what I had seen. He told me of the disaster that had befallen the farming community. An illness known as foot-and-mouth disease had broken out on some farms in the area and as this disease was incurable all the animals had to be destroyed. Not just the ones that showed the signs of having got it but all the animals with split pastern feet, (two distinct hooves on each foot split in the middle), this included Cows and Sheep. All the farms were declared off limits to everyone and a strict guard had to be placed around them. It was a devastating time for the farmers; milk and beef herds it had taken years to build up were having to be slaughtered and the way it had to be carried out was even more devastating. Contractors were called into a field on the farm to dig very large deep holes, the animals were driven into these holes and then the farmer and other riflemen had to shoot them. When the hole was full it was covered with quick lime and large piles of brushwood placed over the top and set on fire and kept burning until there was absolutely nothing left.

It was about this time when all the family were summoned to appear at the wedding of my cousin May and it turned out to be a very nice affair with everyone looking resplendent in all their finery. The reception took place in a spacious room above the Red Lion. I cannot remember much about the church ceremony but I do have special memories even to this day about the reception. As was befitting a reception being held above a public house there was plenty of beer, wines and spirits, floating around,. I had no interest in the beer but the wines and spirits were something else. During the proceedings I had somehow had a taste of something I liked- I think it was whisky- and as things warmed up a bit I strolled nonchalantly past the trestle tables tables where the empty glasses were discarded searching out those that were less "empty" than others. One of the tables nearest the floor was almost full of "empties" but it was too near the many pairs of watching eyes, so I waited until one of the other tables had a fair number on it before putting my plan into operation. I started at the far end of the table, picked up one of the long stemmed glasses with a reasonable amount of dregs in it, then another that was also well covered at the bottom and poured one into the other and taking the one with the most in I did the same with the next and the next and so on until I had a wine glass almost full of the varying concoctions. I could hardly wait to sample my surreptitiously acquired cocktail but at this stage it was vital that I remain inconspicuous and to this end I crouched down behind one of the tables and took a sip from the glass, a very small sip but even then it took my breath away and I stayed behind that table for a very long time before finally the glass was empty. I felt exhilarated and made my way back to the end of the table and began to repeat the collection process, this time I didn't get far as some kind person noticed what I was doing and blew the whistle on me. I was taken over to where my parents were sitting and they watched like a hawk for the rest of the festivities.

On the many journeys to and from school I had noticed a great deal of building work taking place in a large field in the lane near home and wondered what it could be. As it increased in size it became obvious there was a new school being built. I followed it's progress with great interest and when it was getting very close to my eleventh birthday it appeared to be nearing completion. Somewhere around this time my parents were informed that I had been accepted into this new school and given the date of it's opening when I would be one of it's first intake of pupils. This was the start of a hectic round of shopping sprees during which my Mother bought me the school uniform, a maroon blazer with a gold piping surround, brown short trousers, a maroon and gold tie, brown stockings with the turnovers in maroon and gold, a maroon pullover with gold piping around the collar and the most wonderful pair of black "Shoes". Shoes not boots, for the first time in my life I was going to wear shoes. I said my goodbyes to my friends and the teachers at the little school where I had been really happy for the past two years or so, I was very sorry to leave but the thought of going to that brand new school softened the blow somewhat. This new school was about a two minute walk from home. There were to be both girls and boys attending but it was not "co-ed", they were in two different parts of the school one at one end and one at the other and the only things separating the boys from the girls were small triangles strategically placed in the centre of the corridors at the half way point. The playgrounds were also all one but with thick white painted lines across the middle depicting where each gender had to stay. I was duly enrolled along with some three hundred or so boys and girls. Although I didn't know it at the time the next three years were to be the most interesting and enjoyable of all my schooldays.

The school itself was obviously very modern and up to date. It had it's own purpose built gymnasium and an almost full size swimming pool. It's attraction for me should need no explanation. There were fields of all sizes to be used for the various sports for both boys and girls. The large playground was surrounded by either the building itself or just plain fields, making it possible to look out of any of the classroom windows and only see fields, trees, and hedges. The classrooms were very light and airy with high ceilings, this gave a totally different dimension to a classroom as I had previously known it. Here was an environment in which I could, and would, study and learn.

I was still very small for my age, compact but short, despite all the exercising, and I knew I was going to have to prove myself. My previous school had been a long way away and none of the pupils I had known were within the jurisdiction of this school at the present time. There were groups of boys walking around together obviously having known each other before. I was very much an outsider and it showed during those first few weeks. With Yorkshire boys you had to be invited to join them in their activities, you couldn't just muscle in. During those first few weeks we attended all the classes on all the subjects, this gave me time to reach a decision on which ones I was going to like and which I was not. Maths, History and Science, were definitely not my favourite subjects, all of which I wasn't good at, nor even fair, I did try to understand Maths but Algebra and such just did not sink in, the basics were all right, but beyond that I was hopeless.

I knew I would most likely have to prove myself and it happened rather sooner than I had expected during one playtime in the afternoon. In all schools there is always someone who is regarded as the 'Cock of the North', someone who has proved to be capable of taking care of himself, here was to be no exception. This particular boy had come from one of the local schools and a great many boys from that same school were here with him. He, rightly or wrongly, took over the mantle of "Top Dog" and of course had his old school chums to back him up. This particular afternoon a number of us were doing the usual larking about and during one of the melees this boy and I made contact, pretty hard contact, and we both ended up on the floor. We got up and he approached me in a very aggressive manner and said, "You should be more careful who you are bumping into unless you want a bunch of fives". "Some fist", I replied in an appropriate manner and we arranged to meet after school. He would have been about the same size as me, maybe a little taller- but not much. What experience he had I had no idea but I thought of a saying Dad had quoted to me "Brook no quarrel with any man, but being in, bear it, that thy opponent may beware of thee", and it was my intention to do just that. I didn't think this "Top Dog" was the bullying kind although I had already noticed in those first few weeks that he had a tendency to throw his weight about a bit. Home time came, the word had spread, and there was a large crowd that followed us out of the school gates to the field opposite. We removed our jackets and immediately he took a running jump at me, consequently we both finished up on the floor and were rolling around in the grass. This was not my way of doing things at all, I scrambled clear, stood up and waited for him, and he came at me. This was more like it, I was just getting into the swing of things and he wasn't liking it one little bit, when he was saved from further embarrassment by the appearance of the P/E teacher. He had seen the extra large number of pupils gathering. He grabbed us both by the ear, told the onlookers to go home, and with that marched us back into the school where he kept us for a good half hour and all the time attempting to bring home to us the error of our ways, then just before letting us go he said he would arrange for us to see the head master in the morning, and suggested that one way to settle our differences would be for us to meet in the gym under supervision with boxing gloves. We did have to see the head master and he gave us a right telling off, the teacher put forward his suggestion about the gym but the boy declined the offer, we never crossed swords again but the seeds of mistrust had been sown and from that time onwards he gave me a wide berth. After the furore had died down I was no longer treated like an outcast.

There were two other large schools in Barnsley, one was the Grammar school and another known as Longcar Central, they had more pupils than the rest and consequently monopolized the sporting competitions, none more so than the Borough swimming galas which were held every year in the Barnsley Baths and it was always one of these two that took the honours every time. The older pupils in our school had participated without altering that situation for the past two years but in the third year of our school's existence it was thought we had a team that was in with a fair chance and considered good enough to," bring home the bacon". We had very good individual contestants and a really confident relay team. The relay was the most prestigious event and the team had been going great guns for weeks, it consisted of a John, who was the first leg at backstroke, a Jack (me), on breast stroke, another Jack, the final leg at free-style, (crawl stroke), and on the day we were doing quite well in the individuals giving the top dogs plenty to think about. Then we were called to our race, confident that we were going to win. There were seven teams in seven lanes, three in each team and each swimmer would complete one length of the pool. We took our respective places, John and Jack at the shallow end opposite me at the deep end. In those days there were no starting positions as there are today, we only had the ends of the pool. The starter's gun sounded and John our lead boy set off from the other end on the first leg and I stood on the edge with my toes curled over the side to give me a good grip, he did as expected and was in the lead when he touched the wall below me, as soon as I saw him touch I stretched and pushed hard against the floor's surface straightening my legs as I did so, and, "I almost landed on top of him". There were the usual loud noises associated with any swimming competition all around me but I can honestly say I distinctly heard the spectators groan! When I had pushed off my left foot slid along the tiles and went very wide, putting me completely off balance and I was lucky to fall into the water as I could so easily have fallen onto the tiled surrounding. There are no words to describe just how I felt but I struggled to get my stroke going, it wasn't easy because when I had landed in the water I was absolutely flat, the proverbial "Belly -Flop". I did manage to get into some sort of rhythm and put everything into it but handed over to Jack, in "Fifth" place, he swam as he had never swum before but it was all to no avail he finished in third place. All the training, all the build up, was for nothing, as "I" had made such a mess of everything. What made matters worse was that the whole school had thought that I was the mainstay, but I had let everyone down including myself and it was a new experience for me and one that I have never forgotten to this day.

At sometime during that same year I decided to go to the canal and do a spot of fishing one Saturday afternoon, Jacqueline would have been about three and she wanted to come with me to do some fishing with a small fishing net that used to be mine. I didn't want to be lumbered with a girl who would require my constant attention but I lost the battle, and after she had been suitably dressed in warm clothes and an enormous straw hat with an extra large brim we went to the canal bank. I prepared my tackle, she kept dipping her net in the water where the bank sloped down towards a fairly shallow part. After only a short while she lost all interest in the net and between eating some sandwiches and having a little natter she sat on my coat and just watched. I had brought a few worms with me but the fish were biting and I saw that I hadn't many left so I dropped down on to the bank behind me and started scraping around for some more. I have no idea why I looked up over the bank but as I did so I saw a large splash, it was much too big for a fish and as there were no other people around it could only mean that my little sister had fallen into the water. I ran to the edge of the bank and looked out to where I had seen the splash and much to my relief I saw the straw hat floating on the water and dived in and swam out to where it was and lifted it clear of the water fully expecting to find a tiny frightened little girl underneath, there was nothing! When I had first seen that splash my heart had missed several beats but now it was definitely panic stations, I let go of the hat, turned round intending to dive under just as she popped up right alongside me, arms and legs flailing wildly. There was no need or time for lifesaving techniques, I just grabbed her and keeping her up out of the water did the breast stroke kick until we reached the shallow part. Once on the bank I sat her on the grass while I collected my things and then we set off across the field, she continuously blubbering, and I wondering how I was going to get out of this one. It must have taken all of five minutes since I first realised what had happened before we were back in the house but it seemed like an eternity. Explanations had to wait until we had both had a bath, and when we were both dressed and had warmed ourselves with a hot cup of cocoa nothing appeared to be very much the worse for the incident. There was very little I could say except to try and explain that it hadn't been my fault. Dad sat impassively, whilst I nervously awaited the outburst which I truly believed would erupt at any second, but he remained very calm, much to my surprise and relief. However he did say that all my fishing expeditions would be solo efforts in future. Over the years I have often reflected upon what happened and know that as she was in my care, my sister was my responsibility and it must have been my fault that she fell in.

There were some disturbing happenings in the town around this time, someone named Oswald Mosley, a Nazi sympathiser, had got himself a mob who held the same views, and calling themselves "Black Shirts" they went around most of the cities and towns parading through the streets trying to attract anyone to their cause. They were in full agreement with the dubious goings on in Germany. I didn't know what it was all about but most of the Barnsley area people did and they showed their disapproval of him and his mob in violent confrontations with them at every opportunity. There was one time when I was almost caught up in one of these fracas. I had walked from the other end of town and was making my way home when these Blackshirts, who had been attending a rally in the Civic hall, were attempting to drive away in a coach which had been specially laid on for them. People were standing in front of it, others were trying, with some success, to smash the doors and windows with big hammers and pick axes. There were other roads I could use without having to pass that one on my way home and having no wish to become involved I did a smart about turn and beat a hasty retreat.

My younger brother was born on December the second, the year before I was due to leave school. He was named Peter Brian. Unfortunately I never saw much of him, as soon as he was old enough to notice things, namely big brothers, I was always away in some different county, or hard at work, and very rarely staying at home. He would probably have not had the same interests as myself as there was such a big age difference but it would have been nice to have seen a lot more of him during his younger years.

My fourteenth birthday came and went, I was ready to leave school in a few weeks time and had been getting all sorts of advice as to what I should try do do when it became time for me to leave. Almost all the teachers showed a great interest and gave me the benefit of their experience but the main consensus of opinion centred around my acting abilities and they wanted me to allow them to make representation to certain places with a strong recommendation that I be given a position in one of the dramatic art colleges. I was very interested with the idea and put forward my views to my Father and Mother. He said there was no chance of him allowing a son of his to become an "Actor". Mother on the other hand said it was a good idea and if the teachers were so confident I should do as they suggest and allow them to apply for me. My father disagreed and after many weeks of heated arguments he decided that he would arrange to get me a "man's" job at the estate on his postal round. One day he announced that it was arranged and he took me to the hall.

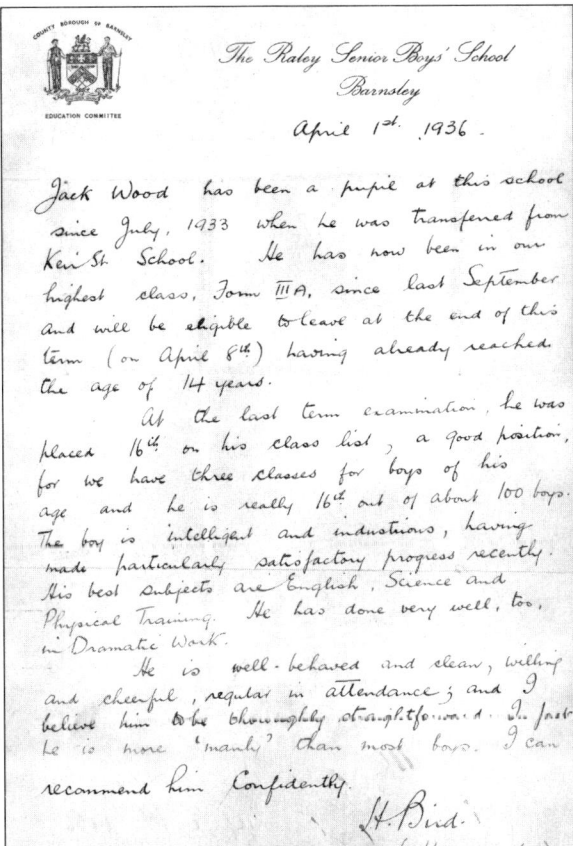

Finishing school report

47

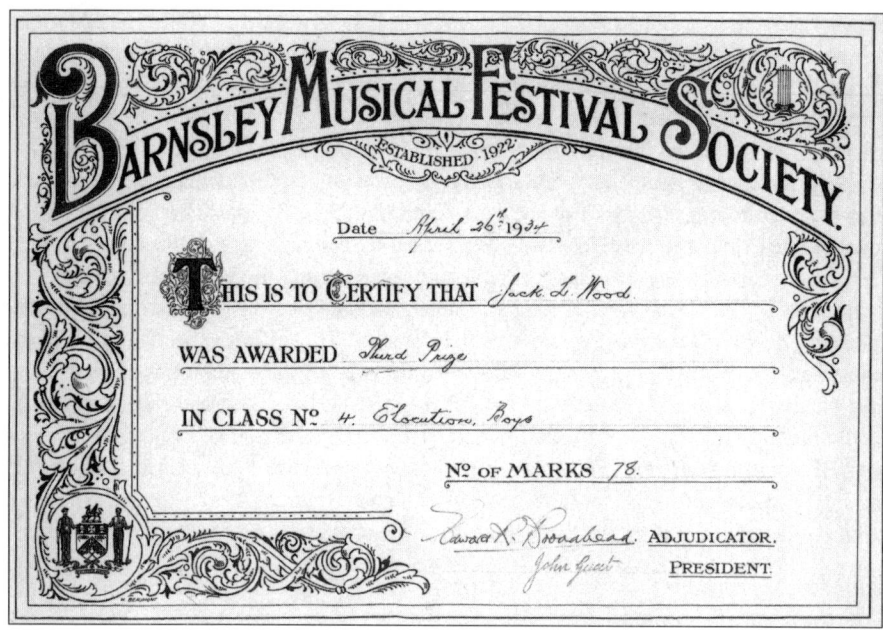

April 26th 1934 - 3rd place out of the whole school

We were met at the door by the Butler who immediately informed me that he was doing us, me and my Father, a great favour for even considering me for a post in his revered establishment. He took us into almost every room, first we went into the kitchen. It was a massive place with long worktop tables and a great big Yorkshire cooking range. There were exceptionally buxom ladies shuffling around in white smocks and white crinkly bonnets, young girls doing various jobs looking as if they were expecting a telling off at any moment, everyone working flat out all the time we were in there. Then we went into the dining room, another large very dull place, it looked as if it was capable of seating about forty persons at meal times. It was here the butler told me that it would be a long time before I would be allowed in here. On to the drawing room, this was the place where guests were entertained and in the evenings the owner and his entourage would sit and sip cocktails and discuss the day's happenings. It was full of dust traps, with curtains hanging from the walls, large chandeliers, fat easy chairs and settees, portraits of all the bewhiskered ancestors hanging everywhere. It was like living in the past. Then into the extra large hallway, where the butler just happened to mention that I should be feeling immensely proud that in about fifteen years time I would be the person answering this great door as the prestigious Butler. Up to that point he had been speaking in a quiet reserved tone of voice until he must have noticed me taking a great interest in the many attractive young ladies coming along the hallway and going upstairs. Then his whole attitude changed, his voice was no longer quiet and reserved, it became loud and harsh, and he said, "And there will be no looking at the girls they will be strictly off limits to you. If you are coming here you must put them right out of your mind". We then went upstairs, not into the rooms, but along the passageways between them where he pointed out where I would find the boots and shoes I would be cleaning ready for use before they were needed the following morning.

48

There were quite a few and it looked like a marathon task to me!

That being the end of the guided tour we ended up back in the hallway, now it was decision time. I would start at the bottom and be known as the "boot boy" which from what I had gathered so far meant being a general dogsbody doing the most mundane tasks. I would have one week-end off in six, with one or two evenings off when I would be able to go into the village. He and Father then went on to discuss when I would be leaving school, and would I be able to start that same week and how, because it would be too far for me to travel every day, I would have to live in at the hall. The discussion having apparently arrived at a satisfactory conclusion for both parties my Father turned to me and asked when was I actually going to leave school, was it in three or four weeks time? I had been listening intently and before I answered I knew I was going to make him very angry but I was fully prepared for it. I simply said, "It doesn't matter when I leave as I have no intention of coming to work here ". There was a moment of absolute silence then he apologised to the butler, telling him it would be all right, he would speak to me on the way home and get me to change my mind. We took our leave and drove home and for the next few weeks I was subjected to all kinds of reasons why I should accept the appointment. It made no difference I was adamant and dug my toes in. Mother never interfered except to say it was my decision and that I had no need to take the job if I didn't want to. Then unknown to anyone she wrote a letter to her brother Edward in Norwich, Norfolk, and arranged for me to go and stay with him. Two weeks later I made the train journey down to Norwich.

Chapter 5

I had, on numerous occasions during my childhood, said I would like to become a boy soldier so when Mother wrote to Ted she informed him of this and he asked his Father, my Grandfather, if he would take me along for an interview if I did come down to Norwich. An interview was arranged for the second week after my arrival and I was really looking forward to it. Gladys and Ted lived in a beautiful bungalow with a general store attached and surrounded by land which Ted had made into an exotic garden, it was a sight to behold with flowers and fruit trees and a large part of it planted with vegetables. The bungalow and shop were constructed of timber and it was on a sparsely populated estate made up of plots of land upon which were built living accommodations, almost all made of timber. Iit was clean and bright, not a bit like Yorkshire, and I knew it was definitely going to be much healthier here. Ted worked as a postman at the general post office in the city of Norwich. This place was three miles out of the city, hence the postal address, Three Mile Lane, and I knew at once that I was going to enjoy my stay here.

On the day of the interview I went to Grandfather's house and we walked to the Royal Norfolk Regiment's barracks on top of the hill overlooking the city. I thought his being present would help me to achieve my ambition as he had only recently retired as Regimental Sergeant Major of the regiment and was consequently very well thought of. I was given a thorough medical examination, no problems there, I was then interviewed by an officer who seemed perfectly satisfied but he then told me that he wanted me to go away and grow a bit then apply again, as he thought I was too small at present. I was very disappointed as this was the first time I had ever been turned down for anything I had applied for. There was nothing I could do about it at the moment so a few days later I found myself a job as an accounts clerk in a wholesale timber merchants office, it would help me to pay something towards my keep while I was staying here. I also helped around the garden and shop and Ted explained about the different plants and how they should be cared for.

Some Friday evenings we went to the village dance hall, this was something else I had never done before and the first time we went I was more than pleasantly surprised as it was a truly remarkable atmosphere everyone was so friendly. To begin with I was a real jerk, my feet didn't do as I wanted them to, but after both Ted and Gladys had dragged me round a couple of dozen times I began to get the hang of the very basic steps. One thing I found to be very different to anything I had ever done before came about when Ted introduced me to some of the local village lovelys, and they were extremely lovely! One in particular was absolutely gorgeous, the real proverbial "Cracker", the only slight problem though; she was tall and slim I was short and stocky but, "Yes, I did take her out a few times". I was having the time of my life.

There was one man on the estate who had a very large plot of land attached to his bungalow, some of it was cultivated but there was a large amount that could only be described as a very bumpy field. I got to know him and his family well. He had a small flat platform truck and an awesome looking motor bike which was a giant of a thing. Even though I could only just reach the footrests he taught me how to ride it, and how to drive the truck on the field. I won't say I found them easy to handle because they were rather difficult but at least I learned to handle both with a modicum of success and was quite proud of my achievement knowing I could now handle a motor bike and a motor car. This same man did car repairs, he would strip the engines down and build them up again; I used to watch him at work and he could see I was interested so he showed me how to do it. I did have a full time job during five and a half days but when it was light in the evenings, as soon as I had demolished my dinner, I would make a bee line for his dilapidated workshop and go every Saturday afternoon and all day Sunday if Ted and Gladys hadn't made other arrangements. He gave me a good grounding in all aspects of car repairing.

Ted decided he would educate me further and gave himself a real problem. He had been first clarinet player in the regimental band and he suddenly took it upon himself to teach me how to play that instrument. He deicided that his first task was to teach me to read music. Having never managed to learn to do this before I knew it would be a struggle. I tried very hard; for Ted as much as me, but in the end he admitted defeat and I decided that I would never try and learn music again.

I was very happy living here with so many people taking an interest in almost everything I did, I was going out meeting people and having an education in the ways of life, something I hadn't done before. I had mixed in at school and with my friends around the areas in which we had been living but apart from that I had been very much a "Loner" and had done very little outside our home life.

Later that year I changed jobs and went to work for a horticultural firm, still as an accounts clerk. It was more pay and much nearer home so not as much travelling. It wasn't quite so exacting as the timber merchants, I had much more work in the mornings but the afternoons were very quiet so I used to leave the office and go into the garden area. They grew all kinds of plants which were sold to distributors all around the country, like rose, apple, and plum trees, and gooseberry bushes, to name but a few. Another much larger area concentrated on growing vegetables, these were prepared to be sold in the wholesale market. I spent as much time as possible with both types of gardener. Whilst I was there I purchased a shrub and gave it to Ted, it's name was "Cupressus Immuni", he planted it in the garden at the bungalow. When many years later they moved to a house near the city they took it with them and it occupied a place of prominence near the front window. However, it grew so tall that it had to be dug up, much to the annoyance of Ted. It was one foot tall when it was first planted, when it was dug up it had reached almost eighteen feet, so it did have a good innings, didn't it ?

Just before Christmas of that year I received a letter from my Mother telling me that uncle Harold had taken on the tenancy of a farm, and that he was trying to work it on his own but it was proving to be too difficult for him. Despite having my aunt Annie to help him where she could, things were too hard for him and so he had asked if I would consider going home and helping them out. I didn't really want to leave Norwich and the lifestyle I had at present.

I was settled and content but pressure was put upon me during the weeks that followed and I returned to Yorkshire and commenced my apprenticeship as a farm labourer. The pay was going to be much less than I had been receiving but it didn't matter as it was apparently going to be paid straight to my Father! I wasn't aware of the circumstances at that time but it later came to my notice that he had been asked to invest in the farm. How much of an investment it was I never did find out. So my sweat and blisters were going to contribute to the repayments and I was casually informed that I would have no need for money as I wouldn't have any time to spend it!

I knew nothing about farming; the only animal I had been personally connected with was Mick my little Terrier. I gathered from the discussions taking place that I was to learn all aspects of the job, both arable and dairy farming, I was told I would find it extremely hard at first and that I would be working very long hours. At the time I didn't have other things on my mind so I concentrated on learning how, and what, to do. There was one thing I knew was going to make my life more bearable than it first appeared. My grandmother had decided to leave her beloved Lodge and came to stay at the farm. Annie was having to do a lot of the work, particularly the dairy side, so Grandma was doing the housework and what was most interesting taking care of all the meals. She was an excellent cook and I have always felt so relaxed and content in her presence.

The first thing I was told was about the most important animal on a dairy farm, namely the cow; it needed feeding, cleaning, and everything done to ensure it's well being and of course it had to have the milk it produced removed. I was told how this was done by taking a wooden stool and a spotlessly clean galvanised bucket. Place the stool just in front of the cow's right rear leg and gently sit down. Place the bucket between your knees allowing the bottom to rest on the floor at an angle, lean forward and place your forehead carefully on the soft part of the animal's body alongside the top of the leg. Your forehead became, in effect, your early warning system, detecting the slight "tremor" that would precede any attempt by the beast to cause you problems.

The part where the milk is contained is known as the "udder", it is situated between the two rear legs, attached to it are four "teats", and to extract the milk these require manipulating in a certain fashion, two at a time. First take a good grip on the two teats nearest the cow's tummy. Place the thumb and forefinger at the top with the other fingers just touching all the way down to the bottom of the teat, then holding the top firmly squeeze with each finger end in turn hopefully bringing the milk down to the end of the teat and out into the bucket.

Milk is a necessary commodity and great care had to be taken in it's production, especially the cleanliness side of it. At all times during the milking process I had to wear a clean white smock, a clean skull cap big enough to tuck my hair out of sight, my hands had to be clean and if there were any cuts on them they had to be covered with a plaster. The cow itself had to be washed in all the places that came into contact with me and the parts of it's body that overhung the bucket. The stalls had to be cleaned and washed after every milking session but just swept out before it began. When the milk was taken from the cow it was very warm and had to be immediately taken to the dairy to be cooled. It was repeatedly run over a galvanised concertina shaped receptacle that had cold water constantly running through it, once it was cooled it was put into a churn and placed in a walk-in refrigerator. All the equipment used during the milking process had to be sterilised twice daily.

The correct sort of food is essential to the well being of the cow because certain foods can affect the taste of the milk. When they are turned out into the fields for the first time after being kept in the byre during the winter months the grass can make the milk taste of the grass. Their digestive systems are very delicate almost anything can upset them and that quickly affects the milk. They are fed on Cow Cake, a mixture of ground corns, dried grass and with a measured amount of minerals, there is nothing a cow likes better than to have a mineral block fixed somewhere in the stall where it can reach it and lick away to it's hearts content. A liberal amount of hay is placed in the troughs after milking if they are staying in, some straw would also be provided as bedding, wheat or oat straw. To complete the bedding arrangements a nice floor covering of sawdust keeps them dry and helps prevent them slipping in the stalls.

All of the above was explained to me in detail to give me the right temperament to look after these animals. Cows are very timid and more afraid of you than you should be of it. The amount of milk they produce can be affected in so many ways, for instance if some is left in the udder at the end of the milking session it will produce that much less the next time it comes to be milked. There is nothing magic about this, the cow produces milk for one reason only and that is to feed it's calf, if any is left in the cow assumes that the calf has had sufficient and does not require the full amount it is at present producing so it will reduce it. With a lot of practice and some inevitable mishaps I mastered the art of removing their produce and learned how to take care of them in the best possible manner.

When the grass was getting too short in the main pastures we had a spare one we used, but it was across the A61 main road, and the first time I drove the cows back to the farm from this field one of them caused me a problem. On the way we had to pass the end of the canal and it was deep and fairly wide. There was very little traffic on the road so it couldn't have been frightened by anything to cause it to do what it did. They were all walking quite sedately when this one decided to have a look at the water. It started running and appeared to pick up speed just as it reached the bank, took a leap in the air and flopped into the water. As it struggled it took itself further away from the bank. It didn't take long for a considerable sized crowd to appear and all manner of suggestions were put to me as to how it could be brought back to the bank. One bright spark turned up with a length of rope and proceeded to attempt to lasso the beast, he wasn't having any success so someone else had a go, in fact several people had several goes. It turned into quite a contest but it soon became very obvious to everyone that Worsbro' Bridge had no "cowboys " living in it's area. It was then that I noticed the rest of the cows milling around on the main road. In all the excitement I had forgotten about them and concentrated on the one in the water. As there were enough people around to take care of that one I took the rest on to the farm and after chaining them up I returned to the scene, having made up my mind to swim out to the cause of all the mayhem and "place" the rope around it's neck. In the meantime some chap had at last been lucky and lassoed it and it was tearing around the rest of the adjoining ground in a blind panic scattering the onlookers in all directions. Why he hadn't kept it attached to the rope I shall never know, but after some considerable time and a lot of shouting and arm waving I got it onto the road and we went back to the farm together.

After six months of travelling from Barnsley very early every morning and not getting home until late it was decided that I should start to live-in at the farm. It was easier in some ways and yet in others it wasn't. I was then available all the time and good use was made of that fact, for instance when things had to be done during the night time I was called upon to assist. If one of the cows was expecting and it looked as if she would deliver before morning our services would be required to attend her. It was nearly always a long night and eyes would start to close at varying intervals as was the case one night when Harold and I were awaiting the arrival of one calf. He was sitting on one of the three legged stools, I was reclining on some straw with my back up against one of the stalls, we had been on watch for quite a long time when I heard a dull thud. I looked over to where he was and he was face down in a really sloppy amount of the stuff that is usually deposited during any night in a cow shed. Avoiding the urge to roar with laughter I picked up a bucket of clean water we had brought in with us in case it was needed, and informing him of my intentions first I poured it all over his head, neck, and shoulders. He spluttered and didn't speak, not one word, and just walked out of the byre and into the house. He returned some time later, lit his pipe, and gradually came to see the funny side of it and together we had a good laugh. The whole episode does prove the point of the saying "You should never fall asleep on the job", doesn't it ?

We had a Bull, and he was retained for the services he performed at varying intervals throughout the year. He was housed where all bulls should be housed, in a proper bull pen. It was inside a separate building and had an exceptionally strong but easily manoeuvrable safety gate. It was made of galvanised round steel piping and so designed as to enable the handler to put a scoop full of cow cake into the feeding trough without going inside the pen, the bull would then put it's head through the gate to get at the food, in doing so it would allow the handler to close the gate and securely fasten it, therefore preventing the bull from withdraw-ing it's head until this gate was unlocked. The whole pen was then cleaned and thoroughly washed down every day. I was allocated the job of handler and did the necessary every day and I always took great care when going into the pen, that is until one memorable day. I put the cake in the trough, closed the gate, went inside and commenced cleaning. I was working on the far side of the wall using a scrubbing brush and had almost finished when I felt hot breath on the back of my neck. Yes, it was his majesty the bull, he had scoffed his cake, turned as he should not have been able to do, and was now inspecting me and my equipment, staring at me with very expressionless soulful eyes. I realised immediately what I must have done. He had a good sniff at me as I was gingerly making my way past him to get all the way across to the gate with the bucket and brushes etc;. I couldn't leave them inside the pen where he could cause damage to himself. He followed my every move with a vacant stare and I kept moving slowly making my way around him to reach the gate. I reached it and pulling it to after me I locked it, breathed a deep sigh of relief and looked out into the yard behind me, and there stood Harold. Apparently he had arrived just as the bull made contact with me and was afraid to do, or say anything for fear of disturbing it. I had closed the gate but hadn't rechecked to see if it had locked, my carelessness could have had serious results for myself, the bull and also Harold. It certainly taught me to pay more attention to what I was doing.

To be able to produce milk a cow has to first have a calf and when the calf is born it is usually left in a loose stall with it's mother, sometimes for a day and a half, it drinks the milk from her which is no good at that time for putting in with the rest of the milk, it is known as "Beastings" it is very thick and discoloured. After the day and a half the calf is taken from the stall and put into a calf pen where some of it's Mother's milk is then taken to it in a bucket and it is taught how to drink. This teaching how to drink business had it's funny side but it was also possible to end up with some very bruised knuckles when performing this deed. You had to place your hand in the bucket of milk with your fingers pointing upwards and guide the calf's mouth towards them, with one finger representing a teat it would take it into it's mouth and begin to suck thereby drawing the milk up the finger from the bucket, it was a fiddly job to start with but gradually it got the hang of it. The calf had spent all of it's life so far taking milk from it's mother's udder and had formed a habit of knowing how to make the milk flow faster into it's mouth; it had only to give the udder a hefty push and it would release more liquid. What you were attempting to do was to make the calf think your finger was the teat but there is no way you could tell it that it had no udder attached to it so it performed as it had always done and would draw it's head back every so often and give an almighty thump at your hand, which in turn came into painful contact with the sides of the bucket, sometimes it would make your eyes water. All boy calves were destined for the cattle market, usually after about one week, and the females were sometimes kept to have calves of their own. On Harold's farm the two to three years it would take before there was any return on the cost of getting them to that stage was not a practical proposition, a quick return was necessary in order to pay all the bills which kept arriving. It meant that all the calves were despatched to the market as near as possible to their first weeks birthday.

Harold and I would usually accompany them on the day the market was open each week, which was always on Thursdays; he to sort out the cash side of things and then disappear into the drovers pub at the entrance to the market place. I would meander around all the market looking at the various things that were there and he would usually give me sixpence so that I could get a cup of tea and a teacake in the market cafe. The whole of the market had a special atmosphere, one that I found to be very enjoyable and relaxing; to walk alongside the rows of pens containing all kinds of animals. There were all kinds of noises as each one added his or her special contribution, together with the auctioneers loudly asking for more bids as they went along the separate pens containing a number of Calves, Pigs, Sheep, or Goats, before accepting the final bid for each of it's occupants in turn. The auction ring was housed in a separate building to the rest and was built to form a circle. The animals, mainly cows, were paraded inside a round metal fenced enclosure where they were attended by one man who at varying intervals would prod them with a stick to keep them on the move. The spectators were all around, some seated others standing, the seated ones were in a kind of semi circle area with seats stretching almost up to the ceiling on different levels. When it was possible to spare the time off on some Thursday's Harold and myself would go to the same cattle market for a few hours just to have a look round.

I had been living in at the farm for almost two months when one of the saddest things in my life occurred. At sometime during one night my Grandmother had a stroke. She was very ill for a long time but she was a strong and very determined lady and this strength and determination saw her pull through, but the stroke left her completely paralysed all down the left side. This was absolutely devastating to my Grandmother as she was unable to do anything for herself. When she was eventually able to come downstairs she had to be carried both up and down in a chair which she then sat in all day. I can imagine how she must have felt having to be dependant upon someone else for everything; she was seventy two years of age when this awful thing happened and she remained in this depressing state without making even the slightest improvement for almost ten years. It became impossible for my aunt Annie to carry on with any of the farm work, Grandma was her first priority and it proved to be a full time job both day and night. It was a very upsetting time for everyone but all I could think about was my very dear Grandmother and how she must have been feeling.

My aunt Annie was very much like my Father in so many things; she was very determined in her ways and had a sharp tongue, praise for anything was very rarely forthcoming but scathing remarks were plentiful if something had not been to her entire satisfaction. I was on the receiving end far too often but for the life of me I never knew why as I always tried to do my best in everything both in the house and around the farm. I must admit my life at the farm could have been much happier if she had been a bit different towards me. I have thought long and hard over the years trying to fathom out what I did to warrant her displeasure but have yet to come up with any concrete reason or satisfactory explanation. Harold was entirely opposite, he would tell me what to do and if I wasn't as successful as he had expected me to be he would say try again and show me the best way to achieve my objective. My aunt's objectionable manner made me feel like leaving the farm on so many occasions, I never complained to anyone but it was a source of extreme annoyance to me when I knew that with a bit more tolerance on her part things could have been entirely different. Harold was on the receiving end of her tongue almost as much as I was but he would agree with everything she had to say and then do exactly as he wanted regardless of the consequences. This was the only thing that spoilt my time at the farm, everything else was great, I loved the life.

Other animals played their part in the successful running of the farm. In those days there were very few motorised methods with which to do the work it was all done by horses. We had two, one was a "Clydesdale", not the heaviest of the horse family but a strong one all the same and good enough to perform most jobs, his name was Prince and he was dark brown, almost black, in colour with some white above his hooves around the four fetlocks. He had a good temperament except when he had been turned out in the field over the weekend, then for the first hour he could be what you might call "frisky" but normally he was very pleasant to work with. He had numerous forms of work and one of his main tasks was to pull the four wheeled dray which was a very well used form of transport around the farm. It was capable of carrying anything up to three tons. There was also a two wheeled heavy cart which could carry slightly more than two tons if the load was not too high, it had much larger wheels than the dray making it much easier to pull in heavy ground, this did the jobs where a smaller base would be better than the big one on the dray. Then there was all the work on the land; the ploughing, the harrowing, and all the things appertaining to the harvesting of the various crops. He had a stable situated at the rear of the cow sheds and an area in which he could run, jump, and loosen up in general if he chose to do so in the stack yard. His stable was a light, airy, roomy place where he was fed and watered but if he needed to go out in the fields to work for any length of time during the day we would take a nose-bag with his food inside it for him to scoff during a break in the proceedings, any water he would need came from the troughs or the streams that were to be found in almost all the fields we worked in. His hardest task was to pull the plough, digging the soil and operating the different types of harrow in preparation for planting or sowing, this could be extremely hard work when the soil was wet and consequently heavy. All the corn and hay had to be cut by machine which he had to pull during harvesting time which all in all made him really live up to his name of "work-horse" and he was always ready for a well earned rest when he was returned to his stable in the evenings. We became the best of pals and I thought the world of him.

The other horse was not a horse as such, he was a pony, he went by the name of Tommy and was pure white, and about half the size of Prince but he was a live wire having his own ideas about everything. His sole job was to pull the milk float, a very light two wheeled cart from which the milk deliveries were made every day, he was at times difficult to put it mildly but he knew his job very well. The person delivering the milk had to go to the houses and consequently had to leave him standing in the street, his main asset was that he would stand perfectly still until he was told to move. He had a stable next door to Prince, exactly the same, being roomy warm and dry and he had the freedom to roam around the stack yard, it was fairly big and he could, and did, tear round it at a breakneck speed giving himself plenty of loosening up exercise. I thought a great deal of him and Prince, and between them they provided me with many pleasant working hours.

There were many things to learn, it was unbelievable just how many there were, but after being taught what to do and how to do them I worked very hard at making myself proficient in almost all of them. Most of it was hard work, some plain common sense, but on the whole it was knowledge plus strength that was required to do them all properly. I hadn't done my usual exercises in Norwich, but I remained reasonably fit so the work didn't pose any problems. I did all of it to the best of my ability, knowing it was doing me good. When Harold and I were repairing, or making new fences, he taught me the correct way to swing a big hammer. The correct way is easier than the one used by most people and having used one incorrectly a few times myself it was rather difficult to adapt to the correct positioning of the hands. This positioning of the hands, before, during and at the end of the strike are the most important part of learning how to use one. After the inevitable hours of diligent practise he must have thought I was doing it the right way because he used to hold the post I was swinging at (a very risky thing to do unless you have explicit faith in the one swinging the hammer). He also took very great care teaching me how to use a long handled scythe, you know the piece of equipment "Old Father Time" is holding in all the pictures of him? This was used to cut long grass or corn in the hedgerows and the headlands. It was a dangerous piece of equipment and in the wrong hands it could prove to be lethal. In time I did handle it reasonably well and used it to good effect without chopping anyone's legs off in the process. Another implement with a long handle was the pick axe and it was used to dig out all the roots and large stones at the edges of the fields (the Headlands). This digging was necessary in order to utilise all the land that could have been unsuitable if it had been left to get overgrown near the hedges. Using the big hammer, the scythe, and the pick axe, proved to be good strength and muscle building pieces of equipment and I used them with great vigour.

Something I did find difficult at first and that was learning how to control Prince when we were doing certain types of field work such as the ploughing. He was attached to the plough with his harness but the only control I had over him was one single length of rope attached to his halter and as I had to have both hands on the handles of the plough the only means of communicating with him was by word of mouth. In order to get him to turn or keep in a straight line he had to be given orders like the word "Gee", meaning move over to the right, and to the left the word "Arv", he would answer to the instruction but not always do the amount of change of direction I intended him to do. I suppose he found the tone of my voice different to the one he was used to, namely my uncles. However we did get used to each other in time but when we had finished a day like that he was ready for a good feed and a good rest, he had most certainly earned it.

Sometimes there was exceptionally heavy work to be done and for that we required the services of a stronger horse. The local council had a "Shire" horse, he was called "Captain", a big, almost white, heavy legged type of horse much bigger and stronger than Prince, and for a small remuneration he was loaned to us for the odd day now and again. His everyday handler was a cousin of Harold's and he always gave us the lowdown on some of "Captain's" slip shod ways of working but as it would have been very unfair to Prince to expect him to do the kind of work we intended to do we used him occasionally. His main work for the council was carting things around the roads and as he needed to be able to keep his feet and have a firm grip on the road surface he had extra large studs fitted to his shoes. These shoes were made of metal and were nailed on to the hard part surrounding the horse's hoof. It didn't hurt the horse when this was being done because their feet, apart from a very soft and delicate piece in the middle known as the Thrush, are very similar to our toe and finger nails, hard and without any nerve. They had to be trimmed at regular intervals just as our nails do; this trimming is called paring and is done with a very sharp knife. The studs fitted to Captain's shoes were very big and came almost to a razor sharp end and this was about one inch across.

One day Prince was required to do some much needed harrowing in one of the fields so we borrowed Captain to take a few exceptionally large loads of manure from the yard to one of the heaps in a field over the railway crossing on West Street. The entrance to the field and the area around this particular heap was very sludgy and slippery. To turn the dray round inside the field with such a heavy load on it would have been very unfair to the horse as the wheels of the dray would sink into the soft soil, so I decided to turn him round at the entrance, on the hard surface of the road, and then back the dray up to the heap, in doing so Captain would have a hard solid surface on which to work when doing the turning. Unfortunately I had cause to regret my decision! Not only was he heavy legged he was what is known in the best of "farming" circles as a "Splatter Footed" one as well. That meant he threw his feet all over the place. We arrived at the field and having worked out exactly what I was going to do I took hold of his bridle with both hands and started to manoeuvre him round in a tight circle. There ensued a great deal of struggling on both our parts when it suddenly felt as if the whole world was standing on my left foot. He had splayed his feet around so much that he had put all his weight on one of his feet and that one was now placed fairly and squarely on my left foot. I had an awful time trying to get him to move so that I could get free. It must have been very comfortable for him because he just didn't want to move despite all my efforts. After what seemed an age he did at last condescend to lift up his foot and then the real trouble started, as he lifted his foot my left foot came up also. I took a quick look down and saw that the top of my boot appeared to be stuck to the bottom of his shoe. I tried to twist my boot around hoping it would come away from his shoe: it didn't. He had at last lifted his foot up but he couldn't stand on three legs for long, so, he put it down again. I felt the bones disintegrating in my foot, at least that is what it felt like. Then he started first taking his foot off the floor then putting it down again straight away, after a lot of "weight ons and weight offs I was quite suddenly free. How long this had taken I really don't know, but both he and I were very upset. I tried to calm him down and we completed the manoeuvre, I was surprised that I could walk. He turned without any further problems and I backed him up to the heap and unloaded the dray and we went back to the farm. After taking his harness off I put him in Prince's stable, gave him a drink and a scoop full of oats then went into the house to inspect the damage. It was quite considerable, but luckily only for my boot. I had taken it off and examined it to find out exactly what had caused that excruciating pain. There was a large tear in the upper part near the big toe and the sole had a two inch gash in it. When my uncle took a look he said that one of the studs from Captain's shoe had gone clean through my boot and must have been sticking out of the sole of my boot and only a miracle had saved at least the big toe, and more than likely the next one to it as well, from being severed. As it was I only had to put another boot on, soak my foot because it was sore and bruised, have a refreshing cup of tea and prepare for the evenings milking session.

The first milk delivery I went on I was taught how to harness Tommy and put him between the shafts of the float, and load two twelve gallon churns of milk in the correct way. They were obviously very heavy and for them to be loaded incorrectly would have meant Tommy having all this weight pressing down on his back which would never have done. The float had two large slim wheels, a body which was light, almost round, with a light but strong metal step that nearly reached the ground at the very end of the body at the back. When Tommy was in the shafts, if you were to stand on this step it would lift the shafts upwards, in so doing it would take the weight of the float off his back and the shafts would move up and down very freely, as they were fastened securely to his harness there was no danger of them coming loose. The churns were placed at the very back end of the body and strapped in therefore ensuring that there was no weight on his back, so all he had to do was pull it, not carry it, and with the wheels being so big this pulling was not difficult at all. Just to give you some idea of how easy it was you could do it by simply placing your hand at the rear of the float and lean on it and it would move. So Tommy thought he was on his holidays doing that milk round:

Sixteen cows being milked twice a day produced a lot more milk than we needed for our customers so the bulk of the production was sold to the Cooperative Society. Our deliveries were made in the mornings and again in the evenings. The morning one was the main one but some people had a half a pint then and another half pint in the evening as they so frequently said "I want fresh milk, not some that is half a day old". I would take a one gallon can with a one pint and one half pint measure to the door, knock on it and someone would appear with a jug or some such receptacle, state how much they wanted and I would then pour from the one gallon can into which measure was needed, pour it into their preferred holder, and with a polite good morning or evening whichever the case may be, I would be on my way. This was a very time consuming affair. Some conversations did occasionally take place but not too often because I was working to a tight schedule and had to get back to do other work.

Some of the hardest days on the farm were taken up by the harvesting of the crops which had been growing during the spring and summer months. We had six fields usually set down to corn and these were the ones that had to be cut and gathered when the weather was fine. Sometimes it was made very difficult when it never put more than a few days together of dry weather. To cut the corn Harold would work with Prince using a machine known as a Binder. I would follow the binder picking up the sheafs two at a time, keeping the bottoms of them about two feet apart I would stand them up to form a triangle with the ground, this was done to allow the straw and corn to have plenty of sun with air travelling through and around it to make it dry. If the weather was kind and it didn't rain for the next few days, the sheafs would be forked onto a dray and transported back to the farm for stacking in the yard or taken to one part of the field and there made into a stack. All the sheafs had to be really dry before they were placed on these stacks, if it was even slightly damp there was a great risk of it overheating and ending up on fire. This overheating also applied to the hay that was made from the fields of grass that were cut and made into stacks but instead of the hay being tied in sheafs it was spread out onto the ground and turned over a few times during the next day or two to allow it to dry thoroughly. There were fields of oats, wheat, and barley, all of which were too much for Harold and myself to do all the work this entailed so others from the surrounding area were brought in to help, casual workers who were paid of course.

There were some jobs I found to be very boring and exceptionally hard work, for instance the potatoes were dug up around the end of September and I had the unenviable task of retrieving them and putting them in a bucket. I followed the plough carrying this bucket and bending my back to it's fullest extent picked up the potatoes and deposited them into it, each bucketful was emptied into a cart and when the cart became full they were taken back to the stack yard to be made into a 'pie'. The ground upon which this pie was to be prepared was levelled out and all the potatoes spread out along it, then when it was large enough it would be covered with straw and given a good covering of soil about one foot in depth, if it was made properly this pie would keep the potatoes free from frost throughout the winter. Other ground produce like turnip, swede and mangold, were treated in much the same way but these were slightly different to prepare for their entry into a pie, they had large leafy tops and long straggly roots which were removed in the field as soon as they came out of the ground. The way this was carried out caused more back aches by walking along the rows and pulling them up with one hand, then each one had the tops and roots cut off by using an exceptionally sharp instrument known as a "bill hook" in the other hand. During the winter months these would be taken from their pie a few at a time and put through a grinding machine, these were then fed to the animals when required. The pigs preferred their's just dropped in the feeding trough whole. One other crop that we grew was known as "kale", it was a dark green and essential for the cows when they couldn't go out because of the weather as it replaced the grass missing from their diet. The pigs and horses would have a root or two sometimes, but this kale was not put into a pie it was simply stored in one of the outhouses.

Another job that took place towards the end of the summer was the Threshing (To separate the corn from the straw). The thresher was placed close to the stack and the steam engine some distance away as it contained a large open fire to make the steam. It required a number of men to work this equipment, some were doing the job of forking the sheafs from the top of the stack to the men on the machine for them to feed it into the actual separating contraption inside the thresher. Others were removing the straw, which had already been through the machine and had the corn removed, and making it into a new stack. I was allocated the task of attaching an empty sack onto the side of the machine and operating a lever which allowed the corn to flow into the sack, when a sack was full I stopped the flow before removing it and replacing it with another and after tying it's neck securely I dragged the full one to a dray and somehow, and I do mean somehow, lifted it bodily onto the dray. Each sack was made to hold two hundredweight, (two hundred and twenty four pounds). Believe me it was some job and I was always ready when milking time came round so that I could have a rest. Threshing days did have their compensations though as it was the general practice for the farmer to provide

60

food for all the workers, this was done twice during a long day by the appearance of a few large baskets containing some real solid food; home made chunky sliced bread sandwiches filled with ham, cheese, or beef, together with enormous jars of pickled onions, all washed down with a never ending supply of ice cold beer, or for such as me, home made lemonade.

Throughout my time on the farm I had some narrow escapes on the injuries side, some I have already mentioned but there was one from which I didn't escape. There was a young man who sometimes helped out on different jobs, he was a nice chap, very willing and a hard worker. One day he was helping me load the dray with manure in the farm yard, we were both using the traditional four pronged fork, he working from the left of the pile and I from the right, facing each other. In our efforts to get it loaded in quick time we must have got in close to each other, I went in to pick up a forkful as he was bringing one up to throw it onto the dray and one prong from his fork went into my hand. The prong pierced the part between the forefinger and the next finger of my right hand and the point of the prong was clearly visible protruding from the back of my hand; a good two inches of it was all the way in, between the two fingers. He started to apologise but I cut him short and suggested he pull the offending point out from it's painful position. It took a bit of withdrawing and at first seemed to be stuck as it was so far in, but eventually it came free. It wasn't showing signs of bleeding very much, but on closer inspection it was agreed I should pay a visit to the local doctor.

It was with some trepidation that I walked the half mile or so to the Doctor's surgery and presented myself to his receptionist. After waiting a few minutes a gruff voice called out my name from a room behind the receptionist. I entered the room and saw a big man sitting behind a large desk, I proffered my damaged hand but he must have thought I wanted him to shake it as a greeting, he brushed it aside and said, "What's the matter with you?". I then told him why I had put out my hand, he had a look, grunted, stood up, and from a cabinet nearby took a bottle. I just managed to see the name "peroxide"on the side of it as he unscrewed the top, then from somewhere he produced a long thin stick, longer than a normal pencil and much thinner, wrapped a small amount of cotton wool around three quarters of the length of it, took it to the sink and poured a liberal amount of the peroxide over the cotton wool and holding my hand in a grip of iron turned it face down and pushed the stick all the way through the hole between the two fingers and proceeded to move it around in a circular motion inside it. Now I don't know whether you have ever had the misfortune to spill any peroxide into an open wound but if you have then you will have some idea what it must have felt like for me. Discoloured white stuff was bubbling out of both ends of the hole, a mixture of manure, peroxide, and blood, then after quite a long time he withdrew the stick completely, had a quick look at the damage and said, "There!, I think that will have got rid of it but if you have any problems come back and see me. Keep it clean and don't cover it up at all". I remember thinking at the time how on earth I was going to manage that with the amount of dirt I came into contact with every single day and arriving at the conclusion that it would be an utter impossibility.

So far I have only dealt with the harvesting of the crops but they had to be planted first, this in some cases was also a backbreaking job especially setting the seed potatoes, the soil was prepared in the normal manner, it was ploughed and harrowed then a plough with a dividing share made a kind of trench in straight lines all the way across the field, a cart full of manure was then driven alongside these trenches and a man using a fork gave them all a liberal amount, when they had all been treated in this way the same person walked along each of the rows distributing the deposited manure evenly along the whole of the trench. The person nominated for the actual setting would fill a bucket with seed potatoes and walk along inside the trench placing them about one foot apart, firmly embedding each one in the manure, and carry on doing this until the end of the row was reached or the bucket became empty, in that case it meant a walk to the cart and refill it, when each row was set the plough was used to fill in the trench. Harold did the ploughing side of it and I did the rest.

The sowing of the many types of corn was dealt with in an entirely different way, the soil was ploughed and disc harrowed but then gone over quite a few times with the chain harrow to make it very fine. The actual sowing was done by hand, a woven wicker basket full of whatever seed was required was strapped across the front of the chest of the man doing the sowing. He would start at one end of the field and fill both his hands with the seed and commence a steady walk forward and throw a handful in a wide arc in front of him, as each foot came forward he would throw whichever handful was next, all the time taking a handful from the basket and trying to keep in a straight line across the field.

My aunt Annie and uncle Harold regularly attended St. James's church on West street. It was very conveniently situated almost next door to the farm. Harold was in the choir with his powerful bass voice, Annie sat with the Mothers' Union part of the congregation as she was a working member of the union. I was now a member of their family, so to speak, and they suggested I start to go with them to the Sunday evening services. I hadn't been to any church service since leaving the Scouts but I had a friend who was a member of the Church Lad's Brigade at this church and it was he who cajoled me into joining the brigade, and regular attendance at church was a requirement. They had a military type band; kettle drums, bugles, and a base drum. I took on the role of a bugler, and after plenty of studious practise got quite an expert at knocking out the tunes by ear. The friend I mentioned also played the bugle and he was another Jack, he worked as a dairy hand with a farmer who's farm was known as Rockley Old Hall farm. He and another dairy farm hand, a Colin, who was also a member of the CLB, were both to become very good friends of mine. It was nice to go to church, I fitted it in with the duties on the farm and enjoyed it but this church going had another very interesting side to it as there were always some very attractive young ladies in the congregation. So far, except for the short interlude in Norwich, I had been something of a recluse and I thought it was now time for me to spread my wings.

For most of the younger members of the church congregation the Sunday service was usually the prelude to a nice peaceful walk in the countryside. When the weather was fine we would come out of the church around twelve noon and a group of us, boys and girls, anything from fifteen to twenty strong would make our way to the cricket field before going past the mill and along the wagon road to Rockley Woods, then walk between the two reservoirs and cross fields where cows were grazing and birds of all kinds were singing and flying around. It was a delightful place, so peaceful, and a far cry from the mundane toil of everyday life. The walk was interspersed with uncontrolled laughter and the shrieks of the young ladies. There wasn't a great deal to laugh at in those days and being out in the freedom of those woods and the magnificent countryside made it all seem worthwhile and we certainly "let our hair down". I became very interested in one or two of the girls which I am pleased to say was reciprocated, one in particular became a really good friend and we were to spend quite a lot of time together.

Church lads brigade 1936 - Jack is on the back row in the centre

My two friends, Jack and Colin, only worked the dairy side of the business whereas I did all the field work as well, so they had much more time to spare than myself. They would come to see me in the evenings sometimes but more often than not we ended up sitting on the garden wall at the front of the farm house. Occasionally our combined assets would stretch to being able to purchase a penn'orth of chips from the fish and chip shop which was conveniently situated in a wooden hut at the entrance to the field opposite the farm, but this was as far as we were able to go as I had usually been doing some kind of work and it had been late before it was finished.

Suddenly, without any warning my organised life as a farm labourer came to an abrupt and totally unexpected end. It was the month of May in 1939 and unknown to me discussions had been taking place between my Father and Harold for the past few weeks and to this day I am not absolutely sure what they were all about. I gathered it was something to do with the loan Harold had obtained but despite my enquiries I was never enlightened as to the actual problem. On the whole I really enjoyed my stay at the farm, Harold was always helpful and did his best to make me want to stay there permanently and make a career out of farming. I had worked there for almost three years and I am convinced that without having done so I would not have known how to cope with the many awkward situations I was to encounter in the difficult years that lay ahead. Harold had a certain outlook on life which, unknown to me at the time, I had automatically copied. He had a dry sense of humour and an ability to overcome disaster.

When I knew for certain I was going to leave the farm I applied for a position in a whole-sale grocer's warehouse as a trainee manager, during the interview it was explained to me that I would be given training in all aspects of the position and what it entailed. I had just turned seventeen and was looking for something with career prospects and this sounded as if it had possibilities, so I commenced one Monday morning full of expectations.

The whole business centred around small grocery shops, the shopkeepers were the hub of the business and were cared for exceptionally well. The orders were made up for delivery by the warehouse staff which consisted of four women and three men, three delivery drivers and one full time representative. It was very much a family business and an excellent one too according to the long serving members of the workforce. The actual work in the warehouse was not hard, simply repetitive. The fairly large building consisted of a ground floor and a first floor, with the first floor having a number of hoppers, metal constructions shaped like a funnel with a square shaped box on the top, the funnels extended to long bench like tables on the ground floor. These boxes would be filled with the ingredients which were to be prepared, commodities like sugar, rice, dried peas, coconut, tea, and many other such things. On the floor all around the hoppers were one hundredweight sacks containing these products that had been packed ready for despatch. It was a very busy place when everything was in full flow and highly organised, as each person concentrated on their designated task.

I thoroughly enjoyed what I was doing as it was such a very friendly and pleasant atmosphere in which to work, the staff in the warehouse were easy to get on with as were the members in the office which included one of the partners of the firm. I liked the situation and was determined to make a good impression so that they would select me for the managers job but what I didn't know at the time was that I would be unable to carry out what I envisaged.

Somewhere about this time my Father succumbed to the constant pressure from Mum to find a house more suitable and he managed to rent a house in Worsbrough Dale so we moved.

It was a three bedroomed house at the end of a terrace of four, it had a bathroom complete with toilet and for the first time in our lives we had a water toilet. It had a very small front garden and a small back yard with just enough room to hang out the washing. The interior was well set out with decent sized rooms and overall it was quite nice but but it's situation wasn't going to be very helpful to Mum when she needed to go out anywhere, especially as Peter still required the services of the pram, as it was three quarters of the way up a very steep hill; an incline of about one in five.

And so my years as a child came to an end just as the world entered one of it's darkest times. The 1930s had been a hard decade, but as the shadow of impending war fell across Britain an unease grew about what was to come.

Chapter 6

In March 1939 my Father joined the Territorial Army. The government had been running an advertising campaign for men to join this part time army and he had thought for a long time that there was going to be a war. I had been far too busy to even think about such things, but when I started working at the warehouse he persuaded me to join the same T./A. regiment as himself. The training depot for this was in a small village called Wentworth about ten miles from Barnsley, there was only one training session per week and that took place every Friday evening at 6-30 in the drill hall, at the entrance to the country estate of Earl Fitzwilliam. I applied to join and was invited to take an interview on one Friday evening, my Father took me with him when he went for the training session and accompanied me to the interview. It was pointless, and I

TA Uniform

took the mickey out of the two 'puffed up' interviewers, but they accepted me. The interview was to set me thinking, what had my Father got me into, were these types of person the one's I could expect to be working with or were they just an exception? I was soon to find out that my fears were not unfounded. I turned out to be the youngest man in the regiment and that remained so for quite some considerable time. I was inaugurated into the regiment, and given a number, 1463349, which was to accompany me throughout my days in the army. I was told to report each Friday at 6-30 p.m. for training, at which time I would be paid the sum of one shilling for each attendance. That shilling for just three hours was good because I was only receiving fifteen shillings for a forty eight hour week.

I cycled to the drill hall after finishing work at 5-30, the journey took me through a few villages, Worsbrough Bridge being the first one, and up and down dale quite a bit but it was good all round exercise. During the first session I met a young man who came from Barnsley as well. His name was Brian and he also made the journey on his bicycle so we made arrangements to meet up at the cutting edge on the Sheffield to Barnsley road every Friday evening and ride together. We became very good friends and our friendship was to continue for many years. We got into the habit of calling at a fish and chip shop on the way back home in a place called Birdwell which was about four miles from Barnsley. The cycling was all right in fine weather but when it was raining it was anything but pleasant, we both had suitable raincoats but trousers, socks, and shoes still got wet and it was rather uncomfortable doing a training session squelching around in wet socks and shoes for three hours.

After a few attendances at the drill hall we were issued with a Glengarry, a type of cap that sits perched on the side of your head, and a Royal Artillery brass badge to fix on it, we were all destined to become Anti-Aircraft gunners. In the hall there was an anti-aircraft gun all equipped for men to do the necessary training, together with all the other equipment it needed to become fully operative. The older members trained on the gun while we, the younger one's, had some practice with the rifles. There weren't enough rifles for one each so we had to take it in turns to have a go but it passed the evening away. I had a gut feeling that everything was not as it should be, because listening to the many conversations taking place around the room I overheard the men from the village talking amongst themselves and not including others who came from a different area. I did get the impression that this was like some game being played out by the village members and done in some way to suit themselves. One evening when we were at home I told Dad how I felt and asked him if I could join another unit in the T./A., preferably an infantry unit, but he said there weren't any others within travelling distance. I took his word for it but I do think if I had been able to make further enquiries I would have found one. I did consider going back to Norwich, now I would not be too small for the Royal Norfolk Regiment but it would have meant leaving the job I had only just obtained so I didn't pursue the matter further, in hindsight I regret very much not having done something.

We were called a Battery, one part of a Regiment. We were split into four sections which were named after the place or area where the majority of the personnel in that section came from; Wentworth section, Elsecar, Stubbin, and all those from the large area around Barnsley and district to be known as District section. When these sections were built up to full strength it was hoped there would be in excess of sixty men in each but at that time more volunteers were required. My Father was given two stripes, a Bombardier, two ranks above a Gunner of which I was one. He did have previous military experience but was placed much lower in rank than some of the village personnel. I am sure it was simply a case of who you knew and not what you knew. In our section (District) were officers who came from the village. Apparently there was no-one good enough for a commission out of our lot so they were brought into ours. I, along with many others, hoped we would never be in a situation where we would have to rely on some of those officers. Nearly all the non commissioned ranks were given to those without any previous experience and in many cases I would go so far as to say, without the brains to go with them.

First uniform for the Royal Artillery 1939 - Aged 17

67

In August of that year we all received an official notification to present ourselves at the hall on the 25th day of that month in order for us to undertake one month's training at a camp near Heddon airport, Hull, Yorkshire. I had to show the notification to my employer who gave me the time off and assured me that my job would be there for me when I returned. Our section had been allocated a camp on a fully operational farm about two miles from the airport, two of the others were given similar places and all three were to live under canvas (tents), but the fourth was actually on the airport itself. They had wooden huts to use as sleeping accommodation and cookhouse . You may have guessed it, they were the village section. Our spot was in a very large field with the main farm buildings being just outside the entrance to the field, all except one building which had housed a load of store cattle, that was inside near the entrance gate. There were four six inch ex-naval guns at the far end of the field, they were evenly spaced about fifteen yards between each one forming a semi circle. At the rear of this semi-circle was a large box containing ammunition which on closer inspection turned out to be 'dummy'.

Not to be maintained in duplicate.   Army Form E 623 B.

TERRITORIAL ARMY.

IMMEDIATE AND IMPORTANT.—NOTICE TO JOIN.

No., Rank and Name *1463349. Gnr. Wood. J. L.*

Unit *270/91st A.A. Regiment R.A. (T.A.)*

In accordance with an authority signed by the Secretary of State, you are hereby called up for service in accordance with the agreement entered into by you under Section 13 (2) (*b*) of the Territorial and Reserve Forces Act, 1907, and you are required to report immediately at

the Drill Hall, Wentworth

Should you not present yourself as ordered, you will be liable to be proceeded against.

Place *Wentworth*

M W Briggs   LT. COL. R.A. (T.A.)
COMMANDING 91st A.A. REGIMENT R.A. (T.A.)
                                                         Adjutant.

Time *6 P.M*

Date *25/8/39*

                                                              Unit.

N.B.—This notice to be sent by hand or by registered post in a plain envelope. (A.I. D419 will not be used.)

(9921) Wt.11172/211 500,000 4/39 A.& E.W.Ltd. p.698 Forms/E623/11

Called up for training camp 25th August 1939

68

After everyone had taken a quick look round what was to be our place of residence for the next four weeks we were formed into groups to put up the marquee which was to be used as the cookhouse, and a few bell tents for sleeping accommodation. It was all very confusing to start with as no one had erected one of these before, but we soon got the hang of it. One of the bell tents was allocated to the quartermaster, the BQMS., (battery quarter master sergeant), he dealt with all the small equipment like uniforms and personal gear and when he had settled in we all trooped over to see him and were issued with the necessary eating utensils, a waterproof groundsheet which also served as a mackintosh, one satchel containing a gas mask, a regulation kitbag, and one large and one small canvas bag which when filled with straw became ur pillow and mattress.. We should have been issued with a complete uniform and various other items of clothing on that first visit to the quartermaster's tent but unfortunately he didn't have any. When we had received the papers to attend this camp we were also sent a list of the things we had to bring with us like a strong pair of boots, plenty of socks, underwear, shirts, towels, shaving equipment, and some articles of warm clothing. Our civilian clothes were kept in the suitcases we had brought with us, all except the clothes we were working in. Fortunately I had brought a pair of overalls with me but some only had light clothing which was very unsuitable, so with the quartermaster's cupboard being as bare as "Old Mother Hubbard's" things were looking rather bleak.

Our sleeping accommodation was organised, the cookhouse was operational, so when a large metal triangle began to clatter announcing that our first meal in captivity was ready we grabbed our utensils and quickly formed a queue outside the cookhouse. This gave us time to inspect the eating utensils which consisted of, one large enamel mug, and the usual knife fork and desert spoon, an almost square stainless steel object which upon closer inspection revealed that it came apart into two separate pieces. The object was known as a Dixie. A demonstration was given as to how the Dixies should be manipulated in order for the food to be deposited inside them. On the actual demonstration the potato from the container shot from the ladle and into the dixie. When we all lined up things didn't go quite according to plan. The cook would do his part but not always in line with the dixie, or the man holding the dixie wouldn't have it straight. Consequently more food finished up on the floor than inside it and every time there was a "miss" each one would blame the other. When you had collected the main meal, pudding, and tea, it proved to be quite a balancing act to keep everything in it's place whilst finding somewhere to sit on the grass. Those dixies just wouldn't keep level and one unexpected swivel meant all it's contents were lost. That first meal was a foretaste of things to come but we all thought it couldn't get any worse.

After a short rest we paid another visit to the quartermaster's tent and were issued with two very rough feeling blankets. These were taken to the marquee and then we were set the task of sandbagging around the guns and other equipment. This sandbagging was necessary to give protection to the men operating them and it took a lot of soil and sand bags. Before we retired for the night there was just one more queue to be formed in front of the cookhouse with enamel mugs in hand, into which was poured "Cocoa". It tasted awful but at least it was hot and wet.

The other pieces of equipment required to operate the guns successfully were a Height Finder, which as it's name suggests was to find the height, a Range-Finder, for the distance away, and something known as a Predictor. The information from the first two was entered into this predictor together with the estimated speed and wind velocity, it then transmitted these combined findings to the guns via an electric cable which was powered by a generator. Everything was encased in the sandbagged surround; even the generator which was on a trailer.

The night passed without incident, and in my case without much sleep, but I suppose sleeping on a hard floor was going to take a bit of getting used to. The blankets were rough and rather itchy to my delicate skin, the pillow seemed to get harder whenever I moved my head and that field surface left much to be desired. However it all ended at six-o-clock with the unfamiliar call of a number of NCOs, walking through the camp "requesting" all within ear-shot to "Rise and Shine". Which we did, some more reluctantly than others. The first thing to be done was have a wash. There were only six bowls and six buckets with cold water and the ground around the bowls soon became like a quagmire. All the time the NCOs were calling for more haste, badgering and bullying; it really was a shambles. Eventually we were all told to assemble in the centre of the camp. As we had not yet been issued with P/T kit (physical training), we were only going to do a few short exercises to get us in shape for the work that lay ahead. That sounded ominous, but we weren't made to do anything too strenuous and it was soon over. The next thing was breakfast, we had to pick up our eating utensils and form a queue in alphabetical order. Breakfast consisted of, one small rasher of bacon "crozzled", one runny pale egg, some tomato skins, two chunks of bread and one mug of the apology for tea, all preceded by a large dollop of milk-less stodgy porridge. Thus fortified we went back to the sleeping quarters where an NCO showed how our beds were to be made up every morning before we went on parade.

It was then time to form up outside in our working clothes, taking our gas masks with us which we were told must be taken with us at all times from now on. We were split into groups and detailed for certain jobs, some into the cookhouse, others to putting up a strong fence around the perimeter of the field with large poles and barbed wire. The solitary gate into the field was reinforced and a very strong chain used to keep it closed. There were a lot of comments being passed as to why all these precautions when we were only going to be here for one month. When the fencing had been completed there were to be two men put on guard around the guns day and night, and one guard on the gate, all of them changed every four hours. The last group of which I was one, was given the task of digging two trenches, eight feet long, four feet wide, four feet deep, about twelve feet away from each other. A solid timber pole was knocked into the ground at each end of the length of both leaving about two foot six inches protruding above the ground, then two long tree branches some ten feet in length and six inches in diameter were nailed to these upright timbers across both trenches, these were to be our "latrines", (toilets), and a long canvas sheet was fixed around each one with an overlapping gap for the entrance. My Father was in charge of this detail, I ended up doing quite a lot of the digging and he watched me like a hawk. When all the tasks we had been set were completed we had lunch and then congregated in the centre of the camp between the tented area and the gun emplacement's, where we were told to clear the area of anything causing an obstruction as this was now to be used as our parade ground where all the assemblies, marching drills, rifle drills and physical training sessions were to take place. Since we had arrived at the camp we had been doing all the things necessary to make it habitable and having spent almost twenty four hours here experiencing some of the trials and tribulations that go with living in a hastily formed army camp it was time to concentrate on the job we were sent here to train for, namely Anti-Aircraft Gunners.

Again we were split into groups, some to be trained on the guns, others on the height finder, range finder, the predictor, and the generator. A few of the younger ones such as myself, were to go round and have a go on everything. The ammunition was "dummy" but it was the same shape and size as the real thing and just as heavy, picking them up and placing them in the breech was awkward with fingers being easily trapped, and having to use a clenched fist to ram them home into the breech caused more than one person to be walking around for the next few days with very sore knuckles. The range and height finders were easy enough to operate it was just a matter of knowing how to use the different dials to obtain the correct readings for these to be passed on to the predictor. My attempts to understand and operate that last piece of equipment were not very encouraging, it was all explained to me many times but it just didn't sink in.

We trained all afternoon, then it was time for dinner.

After dinner It was good weather and still daylight, most of the men were sitting around enjoying a cigarette and having a chat; we weren't allowed out of the camp but as we had been hard at it since six in the morning it seemed quite sensible to have a rest and take it easy for a while, until the sound of the triangle being battered again echoed around the camp. It was the alarm telling us of an expected air raid (we had been told this may happen) which meant we had to man the guns and very quickly too. Everyone started running around, the Officers and the NCOs were shouting orders, the metal triangle was clanging away relentlessly, some of the men had been in the marquee with their boots off, others had even more off than just their boots and they were finding it more difficult than the rest of us, after all it isn't easy trying to run and put your trousers and boots on at the same time! All the shouting and bawling wasn't helping matters either but we did eventually make it to our allotted positions, even though it had taken an awful long time. We stood in our places and awaited further orders, and then came the expletive filled assault on all our characters. What was most surprising was that it all came from the Staff Sgt; who up to that point I had thought was a really nice fellow! We were told the next time we heard the alarm, things had better be a lot different otherwise we would find ourselves in serious trouble. We were then allowed to return to the marquee, it was almost dark by this time, someone lit the Alladdin paraffin lamp and we sat in it's brilliant glow discussing the events of the past forty five minutes or so. We had just settled down nicely for bed when the triangle started it's horrible racket once again, shouts of "Air Raid" were coming from all parts of the camp so we got dressed as quickly as we could and galloped off across the field, and that's when we found that running across a very uneven field in daylight is one thing, but to do it in the dark is a different kettle of fish altogether. Toes were being stubbed, others simply fell over, some stopped to get their bearings causing a massive traffic jam, and all coupled with the strong language usually to be heard outside a pub at turning out time. It was so dark the sandbagged area around the guns was not even visible, just finding and getting into them was extremely difficult, still we all made it and although it had been very stressful we were feeling pretty pleased with ourselves, much better than last time we thought. Unfortunately our mentor was not of the same opinion and he told us so, going on to explain that wherever we were when that alarm sounded, whatever we were doing and what state of dress we were in there must be only one objective in our minds and that was to get to those guns as quickly as it was humanly possible. We were told it was quite possible to run with your boots and trousers in your hands and put them on when you reached the gun pits, "After" everything else was ready and in full operation. We were then dismissed and returned to our beds hoping there would be no repeat performances, not for the rest of that night anyway, there wasn't, but by now it was well turned midnight and reveille was at six-o-clock. The next day was very much the same. Every day after that was very much the same with training and more training, marching, rifle and bayonet drills, and air-raid alarms a plenty at all times of the day and night.

As the days passed I got to know my fellow sufferers much better and I was able to make friends with one or two, there were others though who didn't seem as if they wanted to make friends with me but this didn't worry me at all as I had already adopted a "Couldn't care less" attitude, but one day someone happened to mention that the reason for some of them being "Stand-Offish" was simply because I was the son of the bombardier who took us for P/T, rifle and bayonet drill, and marching drill. This thought had never entered my head before but thinking about it I could understand what they were alluding to, you see when my Father was giving this instruction and orders he wasn't what anyone could call diplomatic. A lot of the unit thought that their complaints about my father would get back to him if I heard them, so they stayed away from me. It took me a while to solve this problem.

When we were doing drills and exercises he would always single me out and make sure I was doing the things to the very best of my ability; he knew what I was capable of, and made sure I came up to his expectations. The physical exercises were no problem to me as we had been exercising together for years, but the rifle drill was entirely new and I had to work hard to master it. Although he and everyone else could see I was doing my best he kept pushing me for greater effort, and it became obvious to anyone with half an eye that far from doing me any favours he was doing just the opposite and making me work much harder than all of them. Once this fact was established it became much easier for me to communicate with most of them. What they didn't know was that out of the six days we had been in camp I had never spoken to him at any time other than on the parade ground.

We had been in the camp six days, things were beginning to fit into place and most were getting used to the routine of army life. I was really enjoying it and looking forward to the next three weeks there but it seemed as if there was going to be a war! Sure enough, three days later the British Prime Minister, Neville Chamberlain announced on the radio that "...we are now at war with Germany". This put our situation in a totally different light. The Colonel had us all on parade and informed us we were now "called up" for the duration of the war and under direct orders from the department of the Ministry for War. This caused all kinds of problems, especially for the married men amongst us. There was the knowledge that their families were going to have to manage on a serious drop in the amount of money they could expect every week. Also, some had businesses and you can imagine how they must have been feeling. There were a lot who obtained interviews with the commanding officer in an effort to obtain their release but most were unsuccessful. I, on the other hand, had no immediate commitments. I was single and I felt sure that my Mother, Jacqueline and baby brother Peter, would in some way be helped by my Father's employers. I had agreed to have half my pay deducted in order for it to be paid to my Mother every week, but as my total pay was only seven shillings and sixpence half of that wouldn't stretch very far.

My father had foreseen what was coming as the Nazis had taken a stranglehold in Germany throughout the 1930s, but few in power in this country seemed to have taken the threat seriously until practically the eve of war. Winston Churchill had made an official announcement in 1934 stating, "We have never been so defenceless as we are now". Our government's comparative inaction in the intervening years had allowed the tragedy that was about to unfold.

Things were looking very bleak; we didn't even have uniforms, one glengarry with regimental cap badge, and one knapsack with a gas mask inside it, that was all we had. But the most disturbing thing was there not being enough rifles and the few there were we hadn't been instructed how to use. When any rifle drill had taken place it was all, slope arms and march with it on your shoulder. It would have been extremely difficult to have fired them anyway as the ammunition we had for them was only the "dummy" kind. There was also not one round of live ammunition in the camp for the Ack-Ack guns. The reason given was that both rifles and ammunition of any description were in short supply.

After about a week this ridiculous situation was really brought to the fore when eight of us were given a special job to perform. One morning we were taken to the Needlers chocolate factory in Hull. It was an imposing building, tall, wide and had a flat roof. We had taken with us, some sandbags, and four pieces of wood shaped like a "Lewis" gun which in those days was the best automatic weapon available and the most widely used in the British army. These bits of wood were painted in camouflage grey and from afar they would look like the real thing. From somewhere, eight steel helmets were produced and we were issued with one each. As soon as we arrived at the factory we dropped our kit off and then we were shown up to the flat roof, taking the empty sandbags with us, where an officer who had accompanied us explained what we had to do. The roof had four corners and at each corner someone had dumped piles of sand and it was our job to fill the bags and form a square about three feet high, leaving a space for an entrance. We completed all four corners and then went back down the stairs. These stairs spiralled up through the centre of the building, I have no idea how many there were but simply walking slowly up them to the top was quite an effort. We had a cup of tea and a sandwich in the factory canteen before being told exactly what we were going to do. We would be staying here for a few days, accommodation had been prepared in a nice clean spacious room with eight camp beds, washing and toilet facilities were nearby and meals would be taken in the canteen. There would be no leave as such but when it became dark we were at liberty to take a walk around the city. The reason for our being here was to boost the morale of the civilian population. The idea was that when the Air-Raid sirens sounded we were to take the wooden guns and run up the stairs as fast as we could, two of us to each corner, and place the Lewis Gun replica on top of a tripod , making sure we and the gun were in full view of anyone passing down below. The tin hats would be on our heads, gas mask satchels strapped across our chests and it would look as if we were prepared for anything. I suppose we looked authentic from a distance. Our stay was very pleasant, the meals were excellent and the ladies who served us were generous to the extreme. The officer who came with us returned to camp and we were left very much to our own devices. We used to take a stroll around the factory and could have any of the goodies being made that we fancied. Chocolate was by this time rationed and, as with most things, was in very short supply. We enjoyed our stay but all good things have to come to an end sooner or later and after two week's, having done our moral-boosting bit, we were relieved by eight strapping young men who would now be able to enjoy a slice of the good life. And so, very much to our displeasure we were transported back to camp.

We arrived early in the afternoon and noticed that the inmates had been very busy. The coal miners had put their civilian occupations to good use by digging and shoring up underground tunnels, just behind the gun emplacement's which made somewhere safe for the gun crews to take refuge if, and when, necessary. They weren't very long but they were high and although they were underground they were still fairly light and airy. The field was now completely encased in barbed wire and strong fencing, there had been a boiler installed so hot water was now readily available and buckets and bowls for holding that water were plentiful. A few days later uniforms arrived and we all received a full compliment of army issue kit. The vests, pants, and khaki uniforms were rough to the skin and irritated quite a lot until you got used to it. The boots were hard and didn't give at all, subsequently they caused a great number to have very sore feet. But after a while we got used to them.

Things were looking up, especially when we were able to practice our skills on the guns in a more positive manner. Arrangements had been made for an aeroplane to tow a target through the sky within our range in order for us to get used to following and tracking things, it was known as a sleeve and was attached to the plane with a very long cable. The height, and range finders had something practical to work on, and when they passed that information on to the predictor they in turn passed it onto the guns, so everyone was getting some much needed practice. When we were informed of the day and estimated time for the arrival of the plane we would all be waiting in the gun emplacement's long before it was due with everything prepared and ready to prove we could do the job when necessary. It was at this particular time when I was to realise that I had exceptionally good eyesight. Everyone was on the lookout to be the first person to see the plane, I saw it, and pointed it out. Even then very few could actually see it but I put the height finder on it and called out the bearing and height which enabled them to pick up on it. As it was so important to be able to get on target quickly and accurately, seeing it quite some distance away made it possible to commence firing earlier. When after a few consecutive days I saw the plane long before anyone else I was automatically given the job of height finder number one, and chief Spotter. A nice steady job with very little hard work attached to it. I was very pleased! "Idleness is nothing unless it is well carried out", I liked to say, and here was a good example.

Every day we had the usual things to do, drills and more drills, with P/T first thing in the mornings, my Father was involved in all of them and consequently he received the reward he deserved, he was promoted to Sgt. and not before time either. We had plenty of air raid alarms but nothing of the real thing, it would have been very frustrating as we had no ammunition but our speed at manning the guns in quick time improved considerably. I still had an attitude complex, in that I would show my disapproval at some of the things I was made to do. I must have rattled one Sgt. on too many occasions and he decided it was time to show me who was boss by putting me on night guard duty around the gun emplacements. How he got away with it I shall never know, but he did this every night for one whole month with no breaks in between.

After my nights on guard duty were over, I was just getting used to sleeping at night again when our tent collapsed in a storm. Unbelievably, I was so tired that I slept on as most of the other residents fled for dry cover. We were moved to the now vacant 'bullock shed' for the time being. The shed was very wide and there was a spacious walkway down the centre, this walkway gave us room in which to bring water inside and fix up the bowls, making it ideal for washing and shaving. By this time it was no longer nice weather and washing outside in the field could be extremely cold first thing in the morning.

At sometime during the next few months we moved from the Hull area to a fully operational anti-aircraft gun site, including live ammunition, and proceeded to do what we had been trained for. It was close to a village called Immingham in Lincolnshire, on the opposite side of the river Humber from Hull. The guns were 3-7's, a really good weapon but we were going to have to learn how to handle them as they were a far cry from the small naval guns we had trained on. It was a nice camp with large wooden huts for sleeping quarters, dining room, and a fully fitted cookhouse. The guns were in a large sandbagged area much bigger than the one we had made in the farmers field. It took us only a short time to get the feel of them and when the bombers came the first night we were there we gave a good account of ourselves. When an air raid was in progress and the crews were in operation, it was a noisy, hot, smelly, nerve racking time. The smell came from the cordite the shells produced as they were fired; it got in your eyes and throat which wasn't good when everything was being strained to the limit. During the first few months almost all the raids were made at night so I didn't see the planes first very often, it was usually the searchlights that picked them up and once they had got one the lights criss-crossed until the plane was trapped in the centre of a number of them, it was then that I had to do my job by manoeuvring the height finder onto the gleaming silvery speck in the centre of the crossed lights, twiddling a few knobs and calling out the height to the predictor crew. We could see where the bombs were falling as the whole area would be lit up with the fires burning on the ground. The destination of the aircraft passing above us was either the fishing port of Grimsby, or Hull, neither of which were very far from us.

Things were fairly quiet when one morning an army lorry towing a box like trailer drove into camp and parked outside the Quartermaster's hut. The trailer was uncoupled and we were told to bring our gas masks and line up facing it. Someone sorted us out into groups of twelve and the nearest group were ushered into the doors at the front of the trailer, when they were all inside the doors were closed. We knew it had something to do with gas training but that was all we did know. The first group were in there for quite a long time, then the doors opened and out they came coughing and spluttering, their eyes red and tearful. My group were in next and once inside we were told to put on our gas masks and breathe normally. I could just make out through the mask visor that there was some kind of hazy smoke beginning to float around. All the time the man was giving a running commentary about the type of gas he had just released into the box we were in. I don't think much attention was being paid to what he was saying. I couldn't help wondering why the first lot had been in such a hurry to get out and why all the spluttering, because what we were doing was easy; the masks seemed to be working as I couldn't smell anything. The man was still prattling on when he said something which sounded to be important, "when you are told to remove your masks you must continue to breathe in the normal manner. I don't want any of you gulping the stuff, there is no need to panic but the doors will not be opened until a certain amount of time has elapsed". Then he spoke the words "take your gas masks off". That is when I knew why the first lot had been so eager to leave the confines of this pokey little box. One tentative sniff was all it took, it went down the back of your throat and into your eyes. It was no use trying to keep them closed, it still managed to get at them. There was an impulse to open your mouth, then as soon as you had done so you realised immediately why you should most definitely have not done it. All your teeth started to ache and all the time you were getting shorter and shorter of breath. It was getting perilously close to the panic he had said there was no need for when the doors finally swung open and we, just like the others had done before, dived out as quickly as possible and then came the coughing and spluttering. It took quite a few hours before the effects wore off and even then the pain in the teeth and gums remained for almost twenty four hours. Altogether not a nice experience at all. We were later informed that we had been exposed to three types of gas all of which were probably the ones we may have to come up against at any time in the near future.

Many hours were spent just waiting around for the alarm to sound and every day some personnel were allocated leave and were free to do as they wished. Those remaining on camp had various ways of passing away those hours. There were "Tortoise stoves" in every hut; large cast iron objects with a metal pipe running from the top of them out through the roof, they had to be constantly fed with coke and gave out plenty of heat but their main asset apart from keeping the place warm was to enable us to make really brilliant toast at any time of the day or night. Other forms of relieving the boredom were of course letter writing, letting family and friends "Not" know what you were doing but keeping them happy with a line or two of well chosen words, although I wasn't good at this. I was however a real nutter for a game of cards once I had got the hang of the games. We played Pontoon and Brag but the game that I really got my teeth into was Solo. As soon as I had been taught the rudiments of the game I was hooked. It requires four persons to form a Solo school and there were quite a few foursomes in operation but I was incorporated into one that took all the games very seriously indeed.

I had kept in touch with the young lady from Worsbrough Bridge. She wrote to me regularly and arranged to visit me at the camp one Sunday. The officer in charge allowed me to have time off when she arrived in the early afternoon. We toured the surrounding area and had tea in a small cafe. It made a pleasant change from the normal routine but on my return I took a lot of stick from the guys. It didn't bother me too much, after all I was the one who had the time off and had spent the afternoon in the company of a very attractive young lady, so why should I be bothered?.

It would have been towards the end of the summer when we moved to a place called Goxhill. It was nearer to Grimsby, still on the same flight path but a much better camp all round. It was more permanent with solid timber constructed huts with more room inside than the previous ones. There was plenty of room to move around and bags of space in which to store our kit. Here we had to put everything in it's proper place, clothing to be hung up, eating utensils put on display on a shelf above the bed, and all beds made up when not in use, it was much more "regimental" but I think we were all relieved at being in nicer quarters. The gun emplacement's were purpose built and the guns themselves had armour plating fitted to the front and sides giving much greater protection for the crews. They were of a bigger calibre than those we had been using, these were 4-7s with a longer range and higher velocity shells which were a lot heavier but they didn't have to be rammed home by using the fist. The extra weight did cause some problems for one or two of the loaders but it was only a case of picking it up and walking a couple of yards before lowering it into the automatic loader which when operated pushed the shell into the breech, that part of it was much easier and there were no bruised fists and knuckles.

In one of the huts there was a piano, I had noticed it when we first took stock of our new home. It was "old" and very much out of tune. I waited a few days and not having seen anyone manipulating the keys I went into the hut one evening when things were quiet and had a go. Soon I had a most appreciative audience making requests for certain tunes. I did my best with the very limited repertoire I had. Plenty of wrong notes were being struck but funnily enough no-one appeared to mind. There were a number of popular tunes around at that time and were sung with great gusto in and around the camp, "Lily Marlene", "Over the Rainbow", "The Nightingale Sang in Berkley Square", and of course "The White Cliffs of Dover". I didn't join in the singing for very obvious reasons but I thumped the tunes out to the best of my ability and it helped to relieve some of the tension which always seemed to be around those days. After that first night I was very much in demand and I was more than pleased to oblige.   During the next few months things got much worse in many departments. The air raids began to take place during daylight hours as well as at night, which made things more difficult. We had the attentions of the inoculation squads, and the little box and it's accompanying different types of gas dropped in on us at frequent intervals. However, now the planes were coming over in daylight I came into my own picking them out early and we were up and firing long before anyone else in the other gun sites around us. As we had moved to a larger camp the whole Battery were all combined.

Some strange things nearly always seem to happen when a large number of men are cooped up together. So far the men from the T/A days had been sufficient to carry out all the necessary duties to be performed, then the strain of having to be awake during the daytime and sometimes all night as well began to have an effect on most of them. More and more were falling ill for some reason or another and frequently there were so many off at the same time it became difficult to muster enough people to man the guns. It was then we received a new intake of conscripts. I didn't have much time for some who were in the battery from the T/A days but this lot who came to join us were on the whole a lot worse than them! I suppose it was to be expected really; they didn't want to be here and they resented it. A lot of them made no attempt to fit in, and it made things difficult all round. It was only after living and working with us for a few months they began to appreciate the kind of job we had to do.

When we were in this camp we had a busy time all round, it was at the height of the bombing campaign, every night and sometimes during the day was taken up by attempting to knock the blighter's out of the sky. We had some success but the town and docks of Grimshy and the city of Hull took one heck of a bashing. They were so close together being separated only by the width of the river Humber. The whole sky for miles around had a deep red glow from the hundreds of fires that were burning. We were aware of the terrible time these people were having as sometimes the planes were overhead from as early as seven in the evening and kept coming until around five in the morning. Many daylight raids began almost as soon as the night ones ended. Our guns and the men working on them were stretched to the limit, but when the planes came in their droves the height would remain constant so once I had established the height and the predictor was working from it I would work with one of the gun crews loading and bringing the ammunition up into position.

As I have said, things were stretched to the limit and the upper echelons of power knew that no-one can be on duty day and night without suffering some form of distress so they arranged for a rota to be prepared, and every night some personnel were relieved from duty, not to be allowed out of camp, but to take a rest and recuperate a bit. I had done quite a long stint when it became my turn to have the night off and I lazed about that evening knowing that when that inevitable alarm sounded I could ignore it and get into bed when I was ready and have a full nights undisturbed sleep. It felt great and I made the most of the opportunity. A raid was in full swing but I snuggled down under the blankets and dropped off to sleep almost immediately. I stayed asleep until those who had been slaving all night came in and disturbed it. As I opened my eyes I thought what a noisy lot they were and when I began to focus properly I could see that they were all around my bed, pointing, laughing, really enjoying themselves and it appeared to be at my expense. I inquired why they were looking at my bed, then they told me of the nights happenings. There had been a stick of bombs dropped across the camp, they had straddled the huts missing all of them but there were three large craters in between some of them and our's was one of those. I had slept soundly through all of this and never heard a thing. After taking a look on the floor I saw all the cutlery that should have been on the shelf above the bed scattered all around and so was everyone else's. I was going to have to be very careful or I would soon be getting a reputation for being able to sleep through just about anything.

In between these goings on parties of us were taken to a small arms firing range where we were at last given the long awaited opportunity to shoot our rifles and have a go on the latest automatic weapon; the Bren gun. I seemed to have the knack of getting a good score on both these weapons and my aptitude was duly noted. When things were a bit quiet we were given lectures on aircraft recognition and first aid. I had acquired books on both these subjects as my job as Spotter was not only to obtain the height but to be able to distinguish friend from foe.

Somewhere about this time I was promoted and given one solitary stripe; I was now a Lance Bombardier, one step up from a Gunner. As the new intake got used to most of the jobs and became capable of taking over from those who had been doing them before we were pleased to hear that some home leave could now be arranged and I went on a long weekend the first time, leaving camp at six in the evening. We were a long way from my home town, money was scarce, the railway station was miles away so I checked the map and decided to "hitch-hike". It being daylight helped me and I arrived in the house just before nine thirty that same evening. It had been much easier than I had anticipated as the car drivers were very obliging and some even took themselves out of their way to drop me off in places where they considered I would have the best chance of obtaining another lift. It was very nice to see Mother, Jacqueline and Peter. I hadn't seen them since the day I left for that one month camp which seemed a lifetime ago. After that I went on quite a few weekends seeing the family and my lady friend. Just a few weeks before Christmas I was one of those allocated one week leave for that coming holiday. As soon as I got to know I wrote and informed my Mother and I could tell by her letters they were all looking forward to the day when I would be arriving home for one whole week. That day came, the house was beautifully decorated together with the most attractive Christmas tree covered in all kinds of decorations, some which Jacqueline and Peter had made themselves, it looked smashing. I spent most of the week visiting relatives along with Mother, Jacqueline and Peter and I managed to slip in the odd hour or two with my girlfriend. I am still of the opinion that I was very immature, despite all the "Man's" work I had been doing during the past two years and the uncomfortable nerve-racking situations I had found myself in at times. There was something missing in my assessment of life in general. Maybe it came from the fact that I had a 'couldn't care less' attitude towards most things.

I returned to camp to find that the raids had increased in their ferocity and there had been requests made for some added protection for the docks in Grimsby. Apparently some of the daylight bombers had been swooping low and strafing the area around them causing serious damage to people and property. As I could handle an automatic weapon I was given the dubious priveledge of taking five men to the docks. I cannot be certain which weapons we took with us, they were either the Lewis gun or the Bren but whichever it was we took three, with a good supply of ammunition and set up sandbagged positions inside the dock, two men to each gun. A small hut was provided for us to sleep in as the problem only occurred during daylight hours, and a cafe was compensated to take care of our food requirements. It was intended that we should spend a few weeks there but it was very boring waiting for something to appear and not one object came within firing range. One evening, after dark, I took a stroll along the quayside where the trawlers and smaller fishing boats were moored and got talking to one of the skippers of a trawler, he asked what I was doing there and when I explained to him the reason he invited me onto his boat to have a look round. It was fascinating following his running commentary on the equipment, what it was used for and how it was used, I never realised how much work went into bringing those pieces of cod and haddock into the fish and chip shops. It was obvious the task of doing this was a skilful, very hard, and certainly dangerous type of employment. The Skipper said the crew had prepared their evening meal and I was welcome to join them. I couldn't really refuse. I had already been to the cafe for my dinner before I set off for the stroll but as you must have an idea by now of the enormity of my appetite one more mouthful or two wouldn't overfill me. We went down into the living quarters and I was invited to sit at a long freshly scrubbed wooden table, upon which were placed plates full of thick chunky pieces of bread. Other members of the crew were sitting down when a plate the size of a meat dish was put in front of me full of large thick pieces of "Whiting". The condiments and the plate of bread were passed around and we began to eat. I had never tasted fish like that before. It was wonderful, my plate had been very full to start with but when I had finished it didn't need to be washed I had wiped it clean. They could see how much I had enjoyed the meal and they were adamant that I should return the next evening for more of the same. I said I would look forward to doing so. Then, would you believe it, a truck arrived early the next morning to return us to the camp. The Battery had a completely different duty to perform. I do remember my visit to that trawler, meeting those friendly fishermen and I can still taste that whiting and those man sized chunks of bread. It had been a time not easily forgotten.

It had been intended that we should have stayed a lot longer on the docks but this sudden change had come about quite unexpectedly. A lot of guns, vehicles, and equipment such as we were likely to need were all in readiness; we were about to become a "mobile" anti-aircraft battery. As knowledge and the instruments to obtain this knowledge had become much more sophisticated it was now possible to ascertain where the raids were most likely to be going to take place, and acting upon this information we would be told where to go. It was then going to be our job to get there as quickly as possible and be in readiness for the expected attack in that area. The powers that be didn't always get it right but more often than not they were spot on. The guns were the same as the ones we had used at Immingham, 3.7's. The 3.7's were adapted for wheels and could be made mobile in a very short time. Their hard-standing legs could be elevated and two large wheels with air-pressurised roadworthy tyres attached to the base and they could be transported quickly at the back of a powerful "Scammel" or "Matador" towing truck. Once we began touring we went to many towns and cities in different parts of the country as far apart as Sheffield and Norwich. We had all the equipment for the task being towed along behind us, together with tons of high velocity ammunition. We travelled at anytime during the day or night and would arrive at a place and get set up ready for the expected raid. It was surprising how quickly we managed to be up and firing. It was much more interesting than staying in a camp but a lot harder in every way. We had all the equipment to prepare, and put up the tents ready for sleeping and cooking in.

I cannot be certain how long we were doing the mobile job tearing from one place to another but I think we had been at it for at least twelve months when someone must have decided we were in need of a rest and we left the guns and were deposited in a camp in Derbyshire. The next thing of interest for me came when I was detailed to take twelve men on a kind of survival course. The idea was that we should do everything as if we had no outside help other than to be taken to this place, given rations for four weeks, and some equipment. We were taken by truck to a hill about nine miles outside the city of Derby, where we put up the tents and had a conflab as to what would be the best way to make our stay comfortable. It wasn't going to be easy as it was the middle of winter and dark around five in the evenings and still dark in the mornings until about seven. We had been given certain things to do and told to obtain as much information about the area as we could. We were certainly going to need the maps and the compasses we had been supplied with. We were on a very high hill with woods and open spaces all around and the tasks we had been set would require plenty of walking in order to carry them out. After the discussion it became obvious there wasn't a cook amongst us so I said I would do my best to provide nourishment for all along with all the other things I had to do like keeping the squad organised and functioning properly. I couldn't help thinking what a time to be playing Boy Scouts!

The tasks were being done without any problems. It meant one heck of a lot of walking and organising but we were well in front of schedule. I suggested we contact headquarters and ask them if it would be possible for us to have the services of a truck and driver for two evenings a week so that we could go into Derby and have a look round as there was very little we could do when it was dark. I had a phone number in case of emergencies so I contacted the duty officer and eventually he agreed. A truck and driver was put at our disposal and it was arranged for him to pick us up about seven in the evening and take us into Derby, and come back for us at midnight. The first evening we had a look around and we located a chippy near the spot where he dropped us off. Some liked a drink or two so they went off in search of a pub while I and two others went to find some sort of entertainment. We hadn't gone far when we came across the Plaza Ballroom. It wasn't very well lit from the outside because of the blackout restrictions but it looked okay so we paid at the door and went inside. It was great and we danced to the strains of the Billy Meyerl orchestra. They had a young lady singing with them, and she was good, in fact it was a very nice entertaining evening.

When we made these trips four men had to stay behind to take care of the camp but we had organised things so that everyone had done one trip in the first three outings. The fourth of these was on a Friday and when the drinkers arrived at the hall one of them came inside and gave us some disturbing news, he said it had been snowing hard and the roads and footpaths were covered. I went to the door only to find it was worse than I had imagined. There was a gale blowing, the snow was coming down very fast and getting heavier by the minute. There was no way the truck would be coming for us so we left and set off to walk the nine miles back to camp. The snow was so deep it came up to our waists in places, the wind was very strong and bitterly cold. I was thinking that I was the one responsible for this situation we now found ourselves in, now I had to make sure no-one suffered any serious problems because of this predicament. The first mile was downhill then it levelled off for another five miles or thereabouts. The wind was so powerful it was blowing the snow into high drifts and after that first mile we were travelling through countryside with open roads and footpaths and fields and trees on either side. We went through a small village which I have learned since was called Little Eaton. There were no lights anywhere on the road or in the houses. The thought of people being tucked up in bed nice and warm did nothing to make our horrible journey any easier. At that stage we had some four miles to go, partly on the level but a long very steep climb for more than one mile to reach the camp. We ploughed our way through the remainder of the journey, arriving at nine in the morning, absolutely shattered but relieved to have made it with only aching limbs to worry about. The camp had withstood the onslaught and seemed none the worse for having done so. The other four prepared breakfast while we changed into some dry clothes. After breakfast it would have been the most sensible thing to take a well earned rest by going to bed for an hour or two but it was vital we complete a scheduled operation that day and to do so meant we would have to face the elements again but only for a short distance. We were back just before dinner in the evening. Despite that little hiccup we returned to battery at the end of the four weeks, I put in a report with all the relevant bits of information we had been sent to obtain and received a good review for our efforts.

Later that year when the weather was entirely different, the whole battery went to a purpose built camp on the west coast of Scotland where we had time to relax, but were also lectured on health and hygiene in foreign countries. We were travelling without the guns and then we were sent to do some special training as part of our preparation to leaving for abroad. The place was south of Poole Harbour in Dorset, the actual camp was in Swanage just beyond the bay. The tents were pitched behind a beach in what could only be described as scrubland. There were more mosquitoes around than you would expect to find in places with a high risk of catching malaria. We had no mosquito nets but could certainly have done with some as everyone suffered from their vicious bites. The first full day there we were taken on a fact finding mission exploring the surrounding countryside. We went through wide streams that were choked with debris and so soft underfoot that the shorter members were in serious danger of sinking out of sight. The fact that we had full battle-dress on didn't help matters and we were all carrying some kind of weapon. This particular foray into the wilds of Dorset was under the command of a Major who had joined us from another regiment some time ago and for some reason he wasn't highly rated by most of the men, but when he took over carrying one of the bren guns from a man in difficulties, even though he wasn't young himself, our view of him changed. I had no idea there were such awful places on the south coast of England it was like being in another entirely different world, we were out for almost four hours and everyone breathed a sigh of relief when we were back in camp.

However it wasn't all doom and gloom. Over the top of a high banking of sand and shrubs

81

alongside the camp was a beautiful beach which stretched a long way to the right and left as you looked at it, on the left was Swanage bay, and on the right it tapered off alongside a long piece of land which curved progressively round to the left and came to a point at it's end, and was aptly named Peveril Point. It formed a peninsular where the land ended and jutted out into the English Channel. Late one afternoon when the daily jaunt had been completed, two or three of us took a stroll along this beach, the sea looked inviting and the weather was nice and warm which prompted me to think it should be warm enough for a swim. One of my closest friends a young Scottish chap called Patrick (Pat) was with us and I knew he was as fond of the water as I was, so I convinced him that it was a good idea and we went back to the camp and changed into our costumes. There followed a quick but careful scramble over the sand dunes in our bare feet and we were in that cold refreshing water, it was marvellous. The others who had been with us on the beach had disappeared but we had a good time larking about and enjoying every minute of it, then in the midst of all this Pat stopped fooling around and said "Look at the beach". The tide had apparently changed and was now taking us out to sea. We couldn't swim back to the beach, as the tide was far too strong. We were going out so fast the only way to deal with the situation was to swim with, and across, the tide. In that way we weren't wasting energy. But it was still very hard work and we seemed to be making very little headway, the beach was barely visible and the point of the land on our right was getting ever nearer. It was absolutely vital for us to arrive at some spot on the land before we rounded the point or we would be carried out into the English Channel. The land on the way out to the point began to come nearer and was bending round almost in front of us, that was when I knew we were going to make it. After what seemed to be an awful long time and a lot of determined hard pulling we finally scrambled out onto terra firma.

After a few more weeks the weather began to change and it became much cooler as winter approached. We weren't sorry when we said goodbye to the mosquito infested land of the county of Dorset and moved to a place farther north, in Leicestershire.

My Father had been transferred to another ant-aircraft regiment soon after we returned from the camp in Scotland. He spent some time operating on the guns around Coventry and Birmingham before he was sent to India where he served for a year or two as a Quartermaster Sergeant. Neither of us were great letter writers and I didn't receive any from him until he was on his way home at the end of the war.

Our first impression upon arriving at the new camp was that we were now in a rest camp. Although we were once again on a farm, this time it was not a working one and all the buildings were set aside for living quarters and a very large cookhouse plus recreation areas. My section were on the top floor of a barn. There were very few parades and no training as such so our 'Solo' school was able to flourish unhindered and a great many interesting games were played. I settled down and was just getting used to the peace and quiet when I was detailed along with seven others to go on an intensive training course at a well established specialist training camp somewhere south of where we were at present.

We arrived at the camp just before lunch on a Saturday morning. It was situated in the grounds of a large country house and there were forty or fifty other men from various regiments. Some were of the ant-aircraft breed like us, others were from infantry regiments. The sleeping quarters were located in three large marquees. We were paraded and split into three squads, each squad was allocated one marquee. We had a short time to settle in and then went into a lecture room in the house. When we were all seated a Captain told us what we were going to do during the next seven days and given the layout of the grounds, the daily routines were explained and we were told that notices would be displayed in all the marquees showing the itinerary for each day. We were casually informed that this itinerary could be changed at any time. Reveille would be at six each morning. By the time the lecture ended it was dark and dinner time, and what a meal; we had never been served up meals of this calibre throughout our whole service. After a short break we were taken back to the same room and enjoyed an excellent lecture complete with demonstrations on First Aid in the field. Each squad was given a large first aid pack which had to be taken with them each time they left the camp. This pack was to be the responsibility of the senior member in the squad. To round off the evening we had an hour and a half being shown how to read a map in daylight and in the dark. About nine-o-clock we were dismissed and returned to our quarters.

On the next day, after having had a good night's sleep, we woke and "leapt" out of bed in great anticipation of the day's forthcoming events! We put P/T kit on and lined up on the parade ground where we were put through a rigorous round of exercises. The selection panels at each of the regiments apparently knew which persons to select for a course of such intensity as there were certainly no slackers here. Then it was breakfast time, a quick trot back to quarters, change into full battledress and make up beds then on parade at eight. The above sequence of events would be carried out on most of the days we were there. The officers made an inspection of their respective squads, our ammunition packs were filled along with the back pack to the regulation weight to be carried and we set off, on a brisk six mile route march. It was a cold damp morning but no-one seemed to feel it. On returning there was a short break and then onto rifle and bayonet training where we were to experience how vociferous our instructors could be. It was not vitriolic language, but short, sharp, and very much to the point. After an hour and a half we were all more than ready to march off and prepare for lunch.

After lunch there was a short break of about fifteen minutes and then on to our first introduction to the assault course. We were directed onto a high mound of grass overlooking the course, it was really and truly awesome! There was an array of pipes, nets, tunnels, platforms, walls and ropes. An instructor went through each obstacle explaining what we were expected to do. Two instructors then gave a practical demonstration as to how it should be done giving a running commentary as they did so. Then it was our turn to try it. The first time around was feel your way time; instructions came thick and fast but were reasonably polite and voices were not raised in anger. Anyone experiencing difficulties at any one particular obstacle was shown how to overcome them. When everyone had managed to complete one circuit we were lined up and did it all over again. When we had done it all a few times it was almost time for dinner so we were marched back to the sleeping quarters, absolutely filthy and very wet. Later we received another very interesting lecture on foreign weapons and how to operate them, the different types of uniform worn by the opposing forces and how to identify their heavy armour. Then it was time for the big clean up, uniforms, rifles, and boots. The rifles had to be cleaned and ready for inspection at eight thirty that evening so they were the first to be done. Uniforms were next, they were wet through and covered in mud so we scraped off as much as possible and hung them up to dry as best as possible in the confined space. The boots had to be washed to remove all the mud and then dried. During the rifle inspection we were told that every evening rifles and boots must be cleaned perfectly. The rest didn't matter just as long as we shaved and made sure we had a clean dry pair of socks to put on every morning. The evening's cleaning session had taken up the best part of the night and that was the end of day one, and into bed for an hour or two.

Monday consisted of a fourteen mile run, followed by practice on the firing range. Tuesday came and we were told to do a six mile run and upon returning to the camp we had to do a complete circuit of the assault course and then run eight hundred yards to the firing range where an instructor would be waiting to direct each man to a firing position opposite a target. We then had to fire five rounds at that target. The first part was a six mile run, mostly on the roads, and I was back and onto the assault course first. There was an instructor standing beside the high wall and he gave me a hand-step lift. I got round the course and ran to the firing range. The instructor there told me to take up a position for number one target which I did and fired the five rounds. When I finished the instructor turned to me and said, "Well done, you put the five rounds in the bull and all five within a one inch diameter". There had been very few opportunities for any practice back at Battery but what little bit we had done on the rifles and the bren gave me cause to think I could handle them, and now I realised that this was something I was very good at. Being the modest chap that I am I was to let people know it! Afterwards we did some unarmed combat instruction. After being told and shown what to do and how to do it we were paired off and told to have a go. Some of the "practice" got a bit out of hand and the instructors had a full time job just keeping the peace. After lunch it was back to the dreaded assault course where in sodden and muddy battledress we were put through our paces all afternoon. Then we were dismissed and told we had finished for the day which sounded great except that anyone who had taken the trouble to read the itinerary for tomorrow would have known that a midnight manoeuvre was planned for tonight, so having time off now didn't alter the fact that we would be working when we should be sleeping. Dinner was taken as usual and the cleaning and scrubbing was completed before rifle inspection at eight thirty and we all got into bed for an hour or two, not actually sleeping only resting.

The instructors duly arrived at midnight and we were dressed in full battledress and ready in no time at all. We were paraded and each squad split into two sections and shown how and where to put camouflage on hands faces and steel helmets. Each section was given a different route and issued with torches, maps, and a compass. An object had been placed at a specific spot, and the map co-ordinates were given to the section leader and he was informed that it had to be found before the section returned to camp. We were going through countryside that was anything but easy with pot holes, fallen tree branches, boulders, and deep mud. The incessant rain didn't help matters either. We were tracked at a discreet distance by two instructors. We eventually found our object and were back in camp around six-o-clock where we were told to remain in full battledress. After having breakfast and an hour off for a bit of a rest it was back onto the assault course. This time the instructors were calling for more and more effort. When we had all got round it we went back to the beginning and did it all again then on to do small-arms instruction. This included stripping a bren gun. Then it was rifle and bayonet practice for about an hour. After lunch it was the lecture room again and more map reading The instructors also explained to us that although it had been a long day, working all hours would sometimes be neccessary and we needed to be prepared for that.

Thursday turned out to be a nice long trudge around the countryside. Each squad was told to follow an instructor. We followed him through the wood, across fields, over fences, through hedges, and "through" streams, across a rickety bridge and over more fields. Legs began to ache, tempers frayed, and it was a relief to all concerned when the camp gates came into sight. I think everyone, including the instructors, were of the opinion they had received enough punishment for one day and we were dismissed allowing us to get cleaned up. Later we were all given a frank assessment of our progress so far and whilst there was much criticism , the instructors seemed to be quite happy with how things were developing.

Friday began on the assault course then a short break and onto unarmed combat for about an hour then more practise on the firing range. Before we went for lunch all three squads were taken into the rear of the house where there was a swimming pool, an officer explained that we were going to use this pool to make the river crossing which had not been possible in the river because of the flow. He went on to give details as to how this crossing was to be carried out. A strong rope was to be attached, about eight feet from the floor, to a metal pipe situated on the wall at the rear of the shallow end. This rope would then be taken by someone who was a strong swimmer up the pool to the deep end where he would get out and fasten it to another metal pipe fixed on the wall at that end, the same height and distance from the edge of the pool as the one at the shallow end. Then each man would use the rope to pull himself along until he reached the deep end where he would be given assistance to get out. He went on to say "You are all in full battledress, with rifles, and bayonets, your clothing will get wet and soon become very heavy but everything will be all right if you keep a tight hold of the rope". The men from our regiment knew how fond I was of swimming and were very quick to volunteer me to swim with the rope but I didn't object as it looked a doddle. However, for some reason I wasn't happy with the set-up. Apparently they had never done this exercise in the pool before but felt it should be easier, especially for the men who couldn't swim. I looked to where the ropes would be tied to the pipes and tried to visualise what it would be like when the men were using it, I had this funny feeling that it wasn't going to be as simple as they were trying to make out.

As soon as we returned from lunch I took all my gear off and put my swimming trunks on and then got dressed again. When we were taken back to the pool I saw the rope at the shallow end had already been tied, it looked to have been tied high enough and there didn't appear to be any problems there, it was fixed to the pipe which was in the middle of the wall and when the other end of the rope was taken up the pool it would be down the centre, splitting the pool in half lengthways. The loose end of the rope was tied around my waist with the knot at my back. The rest of it was coiled round on the tiled surface at the shallow end. I lowered myself into the water and started to swim. It was fine until more rope entered the water and obviously sank to the bottom, the weight increased considerably and I had to pull out all the stops just to keep moving, but I reached the wall at the deep end and climbed out, unfastened the rope from around my waist and then dragged it towards me and clear of the water so that I could reach up and tie it to the pipe. Eventually I managed to tie it and pulled it as tight as possible, remembering there had to be enough slack at the shallow end for the men to reach up and grab hold of it. As soon as it was tied I went near to the wall and removed my gear and left on only the swimming trunks. That should now have been the end of the proceedings as far as I was concerned but somehow I didn't think so. I stood and looked on as at the shallow end one or two of the instructors were helping the men to grasp the rope and lowering them into the water. I thought that they were putting them in much too close together. The instructors were piling them in so close that as they started to move along the rope they were practically touching each other. When the first man in had reached the middle where the depth was six feet, the others were pushing up behind him and with all that concentrated weight the rope began to sag and instantly dropped below the water level. That first man was keeping hold of it but both his hands were by this time below his knees, suddenly his head and shoulders disappeared and the three or four behind him were on the verge of disappearing but still the others kept on pushing forward. What happened next has been indelibly imprinted on my mind ever since.

When I saw those men disappear I knew my fears were not unfounded and I immediately dived in and went for that first man who by now was well under. He had let go of the rope and did his best to drag me under with him but I got him to the side where willing hands dragged him out. I went back and the first one I came to was altogether under. I got underneath him, stood on the bottom and pushed up but he didn't help matters by grabbing and pulling at my arms, but I got him to the surface and dragged him to the side where he was lifted out. I went back, the next one had sunk to the bottom and floated into deeper water but he offered no resistance and after I had got him to the top it was easy to float him along to the side. The next one must have been a lot taller than the others as his head was just about visible and he would not let go of the rope, he was clinging to it. I grabbed his webbing and tried to pull him clear but there was no way he was going to let go of that rope. It's not easy trying to keep yourself afloat and hold someone else up and twist their fingers at the same time to make them let go. I did drag him to the side but it seemed to have taken a long time, especially as I knew there were still others in trouble. I went back for three more and then I looked to see if there were any more but I couldn't see any. There were still men holding the rope and they were just short of the middle. As I got out someone untied the rope I had attached to the pipe at my end and men at the shallow end pulled it towards them. This enabled those still holding onto it to be dragged clear and into the shallow part where they could stand up without any assistance.

The instructors had at last got control and ordered everyone to go to their respective marquees. I was surrounded by men congratulating and thanking me but I didn't say much. I showered, got dried and dressed and went back to the marquee where we rested until dinner. The instructors were noticeable by their absence at dinner; the pool problem had upset everyone and there was no further instruction that day. After rifle inspection the three officers in charge came to see me in the marquee, they thanked me for what I had done. If it hadn't been for my swift actions they and others would have been in serious trouble.

Saturday's parade was very subdued after the previous day's happenings. The itinerary had obviously been changed as we were marched out of the camp and proceeded to take a brisk march along the main road, round in what must have been a circle finishing up at the camp gates about three hours later. This kept us occupied until it was time for all of us to return to our respective units, after a good lunch and a short speech from the camp commandant. I had really enjoyed my time on the course. It had been daunting and severe but was pleased at having learned such a lot.

When we had gone away our camp looked and appeared to be like a rest camp but from now on was to be used for some of the training we had been receiving. An effort had been made to construct an assault course although it was nothing like the monstrosity we had so very recently encountered. Also an area to be used as a short distance rifle range had been arranged and sandbags had been used to form protective units for hand grenade practice. The next day was spent designating responsibility for all the training to be done, the officers and NCOs were to oversee each day's training but the actual training was to be given by those who had been on the course.

Only recently our ranks had been swelled by the arrival of a new batch of recruits, most were from the north west of the country, and some of them had proved to be really difficult people to get on with. There were now about sixty men in our section and I strongly suspected some would give me some problems. Knowing that I could expect trouble kept me on my toes and during all the different forms of instruction I kept a beady eye on them. I do believe the fact that I was much younger than almost all of them could have gone against the grain a bit, and it became necessary for me to be extremely authoritative when giving every part of any instruction.

I took the work very seriously, doing my best in all aspects of it. I planned everything on the basis that if I thought that I myself would experience the slightest difficulty in being able to carry out some task I was intending to give them then I would certainly not have it on the agenda. It is one thing to try to bring people up to a reasonable standard but another one entirely to have them go beyond their capabilities.

We had been back from the course just over three weeks when the grades for those who had been on the course were posted on our camp's daily notice board. My name was at the top, with an incredulous grade of 1.A.1. and it caused quite a stir. I knew I had done better than average on everything we had done and been top in more than one activity but I never expected such a high grading as that. It was the highest it could possibly be. Later on that day I was sent for by the Commanding Officer, he told me he had been in touch with the camp Commander of the course we had been on who had told him they were the highest grades ever given to anyone on the course. He congratulated me and said how good it was to have someone in his battery obtaining such a report. I was also told that I would be receiving an appropriate promotion in the very near future.

The matter of the promotion was something to look forward to. I hadn't been promoted above my present rank because there were very few opportunities in the battery and I wasn't a conformist. Now, I had received specialist training and come out on top in most aspects of it so a promotion would seem to be appropriate, and the extra pay would certainly come in handy.

Certain areas and buildings were set aside for special training to take place. One such building (a Barn) was used as a lecture room and its construction was arranged on similar lines to the auction ring in the cattle market I used to go to during my time on the farm. This room had a straight wall down one side and half of the side opposite was taken up by wooden bench seat's arranged in a semi circle. There were rows of these seats stretching from the floor almost up to the ceiling and on a gradual slope backwards. This enabled everyone to see what was taking place at ground level. The floor was made of timber and extended the full length of the room where at each end there were large barn doors which were closed during any of the lectures.

About eight week's into the training I arranged to give a lecture and a demonstration on the Bren gun, how to use it, strip it down, clean it, and cure any problems that may arise. One such problem was how to remove a jammed cartridge case if it occurred during firing as it had to be removed before firing could recommence. There was one special piece of equipment with

Jack in his Bombardier uniform, showing his stripes off. 1941.

which to do this job, known as a "jammed cartridge case extractor". On the morning of the day of the lecture I went to the camp armoury and collected a Bren and asked for an extractor, the armourer searched his place and couldn't find one but he said he would try to get one from another armoury in time for the lecture.

In the afternoon I assembled the men and we went into the lecture room. The whole section were present, some sixty men. There was no table in the room which made things difficult for what I had in mind so I had to stand on the floor facing them and hold the gun in my hands with arms outstretched as I went through all the different stages of each job. I held the parts of the gun up in the air so that they were able to see and understand exactly what I was doing at each juncture of the proceedings. I was finding it extremely difficult to hold the gun in my arms all the time, especially the stripping down part of it, as I didn't have enough hands and overall it was rather heavy!

The first part of the lecture was almost over when I asked one of the NCOs to go to the armoury and bring back the extractor. He returned a short while later without it. The armourer sent his apologies saying he had asked around but had been unable to get hold of one. This was a problem I could have well done without and I was going to have difficulty demonstrating properly without this piece of equipment. I didn't want to have to stop and leave it to another day and I thought that maybe with more detailed explanation I could show them how it would have worked. So I decided to give it a try. I placed the gun on the floor pointing down the room away from the entrance door behind me. The door at the other end was securely fastened. I was standing up facing the seats and I went on to explain that the method for using the extractor would have been to place it in the breech behind the jammed cartridge case, and that the rear end of the extractor was exactly like the rear end of a .303 cartridge but the front end had grips which opened outwards enabling it to grasp the rear end of the jammed cartridge case and draw it clear. To carry out this operation you would first open the bolt and pull it back as far as it would go then place the extractor in the breech and push the bolt forward. The grips would then open out and grasp the rear end of the cartridge case, then pull the bolt back to it's fullest extent and hopefully the jammed case would be drawn clear, then examine the barrel to check if it had been scored. If it hadn't, put on a magazine and resume firing. I had explained what would have been done now all I had to do was try and demonstrate how to do it. I laid down at the rear of the gun, which was standing on it's two front legs, lifted the butt into position and placed my right shoulder up against it and began to go through the practical part of everything I had just explained, giving a running commentary as I did so. I said in order to make it more authentic I was going to use a Live round in place of the extractor, and I took one from my pocket and placed it in the breech. After only a few minutes into the demonstration the men on the right behind me shouted that they couldn't see anything as I was blocking their view, but there was nowhere else I could position them in the seats so instead I turned the gun round to point towards them but by doing this there were men immediately in front of the barrel some four yards away.

Now, it is an unwritten law that you never point a weapon at anyone, except of course during rifle and bayonet drill, but at any other time it simply must not be done. I was well aware of this law so I laid down again and put the butt to my shoulder, looked straight ahead along the barrel and saw that there were three men in both of the two bottom rows of seats that were almost straight in front of me, I stood up and went across to these two rows and moved the three men in the first one and the three in the second to either side of what I considered to be the area at which the barrel would be pointing. The men in these two rows were now even more squashed but asked them to stay where I had put them. I laid down behind the gun again and was going over all I had been saying before when I looked forward, only to see that the men I had just moved in the second row had sidled back and were once more sitting directly in front of me. I stifled my annoyance, got up, and moved them again. this time I didn't ask, I told them in no uncertain terms not to move. I got down once again, put the butt to my shoulder, looked along the barrel, there was no-one in sight, so I said "I have eased the bolt back to release it and I am now allowing it to move a short distance forward",but then the bolt closed, as it did so there was an almighty bang. The gun had fired!

I looked straight ahead along the gun barrel where my worst fears were confirmed, there was a man sitting in the second row straight in front of me, he and one other had moved from where I had put them only moments before. I didn't stand up, I just laid there looking at him, then I saw a dark red, rapidly expanding, round blotch appear about six inches below his right knee. I jumped up and went towards him but by this time he was surrounded by men and I couldn't get anywhere near him. As to be expected, there was a lot of noise and confusion, someone ran off to call a field ambulance and it wasn't long before it arrived and took him away. I had wanted to speak to him but I didn't get the chance to do so. Someone who had managed to get close to him said that it was a flesh wound, the bullet had entered his right leg at the side of the bone and come out in the top part of the calf. He assured me it wasn't too serious, but I knew that for me it was very serious.

A short time later an officer came and asked me what had happened. I tried to explain the circumstances but it wasn't a good explanation as I wasn't thinking straight at all. However, he appeared to understand and told me to go to my quarters and stay there until someone came to see me. I did so and three of my friends walked with me trying to cheer me up but I didn't hear half of what they were saying. I stayed in the sleeping quarters for one whole day, only leaving it for meals and to go to the washroom.

The next day I was interviewed by two officers, not ones from our battery, they were total strangers and they took a statement from me. I kept asking if they knew how the injured man was but neither of them seemed to know, or at least they weren't prepared to tell me. I asked if I could see him but all I could get out of them was that I would see him all in good time. A few days later, I can't recall how many, I was taken to a hospital, under escort, by the same two officers and two bombardiers. We all went to a ward where I saw the man who had been injured sitting up in one of the beds, there were two officers standing by his bed and I was told to stand just inside the door, I made a move to go towards the bed but the two NCOs held me back. One of the officers at the side of the bed turned to me and said that I was not allowed to speak to the man, that I was only here so that he could identify me in their presence. I was annoyed at the way things seemed to be going but I found out why later when I was taken to a room in the camp and interviewed by the same two officers who had been at the bedside in the hospital. Some of their questions gave me the answer, the main one's were, " Do you hold a grudge against this man?". "Has he at any time offended you in any way?". "Have you ever fallen out with him for any reason?". "Do you dislike him?". Then they went onto the accident itself and wrote all the details down. I found out later that they had asked the man the exact same questions including, "Did he think I had any reason to want to cause him any harm?", apparently he had given the same answers as I had but until they had received the same answers from both of us and some independent witnesses, they were treating the accident as having been done deliberately.

I never did see the man- he didn't come back to the battery. I have tried to analyse what happened that day over the years without ever reaching any totally satisfactory conclusions. It was entirely my fault the gun fired for attempting to do something without an essential piece of equipment. I hadn't wanted to leave that particular part of the demonstration for another time as it brought the lecture to it's final conclusion. I had thought if I explained things in detail a few times it would be possible to show how it operated. It had been my intention to allow the bolt to move forward slowly, holding against the pressure it would produce, until it was just over halfway along the breech and then explain that the extracter would have now grasped the end of the jammed cartridge case and it could be withdrawn after the bolt had been pulled all the way back. I didn't have the chance to explain any of this because the bolt shot all the way forward. I can only surmise that I lost concentration in regard to what my right hand was actually doing and allowed the bolt to close. In the end it doesn't matter "How" it did fire. If I had not been so stupid as to have used a live round for the demonstration it would never have happened. No excuses, I accept full responsibility for my actions and regret the whole incident.

After all the evidence and the respective statements had been collated I was informed that I was to be court-martialled. During the weeks that followed I was confined to the camp and had one or two interviews with the officer acting as my lawyer but he didn't appear to be taking a serious approach to the subject. We went through my background up to the time of the accident and all I could get out of him was, there is no problem the sooner we get it over with the better. What I didn't know at the time was that he was in touch with the prosecuting officer and they were discussing everything together. I do believe now, that the outcome had been decided long before we went anywhere near the court. The incident put paid to my promotion though, as I discovered one day when it was posted on the notice board. It wouldn't have been approriate under the circumstances, but I was still disappointed.

When I appeared before three independent high ranking officers at the court-martial all the relevant facts were presented to them and two men who had been present at the lecture gave their version of the events leading up to the accident. My commanding officer, the Colonel, gave evidence on my behalf, but the court martial decided that they had no choice but to reduce me to the rank of Gunner. I felt I had got off lightly and I was now able to get back into the routine of normal every day duties.

We moved to Wales, to a place called Margam Sands, unsurprisingly by the beach, near the town of Port Talbot not far from Swansea. We had no Ack-Ack guns and it looked as if we were preparing for a move a bit farther afield. We engaged in quite intensive training, both fitness and weapons proficiency, and were also supplied with an array of medium and heavy Army lorries so that we could all learn to drive them.

After only about two months of having had it taken from me, I was once again the proud owner of one solitary stripe and conducting some of the early morning physical training sessions again. Unfortunately the change in my circumstances was not to be allowed to continue for very long. We had been working hard at all the different forms of training and after a few weeks we were split into squads one particular evening and told to be on parade in full battledress, (without weapons of any kind), at nine o clock to carry out a night manoeuvre. We had already done some of these, they were carried out in and around the camp and we were split into squads to foster our ability to work in ad-hoc teams. The squad I was in that night had to guard against intruders at the top end of the camp. I remember it as being an exceptionally dark night, no moon, and the sky was overcast. We were quite close to the huts and organised ourselves so that we could see down and in between three rows of them. Somewhere around midnight the men on the outer edge of our squad came under heavy pressure from the opposition. They appeared to be containing them when suddenly, without warning, we at the other end were almost overpowered by what was to turn out to be the larger part of their squad. During the melee I was bundled over and fell heavily, so heavily in fact it rendered me unconscious. When I was eventually found, and regained consciousness I was in so much pain that I was taken to Bridgend Hospital. I remember being checked over by someone and then put into bed in an almost empty ward. Although I was no longer unconscious I was still in a daze and I remember very little about the first twenty four hours in that hospital.

The pains were coming from my neck, head, and right shoulder. I had been knocked over and had landed on my right side and it is more than likely that my head had struck the floor with such force as to knock me out; the ground around there was rock hard and it would have been similar to landing on concrete. A support was put on my right arm and I was told I had suffered a shoulder injury and that there was some damage to the spine at the base of my skull and that the supa spinatus muscles across my shoulders and around my neck were seriously damaged. I was told that I could expect to have problems from them. When I had the temerity to ask, for how long could I expect them to cause me these problems, I was informed it would probably never go away and in fact it could get appreciably worse as time went by. After I went back to camp I was feeling rough and I couldn't do any work, neither could I go into town for a night out. When the use in my shoulder and neck came back after about two months I gradually started to feel better.

The firing range was being used a lot as everyone needed the practice so when feeling fit again I decided to have a go. I took my rifle to the range, loaded it, took up a firing position, fired, and almost screamed with the pain from my shoulder. The rifle had done the usual kick back and nearly taken my shoulder with it. The amount of pain was unbelievable and it felt as if there was something broken at the front of the shoulder. The shoulder had been more seriously damaged than I had been led to believe and was no longer able to withstand the force from a rifle recoil. This meant that I would no longer be a "Crackshot". I had been very proud of my prowess with the rifle and to realise I no longer had it was something I could hardly bear to think about. A few days later I went back to the range and made a concerted effort to fire using my left shoulder but holding the rifle was awkward, hand and arm positions had to be changed and when it required reloading it had to be taken away from the shoulder in order to pull the bolt back to eject the spent cartridge case. Removing the rifle between each round fired was a time consuming job and meant having to re-aim every time, there would be no rapid fire coming from my rifle in the future. The change in the use of eyes was also a nuisance as I found it extremely difficult to close the right eye and leave the left one open, I did however get used to it after a fashion and reached a reasonable standard of accuracy but nowhere near what it was before.

Chapter 7

A few weeks later the hectic round of training subsided and we were preparing for our departure. One day in the very early hours of the morning we uprooted and made the long journey to Liverpool docks, arriving in mid afternoon. We unloaded and hung around on the quayside. After quite some time we were called to order and filed up the gangplank of a beautiful liner named the "Brittanic". This "floating hotel" was to be our home for the next few days and the means by which we would be transported to our unknown destination.

Once on board we were taken to the upper deck and the naval staff brought each one of us a hammock, explaining how these were to be slung. Once this was done then all that remained was to get into it, that is when more problems came to the fore. Getting into it wasn't too bad but staying there was a different kettle of fish altogether. We were climbing in, spinning round, then the thing would close up and start twisting from side to side. This was when most of us were shot out onto the deck. I had persevered and had almost got the hang of it when my name was called out over the ship's tannoy system telling me to report to the bridge. I was directed to it by a seaman and when I arrived I saw one of our officers talking to a naval officer. They both turned towards me and the naval officer asked if I would volunteer to man the gun in one of the two round turrets which were at either side of, and level with, the bridge itself. Apparently the gun in question had no kick, it was attached to a stand in the turret, and when it was fired it had a tendency to pull away from you. I agreed and the naval officer took me down to the lower deck, round the bottom of the bridge, and up a ladder with quite a few steps which lead into a round armour plated turret. There he gave me a run down on how to operate the gun and once again re-assured me that it definitely had no kick. He told me that I would have two companions throughout the voyage, both from different regiments. We were to be provided with the appropriate clothing. It would be left to us to work together organising and deciding which two would be on watch but there must always be two of us awake in the turret and the third man was at liberty to take a stroll around the ship. I was a given a tour of the naval ratings' mess and washrooms and then introduced to the two men I would be working with for the duration of the journey. Then we were told to go and collect our kit bags and come back to the mess hall. When I returned we were given a marvellous meal and then we made our way to the turret . The climb up that steep straight ladder into the turret hadn't been easy the first time but humping the kit bag, the clothing and the blankets, proved to be too much all at the same time so I had to make two trips. It was almost dark by this time so using a powerful torch we each picked a spot, arranged our kit, and got down to organising things. The two men seemed okay- we got on well together straight away- and it was easy coming to amicable arrangements to suit all three of us. One would leave the turret to stretch his legs whenever he felt like it but it was arranged that most of the time all three of us would be in the turret either talking or dozing. We were still in the dock and it was quite warm here but there was no telling what it would be like out on the ocean. I had the distinct feeling we would need all the warm clothing.

Around midnight there was a great deal of activity, the engine sounds became much louder, orders were being given, the ship began to throb, and then we were on the move. It was my turn to rest for the next two hours but watching all that was going on was much more interesting than having a nap. I had never been on such a large ship before so it was a new experience for me. I noticed the throbbing of the engines and also a slight rolling sensation, not much, but enough to notice and soon we were out in the open sea all alone. It was a clear night and the silvery waves from the bow of the ship as it ploughed through the water were easy to see. There was very little to look at but we all stayed awake that first night and it was soon daylight. After we had taken turns to get breakfast the naval officer came and supervised some practice firing into the sea. I was surprised how easy it was to manoeuvre and there was no kick at all!

The day passed and then during the night we joined a very large convoy of ships; Destroyers and Corvettes, troopships and transports, it was a formidable sight and one which although looking magnificent did bring home to us the seriousness of the situation we now found ourselves in. To the other members of the convoy our ship the Brittanic must have looked a spectacular sight with her four distinctive large funnels and her enormous size. Every so often one of the destroyers would speed around the outside of the whole convoy, like a mother hen keeping all her chicks in order, the corvettes were weaving in and out of the ships as if they were looking for something, turning suddenly from one position to another, they really were very busy little bees, it was all very interesting and no chance of getting bored now there was something to look at. There were ships signalling to each other and the dolphins made a great sight leaping clean out of the water and yet still keeping up with the convoy; they were really beautiful creatures and so relaxing to watch. During the nights the other ships were just ghostly shapes, sometimes disappearing altogether in the mist only to come into view again in a totally different spot to where they were last seen. One such night two of us were straining our eyes making sure we didn't miss anything and with the man off watch not seeming to be sleepy we were having a quiet discussion about something or other when suddenly a naval rating popped his head over the edge of the turret and placed his fingers on his lips motioning to us not to speak. In barely a whisper he said that we were in the Bay of Biscay and moving through a large pack of "U" Boats, everyone must stay awake and alert, there must be no noise.

Needless to say it was a very long night indeed. It was black all around with no moon and drizzling with rain, there was no signalling from the ships and it was impossible to make out just where the destroyers and corvettes were. It was a very eerie silence and just standing there leaning on the rim of the turret made everything feel almost unreal. All the time the three of us were straining our eyes for a glimpse of anything that looked out of the ordinary and the cover was off the gun and it was loaded. The sea was glistening as the liner ploughed along through it and the sound of it's engines could just about be heard making a kind of dull monotonous throb. Looking out and trying to take in the whole area close to us and then scanning the distance in a wide arc put a great strain on our eyes and there was a tendency to see things that weren't there. All in all it could be described as not having been a very pleasant ten hours or so but then dawn came. The naval rating paid us another visit, but this time he brought information which cheered us all as we were now out of danger for the time being.

Our journey took us around the Iberian peninsula, and remained uneventful until we had just entered the mouth of the Mediterranean Sea. On our immediate left we saw a myriad of lights, thousands of them, standing out in the dark. They were on land and the place with all these lights could only be Spain, which although sympathetic to the Nazis was neutral. To those of us who had been in Britain all the war it was an awesome sight. When eventually it became daylight one other thing we did notice was that the Mediterranean was actually a crystal clear blue colour. From where we were high up on the side of the ship it looked very inviting. The weather had changed for the better and I was issued with my new warm weather uniform. It consisted of a full compliment of khaki drill uniform, shorts, shirts, tunics, knee length stockings with puttees to match and the old fashioned Pith Helmet. The mystery surrounding our destination was soon solved.

It was a nice warm sun drenched morning when we docked in the port of Algiers. As soon as we had docked we put the tarpaulin cover over the gun "for the last time" and I changed into the khaki drill uniform. We were thanked for having done a good job and wished well in our forthcoming travels. I at least would not be sorry to be back once again on solid ground and I picked up my kit bag and went to find my battery. They were still on the top deck but being formed into ranks, ready to disembark, when I joined them. We hung about a bit but were eventually moved to the gangplank and we trooped down it in single file. As I stepped onto the quay I was thinking I wonder what lies ahead?

We were lined up on the quay side and the Sgt. Major informed us with his inimitable charm that we had a long march ahead of us. After plenty of yelled out orders to form into straight lines and being told to show the onlookers how a real regiment could perform, we set off. By this time it was very hot, the sun was blazing down and we were in our khaki drill tunics and shorts, knee length stockings and those stupid Pith helmets, together with the inevitable full battle dress, gas masks and steel helmets. We started steadily enough then quickened it up and soon it almost became a forced march. As we marched the locals were giving us the once over as they travelled along on their camels and donkeys at a very leisurely pace indeed. It appeared to be the done thing for the men folk around here to ride on the camels or the donkeys while the women folk walked along behind. Almost all of them were carrying something on their heads. These ladies were covered from head to toe in long flowing gowns in only two colours, Black or White. Their heads were covered with a type of scarf, it surrounded all the head with one end piece of it taken across the lower half of the face and tucked in at the other side, only the eyes remained showing as it totally enclosed the mouth, nose, and chin. On their feet were open ended sandals which gave their style of walking the appearance of a kind of shuffle and sway.

The men had drawn leather tanned faces and had a similar type of headgear as the women, wrapped around the top part but without the piece across the lower portion. They had the same kind of robe, again in black or white, but they did seem to favour white more than the women. Underneath this robe, only visible at times when the robe blew outwards, were wide floppy trousers pulled tight round the leg just below the knee. The waist was very wide indeed looking very much like a balloon spreading out from the waist to the top of the thighs. They were usually white and flopped about almost as much as the robe itself and seeing them for the first time as we were they looked really peculiar! They wore the same type of sandal as their womenfolk not that they made much use of them as they appeared to do very little walking. They sat side saddle on a donkey with their legs dangling and their feet almost touching the ground.

Where we had disembarked at the docks was quite a long way from Algiers itself and as we emerged from the quay side I think we were all expecting something entirely different to what we actually saw. There were no rows of houses, no buildings, and the streets were not streets at all only tracks of sand representing roads. There were some houses but not in any order, just dotted about here and there. They were the typical adobe style house looking as though it was only by accident that they were there, all with flat roofs and a decidedly grimy white in colour.

As could be expected we were all perspiring freely as we marched and the sand blown up from the road surface penetrated just about every nook and cranny and stuck to the persperation turning us all into sheets of "marching sandpaper". Wherever two parts of the body rubbed together they ran the risk of becoming so sore that they could start to bleed.

There were trees and bushes dotted about but they weren't green leafy healthy looking plants. These were straggly brown half dead looking objects standing forlornly in that desolate expanse of sand. In the distance men or boys could be seen herding numbers of weary looking camels or goats across the wide open spaces on either side of the road. It was a very unfamiliar and uninviting place.

Eventually we arrived at a kind of camp with a few large marquees erected on a piece of ground just off the road. It had a dilapidated wire fence around it and a gateway but no gate. We dumped our kit and were told to line up to collect our sleeping accommodation. This consisted of a small canvas bag inside which we were told was a "Bivouac" and it, when assembled, would make up into an obviously very tiny tent in which two men were to sleep. My mate Brian and I had decided that we would stick together during the time we were abroad so we collected our's and investigated the canvas bag and it's contents.

Brian was an honest likeable fellow and very calm in almost everything he did which had a steadying influence on me. He was much bigger than me, two or three inches over six feet and about three stone heavier. He also had a higher rank than me, whereas I had the one solitary stripe he had another one to go with it making him a Bombardier. His usual duties were performed on the guns but as we didn't have any at present we were both required to do anything that needed doing.

After assembling the bivuoac we went on parade to collect our first meal abroad. I must say we were looking forward to it as we hadn't eaten since breakfast on the ship. As we held out our dixies, into one was poured about a half a cup of tea, into the other were placed two square biscuits and a four inch square, half an inch thick, slice of corned beef. This was to be our dinner? Everyone was standing around, a look of sheer disbelief on their faces until one of the officers made an attempt to explain the reason for this apology for a meal. He said that our guns and rations had been sent on ahead of us a few weeks before but they had all been lost at sea. Also, the water supply was contaminated so what water we had was being brought from far away. We ate the food, but found the biscuits to be so hard they were inedible.

Brian and I had just about got the measure of the bivouac, it was much too small to stand up in, but once inside, after crawling in and wriggling about a bit, it wasn't too bad. A number of precautionary measures had to be taken. Our two beds had to be made up and manoeuvred into position before dusk, also the mosquito net required fastening securely. Even then when it was time for bed, a thorough examination of the inside of the made up bed was necessary before any attempt was made to get inside it. This land had other inhabitants that liked a cosy bed to have a nap in; Snakes, Scorpions, and Beetles were likely to take up residence before you were. The only lighting available to us for inside the tent came from a small tin that had a candle, as wide as the tin, fixed inside it. Once you were inside the tent, the flame from this tiny candle was put to very good use. If any mosquito's had managed to get into the net, which they did quite frequently, they would congregate at the seams of the net. A quick run up and down these seams with the flame would crozzle all of them in a very short time. We did however become quite adept at taking this tent down in the mornings and putting it up at our next port of call.

The days were very long, not as we had known them at home, dawn broke around two o clock, the nights came in early about five in the evening and as soon as the sun dropped it was dark. The awful smells and the night time noises didn't help us to sleep. The worst things were the crickets, with their irritating noise that went on all day and all night. The flies swarmed around our makeshift toilets, then made for the food area and rubbed their dirty legs together over the top of the food. It wasn't only drinking the contaminated water that could bring on dysentery. These carried every disease imaginable to any place they visited, they could, and did, go to the dirtiest spots in the area, and then on to the clean parts, and in the end everywhere was dirty. We put the fly sprays we had to good use, but their numbers never diminished. They were on your face. arms and legs, buzzing happily all the time. There was only one way to describe this whole area, It was not fit for human habitation.

During those first few weeks we survived on the bully beef and biscuits, and having to be thankful for the meagre water supply. It altered after we had been paid a visit by a couple of food carrying trucks. So things were showing signs of improvement and the atmosphere inside the camp became a lot less tense. I was staring at the entrance to the camp one morning when I noticed an Arab sitting on the floor just a few yards away from where the gate should have been. At the side of him was a wicker type basket, and he was looking intently towards the tents. My curiosity was aroused so I walked across to him. As I approached he stood up and started gabbling in French. This part of North Africa had been under French rule for many years so it was to be expected that the Arabs spoke French as their second tongue. I had learnt a smattering at school. I did gather from what he said and his gesticulations towards the basket, that he wanted to sell me some of the eggs that were in it. An egg with a shell round it, maybe fresh maybe not, but it had the potential for being a heck of a sight better than the powdered stuff we were getting. So I negotiated and eventually came away with a large number of eggs that had cost me two francs each. I had no idea of the price of a local egg, but I knew I could rely on the camp residents to cough up more than three or four times the price I had paid. They were all very appreciative, and snapped up the lot. Brian was fussing about like an old hen when he thought I was going to sell them all without leaving any for us. There was one good thing about shelled eggs, there was no need for a frying pan and a drop of oil to prepare them. It was simply a case of find something with a solid metal surround, crack the shell and drop it's contents onto the metal, and there you had it, one beautifully fried egg. A slice of bread or two could usually be wangled out of the cookhouse. Two fried eggs, squashed in between two slices of bread, a sprinkling of salt, and you could munch away to your hearts content. The Arab paid me a visit every day we were there, and I helped to supplement the food intake of the whole camp, at a price of course!

Despite all the precautions everyone took to keep the diseases at bay, Malaria, Dysentery and Sand-Fly Fever, took their toll, especially the Dysentery. In many cases it proved to be fatal. Brian and I became feverish one night and went to see the medical officer next morning. After giving us the once over he informed us both we had Malaria and Sand Fly Fever. He didn't have to tell us we had Dysentery, the symptoms had already revealed themselves. We were given medicine and retired to the "Bivvy" for a few days rest. We had to get into bed because there were times when we were absolutely roasting, but at others we were freezing. We were in bed, but our boots were conveniently placed in handy positions near the entrance, ready for a quick exit and a gallop across the sand. It was unpleasant and uncomfortable. Brian had brought a bottle of whisky with him from home so, under cover of the blankets, away from prying eyes, we sparingly drank of that heavenly liquid. I still say that drop of Scotch did more to get rid of our problem than all the medicine and it tasted better!

One morning a dozen three ton trucks came and parked inside the perimeter. The cookhouse equipment was packed up, the food store removed to the lorries and we were ordered to prepare to move out. As we travelled along the roads I noticed that the countryside through which we were now travelling appeared to have a lot more greenery growing at either side of the road, most of it seemed to be trees, and quite possibly fruit bearing ones at that. It was a long journey, and the timing of it hadn't been worked out at all well as it was almost dark before we stopped. We had the unenviable task of unloading and putting up the Bivvys, and before all was completed it was pitch dark. We were again in a hard, sandy area, very similar to the one we had just left, but with no dilapidated fencing, and no marquees.

In the morning it was time to take a look round at our new surroundings. We were in a clearing almost enclosed in row after row of fruit trees, loaded with oranges, grapefruit, lemons, apples, pears, olives, and very tall date palms. Fruit had been something we hadn't eaten for a long time. It would do nicely to ease the pangs of hunger. but as with everything there has to be a catch, as anyone who has ever eaten too much fruit will know. We were lucky this place had already been fitted out with reasonable toilets and that they had easy access for a desperate man.

After breakfast, still feeling unsettled, we were paraded in full battle dress, and taken on a fact finding mission through the hot, humid, smelly, unknown area that surrounded us. We weren't marching, just keeping in orderly fashion, checking everything of interest. There were fields of grape vines, and water melons; literally thousands of them in each field. After a few hours traipsing about, we returned to camp and had a meal.

In some places we came into contact with the local inhabitants and I tried to hold conversations with them. Despite the language barrier I got the distinct impression that they disliked the French regime and the control it had over them. They complained of being treated unfairly, and of being arrested for no apparent reason. Their feelings towards us were hard to define; we had been told that some were for us, others strongly against us, so great care had to be taken when making approaches to them. Our intentions could so easily have been misconstrued. I disliked this country intensely. I knew I was not here because I want to be, or for the benefit of my health. On the other hand I did want to see all aspects of it, in order to arrive at my own, and fair, conclusions. So when an opportunity arose for me to visit the capital, Algiers, I took it, and found myself one day strolling through the Casbah (market place) of this ancient town. To my, not much travelled eyes, it was fascinating, and so colourful. With the many market stalls showing their wares to their best advantage, all tightly packed together, leaving only a very narrow walking space between them. The jostling crowds, the inevitable noise, and the all too familiar smells. I enjoyed it immensely, but the way I was having all manner of trinkets, and other appealing looking goods, thrust under my nose by the stallholders, and the incessant tugging at my tunic by what appeared to be a gang of urchins it became too much for me. I decided to return the way I came, and make my way back to the rest of the lads, who incidentally had opted for a look round in the better class area in the hope they would come across something that resembled a pub. Everywhere you looked the French military were very much in evidence, swaggering through the crowds in their larger than life exotic uniforms. It was obvious, by their manner, they had no respect for the people.

It seemed to be hot wherever we were, but there was a time when the heat went away with a vengeance. I feel sure everyone was wishing it would return, and quickly too. We were in camp when suddenly the sun disappeared, black clouds were overhead for just a few minutes, and then, it started to rain. With this rain came the most awful cold feeling. As soon as it started everyone dived for cover. Brian and I ran to the bivvy and dived inside, where we put on our coats and wrapped our blankets around us. I had no idea things could change so quickly and dramatically as they did. One minute we were roasting, the next freezing. The rain was coming down in torrents and the area all around was flooded. Water was rushing through the bivvy, coming in from all sides. The storm then went away as suddenly as it had appeared. The sun resumed it's position immediately overhead, the floods soaked into the sand, and everyone dried out their possessions and got back to normal.

At this time we were taken east into Tunisia. Although to us almost everything; the sights, the smells, the activities, the heat remained the same. The coastline, and the towns that were on it, were more sophisticated in their overall appearance. Here at least were proper houses, with well tended gardens, set in Palm tree lined streets with footpaths, all with some kind of street lighting. We had cause to visit one or two of them in the course of our travels. It was about this time that a nagging toothache decided to become more annoying, and I made enquiries as to the availability of someone who could relieve me of the pain that was getting considerably worse every day. To my amazement I was told there was a qualified dentist in the centre of one of the towns who had been commissioned to deal with any emergency that arose in the British contingents in that area. One morning I was despatched to have it seen to.

The surgery was in a nice clean area just off the centre of the town. The surgery itself looked to be fully equipped and able to deal with any emergency. It seemed odd to find something like this here. I suppose I could only think of the poverty stricken places that were all too prevalent in such close proximity to this modern room. The dentist himself was of French origin and his command of the English language was quite fair. That first meeting seemed to relax me, his positive manner gave me confidence in his ability to perform the type of treatment I required. The problem was one of the eye teeth, not immediately in the front, near to it but slightly to one side. He gave it a thorough examination and said it would be a shame to extract it as it would leave a gap, so over several visits he removed the nerve. He had done an excellent job. That tooth never gave me any more problems, although it did go discoloured after a great many trouble free years.

It was now time for another change of location. We were taken to a place to have a rest. From the outside it had all the appearances of an old fashioned Fort. The buildings were a whiteish colour and made from the same materials as the local adobe huts, and all of them had been severely damaged by shell fire. We were told to select our own places somewhere inside these buildings and prepare them for sleeping accommodation. It wasn't the Ritz, but Brian and I found a spot that was suitable. There was a large square, completely encircled by these buildings except for a narrow driveway in. There was a gate at the end of the long driveway with a guardhouse. We soon settled in, and the solo school had a great time.

We had been there two days when we were awakened just after dawn by the sound of heavy trucks coming up the driveway. We had not been informed that we may have unexpected guests! Two trucks drove slowly into the square followed by a staff car displaying the French flag. The trucks trundled into the square, turned round, and stopped alongside each other about five yards from, and facing, the exit. The driver and the passenger from each truck got out and unfastened some canvas flaps that were covering the back doors, out of which jumped more soldiers. The staff car took up a position alongside the trucks, and the officer got out and immediately started issuing orders, whereupon the soldiers went back into the trucks they had just vacated and brought out twenty four bedraggled looking men. Only two of them decently dressed, the others were in what can only be described as "rags". These appeared to be Arabs. As they reached the ground almost all of them dropped to their knees, put their hands together, raised their heads up towards the sky, all the time mumbling something which was obviously some kind of prayer. They looked a sorry sight and the soldiers dragged them to their feet and proceeded to put them into groups of six.

It was then that the soldiers showed just how brutal they could be. They turned on one of the groups and dragged them across the square, taking no notice whatsoever at the way they were struggling and protesting. They manoeuvred them towards a wall at the far end of the square, which had in front of it six stout posts as thick as telephone poles, set into the ground, about 7 ft high. Two soldiers grabbed one of the men, and dragged, pulled, or pushed, him towards one of these posts. They then took hold of both his hands, forced them behind the post, and tied his wrists together, then tied his ankles together and tied them to the post. The other soldiers paired off and did the same to the other five. The noise from these six came across as a plaintive wailing sound. There was a lot of poking, pushing and jabbing, to get them to stand upright and face the front. Meanwhile eight soldiers, carrying rifles, took up a position about thirty feet from the posts, and facing them. They loaded the rifles, put them to their shoulders in the firing position. The officer was standing just behind them, he shouted a couple of orders, the soldiers fired, and the six men slumped down the posts. The officer drew his revolver, approached the men, and fired one round into the head of each one. They were then untied, dragged to the trucks and "hurled" inside. The rest of the men from the trucks were standing there watching all this taking place. It was diabolical. There was no sign of pity in the eyes of the officer or his men, in fact they all appeared to enjoy everything they were doing. It is one thing to take someone's life, but to enjoy it into the bargain, is beyond contempt. The same fate befell the other eighteen.

As all this was taking place we were not standing around as if we were watching a circus performance. The square was completely empty except for the participants in this macabre situation. We had all stayed in our places, under cover, but we could still see what happened. It was necessary for us to remain undetected, for the time being at least. When all the executions had been carried out, two or three of our officers approached the French one. They had what appeared to be an amicable discussion, and then the French contingent got in their vehicles and drove away. Our officers were immediately surrounded by men wanting to know what it had all been about. Apparently, the French had explained that it was their way of dealing with spies and traitors. We made it clear that we didn't want this kind of thing happening again while we were here. It was the first time I had seen all the men show such a combined determination over anything before, it was a revelation. We were all sickened by what we had seen. The story about getting rid of spies and traitors, was the French version, it was likely to be a way of getting rid of "anyone" that didn't agree with everything they said or did.

Well, we had made our views known, it was just a case of waiting for the execution squad to return, and see what transpired. They did return. Just after dawn, two days later. The trucks were driven into the square and began unloading their latest consignment of prisoners. It was then that our officers moved in, a conversation ensued, the French officer throwing his arms about and getting really hot under the collar. Ours simply talked, but with a firmness that he would have found impossible to ignore. After all his ranting and raving, he suddenly shouted to his men, they put their prisoners back in the trucks, and drove away. And that is the last we saw of them.

After a brief stop in the town of Sousse, which we found to be filthy and parasite infested, we finally pitched our tents alongside an air field. Almost as soon as we had settled down and had a meal I, and one other, were told to go to the air field operations room and report to the commander for instructions. He was an American and we had a taste of their hospitality by demolishing the few cakes they offered us, together with a large glass of ice-cold lemonade before we were given an insight into the operation they were at present engaged in. They were based in England and made regular bombing raids on Italy. When they had dropped their bombs they carried on and landed here. They were again loaded with bombs and did the same thing again, but this time in reverse. Our job was to help load the planes with bombs ready to make that return journey. We were then taken to the field where a number of long range bombers were parked just off the runway and shown how to do the loading. The bombs were massive things and took some manoeuvring into position in the underside of the plane, where they were securely fastened.

The American crew were great to work with, they were fun to be around and there was none of the ever present strict discipline we were used to. They worked hard flying those monsters, and played hard. The food in their mess hall was excellent, and we made the most of it. Cigarettes were plentiful and they handed them round frequently although I cannot say I enjoyed the taste much; they were mainly Lucky Strike and had a taste of their own. We worked alongside many different crews, seeing some more than once during the time we were there. It was one of these crews who came up with an idea that appealed to both of us. They asked if we would like to do one of these trips with them. It would mean us having to operate one of the guns in the body of the plane, but with the compensation of a journey to England, then a few days off, in which we could visit our families, then be picked up for the return journey. They said they would arrange everything but first we had to ask their commander. An appointment was made for us to see him, and very much to my surprise and delight, he said as far as he was concerned we could go, with two provisos. Firstly, that we accept full responsibility for the outcome, and secondly, we must obtain written permission from our Colonel. The first we agreed to, then saw the Colonel and explained what we would like to do, telling him that the American commander had agreed to allow us to go, without placing too much emphasis upon the duty we would have to perform during the flight. The Colonel said No. It would have certainly been an adventure though.

Our next move was to be further inland towards Tunis. Again it was to a camp set in the middle of what could only be described as the desert. It appeared to have nothing for miles around, all sand and scruffy looking trees. However this place was to be something out of the ordinary.

We were doing the usual things, trying to keep out of the continuous heat, and avoid any of the parasites that were all too prevalent in this kind of terrain. The solo school found plenty of opportunity's to enjoy a quiet game or two, so Brian and I weren't finding things too miserable. Then, out of the blue, I found myself in conversation with a chap well known for pulling a fast one on whoever would be taken in by him. As our talk developed he said he had been making an unauthorized tour of the surrounding area, and that he had been astonished to see what he thought was a large compound absolutely full of large crates, only about half a mile from where we were. He had decided to take a closer look, and had seen a lot of men in uniforms walking about inside, carrying what appeared to be automatic weapons on their shoulders. The men were obviously American soldiers, and he wondered why this compound with it's crates should require guards to patrol it. He asked me what I thought about it, and did I think it worth investigating. I was very sceptical but I arranged to go with him to take a look for myself.

We left camp around eight the following morning, dodging the man on duty at the gate, by going across a portion of sand with a lot of dunes that were fairly close together. We hadn't gone far when he said we should be a little more cautious as the compound was only just over the next rise. We came to the rise and dropped on all fours to climb up to the top, taking care not to allow our heads to show above it. This rise was about ten yards from the compound. It was exactly as he had said; a massive place with hundreds of large packing cases in straight rows. It was surrounded by a fence of heavy gauge, galvanised wire netting which was attached to stout looking timber posts. These were at least twenty feet high. This wire stretched right down to the ground and threaded through it was barbed wire at short intervals, from the ground to about eight feet high.

There was only one thing for it and that was to find out what exactly was in those crates. It was clear that any further information could only be obtained during the hours of darkness. The problem was the guards. We could see quite a number of them strolling along between the rows of boxes. With the rows being straight, down the length and also across, wherever they were, top end, middle, or bottom, they had a clear view of the entire row. There were no gates of any kind at this side of the fence, and it didn't look as if there were any lights anywhere. When we returned, the only way in open to us, was underneath the wire. Care would have to be taken with the barbed wire that was threaded through the netting all the way round the bottom part. If we approached from where we were at present, there was a slight rise in the ground leading up to the fence, this could possibly be to our advantage allowing us to work unseen by anyone inside. We returned to camp, entering from the same spot we had made our exit and didn't appear to have been missed. It had been decided that we would affect an entry that same night. In preparation I borrowed a small torch from one of the blokes, saying I was fed up of stumbling over everything on my way to the latrine.

The sun dropped, and it was dark. We met as arranged, and took the same route out of camp as in the morning. We reached the rise we had used as an observation point earlier in the day, and flopped down to assess the situation. From what we could see the area looked peaceful. It was at that point I realised we hadn't taken into consideration the possibility of the guards patrolling outside the perimeter during the hours of darkness. We waited quite a long time to see if that was the case, staring at the bottom of the fence for any sign of movement on the outside of it. Nothing could be seen very clearly and it was with a degree of uncertainty that we approached the nearest part of the fence, and lay down on the slope leading up to it. We had both brought a bayonet with us, knowing we would have to dig into the hard sand to make a hole under the wire. The sand was fairly hard but the sharp steel soon softened it up, and enabled us to scoop it clear with our hands. It needed to be quite a large hole, large enough for us to make a quick exit if need be, and to be able to drag any small boxes through if necessary. All the time we were digging we kept looking and listening. Gradually the hole got bigger, and I had the priviledge of going under the wire to take a look at the boxes.

I crawled underneath, took a hasty look round and stood up. The crates were not very clear to make out, there were large ones that stretched high up, maybe as high as the fence, some twenty feet or more. It appeared as if they had been stacked in sizes, all the big long ones together, exactly how many of these there were wasn't easy to see, but there were quite a lot. The smaller sizes were not stacked high at all, anything less than four feet long were made into stacks, about six feet high, these looked the easiest to get at so I approached one, and covering the end of the torch to allow only a pin point of light, I directed it onto the writing on the side of one of the smallest, gasped, and quickly went on to the next row. I did six rows, then went back to the hole. I had difficulty containing myself when I reached my companion, I wanted to blurt out the good fortune we had stumbled across in this desolate area. We had to replace the sand in the hole and bring the wire down to it's original position, to make sure that the disturbance we had caused was not going to be obvious to anyone taking a close look at it. I refrained from saying anything, the first thing to be done was to get away from here as quickly as possible. We entered the perimeter of the camp in the same way we had come out. Once inside we made straight for the seclusion of the bivvy Brian and I shared. He knew nothing about our excursion into the unknown. I was prepared to tell him but I didn't have to at that precise moment as he was out somewhere. My companion had been almost overwhelmed with curiosity ever since I had crawled out of that hole, and my reluctance to enlighten him before we were safely back, nearly proved too much for him, but now we were back I explained everything. I am certain my voice, even in the confines of the bivvy still had a tremble in it when I spoke. I told him I had shone the torch on the first box label, it had read, "Property of the U.S. Government. 48 bars of Chocolate". The findings in the rest I had looked at ranged from tinned pears, peaches, apricots, grapefruit, sweet potatoes, biscuits, coffee, sugar, milk. All packed in reasonable sized boxes. He listened to all that I had to say and then said, exactly what I had been thinking, "what are we going to do about relieving the Yanks of some of these goodies?".

When the knowledge of all this food had sunk in, it was simply a case of coming up with a practical solution to getting some. Many suggestions were forthcoming from both of us, but the ideas we had about keeping it to ourselves, didn't seem to be possible, so we worked on the principal of bringing in a few more men to help us carry it out. We knew we would have to be careful about the whole setup, as there were a number of our lot who, if they were not getting a slice of the action, wouldn't hesitate to cause us problems. We thought we would need about four more men to help us. It wasn't so much the getting it out of the compound it was more the transporting of it back to camp. The goodies couldn't be carried in their boxes they would have been far too bulky and awkward, so we decided it would be best to take along with us a couple of empty kit bags. There were one or two blokes I had in mind for the job, so he left it to me to choose the four we would need. During the next couple of days I worked on convincing the four men I had picked that this stuff was just waiting to be picked up. In the end they agreed to have a go.

Everything was arranged for the assault on the compound to take place one night after dinner! When the two of us had made that first inspection to see if it was worth while we went in shorts, heavy boots, and short sleeved shirts which proved to be an entirely unsuitable mode of dress. Our knees got scratched from kneeling down on the hard gritty sand, bare arms were not the kind of thing in which to tackle barbed wire, and if we had needed to make a quick departure from the scene, the boots would have been cumbersome to say the least. So it was long trousers, long sleeved shirts and gym shoes. I still had the torch I had borrowed for a couple of nights (just forgotten to take it back that's all) and I asked three of them to bring small torches and something with which to break open any boxes if necessary.

We met up at the spot where we could leave the confines of our camp without being seen. The equipment required had been checked, including two empty kit bags, and we set off. To say there were six of us, the noise we made was minimal and we arrived at the rise, some ten yards from the actual wire fence in good time. It looked rather ominous; the fence, the height of which seemed to tower above everything around it. Even though we were almost convinced the patrols were only at work on the inside, that ten yard gap between us and the wire appeared to be a long way, so we rested a while. Then we ran over to the incline and up to the fence, and flopped down together. The chap that found the compound in the first place and I went forward and dug the hole, lifted up the wire, and the three with the torches followed me inside. I directed them to the ends of the six rows I had checked before, where they would know what to expect and which boxes to look out for. I waited to see them all settled and went farther in towards the middle rows. At one stage during my progress along the rows I heard talking coming from further up from where I was. The guards were obviously patrolling in pairs, and were not speaking in subdued voices either. The three men who were inside the compound had been told if they were seen, not to head straight for the hole in the fence, and to make a noise of some sort that would warn the rest of us, we could then get out through the hole before they reached it, after they had taken a suitable detour. The only concern I had was that the guards might use their weapons on an intruder without first ascertaining their nationality. We had no intention of fighting it out with the Yanks, we were on a very peaceful, but determined, mission.

Quite a few of the large boxes were checked, before I came to the conclusion that what I had been specifically looking for was not in any one of them. Cigarettes, Tobacco, Wines and Spirits, would have made a great contribution to our collection, but those things were not really the type of goods to deposit in an area such as this, to think they might have been, was wishful thinking on my part. Enough valuable time had been spent investigating, now it was to be used to more profitable effect by selecting something from the boxes. The other three men would have located and taken the specific items they had been told to pick up, but I had left off their lists some of the better class stuff for me to choose. It didn't take too long to take one small box of Milk, one with the 48 bars of Chocolate, and one of Biscuits. They were all reasonably small and light , so instead of hanging about splitting the boxes I opted to carry them as they were. When I arrived at the hole with the last one, it was just possible to make out the two kit bags standing on one side and they looked quite full. One of the chaps humped one of them onto his shoulders, the two who had been left guarding the hole carried the other between them, and the rest of us carried a small box each. The hole had been carefully closed, with the disturbance we had caused to the surrounding area of sand painstakingly restored, and the wire returned to it's usual position. We had been away from camp longer than we had anticipated but our return journey was without incident. The next thing to be negotiated was the walk around the inside of the camp. It was necessary for us to have somewhere to share out the spoils, away from a busy spot, so one of the Latrines had been suggested, not an ideal place but we should not be disturbed too much at that time of night.. Two of us stayed with the goodies while the others went to get something from their bivvys in which to carry their share of the spoils. When they came back one had brought a paraffin lamp with him, and we took the tins from the kit bags and shared them out, they had all brought what they went for, and there was enough for us to have two tins of each variety. Just reading the names made the mouth water, remember we had not even seen most of it, never mind eaten it, for years. It was a good haul, including lots of fruit, beans and coffee. Then I opened my boxes. The milk was a let down as the small box contained three large tins of condensed milk, the thick creamy stuff. The other two more than made up for that first disappointment. The Chocolate was what I had expected, forty eight nice large bars of very hard to bite, thick chunky, delicious tasting chocolate. The third box contained forty packets of biscuits, so we were able to take quite a few each. We all took our share and retired to our bivvys. The milk I hadn't decided what to do with, but I took it all with me. That was the culmination of our first foray into the land of the plentiful.

I arrived at the bivvy to find Brian taking a nap. As I have previously mentioned he was not the adventurous type but had offered to help in any other way. I would need his cooperation because all of us had thought it to be much safer if we buried the tinned stuff under our groundsheets. This meant digging a fairly shallow hole under both our beds and putting a thin covering of sand over the top of them, to prevent any of them sticking up, and giving us sleepless nights. The Biscuits, Chocolate, and Coffee, went into my kitbag, a bit bumpy for a pillow but needs must.

The same six made quite a number of forays, bringing back stuff like rice, sugar, pilchards, sardines, and more milk, along with the usual small tins of fruit, chocolate, and biscuits. The sugar, rice, and milk, went to the cookhouse, as they were not easy goods for us to hide, they were much too bulky. This kept the cook happy as he had extra food to work with, and his own bivvy had it's share of the tinned fruit. All went well for a time, we made regular pick ups, ate some of the tinned fruit, and put the empty tins in the latrines every once in a while. This method of hiding the incriminating evidence was quite safe as a layer of the excavated sand was shovelled back into the latrines every day to cover the deposited residue. The Biscuit and Chocolate wrappers were disposed of simply by burning them. Care had been taken to leave any boxes that had been opened in such a way that they were not noticeable by anyone walking past them. We tried to do everything to keep our nightly trips from becoming common knowledge, but as so often happens our secret was eventually out. The other five fellows had friends and as to be expected they shared their good fortune with some of them. These friends of their's were not quite so good at keeping things under their hat as we were, and inevitably the source of our food supplement became known to others, who started to do their own foraging in the compound. This caused problems for all of us as they were not as careful in the things they did as we had been and it was simply a matter of time before it was going to put paid to the whole episode. We were inside one night, when one of our chaps turned a corner and came face to face with one of the guards, who must have been patrolling on his own for a change. It was a stand-off, both so startled neither of them moved for what seemed to be a long time, then he turned and ran and started yelling. The guard gave chase, also yelling. He had all the full equipment on and our lad in his light gear and gym pumps soon got away. When he had left the guard well behind he galloped around a few more of the rows of boxes before making a bee line for the hole. The ensuing commotion had alerted the rest of us to the danger, and we had done the sensible thing, got through the hole and vanished into the night, although we did wait for him to catch us up before we entered the camp.

Obviously we had been in a hurry to vacate the premises, but that didn't stop us from bringing along the goods we had already collected. We quickly shared these out and made our way to our respective bivvys to hide them. I wasn't worried at all, I had expected something like this to happen on every visit we had made. I did wonder what the guard had done, whether he would have to wait until he was relieved at the end of his shift to report the incident, or if he had a field telephone and reported it immediately. Whichever way it had been done I didn't think we would be receiving any visitors before next morning, so the only thing to do was wait and see.

After a good, worry free, nights sleep, we woke to the sounds of reveille and carried on with the normal daily chores. Around nine o'clock an American jeep containing two officers, a sergeant, and a soldier descended on the camp. It stopped outside the officers quarters. One of the officers got out of the jeep and entered the tent. He was in there for quite some time before he came out accompanied by one of ours. The other one from the jeep, the sergeant and the soldier joined them, and they began a tour of the camp, looking for anything that may connect us with the previous night's happenings. They were conversing in quite normal tones, nothing heated or argumentative. The sergeant was trying to appear interested in all that was going on around them, but every now and then he would have a poke at something with his stick, and turn other things over with his boot. It must have been very frustrating for him as he uncovered nothing that would be of any help to their investigation. The soldier was probably the guard who had seen our chap, but he was being much too obvious, staring intently into the faces of all the men in the vicinity, I assumed he was expecting to recognise the fellow he chased in the compound. Having found nothing they left.

About an hour after their departure we were called on parade and given a lecture, and told that if there had been anything untoward going on in relation to our American friends, it must stop immediately. No action would be taken if there was no repetition of some of the previous happenings. At least our rations had been supplemented for a short time, and some of us still had plenty to make sure we needn't starve for the next few months.

When we were in Algeria I had been privileged to visit the capital Algiers, so when the opportunity arose for me to do the same in Tunisia, I jumped on board the truck bound for it's capital, Tunis. These two cities were as different as chalk and cheese, and I was in no way prepared for there being such a contrast when I got off that truck at the end of the main high street in Tunis. That first sight literally took my breath away, it was truly magnificent. It, like Algiers, was under French control, but here the dominance of the French was much more in evidence. It's overall appearance was spotlessly clean, but just looking around gave the impression that here was a place that had not been ravaged by War. In fact it looked as if it's tranquillity had not been disturbed for hundreds of years. The street was long and very wide, with footpaths at each side almost the same width as the street itself. At the top end away from where I first entered, were high gold coloured domes, probably three or four standing close together, not all of the same size. The most prominent one standing much higher than the others. Below, and just in front of them, was a large gateway built of white stone, rounded at the top and oblong in shape, and the full width of the street, it looked very imposing. There were two smaller ones at either side connecting to the footpaths. There were a number of stone built islands all the way up the middle of the street extending to the gateway at the top end, these islands were full of beautiful flowering plants of every colour you could imagine. At intervals along the footpaths and the centre of the street, were exceptionally tall, brightly painted lamp posts, and hanging from each one of them, were three or four baskets full of flowering plants, all with the same exotic colours, as the ones in the islands. On both sides of the street behind the footpaths were open fronted shops and cafes. White painted tables and chairs were spread out on the extremely wide footpaths. Seated at the tables, drinking from glasses or cups, were Arabs in white flowing gowns, with the traditional red Fez or the white Turban, interspaced with coloured material, in blue, yellow, or red. Some were just standing around talking in groups. The women didn't appear to be welcome at the tables as there weren't any sitting at them, but there were plenty walking about, some in white, or black, long dresses, with their heads covered and only their eyes visible. Nowhere was there any sign of urgency, things were moving, but at an exceedingly slow pace. This was the Arab side of things, the French contribution to the street was entirely different.

That particular day we chose to pay them a visit must have been a celebration day of some kind as the air was filled with music, coming from a military band heading down the street towards us. The musicians were mounted on the most striking horses you could ever wish to see, some a shiny, glistening, black, others white, with flowing manes and tails. All of them were taller than normal, in highly polished harness, with various coloured rosettes adorning their headgear. They were obviously highly trained and picking their feet up in time to the music. As I have said they were striking, but nothing compared to the soldiers riding them. They were resplendent in their bright uniforms, and silver helmets with decorative plumes on top, each one displaying a staff with different coloured flags fluttering gently as they made their progress on either side of the small islands. The musicians were followed by other mounted soldiers, making it into a parade of great proportions, and very pleasing to the eye. A big change to anything we had seen for a very long time, it seemed so unreal, as if it didn't fit in with the rest of the surrounding area.

We strolled about, taking an interest in everything. It was very noticeable there was no shortage of food here. A few of us took a seat at one of the tables and had coffee and a crusty sort of bun with sesame seeds on top; it didn't taste too bad either. When the cavalry had passed by, I could hear more music in the background, and although the song had been widely heard and sung, by both British, and German soldiers, for quite a few years, whenever I hear it now it always reminds me of this particular day in my life. It was Marleina Dietrich, singing "La Vien Rose", the beautiful haunting melody echoed round that street, bouncing off the shops at either side. We walked around listening to it, had an icecream, and then caught the transport back to camp. This was to be the last place I visited in North Africa, as shortly afterwards we were on our way across the Mediterranean, to a different country.

Our first duties on foreign soil had been pretty uneventful, apart from a few incidents which had required our undivided attention at the time. The main problems had been, the unbearable heat, the illnesses, which had always seemed to come upon us at the most awkward times, and the ever present parasites, the Mosquito being the one that caused most of us to wish we were anywhere else but here. There were many cases of hardship for everyone, especially the shortage of food and water for the first month or so. However, we did survive, and we must all be thankful for that. After the trip to Tunis it was simply a matter of preparing for our next move. Four weeks later we found ourselves on board a ship, once again ploughing through the beautiful blue waters of the Mediterranean. This time though I didn't have the comfortable feeling of being behind a powerful gun, I took my place with the other fellows on the decks and hoped for a trouble free journey. As it happened it was, but it seemed to be a very long one just the same.

We landed on the shore of southern Italy in the early hours of the morning, but this time there was to be no repetition of the forced march we had endured at our last port of call. Transport was waiting to take us inland for quite a few miles to a holding camp. Very little could be seen of the Italian countryside as the trucks had canopies around them which prevented all but the men seated at the rear from taking a look. The first thing everyone noticed, was the absence of the obnoxious smells that had been so prevalent in North Africa. However there was one thing that hadn't changed much so far and that was the very uneven, pot holed roads we were negotiating.

It was daylight when the trucks drove through the gates of the camp, and after disembarking, we were able to see the kind of place that was to be our home for the immediate future. There were dozens of bell tents erected in an exceptionally large area of what was apparently an orchard., The fruit hanging from the trees varied from citrus types, such as oranges, to rosy red apples, and the most gigantic red, brown and yellow pears you could ever wish to see. As soon as I set eyes on them I promised myself that one, or more, would grace the lining of my stomach at the first opportunity. This camp was to be our home for a short time and whilst there our duties were light, mostly just security patrolling. We made use of the extra time off by playing football and enjoying a game of cards whenever we could.

It soon became time to move on, and take in places further up the country. The first one was in, and around Foggia and then we moved on to just outside Naples. When there was a bit of time to spare it seemed a good idea to pay the place a visit. I, like almost everyone else, had heard the saying "See Naples, and Die". I thought that couldn't be true, so I summed up all my courage and one day, along with a few other chaps, went and had a look round. There wasn't enough time to take in all aspects of it, but I was not enthralled. It was obvious to all of us that the population were having a rough time, the shops displayed very little food because there just wasn't any. The whole tour we made was a disappointment.

Soon we were on the move again. This time we travelled across the country, eastwards, and ended up at a seaside resort called Bari, where we stayed a few weeks and then moved inland where it was much warmer. It proved to be hot and sticky after a week or two and not very pleasant at all. There had been the usual number of casualties from malaria during our travels, but this spot turned out to be much worse than anywhere else. A lot of patrol work was carried out here, where a number of men would explore the surrounding countryside for anything untoward, each patrol taking a different area. After one such patrol the person in charge of it reported to the Colonel that they had come across a local cemetery full of Mausoleums. He went on to say that they had made a close inspection of the insides of one or two of these buildings and had been dismayed to find that the concrete seals were crumbling dramatically, and in most cases there were large gaps, which would allow insects to enter the inside of the coffin. What was also very disturbing was the presence, even in daylight when the patrol was taking a look, of hundreds of mosquitoes entering and leaving them via these gaps. Our camp was within easy flying distance for these pests. We were in possession of a number of large spray canisters, with pump action handles that we had used before on stagnant water holes and the like during our travels. These canisters were filled with mosquito repellent. Parties were despatched to these cemeteries, carrying the canisters and a large quantity of repellent, which they sprayed liberally inside the Mausoleums. Whether it reduced the number of mosquitoes enough in order to have any effect is debatable, but at least something was done. The Mosquito nets around our beds received much more attention when being erected every evening after that.

When we had moved we had moved south, which was quite a surprise to all of us, we were expecting to go north again. Here we were stagnating, little to do, nowhere to go, altogether it was a boring and uninteresting place. Everyone seemed to be moping around looking miserable, but just when I began to reach a state where I could lose my temper over the least little thing, we were called on parade and informed that applications were invited for suitable applicants to leave the battery in the very near future and that the names of the situations available for these applications were to be placed on next day's notice board. I couldn't believe it, although I had no idea what the situations were, this sounded like the opportunity I had been waiting for since the year 1939.

At eight o'clock, a large sheet of paper was pinned to the notice board outside the officers quarters. It soon became quite obvious that I wasn't the only one eager to leave, as a large crowd soon formed. I left them to it until the crush had subsided, then I read the whole sheet through thoroughly, taking in every word. No specific details were given, simply that the notice gave everyone four options. First- Applications would be considered for transfer to the "Glider Pilot's" training school in England. Second- They would also be considered for transfer to something known as "Popsky's Private Army". Third- To be seconded to the Palestine Police Mobile Force. Fourth- To stay with the battery.

The next few days I spent trying to find out what each of the options meant in order to decide which one I intended to apply for. As far as I was concerned there might just as well have been only three options, because the fourth one was definitely out of the question. I asked the officers about the various options, but no one seemed to have much idea about any of it. I realised that I would just have to form my own opinion from what I thought the options meant. The first I considered was the Glider Pilot's, and what they would mean to me. To apply for Glider Pilot training was appealing, especially as I would be sent back to England and would get home leave, but I had heard worrying things about gliders being released too soon by the aircraft towing them and rejected this idea.

The scarce information available about the "Private Army" was very hard to understand. "Colonel Popsky" had apparently formed his own force to do work behind enemy lines but little else was known. I did not like the idea of committing myself to an unknown quantity.

So, that left the Palestine Police Mobile Force. The information to hand was exactly the same as the other two, no-one appeared to know the slightest thing about it. I knew nothing about Policing but, like everything else, I could learn. I had always enjoyed a challenge and this should be no more difficult than some of the others I had tackled. I obtained the appropriate application form, filled it in under the watchful eye of one of our officers, whose comments led me to believe I should have no problems whatsoever being seconded to Palestine.

Brian and I had discussed things at great length, but I could not get him to commit himself to apply with me. He agreed with my choice, but I got the impression he was more than reluctant to leave the battery. I would have been pleased if he had agreed to take a chance, as I was doing, after all we had been together from the days of the T./A,, and it would have been nice if we could stay together. He said he would probably apply at a later date, once he knew I had been accepted. I had mixed feelings about leaving the friends I had made. There were some grand fellows amongst them, I had been content in their company and I was going to miss them when I left.

The few weeks before I left passed slowly, but knowing I was soon to leave helped to overcome the boredom. Then I was told to report to the Colonel one morning. He told me I was to go to a Sherman Tank depot, and that I would be leaving the next day. He spoke to me for quite some time and said he was sorry to see me go, and hoped I would be successful in my application for the Police Force. Then he handed me a sealed envelope, saying as he did so, that it was a personal reference from him to help me when I eventually returned home. I still have the envelope and the two letters he gave me that day. I found his genuine interest in my personal welfare, to be very reassuring.

> To Whom it may Concern.
>
> H.Q. 106 H.A.A. Regiment. R.A.
> C.M.F.
>
> 1463349 L/Bdr. Wood,J.L.
>
> L/Bdr. Wood has served under my command for two and a half years and during that time he has performed his military duties with efficiency and shown definite qualities of command and leadership.
>
> He is most intelligent, hard working and a very good soldier and I can strongly recommend him for employment on his return to civil life.
>
> Field.
> GF/LS
> 10 July 44.
>
> Lt-Col. R.A.
> Commanding 106 H.A.A. Regiment. R.A.

Personnel reference from an lieutenant colonel in his regiment 10th July 1944

Next morning, bright and early, I found myself boarding a truck, along with about twenty other men, bound for somewhere in southern Italy. As we drove out of camp you could hear the sighs of relief coming from my companions. It was quite a long. hot, uncomfortable journey, yet no-one seemed to mind. Eventually the truck drove into a clean looking camp, consisting of large wooden huts, with proper roadways running all the way around them. This was my destination. I wished the lads all the best, dropped my kitbag off and followed it with great alacrity, and stood watching them drive away. It was about six o clock in the evening, and I was ready for some grub.

I stayed at the camp for about three weeks, helping out, until one day I was informed that my application for the Police Force had been successful and that I would be leaving the next day to make the journey to Palestine. Transport was laid on to take me to a port in southern Italy where I boarded a ship bound for Egypt. It was a troopship, known as a Liberty ship, and was one of many that America had loaned to Britain for the duration of the war. They were very basic in their amenities although there were bunk beds to sleep on. I was shown to a place between decks, at the far end of the sleeping quarters, where there were ten other men who it turned out were going to Palestine to join the Police also. I soon made their acquaintance, having so much in common. They all seemed decent fellows and there was one young chap from south London called Peter, who was to become a close friend. This friendship continued throughout our time together in Palestine and long after we had returned home to civilian life. That night the ship sailed and made it's way to Augusta Harbour in Sicily, where it dropped anchor to wait for an escort to take us across the Mediterranean. During the daylight hours there was very little to do except stroll around the deck. The men on board were a mixed bunch, all of them came from different branches of the army and the Royal Air Force, their destinations unknown. Not like the ten of us, who knew exactly where we were going. The first port of call was to be Alexandria in Egypt, where everyone would disembark for their respective destinations. In the meantime we had to wait here in the heat, until our escort arrived.

I now had plenty of time on my hands and I found myself going over the events of the past few years in the army; they were not the best years of my life and yet despite all the problems I did find them interesting and in some cases very educational. I was very naive in the ways of the world, and it showed during those first few months. I did find it hard to adjust at the beginning. The work the battery did in Britain, as anti aircraft gun operators, was rewarding as we did the job to the best of our ability and could see the success we had. But when we went abroad, to North Africa and our guns were lost at sea our whole situation changed. It had been expected that we would be used in a supporting role as anti aircraft gunners in any theatre in which we were required. Instead we were used in any capacity where our meagre services, without heavy guns, could be of some help in varying situations. The powers that be also deemed it necessary to send us to Italy to operate in the same way as in North Africa. I am not the only one who thinks that our services could have been used to much better effect had we stayed in Britain and carried on doing our job as anti-aircraft gunners. I suppose we did some good at times, during our sojourn abroad, but I have only brought to your attention the things I found to be interesting, amusing, and in some cases educational, the rest I have omitted.

We waited in Augusta harbour for a few days, it was boring and extremely hot, and the boredom was only punctuated by Peter and I engaging in extreme diving into the harbour from the top rail of the ship's deck. Early one morning the ship moved out into the Med and joined a convoy. This wasn't anywhere near the size of the one from Liverpool, but it did have destroyers and corvettes doing their very best to protect us. The journey was uneventful and we were able to relax during the daytime and sleep easy in our bunks at night.

When the ship docked in the port of Alexandria, in Egypt we were directed to transport waiting to take us to a camp. This place was known as Amarya Salt Flats, and it was a holding camp for the army. After a few days there we were taken by truck to Cairo railway station, and boarded a train bound for the Holy Land. Once over the border we would soon see what life had to offer each one of us in this land of "Milk and Honey". We left the train at a place called Sarafand, and were transported to another army holding camp, before about twenty of us were taken by truck to the district in which we had been allotted to start our duties as policemen. Peter and I were kept together and found ourselves on our way to Haifa.

Chapter 8

When we were in the camp at Sarafand, except for the men who were permanently stationed there, everyone else was enroute to join the police force. The ten of us who had been together since we left Italy were split up, and only Peter and I were allocated Haifa. The journey Peter and I made proved to be a real eye opener for both of us. Never in our wildest dreams could we have expected the change from the countries we had recently been in, to the one we were now to find ourselves travelling through, to be so dramatic.

Although we were in trucks it was a surprisingly comfortable journey. The main reason for the comfort were the roads upon which we now found ourselves being whisked along at a very healthy pace. They were not made of compressed sand, containing holes in which you could bury yourself, these were made of proper tarmacadam, smooth and clean looking, with wide footpaths on either side, and tall lamp posts at regular intervals. The view from the truck was entirely different to our previous landscapes; here there were very big houses, with large gardens, green trees and shrubs. There were lots of people walking about, and the majority were dressed in european clothing, the men in suits, the women in light coats and dresses. All looking clean and respectable. We passed through many places like this, although the whole journey did take in some desolate parts where the roads did deteriorate slightly, and the adjoining land had more of the North African appearance, with it's bleak stretches of sand and poor looking trees. There was also the pleasant sight of an Arab and his donkey, being closely followed by the inevitable lady.

After I had been in the country a little while I realised that this was a country far in advance of any we had been in before. It was much more affluent. The houses, in general, were equipped with the most modern equipment, some of which was not yet in general use in Britain. Almost every home had a refrigerator of very high standard and a private telephone seemed to be something that was regarded as a necessity whereas in England, only the privileged few were the proud possessors of such a luxury. The majority of the homes had modern furnishings, with different styles of furniture that were not to become available for many years in our part of the world. Of course not all the country was so well off, even in the different areas incorporated into making up a town or city, there were parts where the lifestyle of the inhabitants was very similar to those depicted in biblical days. Palestine was exceedingly cosmopolitan, each nationality having it's own style and way of living. In the case of the Arab, there were two totally different religions, one being the Muslim Arab, the other the Christian Arab. The Christians tended to live in the better class parts of town, usually incorporated into the Jewish districts, or alongside other nationalities. They had a similar lifestyle to that of many europeans, and they and their families, dressed in that same manner. The Muslims,

113

however, appeared to be less well off. Their houses, shops, streets, and areas used for socialising, were as different as chalk and cheese as far as the other parts of the community were concerned, but this was their traditional way of living, as it had been for hundreds of years. Some were town dwellers but the greater part of them lived and worked in villages, and these villages were almost a carbon copy of the ones we had seen in North Africa.

It was these people, living in these villages , who were the ones that could be seen travelling the dusty roads, in their traditional Arab costumes, cajoling the tiny donkey into putting a little more effort into their leisurely pace. They were a proud people, taking care of their appearance, wearing clothes that may not have been altogether new but were most definitely clean. Most walked about with their heads held high, without that dejected look that had been all too prevalent on the faces of the ones we had been in contact with before. They looked to be an entirely different breed, and although we didn't know it at the time, it was going to be interesting and educational having to deal with them and their problems.

The journey took us through many places but eventually we arrived at another type of army camp, where we were stopped at the gate, by a revolver toting policeman. Once inside our credentials were checked and a police sergeant escorted us to huts where we were allocated beds. After unpacking and a wash and brush up we headed for the dining room. As we hadn't eaten on the journey we were all more than ready for a meal, and after a full blown dinner we explored the camp. Apparently it was quite close to a village called Nablus, where the population was predominantly Muslim Arab, and there were also Jewish settlements dotted around a bit farther away. The policemen already there were reluctant to talk about their work, simply telling us that everything would be explained the next day.

The next day came and we were issued with a complete set of police uniform. There was a lot of it. Two pairs of black boots, but only one pair of highly polished black shoes, three pairs of white ankle socks, three pairs of beige knee length socks, two pairs of puttees to match. The uniforms themselves were of the same material as the army jackets and long trousers for winter wear, for summer there were khaki drill shorts and tunics, plus long trousers. Three of everything; vests, pants, and shirts, all made from white cotton, and numerous belts, some leather, others webbing. The webbing ones had two ammunition pouches and a revolver holster that could be attached. One blue peaked cap, and one blue berry, with cap badges, and two dark navy blue ties. One police whistle with blue lanyard, and another blue lanyard to attach to a revolver. One navy blue groundsheet, with fasteners, to use as a cape, and one khaki overcoat.

This was primarily a training camp and a place in which we were to be told what was expected of us in the way of policing the population. There were many lectures and the first ones were about our reason for being here, what we were expected

Palestine Police Force

114

to do, and how we were to do it. Ever since the day I put pen
to paper and signed on the dotted line agreeing to become a
member of the Palestine Police Force I had been trying, without any success, to find out what I had let myself in for. The
very first lecture enlightened me to the point where I knew
exactly the answers to the many questions I had rolling around
in my head.

The first part of that lecture dealt with the country and part
of it's history. Apparently it had always been susceptible to
problems, but the troubles we were going to have to deal with
stemmed from promises that were made during the first World
War (1914-1918). It had always been a source of contention
as to whom the country belonged to, whether it was the Jewish
population, or the Arab population. Both had valid reasons to
support the claim that they were the rightful owners. When
the British government were given the mandate to take over
control at the end of that war, it was inevitable that sooner
or later they would have to decide which of the two would
eventually take over from them. Whichever one they decided
upon, was bound to cause great disappointment for the other,
consequently the British government found themselves to be
in a "No win, situation". The two promises that were given,
the one to the Arabic population was made by Lawrence of
Arabia, in return for the assistance given to him to remove
the Turkish army from Arabia. The second was known as the
"Balfour Declaration" and made to the Jewish population,
again on behalf of the British, by a member of the government. So two promises were made, and inevitably one had to
be broken.

Palestine Police Force

The nearer it got to the time when the decision would be made, the more frustrated both
parties concerned became, and pressure was applied to the British in varying forms, to pro-
mote their eligibility to becoming the rightful owners of the country. Acts of violence were
carried out by both, some against each other, but the main target was anything British. The
Arabs did cause many problems, but the Jews carried out a continuous vendetta against the
British police, the army, and any properties used by the British, in such a manner as could
only be described as acts of terrorism. They made no attempt to hide this fact, even flaunting
the names of the actual groups which had carried out atrocities, be it causing explosions or
murdering some member, or members, of the police or army. This was their way of putting
pressure on the British government.

These Jewish terrorist organisations were not particular who they killed or wounded, they
placed bombs, and fired guns, anywhere, regardless of the consequences. Hundreds of innocent people became embroiled in their activities. The lecture went on to give specific details
of some of their diabolical acts of violence, and they were not very pleasant to hear. The
lecturer told how these terrorists were very good shots, which didn't auger well for anyone in

their sights. He also pointed out it would be against the law, for anyone to fire at anyone or anything, unless we had been fired on first.

Having listened intently to all that was said during that first lecture, it became time for other things. First of all we had our photographs taken, these were put into a book shaped identity card, and told to carry this with us at all times. Then a trip to the armoury where we were each given a Lee Enfield .303 rifle, along with ammunition and cleaning equipment. We had a choice of two revolvers, one, a .38 Smith and Wessen, the other, a Colt 45. I had used both and regarded the 38 as a pea shooter, so it was the Colt 45 for me. It was bigger and heavier, but I had found it to be more accurate. Ammunition was supplied for whichever weapon we chose, before being told to load it and put the spare ones into the ammunition pack on the waist belt. The officer in charge of the detail then said in a very positive tone of voice, that the revolver must "become part of you from now on, it must be taken everywhere and it must be placed under your pillow at night". The rifle would be left in the sleeping quarters, at the side of the bed, unless we were told to bring it with us wherever we were about to go. When not in use it would not be loaded. After having these two weapons presented to us, it was somewhat of an anti-climax when we were handed the only piece of equipment the policeman back home in Britain had to protect the public and himself; a Truncheon. It was made to fit unobtrusively in a special sleeve in the right trouser leg. I think everyone had the same thoughts though, wondering when this apparently ineffective piece of highly polished timber, would be used. Certainly not in any of the predicaments we had just been told we were most likely to find ourselves in around these parts.

Then to complete our full quota of equipment we were issued with a notebook. It looked like any ordinary small book but emphasis was given to this tiny book and it's extreme importance. Only Police work could be recorded in this book. The writing had to be neat and legible. It must be kept clean, neat, and tidy, and each week it would be read and signed by a superior officer. The book was our word and we must be prepared to stand by whatever we had written as it could have to be produced in a court of law.

We were now in possession of all the necessary equipment with which to carry out our duties, the next thing was to learn how best to perform those duties. For the following week's it was simply a case of attending lectures, learning the correct, and safest method, to do just that.

The village of Nablus was within walking distance from the camp, and as the inhabitants were regarded as being friendly towards the Police, I went along with a group and gave it the once over. There were shops of a sort, mostly with open fronts but dark dingy interiors. It was in one of these that I came across something that seemed totally out of place in these kind of surroundings. It was a shoe shop, and I was to find out later that it had a reputation for being the best one in the whole of Palestine. All the shoes were hand made by the shop owner himself, and on closer examination they were found to be excellent. I tried on a few pairs and they had a very comfortable feeling, but when it came to being told the price, I refrained from trying on any more, they were well out of my league, and so rather reluctantly I came away empty handed.

During the next few weeks more recruits were brought to the camp, and soon it became quite full. Every time a new batch came I looked for anyone from my old regiment, but in the end I came to the conclusion that either they had been allocated to Jerusalem or Tel Aviv, or

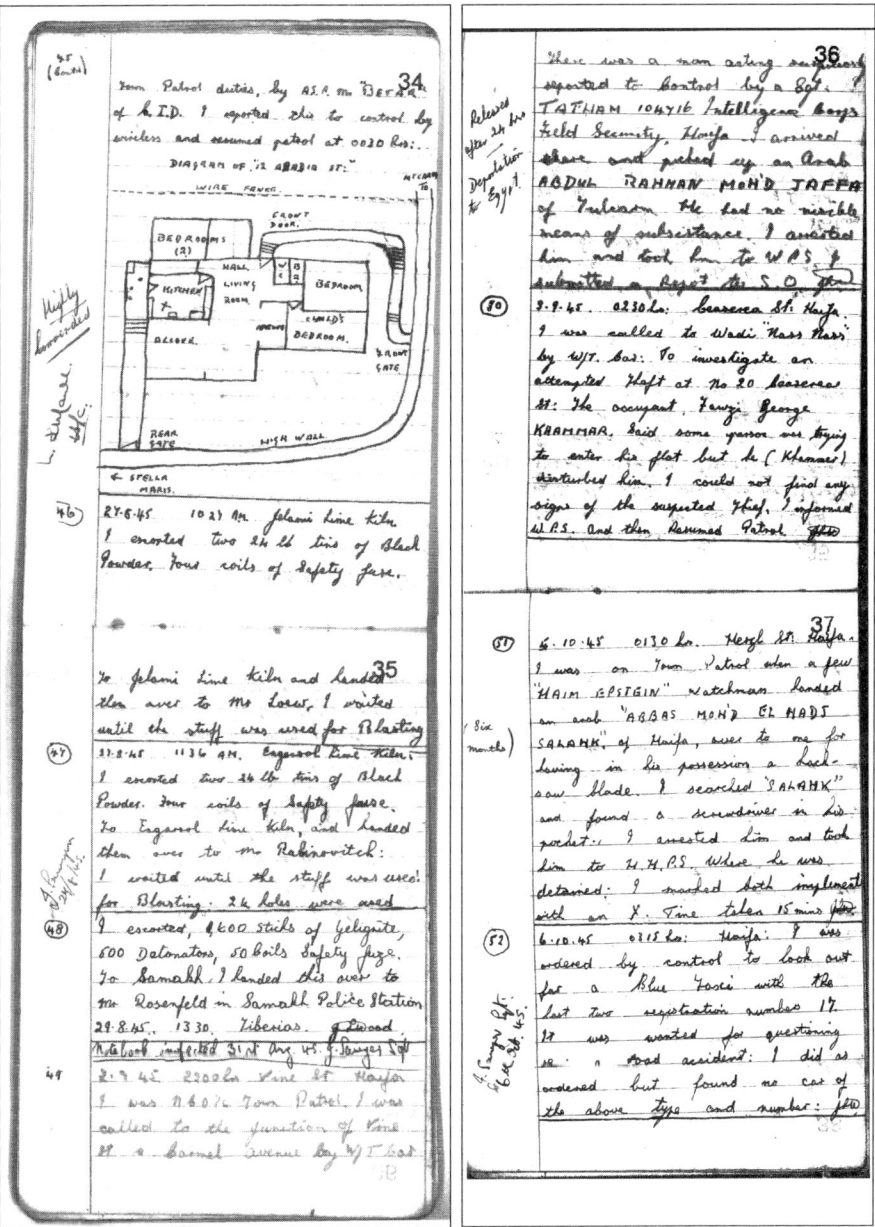

Examples of notebook entries

were not coming at all. I had been very doubtful about Brian applying in the first place, but I had still hoped he would make up his mind to join me.

One day we were assembled, with all our gear, loaded onto trucks, and transported to another camp not too far away. It was very similar in many aspects but with much more emphasis being placed upon our fitness, hence the need for P/T every morning before breakfast, and our skills at handling the rifles and revolvers were put to the test on a firing range. Even after such a long time my shoulder gave me many problems, and it was obvious to me that it would never be able to stand the kick from a rifle, so I used my left shoulder. The revolver was a piece of cake, I still had the knowledge and aptitude to aim and control it, enabling me to be quite a good shot.

This camp was near the village of Jenin, and it was here where we were formed into four groups, to be known as One, Two, Three, and Four Companies. This was done to make things easier to carry out various forms of instruction, and also to bring into our efforts some kind of team work. I was in Four company along with my pal Peter. Time was spent in the lecture rooms, or on the parade ground practicing various forms of self preservation that would be needed. We were each given a police number, this was to be displayed on both the tunic and jacket collars. The numerals in English were fastened onto the right hand side, and in Arabic on the left. Mine was an easy one to remember, in English it was, 3883. They were made of chromium plated metal, which made them stand out and easy to see. Our numbers in the Palestine Police Mobile Force, were higher than those allotted to the other part of the force, they were simply known as the Palestine Police Force and carried out all the normal police duties. We on the other hand were drawn from the army and were here to do exactly as our name suggested; to be mobile, ready to proceed to anywhere when assistance was required, and to carry out day to day mobile patrols covering potential problem areas.

When we had been on the firing range I had a chat with one of the instructors, and he suggested I should purchase a leg holster for the revolver. He said the holster that was issued and made to fasten on the waist belt, was quite suitable for use when wearing civilian clothes but for every day work in uniform a leg holster was much more practical. He was wearing one, and told me where they could be bought and so on one of our excursions into Haifa I purchased a good one, with two safety straps to prevent the revolver from being forcibly removed. There were to be several ocassions in which I was to find myself in a crowded area, and knowing that extra strap was securely fastened added greatly to my sense of well being. The holster itself was fastened onto the waist belt by two straps allowing it to hang down the side of the right leg, where it was held in place by two more leather straps around the thigh. These prevented it from swinging about like a pendulum, allowing me to know exactly where the butt would be at any time, and not having to fiddle for it. I had one more essential piece of equipment; my springy stick from my army days, "Old Faithful". It came in handy many times used as a gentle persuader, but never viciously.

A normal day would see us working on the parade ground or concentrating on what was being said in a lecture room. The country was so cosmopolitan that to attempt to learn all the languages would be impossible, but the two main nationalities being Jews and Arabs, it was necessary to have some understanding of these two, in order to communicate with them. Therefore we had lessons in Arabic and Yiddish, (this being the language of the Jews). Neither were easy, particularly in the reading and writing of them. Arabic was especially difficult, in that the spoken word, could be entirely different to the written one. I worked at both but found I had a certain aptitude when it came to studying Arabic. Once I began to come into contact with these two nationalities it soon became very obvious that the majority of the Jews were better educated and spoke perfect English. There were of course a large number of Arabs who spoke English, mainly the Christian Arabs, but it was not so prevalent in the Muslim community. I did take in enough Yiddish to get by at a pinch, but I put more effort into being able to understand, and speak, Arabic.

This place, Jenin, was pretty central to most other parts of the country, for instance, Jerusalem and Bethlehem, were further south inland, whereas, Tel-Aviv and Jaffa, were more west, along the coastline. It therefore made it easy for us to visit all these places during our stay in this camp. We were taken to all of them by truck and given practically a free rein once we got there. This was on the understanding that we must always be in a group of not less then six or seven, and keep away from any place that was off the beaten track.

As Haifa was much nearer we went there more often. On one or two of the excursions we went to a place a bit further along the coast called Bat-Galim, it was a type of seaside resort with a decent beach, clean sand, and a long stretch of the mediterranean in which to take a dip and cool off somewhat. Part of the beach was cordoned off for the specific use of the police and their families, and a watchful eye was kept over it.

Exactly how long we stayed in Jenin I am not sure. I know a lot of work was done there and the powers that be must have considered us to be ready for a change prior to being let loose on the community, and so all four companies were transported to a very big police station, about eight miles from the centre of Haifa. This station was out in the country and situated on top of a hill, overlooking everything around it. At first sight it looked exactly like an old fashioned fort, with high solid walls, and battlements all the way round, with four observation towers built in to form the round corners of the building, extending to some ten feet above it. This very imposing, and impressive, piece of architecture was known as "Shafa-Amr ". There was a steep road leading up to very solid high doors, and at the beginning of this road was a building used as a guard house, with another gate to enter the road. All the surrounding ground sloped steeply up to the walls on all four sides and about sixty yards from the base of these walls, were two tiers of large coiled barbed wire, covering the entire circumference of the building. It gave the impression of being almost impregnable, and as it could, and very often did, provide shelter for large contingents of the police force, it certainly needed to be.

Once inside it was as near to a palace as anyone could get. All the rooms were beautifully decorated, the sleeping quarters were spacious, light, and airy. The dining rooms were big, spotlessly clean and tastefully furnished. There were two tiers of rooms, the upper ones all had balconies and above them was a parapet which ran all round the top and was wide enough for three or four people to walk side by side around the entire building. On the inside was a quadrangle, some sixty yards square, with a ground surface of hard compressed sand. It was possible from there to walk all the way round the inside, on a wide footpath entirely under cover. It really was some place, and thought I would have no difficulty making myself at home here. I was to learn later that there were four or five of these particular kind of "Fort's" placed at strategic positions in other parts of the country.

When we had moved from Jenin the Sergeants, who gave the P./T. every morning and who gave language instruction, both came with us to Shafa-Amr. This suited me as they were down to earth fellows and I got on well with both of them. Once we were settled in and the lectures resumed I asked the language instructor if he would consider giving me extra lessons as I was very eager to learn. He agreed and arrangements were made for me to have an hour each day (duties permitting). Somehow it worked very well. He taught me the customs, likes and dislikes, of the Arabic nation, both Christian and Muslim. He loaned me his books and I studied them at every opportunity and together with the hour of his personal instruction I took, and passed, the colloquial examination within four months. The reading and writing side of the language I had found far too difficult, but speaking and understanding were going to be of much more use to me anyway.

The officer in charge of Shafa-Amr was a Deputy Superintendent. He had many years service in the force and that experience, together with his determination to make the place a reasonably happy one, albeit a very efficient one, made life there almost like home from home. His immediate subordinates showed great confidence in his abilities, and gave him their unwavering support. Consequently this comfortable state of affairs within those directing things at the top, made for good relations throughout the lower ranks. I found it to be the most pleasant part of my life; I was doing things I enjoyed; with the language lessons, studying the law books, along with the instruction dealing with the duties I was soon to perform. It was a time of learning, and I was never happier than when I was doing just that.

Although it was a nice place in which to live there was very little in the way of entertainment. A canteen provided somewhere to go and relax, it had a large assortment of goods, similar to the Naafi. It was in a large spacious room and sported a billiard table, a dart board, and dozens of smaller tables and chairs ideal for a game of cards or just a cosy natter. I didn't seem to make much use of these facilities as I found the sleeping quarters to be quieter and I could read and concentrate without having to listen to a lot of chatter. I hadn't changed into a Bookworm overnight but it was necessary for me to study at every opportunity. However, one evening I had abandoned the books for a while and had tried my hand at a game of billiards, thrown a dart or two, and relaxed in one of the easy chairs, only to be disturbed by senior officers entering the room proclaiming to all and sundry, to get suitably dressed as quickly as possible, pick up our rifles and ammunition, and congregate at the transport area, in preparation for going out into the countryside to where our services were urgently required.

It seemed as if every available man was loaded onto trucks in quick time, and we roared off into the night. A Sgt had been designated to the truck I was in, and as we rocked and rolled along at a very brisk pace he outlined what the reason was the for the upheaval.

We were on our way to an outlandish village about fourteen miles away. In this village lived a number of large families who were noted for their continual feuding, usually petty squabbles of no real consequence, but about an hour ago a member of one of these families had murdered someone from another family. Under normal circumstances that would have been no problem, all it would have meant was to apprehend the killer, take him away and charge him. This situation was somewhat different as these tribal feuds had their own ways for dealing with some such incident. It was an unwritten law that if someone from one family kills one from another family, the one which suffered the death, would retaliate and take their revenge by killing someone from the offending side. This could, if not defused quickly, see the start of an all out war between the two factions and their friends, something that had to be avoided, and that is why we were going out to stop any further killings. We would have to be alert all the time we were at the scene, or we could find our efforts to help taken as interference by the offended party.

Upon arrival we were quickly deployed to surround the whole village with men to patrol as near to the houses as possible to prevent anyone getting in or leaving. Some officers were sent into the village to operate inside the narrow streets and walkways, and to check and prevent any movement between the houses. I seemed to have drawn the short straw, and was one of those selected to operate inside the village.

There were no lights visible in the village, there was no moon, everywhere was pitch black and visibility was down to no more than twenty feet. It was almost impossible to distinguish anything with any degree of certainty, the rest of our squad were only dark shapes as they moved around. We were to go in groups of four, enabling each man to be covered by another man all the time.

As we patrolled, every so often we changed over to add a little variety to the proceedings, because traversing those alleyways, had a tendency to make anyone feel claustrophobic. The unappealing smells from cooking and other things that were bound to be present in a place devoid of a suitable drainage system all contributed to making our presence here very unpleasant indeed. We had been in such a hurry to leave Shafa Amr that no-one had come prepared to deter mosquitoes consequently we were all at their mercy and getting bitten on face, neck, and hands.

The word went round that our senior officers were holding discussions with the Mukhtar (head man of the village) to get him to use his influence with the offended family to forego their "right" to retaliate. Apparently he was reluctant to do so as it could make him appear to be taking one side in the dispute. Some good did come out of the discussions though; it was agreed that if the man responsible for the murder were to give himself up to the police the offended family would not do anything if they saw justice was being done. Unfortunately, the offender had gone into hiding somewhere inside the village and apprehending him would prove extremely difficult as no-one would be prepared to inform us of his whereabouts.

About two-o-clock it became daylight. One or two of the gates at the front of the houses were tentatively opened a little way, and as they were not pressed to close them, some of the inhabitants came out onto the street. A watchful eye was kept on them but care was taken not to show any antagonism towards them. After all they were most probably innocent parties caught up in this tragedy. At some stage an old man came towards us carrying a tray with small cups on it, he only spoke Arabic, but it was obvious that the cups contained coffee, and he invited us to take and drink from them. Like everyone else I was thirsty as no water had been brought with us, but I couldn't help thinking where, and how, that coffee had been made, and in what state of cleanliness those tiny cups had been when the coffee had been poured into them. I therefore declined his offer, although his actions were really appreciated. Even though it was now daylight the time dragged and everyone breathed deep sighs of relief when the order came for us to return to the trucks ready for the journey back to Shafa-Amr. It was seven o clock by the time we were all on board and on our way. The man responsible had given himself up and was now being taken into custody. As far as we were concerned that was the end of the story.

A few days later I was called into the office and told I was to start a one week tour of duty in a small police station on the west side of Haifa. It was aptly named Western Police Station. This was being done so that I could be shown how a station operated. Also, as I was to be working mainly on patrol duties it would give me close contact with the population enabling me to have first hand instruction on how to deal with the many nationalities that resided in that particular district. The duty was to commence at ten p.m. that evening, and I was taken by pick up truck to the station and introduced to the station officer, an inspector, and told I would be collected around six thirty the next morning. I spent the next half hour being shown around the station, and taking a look at all the paperwork on the desk Sgt's table, which included the station diary in which all incidents were entered as they occurred. Then another constable came in and reported for duty, the inspector brought him across to me saying that this officer was the one I would be doing the patrols with during my time at the station. All the men working here were members of the regular force, and in most cases had served for quite a few years. I didn't know it at the time, but I was to have my first experience of how we, in the P.M.F., were regarded by some members of the regular force.

The constable and I left the station shortly after ten o clock and started the patrol. We were in a nice clean area, with wide roads and streets, which had tall lamp posts at regular intervals. There were footpaths on either side with low walls separating them from the front gardens of the houses. This first part we went along consisted mainly of houses, and when I enquired about the people living in them, he said they were a mixture of all kinds of nationalities. His reply was terse, and I got the distinct impression he was not overjoyed at being lumbered with me. For the first hour, when he did have reason to speak he made it obvious he was not speaking 'To' me, but 'Down' to me. We made progress along the road, and at a junction it came to a kind of circle and branched off at either side of it to form two roads. I saw that exactly opposite us on the other side of the circle was a large imposing building with the Union Jack flying from a flag pole in the front of it. This, he informed me, was the home and offices of the British Consul, and we would make at least three checks upon it during this patrol; it being a prime target for the terrorists.

When we had taken a look at the building, front and rear, we turned around and walked back the way we had come from the station. Apparently that was the end of the area which the station had to control, so we walked back past the station, and out into a much more sparse area with some houses at intervals on both sides of the road. They were still the same style as the others but had much larger gardens with long driveways leading up to the house. Although it was not so heavily populated the lighting was the same, making things stand out clearly in all directions. This lighting held a kind of fascination for me as for the past few years everything had been conducted without any lights at all. Here it looked entirely different and I was finding it hard to get used to. We walked along for quite some way, only stopping to check -and in some cases try- the doors, of a number of factory type properties. These were buildings congregated in small groups. All the doors on each one of them had to be tried before we resumed the patrol. It took time but soon we were once more out into the brightly lit roads and streets. It was just after midnight when without any warning the road widened out and became almost straight. At the end of itcould be seen the most spectacular building you could ever wish to see. The front which gave the impression of being the entrance to a palace. It reached into the sky with a myriad of lights of differing colours on all sides and across the large frontage. There were wide steps leading up to double fronted doors which were open and standing at the front of them were two men in evening dress, with white gloves and white dicky bow ties. They were greeting everyone as they entered. As we were walking from the end of the road towards it I could see the far end of the building. It stretched out into the sea, and was built on legs. Looking at it from where we were it was massive and very imposing.

The constable and I approached the entrance, went up the steps towards the two men, where he just nodded his head, and walked straight in. It was obvious he had done this many times, and appeared to have the respect of all around us. We went inside to a reception area which was spectacular; very wide with an exceptionally high ceiling from which were hanging three or four chandeliers. The powerful lighting making them sparkle and glisten. There were men and women everywhere, dressed in their finery, with a large number in evening dress. We negotiated the many groups standing around in conversation, went through more large doors, and came out into a room that was even more spectacular. It was a hive of activity with everyone seeming to be talking at once, all standing or leaning across baize covered tables, some of which were round, others oblong. I had never seen anything like it before, but it didn't take a genius to realise what this place was: it was a Casino! We spent quite a long time in this room, and then moved on into more rooms where people were sat drinking and talking. It seemed as if we had the run of the place. Eventually we left amid more nods and smiles, the doormen were especially profuse with their parting remarks, wishing us both a pleasant evening. After this we patrolled another higher class area and then returned to the station to have a break. It would have been around two am. We went into a back room where he made two cups of tea then went to his locker and brought out a parcel containing some kind of sandwiches and began to eat. I didn't know about the break and consequently hadn't brought anything with me. I drank the tea, watched him eat, and began to speak about the patrol we had just done. I asked him how the Casino was allowed to operate when gambling was forbidden. He said the people concerned had the backing of the top brass, and providing we didn't find any other things wrong it could continue. He went on to say that we had to keep our eyes open for anything that seemed out of the ordinary, such as a certain type of lady hanging about in the foyer, and anyone under the influence of alcohol looking as if they might cause trouble. It was here I ventured to say, that kind of problem was surely the responsibility of the owners of the place. His answer was, "Trouble is our responsibility wherever it is, They will deal with it if we are not there, but they would call us to deal with it outside anyway".

He became more talkative and asked me where I had worked in civvy street, and had I come straight from there into the P.M.F. I told him I had worked as a trainee warehouse manager, and yes I had, apart from a short interlude of five years when I was in the army! I made no attempt to elaborate and although I was well aware he had more police service than I had, it was obvious he had thought I was a complete novice. He was only a young man, probably a couple of years older than myself. The reply he had just received must have made him realise I had quite possibly seen and done things that he had never dreamed about.

We left the station after about half an hour and resumed the patrol. The first place to be checked was the British Consulate, then we went into different areas. It was broad daylight by now and many more people were walking the streets, most of them dressed in European style clothing, with the odd few in the flowing robes of the Muslim Arab. I did notice that even though we were walking amongst these people not one of them acknowledged us. He was walking in front of me at a very leisurely pace, on the outside of the footpath. He appeared to be closely observing each one as we passed, but not in a friendly kind of way. I must admit I felt decidedly uncomfortable. I know that as yet I knew nothing of the circumstances that prevailed in this troubled country; it may be necessary to present a hard line image in order to gain respect, but I would have thought it could project just the opposite to those whose only problem was to find themselves caught up in the troubles.

Later on we made contact with a couple of "Ghaffir's" (night watchmen). They operated under police supervision and were issued with the standard police whistle. My companion said they were a great help, sometimes, and at others they were more of a hindrance, as they tended to disappear off their allotted beat for an hour or two. In the dealings I was to have with them much later in my career I found them always to be a great help. There was to be more than one instance when their devotion to duty brought to my attention matters of importance.

It would have been around four a.m. when we made a slight deviation off one street, and we came to the premises of a baker. They were just preparing the baking for the day, and invited us inside, where we were each given a steaming hot cup of coffee and a scrumptious tea cake. After that short interlude we went practically all the way round the area once more and made our way back to the station.

That first tour of night duty ended, and I was taken back to Shafa-Amr for a well earned sleep. The following two nights went off very much the same as the first except for the fact that the constable appeared to have come to terms with having me around and was much more talkative. He explained many situations I might find myself in, who to trust, and who not to. During the third night he told me that he had come to the end of his tour doing that shift and as from tomorrow he would be on at six in the morning until two in the afternoon, and that I was to do the same. This change of times was known by my superiors, and I had one night in bed and was then taken down by truck, in time to report for duty at six the following day. The streets had been getting quite busy just before the night shifts had ended but now, at this time in the morning, they were positively heaving. The whole place had taken on a completely different dimension. There were cars of all shapes and sizes, buses that seemed to have more people hanging onto the open doors than were actually inside them. Taxis were weaving their way in and out of the traffic at death defying speeds and making very good use of their horns. Along with all this were the cyclists, riding anywhere but where they were supposed to.

The constable strode purposefully along, not hurried, but with a determined stride and seemingly oblivious to all that was going on around him. I followed, in the same manner, only stopping when he did to explain something to me. Although there were a lot of people about it was very rare for us to have to change direction as we walked as everybody gave us a wide berth. It was not a pleasant atmosphere by any means and one that was going to take a lot of getting used to.

Those daytime patrols were much easier than the nights, there weren't all the doors to try, or specific premises to check. On the other hand calls had to be made to a number of "Cafes" where we had to enter and look around to make sure everything was running smoothly, and anticipate any trouble that may be brewing, like someone showing signs of having had more than his fair share of alcohol. Now it was daytime the sounds of music coming from various places filled the air. Even though in some cases different rhythms were vying with each other for supremacy, all in all it was quite pleasant to listen to, and I found myself inadvertently tapping my stick on the side of my leg to the beat. One thing about this shift was the amount of time we had to spare and I was able to take a much more detailed look around. I have mentioned the houses but there was one in particular that took my attention. It was massive, standing on a hillside in it's own grounds, just seperated from the sea by the road. A low wall surrounded the gardens. A large gate opened out into a driveway that weaved it's way upwards to the entrance to the house. The house itself was truly magnificent, dominating the whole area, with views out across the sea from almost all angles. All the ground was covered with shrubs, small trees and innumerable flowering plants of varying colours and contrasts. I must have been staring at this beautiful place, so much so, that it prompted my companion to tell me a little about it and it's occupants. He said this was no ordinary family living here, the owner was one of the most important men in the Arab world. His Arabic name was the, "Khai-Makham". There were many such striking buildings and places, but this house seemed to have an entirely different effect upon me.

My time on the beat came to an end, and I was once more one of the lads doing the every day duties in Shafa-Amr. It had been an experience, having learned a lot and yet I was disturbed about many things.

A lecture was in progress one afternoon when it was cut short for an announcement to be made. There was to be a trip out into the countryside after dinner had been taken. All available personnel were to report in full kit with rifles and a full supply of ammunition to the transport unit at seven o'clock. It was important for everyone to apply, and take with them, a supply of mosquito repellent, as the area in which we would be working was a breeding ground for our friends. We were informed that we were going to a river that was quite close to the country called Transjordan, our neighbour, and then given a detailed lecture on the reason why we were about to make this journey and how we had to conduct ourselves. It was said that there had always been a certain amount of smuggling across the border between the two countries and tonight a much larger than usual consignment of drugs was supposed to have been seen making it's way, via a camel train route, towards one of the unauthorized crossings into Palestine. It was expected to arrive at our side of the river sometime during the night and we were to intercept it. It could be taken for granted the came train would be heavily armed and prepared to defend their goods against all comers. With it being so dark it would make it almost impossible to see them; the camels would have their feet encased in hessian material to prevent them making noise at they walked along. However, no matter what was done to the harness and the load it was bound to emit a grating and a rubbing sound as it swayed from side to side, so it should be possible to hear them approach.

It took quite a long time to reach our destination and the weather wasn't on our side as it was dark with no moon to shed any much needed light, and the heat was almost unbearable. This kind of night would be ideal for those responsible for our being here. We left the transport some distance away from where we wanted to be, and were directed to the high sloping bank of the river and told to spread out along the top of it, laying down just behind the rigge so that we could observe beyond. This river extended for many miles and was very deep in most parts, but here it was shallow enough to be forded. After we found suitable positions we awaited our targets. Waiting where we were was uncomfortable due to the area being full of rotting vegetation, especially near the water's edge. The stench was almost overpowering. Our position laid on that hard dirty soil made things very uncomfortable indeed and even though we were all wearing long trousers and long sleeve jackets the incessant attentions of bugs and creepy crawlies could not be avoided.

There had been great stress put upon the necessity for complete silence while we waited, and all these distractions giving cause to itch and change positions constantly made that extremely difficult, but we did have one thing to be thankful for because a couple of week's ago we had all been issued with the army type water bottle and in this heat it's contents were more than welcome. Even though the water was warm it relieved the awful dryness in the throat. It would have been somewhere around nine thirty when we had arrived and the seemingly end-less night passed uncomfortably. There were a few false alarms when someone thought they had heard the sound of creaking leather but there was no sign of any camels, or anything else for that matter. In the morning we upped sticks, and made the long journey home. Maybe the information that had been received was incorrect, but there was also the thought that our presence had been noted and relayed to the intending travellers. For us it had been a wasted exercise, and an uncomfortable one at that, but it was all part of the type of work we were expected to do.

There was always plenty to do here in the depot, most of it being training and although there was very little time for recreation, the atmosphere was friendly. I had my books on Law, and Arabic to concentrate on and I had never felt more relaxed and at peace with myself. All the thinking and wondering I had been doing for the past year or two was all behind me, I now had a clear head, the way forward was here in the police force and I intended to make the best of it.

No matter how much work and training there was to do time had to be allowed for other forms of interest, and although the little matter of our safety had to be taken into serious consideration, and vigorously impressed upon everyone, some leave was organised enabling a certain number of men to be taken into Haifa every evening. A truck was laid on with the dropping off and picking up points being near to the police H.Q.. A suggestion was made that walking about in groups would be sensible. Trouble could be just around any corner, and the troublemakers knew us, but we had no way of identifying them. It was more than likely that during our evenings out we could be brushing shoulders with people who positively hated us and all we stood for, maybe even active members of one of the terrorist organisations. It was hardly an ideal situation but one we would have to contend with if we wished to take advantage of the opportunity to see the town in which we would spend most of our time working. Having taken all the above into consideration, late one afternoon Peter and I, along with others, put on our best civilian togs, took great care fitting the revolver and holster into a position on the waist belt where it made the least bulge, hopped aboard the truck, and made the journey into town.

The Police H.Q. was in the lower end of town almost opposite the docks, in a road called Kingsway. There were many different nationalities living in the area, but very few Jews, they seemed to occupy the upper parts of town and most of their shops and restaurants were in the better class streets. This wasn't a bad place to commence our explorations; there were shops and cafe-bars to suit most tastes. These cafe-bars, were a type of pub in which it was possible to purchase tea, coffee, sandwiches and cakes, but the main activity centred around the bar where all kinds of alcoholic drinks were served. Some concoction representing beer could be had, but in no way did it taste anything like it's namesake, but as it was the only one available, large amounts of the stuff were consumed by both the police and the army. The party we were with gradually grew smaller as they selected which establishment they were going to try first, till in the end only Peter and I were left to stroll round on our own. We had a good look at anything we found to be interesting, and after seeing all there was to see in Kingsway we went up a very steep hill leading away from the docks. There were tall buildings, obviously residential flats, on the left hand side, and on the other were gardens containing shrubs, trees and flowers leading up to properties some distance away. One tree lined driveway was the entrance to a church. It looked quite impressive standing there amidst all the trees and shrubs with their contrasting shades of green. Although it was night time the road was brightly lit and apart from a few shadows here and there it was almost like daylight. We passed the church and noticed a building with lights on, a door leading into it was open, and music could be heard. Even to my uneducated ear it was clearly dance music. As I hadn't heard this kind for a very long time my curiosity got the better of me and I went along the pathway to the open door to investigate. I asked a lady, who was seated just inside this door, how it was they were playing British style dance music. She explained that this was the church hall and it being an Anglican church, one evening each week was allocated to the British residents of the town to hold a dance. After enquiring who we were, and where we came from, she graciously invited us inside, saying we would be made welcome at anytime. As we went through the door and into the room a dance was in progress, we must have looked like two fish out of water the way we hesitated and stopped just short of the dance floor. All heads turned towards us and the majority were female. That first few minutes just standing there, in what appeared to be complete isolation, had me wondering if it had been a good idea to accept the lady's invitation. There was no need for us to worry though as we were soon whisked off to a table containing refreshments by a woman who must have noticed our dilemma. That broke the ice and we were soon chatting to the people around the table. By this time the dance had ended and seats which were placed around the side of the room were taken up by the girls and women who had been dancing. It was quite an array and one we had not expected to see on our first visit to town. I do believe we were the subject of more than one conversation during our short intrusion upon their usually uninterrupted evening. I say short because we had to leave in order to catch the transport back to the depot. The time had been taken up answering the many questions about where we had been, what had we been doing, and would we be coming again next week? To that last question, we said we would if we were off duty. So, we hadn't had a dance, but time was against us. It had been a pleasant experience and I had high hopes of being able to repeat it soon. On the walk back to the truck we decided to keep our new found oasis strictly to ourselves. No sense in having the place cluttered up with heavy footed policemen!

Sometime later that week we were to go within a couple of hundred yards of the church hall, but for an entirely different reason. Shortly after breakfast one morning almost all the contingent from Shafa-Amr was assembled, in full gear, rifles and ammunition, plus steel helmets, and made a hectic journey to Haifa docks.

Twenty five officers, myself included, were ordered to take up positions on both sides of a steeply sloping ramp that lead down to the water. We were ordered to just stand there, rifles loaded and at the ready. At the end of the ramp was a boat, about fifteen yards from where we were standing, it was overflowing with people. I had no idea how many but it looked too full to be safe. They were leaning over the side, hanging onto the rails, and some were making attempts to get off and come onto the ramp. It was very noisy with screams and shouts coming from these people on the boat, directed at us. They were a dishevelled crowd; the clothes they wore were mostly rags, with gaunt faces and staring eyes. Many children were struggling to avoid being squashed in between the adults. It was just one mass of grey faces swaying from side to side.

Before we had left the depot we had been told that we were going to prevent a boat load of illegal immigrants from landing at the quayside in Haifa. These were Jews who had managed to escape from Europe where they had been subjected to untold horrors by the Nazis. Their intention was to take up residence in Palestine, being regarded by them as their rightful home. This the British government was not prepared to allow, and was insisting the boat leave the dock and travel elsewhere to unload. It was to be our job to make sure that these people did not leave the boat.

The rest of our contingent were positioned around the dock almost rubbing shoulders with each other. If by some concerted movement on their part we were to be overrun on the ramp, our lot standing well back would be able to contain them. At that time there appeared to be very little we could do except stand there and absorb all the abuse that was being directed towards us. The position they found themselves in, having definitely negotiated and overcome many dangerous situations to reach here, was so devastating they could hardly be blamed for showing their disapproval in any way open to them. From what we could see it was a stand-off, until one of our senior officers walked slowly down the centre of the ramp exclaiming to us loudly that if any one got off the boat onto the ramp they must be shot, and if a large number looked like getting off together, then we must fire into the bulk of the passengers. At that time more and more were scrambling up the sides of the boat and things began to look extremely dangerous for those who were doing this, as the boat had developed a decided list, and looked as if it could actually spill it's passengers onto the ramp or into the harbour.

That order, when it was given, didn't even make me have to think. Nothing on earth could induce me to fire on unarmed, defenceless, men, women, and children. It was a problem though, I would have to deliberately disobey an order, and what the outcome from that would be I hadn't the faintest idea. Having thought long and hard about the situation that morning for many days and nights since, I can only hope that the explanation I have offered myself is the correct one, that being, the order was given purposely in that very loud voice, so that it could be heard by everyone on the boat , and that the thought of being fired upon would bring about some stability to the situation.

We had been there somewhere in the region of three hours when suddenly all our troubles were over. A lorry load of soldiers arrived, they unloaded and took up positions all round the whole of the dock area. This made it absolutely impossible for anyone to encroach upon even the smallest piece of ground anywhere near the dock side. We had become redundant, so we came away and returned to the depot. We did hear later that the boat left the harbour with all it's passengers intact, and none having suffered any injuries. Where they eventually finished up we never found out. I couldn't help feeling extremely sorry that after all that had befallen them in Europe they should be turned away and threatened on the very doorstep of a country they had hoped would give them some security and stability at last. Although my feelings of sorrow at that time could well have been misplaced, as it was possible that some members of that particular boat could have been part of the many problems I was to face later on in my service.

Normal duties were once again resumed and the usual round of enjoying life in the depot soon took pride of place over everything else for a while. The day came for our hoped for return visit to see the ladies in the church hall, enquiries were made as to the possibility of our being granted the evening off, and much to my surprise we were told we could go.

We were made welcome at the door and without hesitation we entered and made our way towards the tea counter. I was feeling extremely nervous and that feeling stayed with me, even when I eventually plucked up enough courage to ask one of the young ladies to dance. My previous efforts at swinging the light fantastic had not been what you could call entirely successful. This place I now found myself in was much more sedate, definitely a different class of partner all of whom seemed to be well versed in the art of dancing to a strict tempo with grace and decorum. Sadly both of which were lacking in my case, as having to concentrate on the steps allowed little time for either! I waited until a waltz was announced and I threw caution to the winds and chose a young lady sitting closest to the table where we were. She was very good and with her help and guidance we didn't do too badly. Once the ice had been broken my nervousness disappeared and I had an enjoyable evening dancing with a few of the young ladies, without any mishaps. Peter, however, was content to sit and drink tea, whilst holding conversations with the older ladies. I was surprised when he had informed me that he had never learned to dance and never wished to. The evening came to an end all too quickly and we returned to the depot.

During the next few weeks I put in extra time on the Arabic lessons to prepare for the colloquial exam. I took it, and passed. Now I could hold very basic conversations and understand a lot of what was being said by the Arab population. There wasn't a great deal of opportunity to practice what I had learned at present, as we very rarely mixed with them at this stage. Shortly afterwards a big change in my career took place.

One morning I was told to report to the commanding officer, who said I was to be promoted to Second British Sergeant, and would take up the duties as such at the end of that week. I was asked to consider it, and to give him my answer later that day. This was something I had never envisaged, I had only been in the force a short while and had not acquired sufficient knowledge of the many duties I was bound to perform. All the Sergeants here had many years service. Their ability and knowledge instilled trust and confidence in the officers they had to work with. These things were rolling around in my head as I went back to the sleeping quarters just before lunch time, where everyone was having a few minutes rest. I told Peter the news and his reaction caught me somewhat off guard, he was very emphatic saying I should not even consider it, when I asked him why he said it would put a strain on the friendship I had with him and the rest of the crowd we went around with. Apparently it wasn't the done thing for the higher ranks to socialise with the constables. My thoughts on that were, what a load of rubbish, and I told him so, taking on some form of responsibility would have no effect whatsoever on my friends or my friendship with them.

Hoping I was doing the right thing I went back to see the Deputy Superintendent and he said the other officers had every faith in me and that my army records showed I had previously held positions of responsibility, similar to those of a Sgt. I therefore agreed, and was subsequently promoted the following week. I was once again taking on yet one more challenge and wondering how I would cope. The first thing I had to do was move my kit from the sleeping quarters on the ground floor, and put it in a double room on the first floor. This was now where I would sleep, along with another Sgt. It was a nice spacious room, with access to a balcony overlooking the surrounding area of the depot.

I didn't have long to enjoy my new quarters though as a few weeks later Four Company were told to pack our bags and transported to a beautiful hotel situated on the top of a hill, known as Mount Carmel. The hotel had the same name, being called the Mount Carmel Hotel.

It was on the highest hill above, and to the rear of, Haifa with spectacular views of the surrounding countryside and the Mediterranean Sea. The hotel was empty when we arrived apart from the kitchen staff, who we understood, were to do all the catering for us. A large room was allocated to the constables, on the ground floor, and the senior officers each had separate quarters on the second floor where I shared a fantastic room, it must have been one of the best in the hotel. When everyone had settled in it was time for lunch. The Sgt and I were informed we would take our meals on an enclosed veranda just outside the side door.

This veranda was underneath, and surrounded by, flowering orange trees. They gave off a very heavy but nonetheless, pleasing, scent, and at the front and both sides it had views of the gardens which extended to the outer perimeter wall and hedge which surrounded the hotel. They were well looked after, containing flowering trees, shrubs, and plants, of all descriptions. The most idyllic place in which to have any meal.

Later in the afternoon, we all congregated in another large room and told that we were here to at last begin to do the job we had been training for: Mobile Town Patrols. We were to operate from the hotel, doing three shifts, of two patrol cars each shift. The areas and routes were explained, also the mode of operation. There was to be no time wasted in getting them into full operation, as my companion and I found out. Six constables, and a driver, were selected for each of us, our transport was to be two fifteen hundredweight open topped trucks, one each, and we were to be ready to leave the service yard at the rear of the hotel at nine thirty that evening.

At nine fifteen we assembled in the yard, and after rifles and ammunition had been checked, together with the first aid kit for each truck, we loaded up. We left the yard just before nine thirty, to go down the long winding road that was Mount Carmel, to our first area to be patrolled. Mine was in the main high street of the Jewish quarter, known as Hertzlia street. My thoughts as we drove down that brightly lit hill, were of the hours we had spent during the past four months in the lecture rooms, being instructed in the art of self preservation, and having it rammed down our throats that we must never allow ourselves to get into a position where we were vulnerable to any kind of attack. Sitting in that truck, all the explanations as to how this could be achieved suddenly seemed worthless: The whole lot of us were sitting ducks. However, this was the way it had to be done, regardless of the consequences. I did not voice my opinions but the officers were all ex-soldiers and were quite capable of forming their own without any help from me. All I could do was to ask them to be very vigilant, so that evasive action could be taken quickly in the event of anything suspicious being seen. I didn't like it at all, these officers were my responsibility, their safety was in my hands, and all I could do was to rely upon them to keep a sharp lookout for impending trouble. It reminded me of the predicament we in the army had found ourselves in at the outbreak of the war. Then we were short of almost everything, and what we did have was in most cases inadequate and totally unsuitable for the job it had to perform. This country had been troubled for many years, but it was obvious that the situation was going to change for the worse in the not too distant future. The equipment that was available to us here was certainly very inadequate. I would have thought that now the war was nearing it's end, there were bound to be many armoured cars surplus to requirements, they would be suitable for the type of work we were doing, and able to give to the officers on these patrols the protection to which they were surely entitled. Having said all that we had the job to do, with the equipment provided so we negotiated the hill, Mount Carmel road, arrived at the commencement of Herzlia street about nine forty five, which was the designated point at which our patrol was to begin, and got on with it!

Not one of us had been in this part of the town before, it was predominantly Jewish and most of the beautiful shops, restaurants, theatres, cinemas, and hotels were owned and run by them. The street was very wide, with extra large pavements, tall, flower decorated, street lamps provided the lighting, making it appear to be broad daylight. There were small off shoots, alleyways, leading to the rear of the properties, but even these were well lit. At intervals along the pavements were small built up islands, all with plants and flowers growing in them. It was a truly delightful sight to behold. The bright colourful shop windows displaying their wares, the restaurants tastefully decorated both inside and out. People could be seen through the large curtain free windows enjoying an appetising meal, but the main source of the business seemed to be conducted outside on the huge pavements; tables and comfortable looking chairs with brightly coloured parasols seeming to encircle the whole table, giving an air of seclusion to the customers. Immaculately dressed waiters weaved their way between the tables It was obvious to all of us that this was the hub of the sophisticated lifestyle any self respecting citizen of Haifa aspired to.

We had arrived at the time when everything was in full swing. On a normal day such as this, things didn't come alive until around ten o'clock in the evening. Now it was full to overflowing. Most people were dressed in european clothes, but many languages could be heard. The traditional Arabic dress was noticeable by it's absence. I suggested to the driver that he drive as slowly as possible down the centre of the street, it was quite a long street and must have taken us some three or four minutes to reach the other end. Our passage did not go unnoticed, far from it, we were ogled at all the way along, some gave us looks of sheer hatred, others of disdain, some simply stared without any kind of expression at all. To have a truck full of armed police officers driving slowly past where you were probably taking a well earned rest from your daytime endeavours could not have been very pleasant for anyone. What we were doing was nothing short of intimidation. It was the intention of our superiors to make a show of strength in this fashion but it only showed how weak we actually were. After we had arrived at the end of the street, we turned around and repeated the performance in the same manner, moving very slowly. One manoeuvre was sufficient for now, it would have to be done twice more before the end of the duty. We made our way through more roads, not as slowly now, but not speeding, we had to be able to see the area. The first part was made up of nice wide tree lined roads and streets, with large gardened houses on either side. At this time of night there was very little traffic about; a few buses, and the odd car or two. Then we came out into a district I knew, as it had been part of the foot patrol I had done from Western police station, it was Kingsway. Another nice road, but nowhere near as good as Herzlia street. This was a more cosmopolitan area, there were Greek and Italian restaurants and bars, some small hotels catering for all nationalities. It was a more relaxed atmosphere, everyone congregating together in what were usually noisy groups, the pavements had tables and chairs and were occupied to the extent of being overcrowded. It wasn't very well lit, and only one side of it had shops as the other side opened out into the dock area.

We drove along receiving the occasional stare or glance, our presence appeared to be of no consequence, and considering that it must have been the first time anything, remotely resembling a show of force in this particular manner had passed that way before, it was received as if it had been an everyday occurance. The farther we travelled along, the more populated it became, with larger shops, cafes and bars. We stopped short of the end of the road as that was where the Arab quarter, the "Souk" began, and made our way back to where we had first entered Kingsway, we had approached it from one street that came out about halfway along it and turned right, had we turned left, we would have done the lower end first. We now found ourselves making progress along that end and in doing so we had to drive past the Haifa police head quarters, an immense building. It had it's own guards, but we had to check the surrounding area at least three times during our tour of duty. At this end of Kingsway were the offices and home of the British Consul, another place of extreme importance for us, which once again had to be thoroughly checked at least three times. Having done so we travelled along the exact same route I had experienced during the foot patrols, passing Western police station which looked calm and serene, where no activity could be seen in or around it, and then on into Bat-Galim. It was quiet with very few people about, probably most of them were in the Casino which we crawled past. I acknowledged the waves and nods from the two doormen, and gave my companions a brief resume' of the interior and what was likely to be happening there.

We made progress and came to the business district, the one with the factories. There were no lights that could be seen, they were just as foreboding in appearance as they had been the first time I patrolled them. These places invited the break-in specialists. It was going to need careful scrutiny each time we paid this area a visit. We left and went further down the road out into a residential area, this included the beautiful house I had shown such an interest in before. After touring the connecting streets we returned to the beginning of Kingsway where I had noticed a fairly clean looking cafe, it was time for refreshment, and an opportunity for me to study the map, and work out where we needed to go next. It was the duty of the Sgt to plan out the route for the patrol, it had to be planned so that the trouble spots were visited in a methodical way, but at varying intervals. This was done so that no one could forecast where the patrol would be at a certain time. I had prepared all this before we had left the hotel, but an occasional recourse to the map was inevitable.

The British Consulate, Police Headquarters, and Herzlia street had all been done twice when we took the road back up to the hotel and made a run round the area. By the time we returned to the town it was daylight, about three thirty a.m., so we did it all again. Herzlia street had quietened down, the cinemas and theatres were closed, the restaurants were tidying up, but the cafes and bars were all in operation for the daytime customer. There were still quite a lot of people about, most of them looked as if they were going to work, or that they had gone out the night before. There were more people walking along the footpaths, more buses and cars. It was apparent the working day started in the early hours of the morning, with an early finish in the afternoon. An entirely different lifestyle to what we were used to, adopted because of the unbearable heat that engulfed everything and everyone as the day progressed. The patrol continued until six o'clock, and we returned to our billet. I had two duties to perform before calling it a day; the officers' rifles had to be checked to make sure they were unloaded before they were taken into the sleeping quarters, and my report on the night's happenings made out for the senior officer in charge. The report was very short! After a wash I headed on to the veranda for breakfast. The other Sergeant was already there, he said they had a quiet night except for having to deal with a punch-up in a cafe bar in the early hours which had livened things up a bit.

The night patrol continued for six nights, then we went on the early shift, six a.m. to two p.m. A truck was still being used to take anyone off duty into town at seven in the evening, and bring them back at ten thirty. That first night I was off it was the night the dance took place so I decided to partake in it. I went down with the rest and after having one drink with them, made my way to the church hall, alone. With doing the patrol in that area for almost a week I now had much more knowledge of the places close by and hoped my civilian clothes would make me less obtrusive. Questions were asked as to where my friend was, I made some excuse and because I felt more at home there now I found it easier to choose partners to dance with. On a previous visit I had two or three dances with one particular young lady, and this night we had a few more. She was an excellent dancer and I felt comfortable in her company. During our conversations she told me she was a self employed dress maker and although she held a British passport, she was of Armenian descent. The evening passed all too quickly and after confirming my intention to be at the dance the next week, I returned to the billet.

On one of the early shifts, everything had gone smoothly until about ten in the morning, then shots were heard coming from a street we were approaching. As we got nearer the shots began to come in rapid succession, like automatic weapons fire. I asked the driver to slow right down as we got nearer. It was a good job I did, because as we rounded the next bend and turned into the street, we came across a black American soldier standing in the middle of the road, spraying bullets in an arc in front of him towards the houses and gardens at either side. I told everyone to hang on and got the driver to reverse back round the bend out of the line of fire. This done, I told three officers to carefully cross the top end of the street and take cover behind the large concrete gateposts at the beginning of a driveway, emphasising they must not open fire unless they heard me give them a positive order to do so. I watched them get into position, then told the other three to move into the street and take cover behind something solid on the opposite side to them. We were in one of the better class areas, and thankfully all the houses had very long wide gardens in front of them, with large concrete gateposts adjoining the footpaths. At that moment I was crouching behind one of these posts on the bend, I had asked the driver to stay with the truck but to take cover alongside it just in case the soldier decided to go walkabout. The soldier was still standing in the middle of the street and facing us, not making any movement with his feet, simply swivelling from side to side, keeping his finger on the trigger. Bullets were flying everywhere, the sound of them ricocheting off the road surface and other solid objects in his line of fire, was very disturbing. On the soldier's left, and to his rear, was an army truck. It had canvas covered sides, the back of it was facing us, with a canvas flap fastened down preventing anyone from seeing inside it. I didn't have a satisfactory view of the proceedings from where I was, so putting my best foot forward, I scampered down the right hand side, and dropped down behind the gatepost of the fourth house. From here I did have a good view, and so did the soldier, he saw me and changed his direction of fire towards us. I waved to the others to stay down, there was nothing we could do at this stage, and it was no use becoming exposed to anything. I was now able to take a closer look at the soldier, in between bursts. He looked confused, he carried on firing but kept turning his head to the left and then to the right, as if he was looking for something or expecting something to happen. Then he stopped firing and ran towards the back of the truck and jumped inside, and keeping out of sight he began to fire directly towards us. He must have had spare magazines as he was keeping his finger on the trigger all the time, appearing to do so until a magazine was empty. There would then be a short lull, time for him to attach a full one, and it would start again. I was trying to think what he may do next, if he decided to leave the truck, and ran I would be able to take a shot at him. I didn't relish the thought but if it looked as if someone was directly in the line of his fire, and could be hurt, then I would have no option but to try. Until things took a turn for the worse, I didn't intend making a move as he had a powerful weapon, and a spray from that could chop the legs off anyone that got in the way. All this was going through my mind when I heard the sound of heavy trucks approaching from behind us, then three army trucks came into view from around the bend and entered the street. Almost immediately they stopped, an officer and a number of soldiers got out and using the trucks as cover adopted firing positions. The officer started calling out to the soldier in the truck, who could still not be seen as the rear flap was down, but he kept on firing, only in our direction though. The officer continued shouting, and after a while there was a deathly silence. It was eerie. No-one moved, nothing was said, everyone appeared to be waiting for something to happen. After what seemed an age, the officer and two men ran towards the rear of the truck, in zig-zag fashion, they stopped just short of the flap, waited a few seconds, then one of the men went nearer and cautiously lifted it and looked inside, he then jumped into the truck and came out almost immediately, saying, "it's all over, he has shot himself". I had a short conversation with the officer, who told me the man had escaped from a security compound, driving away in the truck! He didn't elaborate on the subject, and as there was no longer any need for us to stay there, we got back onto our vehicle and resumed the patrol. I made the necessary entry into my notebook, detailing the relevant facts, and the amount of time taken up by the incident. I think all of us on the patrol were feeling rather depressed at the outcome, but at least we could take some form of consolation from the fact that our arrival on the scene contained the soldier long enough for the others to arrive. So we had helped, in an observation role, rather than an active one, and we were all in one piece!

With the town patrols working three shifts it made it impossible for me to further my education as a dancer on all but one of those shifts. When I was on afternoons or nights the starting or finishing times did not allow it. I did however manage to wangle the appropriate evening off when on days. The excuses I was having to make to my companions on the truck taking us in to, and returning from, town, about my reasons for leaving them in the bar were beginning to wear thin and I knew it wouldn't be much longer before my journeys to the dance hall became common knowledge. Peter, in his wisdom, had already pointed out the problems it could cause. Taking advice from others was not one of my strong points, so I continued my excursions whenever possible. My dancing partner, that's how I began to refer to her, was hard to convince of the reason for my absence on two week's out of three. Nevertheless, when I did make it, and put in an appearance, she tried her best not to appear too disappointed about the times I had to miss, and ensured I received plenty of tuition while I was there, which pleased me.

Well it had to happen, we left our life of luxury in the Mount Carmel hotel, and returned to Shafa Amr. The town patrols would now be carried out from here as all personnel had been withdrawn from the hotel for security reasons. There was to be one big difference and that was from now on all patrols would be enlarged to accommodate a number of armoured cars. One would be accompanying each of the trucks. These were really four wheeled Scout cars, with a short wave radio and one Bren gun. The crew were surrounded by armour plating which made their position more safe and secure. We regarded the radio as the most important addition to the patrols, as it meant we were in contact with base all the time we were out. It also helped knowing there was a powerful weapon such as the Bren to cover our backs. The Scout cars had the protection of the armour, but they were still very vulnerable to being blown up by specifically positioned mines or the like, and their crews could not abandon ship as quickly as we could.

At every opportunity I would go to the church hall and meet my dancing partner. I had some time off when there was no dance on, as day time trips into town were now organised as well as the evenings. We discussed this, and arrangements were made for us to meet up at various locations. All her dressmaking was carried out in the homes of the people having the dresses made, and while she was there she was treated almost as one of their family, taking all her meals with them, seated at the same table. On one ocassion when we met up, she said would I mind going with her to one of these homes as it was very important she get on with making the dress for the daughter of the family. It was with some apprehension that I entered the house, introductions were made, and from then on I was treated as a respected guest, and invited to partake of a meal with them. That was the first time I had done this, there were to be many more. The majority were in the homes of Christian Arab families but there were also Jewish ones as well. I must admit my nerves were a little on edge on many occasions "cohabiting" with the Jews although the ones I met in those homes were very nice people. The more I saw of Anna, the more interested I became. She spoke quite a few languages and was able to help me in learning Arabic.

She told me of her work in Egypt where she was employed by the British Ambassador's wife as lady in waiting. He was a Lord. She was well acquainted with all the top Arabic singers, male and female, in Egypt at that time, and knew them all personally. She was also well known and respected by most of the Arab royal families, Kings, Princes, Princesses, Emirs and Sheikhs, in all the surrounding countries. Her brother and his wife and one daughter, lived in Jerusalem, he was a solicitor, and was later to become a barrister, a judge, and very much later, Governor of British controlled Cyprus. Her sister and husband lived in what was known then as Transjordan, he was the personal bodyguard to Lawrence of Arabia, fought alongside him in his campaigns and was one of his closest friends. Most of the business people, Jew, Arab, and Greek thought very highly of her. I started to think about all this; I was only a policeman, and not a very important one at that, how was I going to fit into her world with all the experience she obviously had. I was not in the same class to which she was used to, far from it! I did think long and hard, but when I spoke to her of this, she expressed her high hopes of what we could achieve together. She did seem at ease and totally relaxed when in my company, so we continued with our relationship and I was to see her at every opportunity.

Now that we had the company of the scout car all patrols in some way seemed easier. One night on our way to check over the Mount Carmel area we were approaching one of the more densely populated districts in a high class suburb, just below the top of the hill. Arrangements had been made with the scout car commander for them to follow the truck, and if he received any radio messages that required our immediate attention, he would flash the car's head lights twice. This would be the signal for us to pull into the side of the road and stop. This was to be the first time this form of communication was employed. The street we were in was fairly well lit but the two flashes that came from behind us were plain for all to see. Our driver pulled in and stopped, I got out and went to the car where I was told a message from headquarters had been received, informing us of a shooting that had just taken place at a house in a street not far from where we were at present. Nothing specific was known, and no further information was given except that we were to approach with extreme caution. I told the car commander to follow the truck and when we reached the street to drive in a short distance, then mount the kerb onto the footpath on the right hand side, almost opposite where the truck would be, stop and switch off the engine, turn off all the lights, and keep the radio noise to a minimum. If there were any further messages, to give them to my driver who would be waiting in the truck and he would then bring them to me. Having made sure he understood, I resumed my position in the truck and went in search of the street in question. It only took a few minutes for us to arrive. The street was slightly downhill with a continuous bend to the left all the way down. There were some bungalows and some houses, all with long gardens and small surrounding stone walls. The gardens had trees and shrubs making it awkward to see very much from the road. Very few lights could be seen in any of the houses and there was nothing visible that gave any indication of there having been a disturbance of any kind. My first thoughts were, was it a trap? I sent three officers to go down the right hand footpath, telling them to keep close to the inside near the garden walls, and to take nothing for granted, expecting problems all the time. The other three I took with me down the left and we came to the house with the number we had been given. They took up positions near the entrance to the driveway and just inside it, keeping well out of sight. Still there were no signs of anything having taken place, the house appeared to be in total darkness when I approached the front door and rang an electric bell positioned on the side of the door frame. I heard it ring but nothing happened, so I put my finger on and held it there for quite some time before a light came on and a woman opened the door. Then I knew it wasn't a trap, she was very distressed and crying uncontrollably. When she saw the uniform she asked me in and led the way to the kitchen, saying as she did so that her husband had been shot by someone who had come to the back door. When we reached the kitchen I saw a person on the floor on his knees leaning over someone laid on the floor. I could see the man lying on the floor had an injury of some kind, and there were considerable amounts of blood around him and more splashes of it on the floor leading from the door. The man leaning over him turned to me, gave me his name and introduced himself saying he was a doctor, and lived close by. The man's wife had called him in after the shooting. He also said that he had called for an ambulance, but it didn't look good. I went out of the kitchen and found the woman in a room with her two children. I said I was very sorry for what had taken place but it would help if she could tell me exactly how it had happened, about what time, and would she tell me first if she knew the person who had done the shooting? She answered by saying she didn't know the man, but she had seen him run away down the pathway after the shooting, and that it would have been about ten forty five. It was now eleven fifteen, so if she was correct, half an hour had passed and presumably the culprit was long gone. Nevertheless, I went out and spoke to all six officers, explaining what I knew, and asking them to take a look around the area in pairs, just in case the man had decided to stay around, maybe to verify the outcome. I also informed the car commander of the situation and told him I would keep him advised on any developments as they arose, and in the meantime to stay alert but remain in the car. I then returned to the house and spoke to the woman again, this time allowing her to tell me what she knew. She told me her name and that her husband was a doctor. Her children had been in bed and she was in the living room when the back door bell rang. She went into the kitchen to answer it, and when she opened the door a man was standing there and asked if he could speak to her husband. She asked him to wait, closing the door as she did so, and then went into her husband's study where he was working and told him about the man. He left what he was doing and went towards the kitchen door, she watched him approach it, but before he could open the door a number of shots rang out and he slumped to the floor. She was very upset, and having to go over the whole thing wasn't helping her at all. I had no wish to cause her further distress so I made my excuses and left the room, returning to the kitchen where the doctor was still trying to help her husband. I opened the kitchen door. It had a frosted glass upper panel and on the floor outside I saw six cartridge cases obviously from a small calibre gun. I did not disturb them but made a mental note of their position on the floor. The frosted glass panel had holes and cracks in it. I closed the door from outside and looked through the unbroken part of the panel. With the light from the kitchen being behind it, I could see into the room enough to see the outline of someone approaching the door. That is what must have happened with the culprit able to make good his escape from behind the closed door. The ambulance came and took the man to hospital. I went to the car and told the radio operator to inform headquarters and ask them to ask the criminal investigation department for their assistance. Now that the injured man was on his way to the hospital there was nothing more we could do. I spoke with the woman for a while and explained that C.I.D. were on their way and would do all they could to help her. I went round the officers and told them to be ready to move, but to keep out of sight until then. By this time it was after eleven forty five, we had been there three quarters of an hour when the officers from the C.I.D. arrived. The injured man must have been of some importance as there were three detectives and one Superintendent. I gave the Supt. a brief summary of what we had done and obtained his permission to resume the patrol.

This type of problem should not have been left to us. H.Q. had been informed as soon as we were aware of the extent of the situation, we should then have been allowed to go back to doing the job for which we had been trained; the patrol. Our initial purpose when we had first received the radio message was to attempt to detain the person or persons responsible for the shooting. As soon as we had been told that person had left the scene some ten minutes before we arrived, our services were no longer required, in a practical sense. To give any assistance or help if needed could have been carried out and then we should have left any further enquiries to the qualified branch of the service. We had received no instructions to leave, so we stayed and did what we thought was necessary, in doing so we left the area we were supposed to work in, unprotected for more than three quarters of an hour! All this I emphasised in my report to our depot commander and a few days later I received a reply from H.Q. laying the blame squarely at the feet of the CID and their failure to arrive at the scene as expected. My report was forwarded to CID for their information and I knew It wouldn't go down very well with them; a P.M.F. Sgt having the cheek to complain about their activities. I received a memo from C.I.D. saying we were to be congratulated upon the way we handled the situation. Unfortunately the man died and the person responsible was never found.

The patrols continued on all three shifts, incidents occurred on quite a few, the odd punch up, a vehicle accident or two. British soldiers having to be restrained in the many cafe bars was a regular occurrence. Apart from doing their best to upset everyone, Jews, Arabs, and very often the British police, they always seemed to be of the opinion that some bar attendant or street vendor, was deliberately setting out to swindle them. Some situations were extremely difficult to control, the main problem being that they were also armed as we were, and it was not unknown for them to resort to using their weapons against us, it happened on more occasions than I care to relate.

On one night patrol we came across something that wasn't unpleasant, just the opposite, it was hilariously funny for us, but I am afraid not so for one unfortunate miscreant. We had just worked the area around the casino and checked the government hospital desk, toured the outside of the building including the secure compound where people who had committed some kind of offence were undergoing hospital treatment and then we went into the factory road. One of the ghaffirs stopped us and said he had heard noises coming from one of the properties. I asked him to show us which one, so he hopped onto the truck and took us into a very dark alley at the end of a large building. He pointed to a door up ahead. I told three officers to stay at the side of the scout car while I took the other three. We spread out and crossed the alleyway towards the door, but before we reached it we heard movements coming from a ground floor window. We could just about see that the bottom half of this window was open, then a shoe attached to a foot and leg appeared coming out over the window sill, then followed a rump, then another leg, and very soon the owner of these limbs was standing before us in scruffy clothes with a big black canvas bag. He came towards me and in a breathless quivering voice, said, "Oh I am so pleased to see you, I was looking for my friend's workplace and got lost. I heard you coming and not knowing who you were, and frightened it might be someone wishing to hurt me, I opened that window and found a hiding place inside, then when I saw it was you, the British police, I knew I was safe, and came out to meet you". All this in garbled Arabic, but it wouldn't have mattered which language it was in, it would have sounded just as unbelievable. We took him where we could see a bit better and examined the contents of his black bag. Inside were, a jemmy, a hammer, two screwdrivers, a hacksaw, and various other pieces of equipment. He was only a young chap, probably sixteen or slightly over, he looked to have been rooting somewhere as his face and hands were filthy, his style of dress left much to be desired in quality but he had a fairly long coat with the appropriate large pockets, for a fellow in his profession. After he was given a thorough search for any kind of weapon he was politely requested to turn out his pockets, and place the contents on the floor in front of him. It took him quite some time and he seemed surprised at all the things he brought out; two desk clocks, three silver pen holders, two expensive looking paper knives, and a small amount of money in notes which, handily for us, a piece of string was tied round with a label from the firm that owned the building where we had found him. Despite all this he still tried to convince me of his innocence. I did feel really sorry for him but we dropped him off at Western police station for them to deal with. He gave us quite a good laugh with his charming attempts to bamboozle all of us.

At least once during the night we would be in the area of the coffee wallah, his melodious cup clanking was a welcome sound in th dead of night, and his wares were most welcome. We met up with the one I first had dealings with on the foot patrols. One day he asked me if I knew what some of the regular beat officers were doing to them (the coffee boys). He went on to say they were threatening to stop them working in their areas, if they refused to give them some of their takings every week. He didn't single out any one person, but I already suspected one of being in on some sort of "scam". It was common knowledge that there was a lot of this kind of thing going on. I had also heard it wasn't only the lower ranks that were involved. I was to experience personally the whole sordid carry on at a later stage in my career. It wasn't always the officer's doing in the first instance, the business people wanted to be allowed to do things that were against the law and were prepared to pay to have a blind eye turned in their direction. I know it was only a tiny thing compared with what was going on, but I always made sure our lot always paid the correct amount for the coffee. The rendezvous with those coffee boys were something we all looked forward to.

Although I had some time for other things, Anna and I saw quite a lot of each other. We had been friendly for quite a long time and we had discussed the possibility of our getting married. I have previously expressed my doubts as to my being the kind of person she would find suitable for her way of life, saying that maybe she was of a different class to myself, and would those apparent differences make us compatible enough to get married? I did find this to be something that was really worrying, but every time the subject came up, which was quite frequently, it was swept under the carpet by her insistance that everything would be all right. So, it was eventually decided that I would apply for permission to get married. This was something that had to be done as I was in a foreign country, and Anna was of Armenian descent. As far as I could see there would be no problems. I made the necessary application, filled in all the appropriate forms, and the reply came back, permission refused! Then came a round of interviews, not requested by me but by at least three commissioned officers, one being the previous commander of the depot, a Deputy Superintendent. The Deputy Supt was the person responsible for my promotion and he had always treated me with great respect and sympathy. He spoke to me in an arranged interview at the depot. He asked me to withdraw my application as I was well on my way to obtaining a promotion in the very near future. To go against the authorities' decision would most certainly put an end to that. When I asked him why the application had been turned down he would only say that Anna was not a fit person for me to marry and that the refusal had nothing to do with me. During the next few days I had interviews with an acting assistant Supt and assistant Supt. These were carried out in the depot and both were on the same lines as the first one. They did not answer my question of why?

There were some things which had given me cause for thought, for instance we had been on trips to places like Jerusalem, Bethlehem, Tel-aviv, Trans-Jordan, and other smaller places. When we went to Jerusalem I did wonder why we didn't visit her brother and his family, as they lived there, also when we went to Trans-Jordan her sister, her family, and her internationally famous husband, had a home there, but we did not visit them either. Although I did ask her about this it was not until some time later that I did eventually find out the reason. For my part I was a Sgt with an exemplary record and I was apparently on my way up and fast so the problem could not be with me. Anna said as far as she knew there could be no reason that she could think of why she would be deemed unsuitable, although when she had been living and working in Egypt, she had been very friendly with a well known lady singer who had been accused of being a double agent during the war. She went on to say that maybe she was thought to have been in some way involved, as at that time she was residing in the British Ambassador's home. I thought this was a little too far fetched, so the mystery remained.

A few weeks went by, I had still not withdrawn my application, and I was surprised to find that an appointment had been arranged for me to see the Deputy Supt. again. This time it was to take place in a more personal environment, a select cafe, of the Supt's choice, and during his own time. He emphasised that it was a police matter but he was discussing it purely as a friend. This, as you can imagine, was not the usual way of doing things. I could see no reason for the change of venue, except maybe the Supt thought I would be more sympathetic to his views in a neutral and friendly atmosphere. We had a very long and interesting conversation, but I was none the wiser afterwards. It was made very plain to me that if I went through with the marriage I could forget any form of further promotion, I would not receive the normal married man's pay, nor would I be given married quarters. I would be married, but in their eyes I would still be a single person, no recognition would be afforded to my wife. He went on to say that if I did go through with it, he personally, would be very disappointed indeed, and that I would be throwing away the opportunity for a highly successful career. I had never taken kindly to being pressurised into doing something so Anna and I decided that the 'top brass' had got it all wrong and the wedding would go ahead.

I had no idea how much work went into preparing for a wedding until we started to get into the swing of things. It was decided that with the situation the country was in at present, the police not being the flavour of the month, it would be prudent for all attending the wedding to wear civilian clothes. I was to have a suit tailor made by a friend of the family, a Jewish firm,and it was splendid. Anna took weeks to make her dress, and to accumulate all the accessories. The bridesmaids, of which there were two, were both very pretty young ladies, one about sixteen, the other about ten. Their dresses were also made by Anna. The one and only page boy was suitably kitted out, he would have been about six, and he looked resplendent in his outfit. As to be expected, Peter was the best man. The principals were ready, the invitations had been sent out, and they all turned up, including the senior officers!

At sometime during our getting to know each other period, after my application to marry had been refused, Anna had informed me that she had two godfathers living here in Haifa. One was Superintendent Cafferata, a very distinguished officer, and what's more, the head of police operations in Haifa. The other I had already met, although neither of us had known it at the time. He was Ibrahim Betar, a Superintendent in C.I.D. Haifa, the one who attended the murder of the doctor on Mount Carmel, he and his wife attended the wedding, but not so Cafferata. He had a beautiful house at the top of Mount Carmel, living there with his wife and family, but we never had the pleasure of paying them a visit. He was high on the hit list of the terrorists, many attempts had been made on his life and so, with regret, he and his family were the only ones to miss the wedding. He felt that if he were there the terrorists might think the chance to get rid of him and a lot of other policemen was just to good to miss.

The wedding service was conducted in Saint Luke's Church, in mountain road, where we had first met in the church hall. The actual wedding and reception were a truly grand affair, our good health was toasted in vintage champagne. The reception was held in the home of an Italian friend, with the victuals being provided, again by an attending businessman. The Italian, his name was Umberto Georgi, had also agreed to rent us the ground floor flat in his house when we returned from honeymoon. There were stacks of presents.

Anna and I took our leave of the reception and went to her friend's house and got changed, then it was a short trip in a taxi to the port of Haifa where we caught a ship to Cyprus. The trip was only an overnight journey and we spent the night on the top deck. It was a warm moonlit night with the Mediterranean, a lovely calm sea, as ever. We docked in Limasol in the morning and took a taxi to Nicosia, the capital. At that time, in 1945, the island was under the control of the British, with the inhabitants being mainly Greeks and Turks, who were living in close harmony together. It was very pleasant then, being able to walk, or ride, anywhere you liked without any problems.

We stayed in Nicosia a few hours and then left to go to the Troodos mountains, in a taxi. We spent a week in the Forest Park hotel in Platrus. I do have more than a fleeting memory of that particular taxi ride, up all the winding roads, the extremely sharp bends, and the very steep drop on one side. To put it mildly it was hair-raising. The weather when we arrived on the island was very hot indeed, but when we got to the hotel in the early evening it was cool to the point of being cold. The hotel itself was really classy, with large spacious rooms and balconies. The views of the surrounding countryside were magnificent. Even though I had previously had my share of fields full of grape vines, and citrus fruit trees, in the army days, we toured quite a few and took advantage of the tasting facilities that were offered. Anna was quite at home, being able to speak Greek and Turkish, although her dealings with the Turkish community were tempered by the memories of what the Turks did to the Armenians. It was common knowledge that they had slaughtered some twenty thousand men, women, and children, during a concerted attack to remove them from their own country.

With it being the middle of September it was extremely hot during the daytime, a slight breeze made it bearable, and we spent a great deal of time just sitting on the balcony looking out onto the green fields and trees of the rolling countryside. It was like living in a different world altogether. We had booked a week in a hotel in Nicosia, and I must say it was with some regret that we packed our bags and made the journey back down the mountain. We decided to leave the capital after three days as it was so very hot, and had a few days in Kyrenia, a beautiful seaside town, where we caught up with a bit more swimming. Then it was time to return to Palestine to see what lay in store for us there.

I was feeling rather apprehensive; I had gone against the wishes of my superior officers and did not know quite what my reception would be because of that. We went to see Umberto Georgi and his wife and sister first, they had made all the necessary arrangements for us to take over the flat, cleaned it out ready for the furniture that Anna had in her own place. It was high quality stuff, the best of English workmanship. She had made arrangements for it to be delivered by a few of her friends, in time for us to be settled in that night. My leave was over at noon the next day so I returned to Shafa Amr, to a lot of ribald comments from my friends, and some not very nice orders from the depot commander. I did not speak to him personally, but received the message from one of his sub-ordinates. I was not allowed to stay away from the depot, and must return after every duty. My sleeping arrangements must stay strictly as before. I was informed by a senior officer, upon whose word I knew I could rely, that the depot commander was one of those persons who did not take kindly to having one of his officers married to what he regarded as a foreigner. The realisation struck me that this was probably what all the resistance had been about.

That first duty was a night patrol. We left the depot around nine fifteen and were in position in the first area just before ten. Any spare time I had during the day had been taken up trying to think of a way in which I could see Anna for a few minutes. I would have the usual times off as before, returning to the depot at ten thirty at night, and most probably a full day off here and there, so all that remained was to sort something out where a quick visit could be fitted in somewhere. One thing was in my favour, our flat was in one of the streets that we would have to pass at least six times during the patrol. There were occasions when the patrol would stop and do a few spot checks if we had any reason for doing so, but this I could put to my advantage. I was able to go in and have a few minutes chat with Anna, just to assure her I hadn't done a bunk, and to see if she wanted anything doing where I would be able to help. I couldn't do this every shift, but did whenever I felt I needed to. The chaps were quite able to take care of themselves for a short while.

My shifts alternated and on one of the afternoon duties, when we were touring one of the residential districts, one which seemed to always give us some sort of problem, we heard the sound of someone firing a small calibre gun. This sound was coming from a block of flats at the far end of the street we were in. We pulled up outside and I took four men with me, went up the stairs and located the flat the shots were coming from. As we reached the top the firing stopped, so we started door knocking. This was fruitless because not one was answered, probably because the occupants had heard the firing as well and were keeping out of the way. Then the firing started again. Now it was possible to locate the exact flat. Motioning the others to stay away from the door, I gave it a good thumping, all I got in return was a loud mouthful of abuse in perfect English! The tirade of abuse continued for a while, intermingled with sporadic firing. The door didn't appear to be all that solid so I kept well away from where there were panels, these would be the spots even the smallest of calibre bullets could be able to come through. So, keeping to one side of the door frame, I politely, and without raising my voice too much, informed the inmate that if he didn't open the door we would break it down. He ignored my plea altogether. We had no idea what we might find on the inside of that flat: If there was anyone else in there it couldn't be very pleasant for them. It wasn't going to be simply a case of stand out of harms way while he called the tune, something would have to be done. Suddenly he stopped firing and without warning he pulled open the door, nearly tearing it from it's hinges. As it opened wide, I saw the look on his face when he could see there was no-one there. He stood in the doorway in full view of all of us. I called out to him to throw the pistol onto the floor on the landing. He waved it around somewhat and I thought he was going to close the door again. He was standing perfectly straight, not wobbling at all and I was thankful that at least we weren't dealing with someone under the influence of drink or drugs. He was tall, well built, well dressed, but looked wild eyed, and most certainly agitated. I motioned to the others to stay back, and with some trepidation I moved out and walked towards him, not slowly, nor hurried, but purposefully. I left my revolver in it's holster, but had unfastened both safety straps, just in case. I held out my left hand and told him to give me the pistol, he made some kind of movement as if he was going to step back inside the room, then to everyone's surprise and my relief, his shoulders drooped, he held out the pistol, and started sobbing like a child. Two officers took hold of his arms and moved him away from the door. I and the other two went into the room hesitantly. We went into all the rooms and found nothing except the sight of many bullet holes; in the furniture, the walls, and the ceilings. It looked a right mess, stuffing from cushions was everywhere, glass picture and photo frames were smashed, and some hanging drunkenly from their positions. Now I knew there were no casualties it was possible to relax and concentrate on him. His excuse was a lame one, apparently he had a falling out with his live in young lady, she had gone off in a huff, and he had thought if he started firing his revolver she would hear it and return. Well she hadn't returned.

142

After searching him for more weapons, we took him to Western police station and handed him over to the desk Sgt, where he resided in a cell for the night. I made out a report and had to appear in court the following day where he was fined, given a severe reprimand, and bound over to keep the peace.

When I had a day or two off, Anna and I paid a visit to Ibrahim Betar and his wife. I was in civvies but her husband must have been making enquiries after the wedding, because after the initial greetings were exchanged he said, "Ah!, at last I meet Jack Wood, the P.M.F. Sgt. who had the audacity to complain about the way the C.I.D. handled the incident on Mount Carmel". He went on to say that they had been a long time answering the call I had made, but there had been a good reason. I didn't like talking shop, but I thought here was a good opportunity for me to explain a little of what a P.M.F. patrol was expected to do, and emphasising that attending situations, even those as serious as a murder, could not be allowed to keep us away from our areas for very long. He said he understood, adding that he thought we were doing a good and very necessary job. Yes, typical C.I.D., good at the "flannel". They had a really unpleasant job to do and he was in charge of most of it, so I don't suppose for one moment that my explanation made the slightest difference towards his impression of our lot. Both he and his wife were exceptionally nice people and Anna and I were to spend some good times in their company. Fortunately the difference in rank and status never entered into anything we wished to do at any time. He was a Christian Arab, and a real gentleman; the type of person almost anyone would find it hard not to get on with.

At this time there was a lot of quarry work being done, out in areas that were a long way from the towns and cities and we had the job of escorting the explosives that were to be used in carrying out this work. Anything to do with causing explosions were things that had to be taken great care of so that they did not get into the wrong hands. It had to be escorted to the place where it was needed and supervised when it was being used. I was notified that this task would be mine for the next few days, seven officers and two Humber scout cars were made available to me. The order of travel was for three officers and a driver to be in each of the cars, and for the explosives to be carried on a civilian armour plated lorry with two civilian drivers. We would meet the truck where it was to be loaded, it would then travel in front with the two cars following. These convoys had been ambushed on a number of ocassions, some I might add culminating in loss of life of escorts and lorry drivers. Some of the roads were not too bad but the majority were simply dirt roads, bumpy, narrow and extremely dusty; especially for anyone travelling behind a heavy truck that was kicking up dust. We required to be able to see in front of the lorry where possible, so we hung back, out of the dust cloud, in order to do so. It wasn't easy and much of the time we could not see anything at all. We couldn't put one car in front because itwould have left it wide open to being cut off. The way we were doing it if anyone attempted to ambush the lorry they would find they had two cars bearing down on them from the rear, with the armed escorts inside. There were obviously ways in which an attack upon us could be successful, but it would require a considerable number of personnel in which to carry it out. So this is the way in which we tried to ensure that if we were ambushed we could at least be in the best possible position to defend the lorry and, of course, ourselves. We could not have wished for a better kind of transport for ourselves, the Humber car was noted for it's resilience, it's ability to travel long journeys in extremely hot climates, and most of all to give it's passengers a reasonably comfortable ride in doing so. This job we were doing would have been easier and much more comfortable if we had been able to travel with the windows open wide but the amount of choking dust that was swirling around us for most of the time made this impossible. The inside of the car was very hot and uncomfortable, but at least we could breathe. Just!

We travelled through wasteland for mile after mile, only barren ground and mountainous hills on both sides. These places were known as Wadis, at one time they would have had water running through them, now they were just tracks between the hills, with many twists and turns. They were ideal places for someone to carry out a successful ambush. Sometimes the terrain levelled out and things could be seen clearly many miles away. On these odd ocassions we came across what appeared to be dozens and dozens of Goats, with the goat herder walking along in the front, closely followed by the herd leader, a goat with a jingling bell tied around it's neck, the rest trotting along in a large clump, spreading out over a very wide area. All the time they were stopping for a second or two to take a tug at a tuft of very old withered grass. It surprised me to see them trudging through these barren spots, with no apparent destination and yet these animals were the main source of the meat diet for a great many people, and the providers of life giving milk, also used in the making of cheeses, and for baking. Another view that gave us the feeling of utter desolation was the sight of a Camel train in the far distance, they were a long way away but we were still able to make out the large loads they were carrying, tightly packed on both sides of them and more on the top. "Ships of the desert" plodding along at a very leisurely pace, their long ungainly stride covered the ground at a spectacular rate.

We arrived at the entrance to the quarry and were directed to a hole in a hillside, a type of cave, where the explosives were unloaded and carried inside. The men were all of Jewish extraction, with the quarry apparently being owned by a Jewish contractor. I took one officer and made as if to enter the cave, where we were informed that we were not allowed inside, and were asked to keep clear of the entrance. It would take about fifteen minutes before they were ready to make the detonation, and we would be informed just before it was to take place, so we stood back. Our instructions from the depot were that we should make absolutely sure all the explosives were used. We didn't want explosives falling into the wrong hands. The officer and I were standing some fifty yards away from the entrance to the cave, how on earth were we to know exactly what was going on inside? Were they doing as was intended, or was some put to one side? Whatever they did we would be none the wiser, standing outside like a couple of obedient little schoolboys. There was no way we could be present at the preparation or the actual firing, so the orders given to us were ludicrous! There was an explosion, something had been blown up. When the stuff had been unloaded the lorry returned to it's base, having no need for our services on the return journey. So our job done, we returned to the depot. As far as we were concerned we had done what we could and everything had gone according to plan. We did three or four more such excruciating journeys. I breathed a sigh of relief when I was given other duties.

Chapter 9

These new duties were foot patrols in the "Souk", the Arab quarter of the town. I went on patrols with one Jewish and/or one Arab constable, not the same ones every time. Going out with the two nationalities gave me an insight into both sides and their differing views on the situation we all had to deal with. One thing I was very positive about, the religious factor would never lead me into any arguments. On this subject I was to find that my wife Anna had very strong views, but I refused to let my judgement be influenced by her; never contradicting, nor agreeing, simply refusing to be drawn into any kind of discussion. It is one thing to have an opinion upon these subjects, but to let it be known what they were in my type of work would have been defeating the objective of trying to be neutral and fair minded in dealing with everyone.

During these patrols which were always carried out either on the day or afternoon shift (no nights at this stage in my duties), I learned a great deal about the area and it's inhabitants. The roadway's through the entire Souk were only narrow, with barely room to walk without having to dodge something, and the overhanging tapestry like shop blinds had to be negotiated through the narrowest parts. It was a hive of activity with different aromas seeming to invade your nostrils at every turn from the different foods being prepared for consumption in the restaurants or the dozens of small stall like shops which could be found every few yards. The most noticeable thing was the leisurely pace at which everything was conducted. Another thing that I found to be very pleasing to my ears was the music, it could be heard coming from many different sources; the cafes the shops the restaurants, the private houses and all kinds of places. It gave the impression you were entirely surrounded by it, and it had the effect of making me feel completely relaxed listening to the lilting, and mostly haunting, melodies.

I was quite happy doing those patrols but one afternoon I was sent for by the depot commander. As I walked to his office I was thinking, what would he be going to grumble about this time. Ever since I had got married his whole attitude towards me had changed and not for the better either. I had already noted that I had been "selected" for those dangerous escort duties, of which most Sgts had only done one. I knocked on the office door, was invited in, and upon entering I gave the usual required salute. Much to my surprise I was told to take a seat. Then came the reason for my being there. The commander began to explain that a "Kibbutz" (a Jewish village), was giving cause for concern and he had been asked to arrange for someone to be sent to investigate it. He went on to say that he regarded me as the one person who could do the job, adding that it would be a highly dangerous task as the village would have to be entered in order to ascertain the full extent of what was going on inside. He told me that the whole operation had to be kept quiet, no-one except the actual participants must know of it's existence. Even he did not want to know of any of the details. He would sanction any requests I made, and provide any help I might require but the job would be my sole responsibility. I could not expect to receive any kind of "back up" If things went wrong. Most worryingly all knowledge of the operation would be disclaimed by the powers that be. He then told me the reasons for the concern, and what was expected of me. I would choose three officers to accompany me. My thoughts on that subject were that it would be very unfair to volunteer anyone without first informing them about what they could expect and of the "dodgy" circumstances under which this particular job had to be carried out. Towards the end of his somewhat uninformative explanations, he suggested I might consider making it a one man operation and doing it under cover of darkness. That way I would only have to take care of myself, without having to be responsible for anyone else, who could inadvertently jeopardize the whole operation. He had shown me on the map where the village was and it was plain to see that the surrounding terrain would be difficult enough to negotiate during daylight, in the dark it could prove impossible, besides which, if this village did have something to hide, the inhabitants would not be foolish enough to leave it unguarded, especially at night. I therefore declined his suggestion!

All done that could be done, for now, I left the office, and contacted a friend of the three officers I had in mind, when asked if they would be on duty the following day, he said he thought they would have no special duties, so I asked him to tell them to meet me in my quarters at seven thirty the next morning.

It wasn't easy to convince the clerk in the main office that I was studying the area and required the use of one or two maps, but in the end I got what I thought would be appropriate and after having dinner I took them back to my room and got to work studying them. The three officers came as arranged the next morning and I told them we had a job to do. I did emphasise the fact that it could prove to be extremely dangerous, and knowing this were they prepared to accompany me? All three had been with me in other situations that had required their full cooperation, so I knew I could trust them, and it was equally as important that they had faith in me. We went on to discuss the entire operation, right down to the finest detail. I told them exactly what we were about to do, not forgetting to inform them of those few sentences from the commander that had me reaching for the bottle of aspirins that I felt sure would certainly be required sooner or later!

I started by telling them about the Kibbutz, which like all the others was under constant surveillance. This particular one had a lot more "comings and goings" than was normal. There were trucks with people in them entering and leaving at all times of the day and night. On the outside it looked just the same as any of the others, but what was going on inside was going to be our job to find out. This would be much easier said than done as we would not be welcomed with open arms by the inhabitants. However I had formed a plan which seemed quite feasible, providing we didn't meet with any problems I had not envisaged. Eventually we decided exactly what we intended to do, and left the rest to providence! Always remembering that we could change the plan at any stage during the operation.

The plan was for all of us to be dressed in civilian clothing, carrying only our police identity cards, one valid correctly dated and stamped day pass, and of course the usual revolver. The taking of the revolver had been something that had caused quite a bit of discussion, until I pointed out that if we were to be seen and accosted, it was well known by almost everyone

146

that we were not supposed to go anywhere without carrying them, and it would make these well informed people extremely suspicious if we didn't have them. The revolvers would at all times stay firmly seated in their holsters underneath each officers jacket. The only other things to be carried on our person would be the ever present, full, water bottle, and a couple of packets of plain biscuits. It was our intention, having studied the maps, to make our way to the farthest point away from the main entrance to the village, look for a suitable spot and enter there. According to the maps which were quite detailed, the terrain around the whole area was very rugged, and appeared to have some kind of vegetation growing in and around it. The village was clearly marked and there were trees and shrubs growing all round the living area. The trees were most likely to be oranges, the shrubs could be almost anything. They would provide us with some sort of cover, although we would not know how much until we arrived there.

A Kibbutz is a small Jewish community. People live and work together in a commune. The houses, at the time of which I write, were built solely of timber, very similar to the old sleeping accommodation huts in the army. The land extended to the rear and both sides of these houses. The commune was practically self supporting, and the workers were not paid a wage as such, but they were provided with their meals and living accommodation, simply working for the good of the community. It must have been very frustrating for them but they lived in hope, and here in these villages, were working towards achieving their independence. Overriding all the good work done in the Kibbutz was a fervent hatred of any kind of authority that appeared to be doing anything to stop them achieving their independence and having the country handed over to them. This was ridiculous, as far as we were concerned we were here to do a job and were not interested in the politics of the country. We did as we were told to the best of our ability, trying to keep the peace and making it safe for law abiding citizens, and yet by simply doing this we were regarded as the enemy. There were a large number of these Kibbutz spread about all over the country, and most of them were situated in areas where access was difficult, usually having only one road into them and the same one to get out. Ideal places in which to prepare and organise terrorism.

I asked my three companions what their duties were for the next three days, and made a note of them. Once again telling them that they must not, under any circumstances, speak to anyone about our intentions. I was going to arrange for all of us to be granted one days leave, have their present duties changed, and organise transport. I would make arrangements for this transport to take us to within about four miles of the other side of the village. From the depot, the village was approximately eight miles, the intended dropping point a further four miles beyond the village, making a total of twelve miles overall. A nice steady hike back to survey the countryside for four reasonably fit young men. Just enough to convince anyone (if we had to), that we were in fact out on a sight seeing tour. I made an appointment with the depot commander and obtained from him four one day passes, one for each officer, and an authorization for a fifteen hundredweight truck, with a canvas cover fitted to the top, together with a driver who would require a convincing reason for taking us to the drop off point, and another reason for proceeding into the town of Haifa. There were to be no dates stamped on the passes or the truck and driver authorization. I kept one map, one without an area showing the Kibbutz, and returned the others to the main office clerk. I made contact with the three officers and informed them we were "on" for the next day, and for them to meet me in the transport area

147

immediately after breakfast, in their civvies. Later that evening I went to the main office hoping it would be empty, it was, and found a date stamp and put the next day's date on the truck and driver authorization. Next I found the transport Sgt and told him I would need the truck the next day at eight thirty, and would he ask the driver to wait in the truck, inside the garage, until I arrived. The next stop was to be the kitchen, it was just before midnight, where I picked up four bottles of mineral water and eight packets of dry biscuits. I had a good look at the map I had kept, trying to memorise all the relevant details for the journey, then hid it inside my wardrobe, and tried to sleep. I must admit I didn't have a very restful night, I was clock watching.

The day dawned, I got up around six, had breakfast and dressed in civvies, put my watch on and checked the time, and put a small compass in my jacket pocket, filled my water bottle, then gave my revolver the once over.

About eight o'clock I went to the office and had all the passes date stamped, then made my way to the transport area where I met the other three already waiting for me. I asked them to check their pockets, just to see if they had missed anything, and to make sure their water bottles were full, gave them one bottle of water and two packets of biscuits each, and told them to get on board the truck and to drop the flap when they were inside. I took my usual place beside the driver. I didn't have to explain anything to the driver as he was an avid football fan and all he could talk about was did I think we were good enough to win our next match against one of the better teams. By the time I had convinced him that we were, the dropping off point came into view. It had been arranged for him to have something to pick up in town making his journey seem authentic. We dropped off and found a place to sit down on some tufts of grass. I gave them all their passes and we contemplated for a while upon what we were about to do. It was a very hot morning, shirt collars were unfastened and ties loosened. Once we had entered the village, if we were seen and accosted it was important that we all knew how to conduct ourselves. The main things being, be pleasant and polite, try to show you are pleased to meet them, and above all if things appear to be going against us and what we had planned, remain calm and collected. If they ask to see your identification, produce it along with your pass, try not to make it appear as if they were taking a liberty asking to see these things. Adopt an attitude that gives the impression we cannot be doing anything wrong. Explain that we were just exploring the countryside for exercise. I reminded them that when we set off from where we were at present, to appear casual, but stick reasonably close together, and not to give the impression we were going anywhere in particular, look for anything that could give us cause for a laugh, and laugh, loudly, but when we were within shouting distance of our objective, cut out the fun and games, keep your eyes peeled and be prepared for any eventuality. When and if, we do get into the place do not touch anything, only register in your head what you do see. Talking must be kept to a minimum and be done very quietly. Where possible hand signals could be used to alleviate the necessity for talk. If we were seen then all conversations would have to be conducted in the normal manner.

I checked the compass, we had a drink and ate a couple of biscuits and then we set off north north eastwards towards the village. The time was almost nine o clock and I wanted to be somewhere close to our objective for about eleven thirty. That gave us plenty of time to dally and deviate from a straight line. Although we were in civvies I had stressed the need for us to wear our strong boots, expecting we would have to travel across land upon which shoes would have been inappropriate, and not giving suitable protection for the feet and lower leg. There was a clump of trees ahead they looked to be about one mile away in the direction we needed to take, so we headed for them.

We walked along hands in pockets, heads down and kicking at any loose object, there was nothing about our demeanour that said we were military men, just the opposite, anyone looking at us would arrive at the conclusion we were a set of scruffs simply meandering the time away. I was worried as to how we were going to affect an entry into this settlement. I regarded it as being almost impossible to do so without being seen by someone at some stage. My companions had enough to worry about without me expressing my doubts on the subject. At this point in time the getting out part didn't appear to be a problem, my thoughts upon that were, if we can get in, there would be no difficulty retracing our steps to get out. When we eventually reached the trees, the next part looked to be decidedly more hazardous. It was still a field but it had large mounds of earth, some as high as six or seven feet. These were something that had not shown on any of the maps, but at least they provided us with a lot more cover than we had anticipated, and we could still walk easily enough even though we had to steer around the bumps. This in it's turn made us appear to be much more casual. We still had plenty of time so we sat down at the bottom of one of these mounds and had another drink. I went to the top of one of the mounds, and picked out a hill slightly to our left, and decided that hill would be our next line of approach. We reached it about ten forty five. The hill had some shrubs on the top and all around it looked like land that had until quite recently been used for growing a crop. This told me that this area we were in was not quite as desolate as it appeared. It must be part of the settlement although there were no fences around it. I walked slowly round the bottom of the hill, and there, straight in front of me, no more than half a mile away, was the village. It was quite a large place, much bigger than I had imagined and it contained a lot more trees and shrubs than I had expected. Now we could see the village, the people in there, if they were looking, could also see us. The living area was to our left, taking up about one eighth of the whole area, the rest appeared to consist of trees stretching the full length of the village compound. Around the outside were smaller trees and a large number of bushy shrubs. Further out than this was an area that was poorly fenced off with a few strands of wire, fastened to posts that were few and far between. Leading up to this fenced part, was another field. The most disturbing thing about it was that we would have to cross it to get to where we wanted to be and it would provide us with no cover whatsoever. As we looked to the right towards the very end of the trees, which was also the southern end of the village, we realised that the hill near which we were standing, bent round towards these trees, it didn't go right up to them but the distance between it and them, was very much less than it was from here. We decided to follow the hill, it would be quite a bit farther but we were in no hurry as we were still well inside our time schedule. We kept close together and moved along the base, stopping every now and again to see how much further we needed to travel. We eventually arrived at a spot some seventy yards away from the trees. From the top of the hill the view was excellent, the ground leading up to the trees had those same mounds of earth we had negotiated earlier on, again some six to seven feet high, we couldn't have wished for a better place to enter. About twenty yards from the bottom of the hill was some of that dilapidated fencing, that was to cause us no trouble. The only thing now was to hope we had not been seen earlier on in our travels. The spot at which we were about to enter was densely populated by trees, some orange and some olives, all were fairly high and with plenty of foliage. It looked from where we were standing that we would probably be able to walk around in reasonable safety, providing we kept a good look out for anyone moving around in the same area. I think we were all looking forward to spending some time in the shade as the heat was becoming almost unbearable. After a drink we set of directly towards the trees, walking positively, not talking, and keeping close together. Before we knew it, we were inside.

All we could see were the trees, they were growing close together and the foliage had about a six to eight feet spread, the only way we could see anything was to look underneath them. We crouched down for a while, just to get acclimatised to our new surroundings, then acting on various hand signals we moved forward, looking around all the time. It was only possible to make slow progress. We must have been inside the perimeter for over an hour when, without warning, we came out into a clearing. It must have been well over two hundred yards in length, and forty or fifty yards wide. The length had a very pronounced slope from one end to the other, and at the lowest end there was a mound of earth stretching the full width of the clearing, some twenty feet in height. It was high, but because it was at the lowest end of the slope the top of it was barely visible above the trees that were all around it. About three feet from the top there were round discs at regular intervals of approximately two yards, each of these discs had a number painted on it, at one end the first one being number one, and progressing to number twenty at the other end. At the bottom of this mound almost stretching the full width of the clearing, were twenty stout looking, round, timber posts, inserted into the ground, leaving about six feet standing out, and about two yards apart. It was what was attached to these posts that made us turn to one another in disbelief. We all knew what we were looking at, and that knowledge put our whole operation in a totally different light. Here we were, standing at the edge of this clearing, looking at a full scale firing range. Without one word being said we knew that because of what we were seeing, it would be extremely dangerous to hang about in this area. If we were to be found anywhere around here, it would be very difficult to explain away.

So with a quick glance at each other we moved back under the trees. It did give us a false sense of security but at least it was a place in which we could hold an impromptu conference to discuss our next move. Any kind of conversation had to be made as quietly as possible, and at the same time a sharp look out had to be maintained. My first thought was to get out of there and return to base with the information, but I was concerned that if we deviated from the plan we would lose our cover story if we were stopped. I told the other officers that our main priority was to get out of here safely and the only way to do that was to have a very good reason for being on their property, and make it sound feasible. As things stood at present we did not have that reason, nor were we likely to find one unless we moved on. I explained that at the moment I had no idea what that may be, but I felt sure something would present itself in due course! Having agreed that we would continue, I checked the compass and we moved off.

We didn't have time to do much thinking about anything as we had only travelled about fifty yards when we came across another clearing. It was once again surrounded by trees. The ground was hard but it was obvious it was walked on regularly, and appeared to have been raked recently, most probably to keep it level. There was nothing at either end of the clearing, but running across the middle were a dozen or more pairs of strong wooden frames, about two yards apart, extending the full width of the area. Suspended in between these frames were Dummies, made from hessian, with shaped heads and stout bodies. These bodies were stuffed with straw as bits of it were showing on all of them. No prizes for guessing what we had stumbled across this time, it was a rifle and bayonet training ground, and a very well used one at that. Our reasons for wishing we were anywhere else but here, had doubled in a very short space of time. We hadn't moved out into the open as we had done with the previous clearing, we stayed under cover and just looked out upon it, taking in everything. We saw at the side we were on, partly covered and almost hidden by trees, what appeared to be an old ramshackle timber shed. It was about fifty yards in length and maybe four yards wide, and had two doors, one at each end, that faced out into the clearing. I motioned to two of the officers, making them to understand I wanted them to move back into the trees, and to the other one to come with me to take a look at this dilapidated building. As we made our approach we could see a fairly long line of narrow and very dirty windows across the front, stretching almost the full length of the building. They were all closed and gave the impression they hadn't been opened for quite some time. Both doors were slightly open, and the hinges on them weren't doing their job properly. I looked into the nearest one, the other chap walked around the back and came out near the other one, and went inside. I followed suit, and saw long rows of solid timber benches, running the full length of the shed, all down both sides and down the middle. On the top and underneath in racks, were long lengths of cylindrical copper piping, and lengths of other metals, some round some flat. There were also metal and woodworking tools of every description and strong looking vices clamped to the benches. All over the place were rifles, automatic Sten-guns and revolvers, in various stages of production. There were heaps of the strong wood for making the rifle stocks, and the steel piping used in the manufacture of the weapon barrels. There was one bench that had tools and equipment, and what appeared to be hundreds of made and part made cartridge cases. In the middle of this particular bench were a large number of smallish wooden boxes, and inside, packed very neatly were bullets of varying sizes for the different weapons. Somewhere in this building there must be a consignment of explosives. This dilapidated, decrepit shed was a fully equipped, and fully operational armaments factory. The officer and I had walked the full length of the building, taking care not to touch anything. I thought we had seen enough so I signalled to him to leave, and we made our way back into the trees where our two companions were hiding. It was not the appropriate time to inform them of our findings, so I motioned to them to follow us and we went a considerable distance inside the trees, away from the clearing. When I thought we had gone far enough we huddled close together and told the other two what we had seen. At this point in time I knew if we were to be confronted by any of the villagers, we would be in very serious trouble. So far we had avoided being seen, but it was only a matter of time before our luck would run out. The responsibility I had for my three companions was weighing very heavily upon my mind, I could not afford to make even the slightest mistake in any decision I would eventually have to make. Then I found myself thinking that we must put as much distance between ourselves and the two clearings as we could. We couldn't just walk straight out so we needed to make our way to the western edge of the trees and take a look. I told my companions I had something in mind but needed to reserve judgement until we had got to the outside edge of the village. Having obtained the direction from the compass, due West, and using eyes and ears, we carefully made our way through the undergrowth. Eventually we arrived, and on taking a good look I suggested we move northwards through the trees until we came to the narrowest bit of open ground between the perimeter fence and the trees. We wouldn't be able to see it without looking out every now and again, and in doing so, we would have to take exceptional care we weren't seen. When we did reach it, we would have to methodically scan the whole area, because it was of paramount importance we weren't seen leaving the trees. It was my intention to leave the cover and walk out into the open at this point without being seen. We would walk out beyond the fence for approximately twenty yards then turn sharp right and do another twenty yards before turning right again, this time we would walk at a slight angle which would once again put us back under the trees. We could only hope we weren't seen during the first and second twenty yard walks, after that it wouldn't matter as it would appear as if we were walking directly towards the trees and the village for the first time, and giving the impression we had in fact just walked over the adjoining land in order to go into the village. The expressions on their faces as the plan unfolded left me in some doubt as to whether they were all in favour of it but in the end it was decided to put it into operation. I had put my brain to the ultimate test trying to find a reason why we should decide to enter their village, and as it was put to the other three I noticed they almost smiled, therefore giving me the kind of reaction I had been attempting to obtain. We were going to say that we had seen their village and as we were so close to it we decided to ask them if they would give us all a nice long cold drink, as the water we had brought with us was almost as warm as we were. If it could be seen that more conversation was expected a joke about the blistering heat may help to relieve any tension.

Discussions over, everyone seemed aware of what had to be done. I was concerned that metal filings could have attached themselves to the soles of our boots when we had entered the arms factory so the two of us who went in were subjected to a thorough examination by the other two. Sure enough, some particles were found lodged between the treads, and meticulously removed from the boot soles. Then we commenced our trek to locate the spot at which we intended to leave our hiding place in the trees. Nothing untoward took place during the journey but it seemed to take a long time before we finally made it, and found ourselves looking out at that rickety fence and the landscape beyond it. The fence itself was about five yards out from where we were in the trees, and was so low it was practically touching the ground. The view behind it gave us very little encouragement for the plan we had in mind. It consisted of a very wide open space of almost totally barren land, with a few clumps of trees and bushes scattered about, none of which could be expected to provide us with the kind of seclusion from prying eyes we would have liked. We moved out from the trees. I went in front and when I thought we had gone far enough out I turned sharp right, walked another twenty yards then turned right again, travelling at an angle towards the trees. The whole manoeuvre couldn't have taken more than a minute before we were back inside them. This time we were not treading carefully and speaking in whispers but holding conversation in a quite normal manner. It will be hard for you, the reader, to even imagine the kind of thoughts and feelings we had as we laboriously threaded our way towards a now inevitable meeting with the villagers. It was now well into the afternoon, the few remaining biscuits we had were unceremoniously munched and the empty packets stuffed into our pockets. The water in our water bottles was, as we intended to announce, very warm indeed, and as it could be required to confirm our story we didn't drink any more.

At first, our progress through that final part of the trees was very slow. Then it became noticeable that they were thinning out. We didn't have to go much farther. The trees ended and we found ourselves walking out into what could only be described as a quadrangle of well trodden soil and sand. Opposite were timber houses, they stretched away to our left for about three hundred yards, leading to a large opening which was the main entrance to the village. I remember thinking that we had arrived at almost the exact spot I had hoped we would. If we hadn't been seen somewhere earlier on in our travels there should be no reason for anyone to suspect anything. We had obviously been heard coming towards this area as there was a small crowd forming a semi-circle in front of us, apparently inquisitive. In the centre of this circle, and standing forward, much closer to us, were a number of men: probably nine or ten. They appeared to be the reception committee, so I approached them with my hand outstretched towards the one who was nearest. I recounted to them our story about being out for a walk and needing some cold water to drink. All the men began to walk towards us and as each one got close enough they shook our hands in a warm and friendly manner, insisting we were very welcome. They all spoke in near perfect English and appeared pleasant enough. As we engaged in conversation we told them we were from Shafa Amr depot about eight miles away, most of them nodded, acknowledging that they knew it. We proffered our identification books and day passes, which were only given a fleeting glance by the chap nearest me, he seemed to be the head man and after he had conversed, albeit in Yiddish, to one or two of the other men, he took my arm saying "come with me, we will see if we can find you that cold drink". Taking me towards one of the houses, followed by three of the other men. I expected my three to follow as well, but having taken a swift look round I saw they were being guided in the opposite direction by the rest of the men, towards the houses lower down. I immediately thought of the old adage, "Split them up and see if their stories tally". I wondered how my companions would cope, and yet I had to have confidence they would stick to the plan we had made. There was nothing I could do about it now.

As our party arrived at the house two men came out. They in turn gave me a pleasant greeting, I replied in the same vein and smiled as I did so. I was graciously invited inside and directed to a wicker armchair whereupon I sat down, making myself comfortable and immediately took a purposeful look around the whole room. All the other members of our party followed us into the room and took up seats which rather disconcertingly were positioned in front of my chair. I had my back to the entrance and was sitting entirely alone. I thought to myself, "ready for the inquisition?". Someone brought a large jug, full of orange juice, poured a glass and set it down on a small table in front of me, and I was invited to drink. This being what the whole charade centred upon, I drank, and didn't pause for breath until the glass was empty, expressing my extreme pleasure at the wonderful cold taste. The glass was filled again and placed on the table. I made some comment about the country being full of flies and mosquitoes, and that the heat was almost unbearable. Saying it in the manner of a joke, I was endeavouring to inject a little triviality into the proceedings. It seemed to work as they also made similar comments and we had a good laugh. I was studying their demeanour; each one in turn, without making it obvious to them. They all appeared to be relaxed, but there was also an air of expectation and determination upon their faces. I took another drink of the orange but this time did not empty the glass, when I had replaced it on the table, the man I took to be the senior one asked me in a very matter of fact tone of voice, where had we come from that morning, in which area had we started our sight seeing tour? To soften the question even more, had we enjoyed what we had seen? I knew then that I would have to be very careful with this fellow, he was adopting the same attitude as I myself did when the occasions arose, making a direct and positive question to be nothing more than someone showing a passing interest. He was expecting a positive answer especially to the part about the area in which we had started the tour. This would give him a very good idea of the direction in which we would have approached the village, and if we had used the route he was apparently thinking of. Our actual starting off point had been discussed and confirmed during the preliminary exchanges that were made when we had unexpectedly entered their village, this apparently hadn't convinced him and he was now pushing for more details. So, it was now up to me to dispel those fears that he obviously had about the direction we had taken after we had set off. I told him we had obtained a lift in one of the trucks that regularly made the trip into Haifa to collect supplies, the driver had suggested we start our hike from there, as he himself had walked the area before and had found it very interesting, with a lot of open spaces to explore and not too far to walk back to the depot. I felt as if I was on safe ground here making it out to be a spur of the moment decision to start from there instead of it having been planned, my companions could not have known what had been said between the driver and myself, as they were in the back of the truck and I seated alongside him. I spoke in a very flippant manner and I could see they appreciated the humorous bits. I told them how we had set a line that would take us due East, our intentions being to hold that line for a couple of miles or so, then to head directly North which would eventually bring the depot into view. We had been in no hurry and had taken more than a few rests using the odd clumps of half dead trees to get out of the heat and glare from the sun. At that stage I think we were all coming to the conclusion that interesting and unusual it may be, but it was certainly no way to spend a day off. We were constantly being annoyed by the attentions of the flies and other parasites, and were hot, sticky, and in desperate need of a cooling drink, so when we saw the village we decided we would call in and spend a while in the shade out of the sun, and as we have said, hopefully be offered a cold drink. With that I picked up the glass, raised it and before taking a drink, said, "we were right in hoping for that, weren't we?".

I hadn't found it easy thinking about, and putting the story together, at the same time making it appear as if I wasn't having to concentrate on the details. Another question from the spokesman seemed harmless enough but I am sure he had an ulterior motive and was looking for something. It was, "what kind of duties do you and your three friends usually have to carry out?". I explained that we were not the same as the regular force which had been in the country for many years, we had only recently arrived from the army where we had been serving in Italy, and that our correct title was the Police Mobile Force, the P.M.F. We were the ones who rode around town on the back of the fifteen hundredweight trucks, keeping the peace and maintaining some sort of stability. A few more questions followed and then I got the impression we were waiting for someone. A short while later three men came into the room, they acknowledged me. They shared a short conversation with the others, in Yiddish, and then left, but not before each of them had shaken my hand vigorously, and wished me and my companions a safe journey back to the depot. What a relief!

I looked at my watch and saw it was almost four-o-clock, I had been in this room for more than an hour so I informed my "interrogation" party that it was time my friends and I began to make a move as we still had a long way to go before we would reach the depot. My chief inquisitor asked if we would accept a lift back to the depot in one of their vehicles. It was at that precise moment my three companions were ushered into the room. I pretended to think about what he had just said and I told him we would be very grateful for a lift as far as the main Haifa road (it would soon be dark and I didn't fancy stumbling around in this type of terrain not being able to see properly). We knew our way from there and could enjoy some even ground walking for the few miles we had to go to end our day of exercise. We all emerged from the house and someone was despatched to collect a vehicle, which duly arrived. It was an open topped truck and after saying our goodbyes and thanking them for their hospitality, the four of us jumped on board and, after waving reservedly as we passed through the gateway, we took a bumpy ride in silence. We reached the road and climbed down, thanked the driver, and strode off in the direction of the depot. We waited patiently until we saw the vehicle lights disappear into the distance, then started jumping up and down with sheer joy, we had pulled it off!

We walked the six miles back to Shofa Amr swiftly. I was still concerned that someone could return to the village who had seen us earlier in the day and they would come looking for us. We kept a sharp look out behind us, and in front, for any vehicle lights approaching. If any were seen we would get off the road as quickly as possible and find cover just in case they had realised their mistake and decided to pursue us.

We made very good progress towards the depot, no lights came up from behind us and reached there around seven-o-clock. A suitable explanation was given as to how I had "forgotten" to show my three companion's day passes when I had booked out that morning and although I was given a quizzical look by the guard commander, he allowed us in. We arranged to go over what had happened in the morning, and I went to have a shower, some food and then wrote my report.

The next morning, we met as arranged and went to my room. We discussed the day's events and I told them how to write their reports. When their's were ready I put them with mine and took them to the depot commander's office where I obtained a suitably sized envelope, put them inside and wrote on it, "Personal, For the attention of the Supt;" and requested to see him. A Sgt went to his room and after a short discussion came out and said that he was busy but that I should leave the report and he would see it in due course. I believed it's contents would ensure that It would be in the hands of the person who had requested it as quickly as possible, and as far as I was concerned my job was done, I never heard another thing about it!

That different and rather difficult duty now being out of the way, it was time to return to the more mundane ones of keeping the peace. For the next few weeks I enjoyed the duties of working in the "Souk" district, patrolling the mainly Arab quarter which incorporated some parts of a cosmopolitan inhabited area. As I have previously mentioned I had done this duty before, but as the days passed I found that I still had a great deal to learn. The Sgt in charge of the police station was a long serving member of the regular force, and took it upon himself to educate me on the workings of the station. I accompanied him on a detailed and very informative tour of the place, taking particular interest in the uninviting "cells", the reason for the Desk Diary, and how and when it should be used, together with all the other necessary paraphernalia that was placed on or underneath that same desk. The amount of paperwork required to keep the station running was phenomenal, every incident that took place within it's stipulated area had to be recorded. The times during which the changeover of the three shifts took place were exceptionally hectic. It was known as Central station and it had overall responsibility for the area, but why it should have been given the name Central is a mystery because it was situated at one of the larger entrances to the Souk. It was built of stone, with an almost oval frontage with three or four stone steps leading up to the solid double doors that were the entrance. It had quite a foreboding appearance really, especially with all the iron bars that were built in to protect the windows. A lot of similar small stations were targeted by the terrorists, but this one being completely surrounded and integrated into the Arab quarter, guaranteed to have heavy pedestrian traffic throughout the day and night, was not troubled unduly. The days I spent doing the patrols and being introduced to the workings of the station, were extremely educational, but those few weeks came to an end and it was back to the fifteen hundredweight truck, the armoured car, and the mobile town patrols.

It was never boring on any of the three shifts. Apart from having to be alert there were always a number of incidents which took place during every shift, some that had to be handled with extreme care, others could turn out to be quite amusing. One incident I recall with particular gravity. It took place during one day shift. About ten thirty the headlamps on the armoured car began to flash repeatedly. That was my signal to stop and go to the car, where I was given a message over the radio from headquarters, stating that there had been an ambush on a very large terrorist group, carried out by the British army. There were many casualties and these were being transported by army ambulances to the government hospital in Bat Galim. The job for the patrol was to maintain order around the hospital whilst I checked on the senior members of the terrorist group: find out where they were being treated, and make arrangements to keep them under supervision all the time they were there. I was informed that sufficient police officers were being sent to the hospital to carry out this task. No further details were given at that time but I was ordered to make a report over the radio, as soon as I had information of any consequence.

We went to the hospital main entrance, where the truck and driver were placed out of sight, near the entrance. The six officers were positioned where they could see and be in touch with the goings on at that entrance. If a crowd formed anywhere near the entrance and looked to be contemplating entering the hospital, they had to be contained. All this time there were ambulances unloading people outside the main doors, from where they were being hurriedly taken inside.

I had to obtain information about these casualties and somehow find out where the most important members of the group were being treated. I was familiar with the names of many of these people, and was thinking that this should prove to be no problem for me, as each person's name and particulars would at sometime have to be entered into the hospital registers. This being the case, there was no better place to start than the enquiries desk inside the reception area, and it was to there I went, armed with pencil and paper, and struggling to put on my most charming and endearing smile. I shouldn't have bothered. The replies I got to the questions I asked, in a very respectful tone of voice, were so rude I find it impossible to repeat them. I was treated with disdain. It was obvious they had all been advised to act in this manner when asked for information. I could see that I was getting nowhere fast, so other methods had to be used.

Having thought for a short while, I decided that I should endeavour to find the wards. I began to make my way along a corridor, weaving my way through the large numbers of staff hurriedly traversing the hospital. Every step I took resulted in more abuse. It was quite understandable they should show such animosity towards me, I represented the establishment partly responsible for their present situation. However, I had been given a specific job to do and if I could somehow succeed in carrying it out the future could be a little more peaceful.

As I made my way along the corridor I noticed out of a window, on a small plot of land between two buildings, a pile of old clothes. I thought it strange for such things to be dumped in a place of this kind, it being so close to what appeared to be the wards where cleanliness was of paramount importance. I was preparing to move off when I saw a door in one of the buildings open and a nurse come out carrying a bundle of similar things. She unceremoniously threw the bundle onto the already fairly large pile and went back through the same door. My curiosity aroused, I made one or two unsuccessful attempts to find another door that would enable me to go outside and take a closer look. Eventually I found one and went to the heap of clothing. What I saw was unbelievable, I had been correct in thinking it was clothing, but totally wrong about it being old clothes, some of it was practically new and the majority of it being heavily blood stained. Strewn around the bottom of the heap were papers, cards, and other items of identification. Some had photographs attached, and nearly all the cards and papers that I could see had numbers on them. At first I didn't realise the significance of what I was actually seeing, and when I did, the realisation was such, that I had difficulty in bringing myself to believe it. The nurses and staff were deliberately removing every piece of clothing from the dead and injured victims, and dumping it on the pile to remove all forms of identification, therefore making it impossible for anyone to identify them, except families and friends. There was absolutely nothing I could do now, it had been made impossible for me to do what I had been ordered to accomplish. I hadn't been welcome simply walking around, there was no telling how I would be received if I were to be found inspecting these articles of clothing, so I made a very hasty retreat, as far as the armoured car and it's radio, upon which I relayed my findings, and the conclusion I had reached in regard to the reason for them.

It was very annoying to know that it had all been unneccessary and a complete waste of time. The ambulances were still bringing their loads, and a contingent from the regular police force arrived. I contacted one of their senior officers and was given permission to resume our mobile patrol, much to the relief of everyone concerned.

I spent the afternoon making out the usual daily patrol report and most of it concerned the time spent in and around the hospital. When the report was completed I took it along to the office where I handed it to the deputy Supt, he read it and said that I had done all I could be expected to do under the circumstances. He then went on to tell me that the British army had been keeping tabs on a number of settlements and at sometime during the early hours of the morning a convoy of trucks and other smaller vehicles was seen heading towards Haifa. It turned along one of the main roads leading away from the town and after travelling a couple of miles, forcibly entered a large army ordinance depot. The army had kept them under close observation during their journey, and as soon as they were inside the buildings an ambush was prepared. Soldiers were positioned all round the perimeter fence, and two large tanks took up positions at the gate. When the terrorists had tried to leave, their vehicles heavily laden with explosives, they had been ordered to stop and surrender or be fired upon. They had ignored the warning, and kept on driving towards the exit gate. It was then the Tanks had opened fire with their heavy guns on the approaching vehicles. There had been a very large number of casualties, many of whom had lost their lives.

The mobile patrol duties carried on for a few weeks more, until one morning I was called into the Superintendent's office and asked if I would consider taking on the duties of station Sgt at the Central station in Haifa on a full time basis. It didn't take any considering. It would mean my having to leave Shafa Amr as a base meaning I would be be able to live with my wife. I would be taking over the duties of the same Sgt who had given me the guided tour only a few weeks earlier. He was being transferred and taking another step up the ladder. He didn't appear to be too surprised when I presented myself at the desk the following Monday morning. From now on, Anna and I could lead a normal life. I could leave home to go to work at the station, and come home at the end of my duty, having first made sure that everything was running smoothly.

The first few days of the new and altogether different duties were strange but interesting. I spent a lot of time at the station in order to make myself fully conversant with all the things I was required to do. There was a full compliment of officers, British (regulars), Jewish and Arab. The British constables had the job of maintaining the desk diary, one constable on each of the three shifts. They were responsible for the workings of the station when I wasn't there, and keeping that diary, up to date. Another on each shift accompanied one Jewish and one Arab constable on one of the area patrols. One Jewish and one Arab went out together on another one. These detailed duties included having one Jewish and one Arab constable doing the work that was necessary inside the station, like taking care of any prisoners in the cells. After familiarizing myself with what to do and when to do it, it was my intention to spend most of my time out in the area getting to know the people for whom I was to be responsible. The language barrier was still a cause for concern, my knowledge of Arabic had increased tremendously but there were others of which I knew and understood very little like Yiddish, Greek, and Turkish. To all these people Arabic was their second language and they understood it perfectly but when the occasion arose for them to deliberately take evasive action in order to avoid being understood they would revert to their mother tongue. Many such occasions did arise and I was well aware of their reasons for doing this. It was very frustrating to say the least but the Christian Arabs, most Jews, and almost all those who owned or worked in the well frequented establishments in the area spoke English. It did make life a lot easier understanding everything that was being said.

The pleasure of leaving home to go to work and returning when the work was done was something I had not known for the past six years. Then there was the great feeling once I had returned home work done, of total freedom. I was able to relax knowing that no-one would suddenly turn up and fill in my spare time with another duty. Gradually Anna and I settled into a routine. She would go to someone's home making dresses for them, and would usually be away from the flat during the daytime. I arranged my duties to coincide with her return, sometimes for lunch but mostly in the evenings. Then we would have a light meal together. She would have had a meal with the family where she was working and I had a little something in one of the eating places in the Jewish district. When I worked the afternoon shift I would come home for a meal around six and then resume the duty until ten. The night shift was easy to organise, sleep when I got home until mid afternoon, then go to where she was working and stay there until we returned together, or my preference was to take a stroll through the area and call in at the station, having had a bite to eat on the way round.

Many of the people who she worked for were Anna's friends and we were invited to their homes frequently to have meals with them. In this part of the world a night out would not start until somewhere around ten in the evening, probably the hot weather was the reason for this. So, duties permitting, we would be dressed and ready for off just after ten, then make our way to our host's for the evening. Some were more than thirty minutes walk away, but it was very pleasant on a nice cool, fresh, balmy, evening, with the scent from the orange blossom drifting in the air. The district we were in and where we usually went, was very clean and brightly lit, with wide tree lined roads and footpaths. It was a residential area with very little vehicle traffic, only the odd taxi now and then, and pedestrians were few and far between. There were no public houses, only houses, most of which were large and detached. It was an ideal place in which to live on the surface but I was always aware of the underlying tension in this country. We were never in a hurry and usually having a conversation about something or other. The road would appear to be empty but it had always been my policy never to take anything for granted. As Anna was at risk simply by being in my company, my eyes and ears were alert to any signs of danger at all times during the many journeys we were to make together. Whenever we went out visiting I always wore civilian clothing. For some it would not have gone down very well if they were thought to be too friendly with someone such as me.

One afternoon when I had time off, Anna said she had a dress to complete at a house in Bat-Galim and would I like to go with her as it would only take about an hour to finish and then we could spend a little time on the beach which was close by. It was too far to walk so we took a taxi. We went through the district where we usually walked, and on past Western police station, the Government Hospital and into the area of the Casino where we negotiated a couple or more bends and came to a stop. We got out of the taxi and I looked at the immediate surroundings. On our right, about thirty yards away, was the coastline consisting of large imposing rocks. The sound of the sea was very noticeable as it came in and smashed against them: It somehow made the stifling heat more bearable. I knew where we were as I had been in the area before but not in such close proximity to the very attractive eye catching building we were now standing in front of. It was this house that had fascinated me when I had seen it from a distance during those first few foot patrols with that constable from Western police station. I had marvelled then at the beauty of it all never for one moment thinking that one day I would pass through it's hallowed portals and come face to face with it's highly respected occupant. Anna led the way up through the beautiful rockery gardens on either side of the winding footpath and as we arrived at the door we were met by a charming middle aged lady who rapturously welcomed us. She escorted us into a large, beautifully furnished room which boasted a breathtaking view of the Mediterranean through the conservatory which occupied one end of the room. Seated in an armchair was a portly gentleman with a cherub like face, giving the impression that here was a man with a decidedly agreeable and most possibly very witty personality. As we entered he arose from the chair and advanced towards us with outstretched hands. First he placed them both firmly upon Anna's shoulders and drew her towards him, speaking to her softly as he did so, she then turned to me and guiding him forward said, "this is my husband, Jack", whereupon he extended both his hands and shook mine firmly, declaring his pleasure at meeting me together. He made me feel totally at ease in his presence. His wife brought glasses of ice cold drinks and we all sat down, Anna preparing the partly made dress and the bits and bobs that went with it. She and the lady of the house were oblivious to every-thing except that dress as they discussed it. Meanwhile our host and I discussed many things; he enquired about my country and how it compared with his. I found this difficult as I knew that there was absolutely no comparison whatsoever, but I did my best to point out the better side of Britain, especially the large areas of countryside with it's beautiful trees and rolling green fields, where cows grazed in peaceful pastures that were all too frequently doused with gallons of life giving rain, making everything a glistening eye catching green, producing a cool refreshing atmosphere. Well, he wouldn't have been able to understand what a "Slag Heap" was, or how the air we breathed was often choked up from household coal burning fires, and for me to describe a "Pea Souper Fog" and it's resulting consequences would have been way beyond his comprehension. He spoke of his love for his country and the intriguing different ways of life that existed. To speak and hold a conversation with someone who is obviously very intelligent and at the same time considerate is good, no matter what the conversation may have been about.

Now that I was living at home, and didn't have to return to the depot every night it was possible for us to visit Anna's long standing friend and her detective Sgt husband in the late evenings when he was at home. We had only been able to go during the daytime and he had always been out at work. He was a member of the Criminal Investigation Department (C.I.D), and heavily involved in counteracting terrorist activities. His successes at this highly danger-ous work had caused the terrorist gangs so many serious problems that he was high on their list for elimination. One evening, about ten thirty, Anna and I made the short journey to their home, a first floor maisonette in a pleasant secluded suburb on the edge of a residential area. He was there, and after a suitable introduction he politely informed me that my reputation of being a somewhat outspoken person had preceded me. He did however condescend not to hold it against me if I would consider treating him as a friend. Here was a man after my own heart, he was witty, and quite prepared to see the funny side of things. We were to get on like a house on fire.

The maisonette was spacious and decorated to perfection, but even though there was plen-ty of room for all four of us to sit down in comfort on large easy chairs, or be seated around a table to have a meal, they both seemed to prefer to sit outside on the balcony. The balcony was big and semicircle in shape, with shiny black painted railings, some three feet high, all around it. It was brilliantly lit by electric lighting from lamps fitted to the wall and two or three standard lamps placed in appropriate positions alongside the railings. It was really beautiful, sitting there in the cool of the evening, the scent wafting all around, and looking out onto the mediterranean with all the twinkling lights from the large ships anchored in Haifa bay.

After that first time, Anna and I were invited to dinner on many occasions. After dinner the conversation flowed freely and time was never a factor there. Police business was strictly taboo as both the Sgt and I had enough of that without bringing it home with us. Nevertheless, I could never understand why he took all his meals on the balcony where he was so exposed to potential terrorist activity. He knew he was a target, but would never compromise on being able to sit out. Nor would he vary his time of leaving for work, or the route he took. It was a well known fact that in order to avoid problems no set patterns should be established. Times, places, and regular habits must all be avoided. His wife, Anna and I questioned him about it, but to no avail.

By this time I had been at the station a few weeks and I had had the opportunity to take more notice of the shops. There were so many different shops, but the majority bore no resemblence to shops as we know them: they had no glass fronts or sides showing off their wares or seperate entrance doors. All the fronts looked exactly like garage doors which when swung open revealed the interior. Some of the occupants were preparing and cooking food for sale over the counter, like Fallafals and Chapatis. The Fallafals were similar to a beef burger but much more spicy; the Chapatis a type of yeast free bread, sometimes used as sandwiches filled with a white goat's cheese called Leboni. A type of Yoghurt was also made from goat's milk called Lebon and eaten by a large number of the population. At intervals along the main street were places of entertainment, the cafe bars being the most widely used. A close second were large halls resembling theatres with a fairly big stage at one end where scantily clad maidens gyrated in harmony to Arabic music. These places could be a problem sometimes as they had a licence to sell alcoholic drinks and this, combined with the raucous and very care-free atmosphere, resulted in brawls which frequently got out of hand.

One establishment situated down an alleyway didn't have an impressive appearance from the outside but inside it was immaculate, with thick pile carpets on the floors, very brightly lit, spotlessly clean everywhere, and beautifully decorated throughout. This place prevented us from having the problems the police forces in Britain have of having to deal with prostitution. In this country it was legalised, confined to establishments such as this which were licensed and kept under strict supervision by the authorities. Although we didn't have the same problems as our British counterparts, daily inspections of the premises had to be carried out. Another side to this strict supervision gave rise to one duty we had to perform in the region of once every month. The "Ladies" had to be collected from the establishment and taken to the Government hospital, where they all underwent a thorough medical examination. The easy way to have done this would have been for the proprietor to be given notice of the date and exact time of our intended visit but this was not practical under the circumstances. Had this been done it was probable that some of the "Ladies" would be absent. Therefore our visits had to be impromptu, and unexpected. There was never a right time to do this job; to arrive when every single one of the "ladies" was not "otherwise engaged" would have been nothing short of a miracle. Once we were inside the place the Madam, proprietor, had to be approached and informed of what we intended to do and when she had condescended to comply with our wishes, which was usually after some considerable time had elapsed, we could then begin to assemble them into some kind of order. The "Ladies" were not very helpful either. Sometimes it could take the best part of an hour before we had everyone looking decent enough to make the short walk to the station. The onlookers, of which there were many, knew what it was all about, and the cat calls and spicy adjectives which were forthcoming from every direction were not all directed at the ladies.

To stand at the station end of the Souk and look along the street was so colourful, with the rolls of dress material placed on both sides of the shops in an upright position, the array of all the different colours was quite startling. The carpet shops were just the same with the carpets draped down the walls at either side, the various patterns and colours producing the same pleasing effect. The greengrocery was positioned on wooden trestles or simply arranged on the floor, there were so many variations of fruit and vegetables, most of which I did not recognise. There was one type of shop that was entirely different to the ones in Britain, the wet fish shop. There were no marble slabs positioned in glass windows at the front upon which were dead fish, with their wide open eyes staring out at you. They did have fish but these were all very much alive, swimming around in very large galvanised tanks inside the shop, just waiting for someone to come and select them. They would then be caught in a net by the proprietor and be prepared to take away. The fish were kept alive because of the hot climate. Every shop had a sun blind and when these were pulled down on both sides of the street they would meet in the middle, forming a canopy over the whole street. Overall it had all the trappings of an open air market place contained in one long row.

Those places were to cause us very little trouble, but all was not so peaceful in other establishments.

Problems galore could erupt at the drop of a hat in the cafe bars and did so on an all too regular basis. Some were fairly mild, but frequently our presence was required to quell a near riot or face a knife wielding lunatic. The people had a preference for long, wide bladed knives, some up to eighteen inches long. A drink or drug crazed, white flowing robed, Arab in full cry can have a disturbing affect on a person's sense of well being. They were dodgy situations and had to be treated with great caution, the man had to be subdued quickly using only such force as was deemed to be necessary, and no more. Alcoholic drink when taken in excess,did result in many people becoming so intoxicated as to cause them to become potential trouble makers. This however was nothing compared to the very serious problems we had to face from some who had been using an innocent looking piece of equipment known as a "Hubble Bubble Pipe". There were many such pipes in all the cafes, owned and provided by the proprietor's for the convenience of their customers. If you were looking at one of these pipes you could be forgiven for thinking it was only an exceptionally large glass "vase". It had a long thin neck which widened out at the top to form a small tray about two inches in diameter, fastened to this in some way was a piece of brass shaped like half an eggcup in the middle of it. This glass "vase" was placed on the floor and almost filled with water up to it's neck, there was a piece of rubber piping attached to the brass fitting and the other end of this piping was left hanging loosely inside this water, alongside that brass fitting there was another similar in shape to which was attached a further piece of rubber piping but this one stretched from there and was pushed onto a mouthpiece. The mode of operation was to have charcoal burning in the brass eggcup and place some tobacco on top of it, then draw on the mouthpiece. This had the affect of pulling the smoke down the rubber piping, through the water, and out into the mouthpiece, and as this was taking place the water would bubble. There was one good thing about this method of smoking, there could be seven or eight of these pipes in operation in a fairly large room, and unlike the clouds of smoke from cigarettes which always filled the "tap room" in our pubs at home, the air was hardly polluted at all. No problems arose from these pipes when they were used in this manner, it was only when they had other substances placed underneath the tobacco, namely drugs. One such drug was known as Hashish. This was not extremely harmful to the user but still against the law. There were others which were extremeley harmful, Opium and Heroin were two hard drugs, although they were not smoked in this way. The "smokers" obtained the drugs from somewhere, and although there were many places where they could be purchased outside the cafe bars I suspected the proprietors of making them easily available to their customers along with the pipes. I cannot remember exactly how many approached me with offers of cash to induce me to "look the other way" when cracking down on the misuse of these pipes.

The mouthpieces for the pipes were small things about two inches long when used for smoking tobacco, but when anyone intended to use the drug it was absolutely necessary for them to use a totally different mouthpiece, these were about four inches in length and slightly thicker. Why they had to be so I never knew but that extra length was the sole reason for my success in reducing the number of drug smokers in my area. It was my usual practice to visit the cafe bars more than once during every patrol. As soon as I entered the cafes I checked the pipe mouthpieces. It wasn't hard to spot the long mouthpieces, and descend upon the nearest one. The first thing to be done was stop the man drawing on it. The proprietor would by this time have seen the commotion and made his way across, apologising for what had been taking place and vehemently denying all knowledge of it. His highly dramatised show of uncontrolled anger aimed at the pipe smoker did nothing to help his cause. No amount of theatricals would convince me that not only was he fully aware that drugs were being smoked, it was a near certainty that he had provided them in the first place. Events such as this were all too prevalent at the beginning of my time as station Sgt, but eventually the message was received and understood. Some did allow this law to be broken in the hope that they wouldn't be caught, and I suppose they did get away with it from time to time. I was not so bigheaded as to imagine for one moment that I had obliterated it altogether. There were some cafes where none of this took place, they were clean and law abiding, but if they had all been like this I would have soon been out of a job or probably ended up directing traffic!

There were other things going on inside the cafe bars which were also against the law, such as gambling. Card playing was okay, but when cash was riding upon the turn of a card then it wasn't, that was gambling! The high class casino at the "posh" end of town was gambling but condoned by the authorities. I must admit to treating this type of gambling in a very light hearted manner, at the same time taking care not to show it. I would walk into a cafe', see a game of cards in progress, note the cash on the table at the side of each player, and move in. Then we would have the same ritual as with the dope smokers, the proprietor would be called over, and disclaim all knowledge of what had been taking place, his hands and arms flailing in all directions, berating the players. I would tell the proprietor to confiscate the cards, and the players to pick up their cash. Always saying that if I came in again and found them gambling I would have no choice but to put them in the cells. It never worked, and I couldn't bring myself to carry out my threat, but they did think they had found a way round their dilemma. The first time they tried it out I immediately noticed how relaxed and confident they all looked. They had adopted a method of scoring using chalk. On the tables at the side of each player were chalk marks that constituted a series of games played. I didn't know how they worked it out but what I did know was that this was their way of keeping me at bay and hopefully allow their gambling to continue. I went round all the tables looking at the chalk marks, went to the bar and asked for a damp cloth, and without saying a word I went to each table and wiped off all the chalk marks. The grins quickly disappeared.

Now on to something much more entertaining, but at the same time very puzzling. Anna and I had been married for quite a few weeks when she told me she had made arrangements for me to meet a very close friend of hers, an "Emir", a member of Arab royalty, only one step lower than a King. It had been decided that we were to go to the Carmelia Court Hotel at twelve noon to take refreshments with him. The Carmelia was about two hundred yards from our flat. It was a large imposing building standing in a prominent position with one half of it's frontage in Mount Carmel road. I dressed in casual clothes, neat but nothing special, then Anna told me that the Emir was a very influential person, and that she fully expected the refreshments to be nothing less than a dinner. I had naively thought we would probably have a drink at the bar, and a natter. Casual dress was therefore out of the question, so I changed into something more appropriate. We left home about eleven fifty, and as we approached the entrance to the hotel I commented upon the number of very large cars parked in the street at the side of it. We went into the lobby where we were approached by the most striking figure of a man I had ever seen. He must have been more than six feet six inches tall, and was holding himself very erect. The style and colours of his clothing were so impressive that I experienced great difficulty absorbing everything, from the brilliantly white turban, with red, green, and orange stripes interwoven through it, to his predominantly white tunic coat that reached down below the knee. The sleeves and front being of different intriguing patterns in varying bright colours. A row of shiny silver buttons fastened at the neck and went all the way down the long front. A broad, bright red cummerbund encircled the waist, and white pantaloons were tucked into the top of knee length shiny black boots. A large ominous looking scimitar hung down at his side, and a curved, sheathed, beautiful bejewelled dagger was held in place inside the front of the cummerbund. All of this, together with a pair of gleaming white gloves, made his whole appearance absolutely breathtaking. His large, well trimmed, black moustache, stood out from his sun tanned face which was wreathed in a broad smile as he greeted us. He spoke to Anna in Arabic. I was given the courtesy of a slight bow before he ushered us through some highly polished double doors. These were ceremoniously opened for us by two men dressed in white gallabias, and the striped coloured turbans. We then found ourselves inside an exceptionally large, brightly lit room. This then was the banqueting hall, in which we were about to be entertained by our royal host, the Emir.

Anna and I were being gently but firmly propelled towards an exceptionally large table in the centre of the room, and although it was necessary to keep moving and to see where I was going I couldn't resist taking a look around at the splendour of it all. Above this table was a gorgeous chandelier with it's myriad of twinkling light's shining down upon it, large glass vases full of flowers were standing on the floor at strategic intervals all around the room, and even though it was daylight outside the curtains were drawn on all the windows, therefore good use was being made of what seemed to be dozens of light's, some positioned in the ceiling others attached to the walls, and these brought out the many different contrasting colours that surrounded the whole place. At the opposite end of the room to where we had made our entrance were more double doors, and standing in front of them were six very tall men, each one dressed in similar clothing to the person who had greeted us in the lobby. They were standing with their legs slightly apart and arms folded across their chest, staring straight ahead and looking very fearsome indeed. The most striking thing to take my eye was the enormous table, it was positioned in the middle and dominated the whole room. There were so many different kinds of silverware placed upon it, all of them resting majestically on a white, patterned, silk table cloth. It looked truly magnificent.

We had by this time reached the far end of the table and because I had been concentrating on other things I had failed to notice someone already seated there. As we approached he stood up and took hold of Anna's hands, bowed, and kissed them both in turn. She said something in Arabic and he replied before turning to me and holding out his hand. I shook it at the same time as Anna was introducing us. When the introductions were over he carried on shaking my hand vigorously and said, that he was very pleased to meet me and hoped we would meet on many more ocassions, and that I was most welcome to sit at his table. He spoke very softly and with feeling, giving the impression he really did mean what he was saying. In spite of his exceedingly high rank and status there was no hint of condescension in his voice. He was rather short in stature and dressed in white flowing robes and a turban, with innumerable gold or silver chains hanging down from around his neck, some to well below his waist. His forearms and wrists were covered with jewelled gold bracelets, and almost all of his fingers were adorned with more than one gold diamond studded ring. The lighting in the room made his every move glisten and sparkle to the extent that I found it necessary to close my eyes from time to time.

There were two other chairs placed at the table opposite each other about halfway down, he turned towards them and motioned with his hand for us to be seated, Anna on his left and I on the right. Someone guided us to the chairs and held them until we were seated comfortably. At intervals of approximately one yard all round the table were men in traditional clothing, sitting cross legged on the floor, backs to the table, about two yards away from it, and facing outwards, each one having a scimitar and dagger. With both hands they were holding rifles, pointing upwards to the ceiling, butts resting on the floor, and sitting as still as statues, eyes fixed in a permanent stare. The whole proceedings had an air of dignity about them, not pomp and ceremony just for the sake of it, we were in the presence of a highly respected person and one who's safety and well being were of paramount importance. I had never been, nor could I have ever expected to be, a guest at such a prestigious function.

We had been seated for only a few minutes when suddenly, and silently, the room was filled with the figures of men, dressed in white gallabiyas, gliding across the floor carrying silver trays loaded with food which they placed with great ceremony upon the table. There were so many different dishes, I hadn't the faintest idea what most of them were, but Anna helped me by giving advice as to what she thought I would like. I managed to eat some of most of it, and hoped it was enough to at least convince our host that I had made a determined effort to please him. It was then I looked around for a drink. I had more than one large glass of water but they did nothing to alleviate the peculiar unpleasant taste in my mouth.

A conversation of sorts was carried out during the meal, all manner of things were discussed but nothing of any real importance. However when the meal was finished a much more serious discussion began, introduced and prompted by his Royal Highness the Emir. He began by asking how many years had I been in the army, what had been my type of work, and which countries had I served in since being posted abroad. Then he asked what I thought about North Africa and in particular it's Arab population. I answered each question in turn without going into detail on any one of them. Then he turned his attention to Palestine, asking how long I had been in the country, did I like it, and had I formed any opinion about the Arabs and the Jews. In reply to the part about liking it, I said I did, very much so, and went on to say that I hadn't been here long enough to reach any decision about the inhabitants. It was at this time the questions took on a more positive note, they became direct and to the point. There were some things where I must have given the wrong answer which resulted in him trying to prompt me into giving the one he had expected. His demeanour remained the same but beneath it all I could sense he wasn't as cool, calm, and collected, as he would have me believe. The main question was, how did I feel in regard to the Jews having Palestine handed over to them by the British?

Throughout all these politically motivated questions and answers I was very puzzled at the show of disinterest put on by Anna. It was not like her at all. There were times when I was debating with myself as to how I should put my reply to a question, and I had looked across at her hoping for some guidance in the shape of a nod or a shake of the head, neither were forthcoming. It was at this stage in the proceedings when I began to realise that the Emir was only interested in what I had to say. I do believe it had been arranged that she would not interfere or attempt to influence me in any way during the question and answer period. The purpose of the meal was for me to tell him who's side I was on, and he obviously hoped, and expected, it would be the Arabs. To what end? I had no way of knowing!

The answer I gave to his all important question was non committal, simply saying that I knew too little to even offer an opinion. Actually I did know for certain the Jews were going to get Palestine, although it was not common knowledge. My replies were neither abrupt nor rude, but I tried to make it clear that this kind of discussion was something I would not allow myself to be drawn into. Gradually this conversation petered out, much to my relief. Seemingly an answer appertaining to something of importance had been required and whether it was the one the Emir had expected or not he had apparently reached a decision. He then went on to say that his father had been with Anna's brother-in-law, Suleiman Saleeba, and Lawrence of Arabia, during the fighting in the Arabian desert campaign against the Turks, and that his country was becoming modernised and leaning more towards the western world. It was now only polite conversation and after a while he stood up and thanked Anna and I for coming, extending to us both an invitation to visit him in his country assuring us that we would be made most welcome.

After everything had been said we were escorted through the lobby and made our way home. We had been in the hotel for more than two hours. As we walked the short distance to the flat I took another look at the large number of limousine cars parked in the street at the side of the hotel. Each one with personnel seated inside or standing near them, and all dressed in the same manner as those in the banqueting room. These were obviously more of his entourage. I could not understand wht we had been afforded such a reception as we had received. In the days that followed I kept my own counsel, but during the ensuing weeks there were plenty of discussions between Anna and myself. I was anxious to know how it had all come about, and the reason for it. All she came up with was the fact that she was a close friend of the Emir and his family, and the reason for the meeting was so that I would have an opportunity to make his acquaintance. As for the highly elaborate set-up she explained that was the way influential Arabs do things. I wasn't convinced but no matter how many times I asked the answer was always the same.

There was nothing I liked better than a quiet night shift. I would be in the station for around nine thirty and organise the work for the constables as they reported for duty. Then a quick check on the day's happenings, and if there was nothing that required my immediate attention I would leave the station and join the seething masses of the Souk population who were already enjoying the delights that were on offer at that time of the evening. Although it was expected that I should always have with me at least one Arab and one Jewish constable I invariably bent the rules, preferring my own company. The first hour or two were very pleasant, the climate producing a balmy warm evening, but as the night progressed it became perceptibly cooler, especially during the winter months. Sometimes it was necessary to wear a long overcoat and gloves. If there had been no incidents of note and nothing to hold me up, I would usually have made one complete tour of the district by about 1.30 a.m. During my journey round the area I made contact with the other patrols. When everything had been done to my satisfaction I would call into the station to see if things were running smoothly before starting out to do another complete tour. This was usually around two a.m., and my first port of call was to one of the cafe bars. I would walk in and have a good look around the place before finding a seat near a table, hardly having time to settle down before someone brought something and placed it on the table. In one it would be a glass of piping hot lemon tea and a chapatti filled with goat's cheese, in another, a small brandy and a bread roll, or three or four bananas and a glass of ice cold lemonade in another. Although I knew the outcome I made a point of offering to pay at each one, it was refused every time but the offer was necessary to keep everything above board.

It was always my aim on those night shifts to get everything organised as quickly as possible and go out into the area where I could obtain first hand knowledge of everything that was taking place. One evening things had gone according to plan, it would have been about ten thirty, when a well dressed Christian Arab came into the station. He walked slowly and calmly to the desk and in a very matter of fact tone of voice, said "I have just killed my wife". He stood there, his face impassive. I asked him where his wife was, and accompanied by two constables and myself he took us to a house in the better class part of our district where, unfortunately, we found his so calmly delivered statement to be correct. We found her in one room, and in another we found something for which none of us were prepared, two young children as well. On the way to the house he had described in detail how he had killed her, but with no mention of the children. His description was such that there was little doubt that he was responsible. We held him overnight and in the morning he was collected by someone from C.I.D. About three weeks later I had to make an appearance in court simply to confirm that he had admitted to me what he had done, and that he had presented himself at the station in order to do so. The man was sent to Acre jail to serve a life sentence. I found this case to be very depressing. I felt sorry for the woman and the two small children, but I also sympathised with the man because there was no doubt nobody felt worse about what had happened than he did, and he would have to live with what he had done for the rest of his life.

When I worked the day shift it was usual for Anna to be at home waiting for me to arrive about two thirty. We would then have something to eat before she went back to the home of the person for whom she was making a dress. One afternoon I arrived home and she wasn't there, I thought it wouldn't be too long before she came so I made some tea and put my feet up. I must have dozed off and was only awakened when she came into the room. I looked at the clock, it was four thirty. I started to ask why she was so late but she cut me short and said she had kept an appointment at a private hospital, where it had been confirmed that she was expecting a baby. To say I was taken aback would be putting it mildly. When the full implications had sunk in, I was over the moon in one sense, and yet in another, I had serious misgivings. Many thoughts crossed my mind and the one that caused me most concern was, were we doing the right thing starting a family in such a precarious unstable country? We had been told by more than one knowledgeable person, that things could become very awkward for anyone staying around hoping to make a permanent home here. I was very uncertain where I would be in twelve months time. We soon settled down and Anna began to make arrangements for the coming months. She had booked into a private hospital in the Stella Maris district. I went with her on appointments a few times and was impressed by the apparent efficiency of the place.

Although occupied with these things she managed to keep me on my toes in the entertain-ment stakes. She told me we had been invited to attend a Police Federation ball, which was to take place in a large dance hall on the Friday evening the following week. In order to give myself the necessary time to go home and make myself look presentable before setting out for the hall I worked a day shift, starting at eight and finishing around six in the evening. As I made my way through the Souk I noticed there was a great deal of activity in almost all of the cafe' bars. It was noisy but there didn't appear to be any trouble. There seemed to be some sort of party going on in one of them though, it was about a hundred yards further along the Souk in front of me, and as I got nearer British army soldiers started spilling out into the road. I heard them calling out my name as they rushed towards me waving glasses of beer. Then I recognised some of them; they were men from my old battery. They were all milling around completely blocking the road and making one heck of a racket. Some were shaking my hands vigorously and I gathered that someone had seen me and informed the others. I never knew I was so popular! Gradually I was propelled inside the cafe and found myself standing at the bar with a pint of beer in my hand, and before I had emptied it another was placed at my elbow. I have made plain to you my views on beer before, but you try telling that to a load of soldiers you hadn't seen for quite a long time. I tried to take my time over every glass but knew I was consuming far too much. Everyone seemed to be talking at once, asking questions and during all this time I was looking around noting all the faces I knew. Some I remembered as being objectionable people to work with when I was with them in the battery! I told them all I was running the police station at the other end of the Souk, that I was married and that I was overdue at home. At the mention of my wife they all requested to accompany me to meet her, but most of them were very much the worse for wear and to take them would have been asking for trouble. In the end I was "allowed" to leave after promising to visit them in their camp sometime during the next week.

Unfortunately, how could I make it to the ball when I could hardly stand up? I staggered along the road, fortunately in the right direction. I was making slow progress with the occa-sional stop to lean on a wall or some such object that would bear my weight, then I heard the familiar sound of the Coffee Wallah and his clinking cups. I made my way towards the sound and came across him walking towards me. At that stage I was in need of a rest and after ask-ing him to pour me a cup, I sat on the floor alongside him. As I finished the cup I asked him to keep giving me a refill every time I emptied one. That sweet tasting liquid was boiling hot, consequently it took quite a long time to consume the amount I felt was necessary to relieve me of the feeling of being drunk. Eventually I thought it was enough and paid him. I was now sober, and after dusting off the seat of my trousers, I thanked him, and walking once more erect and stable, I headed for the dance hall. It was much too late now to go home and have a wash and brush up, so it was straight forward, to face a fully deserved and expected tongue lashing from my spouse. At the door I handed over my ticket and made a bee line for Anna who I noticed was sitting at one of the tables placed around the edge of the dancing area. In a subdued voice I made a reasonably plausible excuse for my late appearance, something about being busy at the station, and much to my relief and total surprise she seemed to accept it. I made a point of not leaning too close to her as I couldn't imagine how my breath would smell from the mixture of that concoction called beer and the black coffee I could feel swirling around in my stomach. I did however manage to take a look around the hall and commented about the number of high ranking officers that were present. Then it was time for me to put my condition to the ultimate test, the next dance was announced, a quick step. We took the floor. Fortunately Anna had remembered to bring my dance shoes and I had put them on. We had quite a few dances of one kind or another, all carried out without any trace of instability on my part. The evening was progressing nicely as far as I was concerned, until the master of ceremonies announced "Take your partners for an Old fashioned Waltz". Anna and I obliged by standing up, taking hold of each other awaiting the commencement of the appropriate music. It began, and for the first few times going all the way around the floor there were no problems, then the beer proved to be stronger than the coffee. After making a number of normal fairly quick right handed turns we went into the reverse movement, where a few quick turns happened to come close together. All I can remember is lying flat on my back looking up at the distorted features of Anna staring down at me in disbelief. Somehow I had managed to relinquish my hold on Anna, therefore not bringing her down on top of me.

She helped me to my feet, without one word of commiseration. I couldn't help thinking that all my attempts at concealing my predicament had now all been in vain. We left the hall almost immediately and during the somewhat hurried walk home I did explain what had happened. I was apologising but my apologies fell on deaf ears, and they were continually being interrupted by scathing remarks, most of them appertaining to my lack of respect for Anna and our friends. That dance and it's disastrous ending stayed with me for an awful long time. The only good thing that came out of it was that from then on my beer drinking came to a stop.

We were still doing lots of visiting and one evening we visited an elderly Jewish couple in the best residential area around the top of Mount Carmel. Although the couple were getting on in years they were a lively pair and we all had a great time. It would have been somewhere around two a.m. when we made our departure. It was a cool night and just right for a pleasant walk down the hill. We had travelled about half a mile when suddenly and without warning I felt very ill, I began to find it very difficult to walk and soon I couldn't walk at all. I was finding it difficult to breathe and unable to straighten up so I slumped over the nearest garden wall while Anna went to make a telephone call for an ambulance. It arrived fairly quickly and took us to a small private hospital that was only about one mile away. I was immediately seen by a doctor who carried out a number of tests. I was diagnosed as having Pleurisy, what that meant I had no idea and no one seemed willing to enlighten me, but I was taken to a small ward and put to bed. I found it extremely hard to get comfortable owing to the wide and very tight dressing that had been wrapped around my back and chest. This, I was told, contained some kind of heat which would penetrate my body into my lungs, they being where the problem was. I was later informed that there were two types of Pleurisy, one known as Wet, the other Dry. I was apparently fortunate as I had the Dry one, this being the lesser of the two evils. Once I had been settled in Anna went home and informed the station I was out of action. Anyway, I made a steady recovery and was allowed home after one week with strict instructions to take it easy for the next few weeks. I did, I arrived home and felt fine, so I went back to work two days later!

About this time, Anna seemed to be becoming worried about her pregnancy and she decided she would like more advice from a doctor friend of her's, a gynaecologist. The only trouble was he lived and worked in Nazareth, and it was a very long way from Haifa. Nevertheless an appointment was made for the following week. I arranged to work the afternoon shift the day before and have the next day off altogether to give us plenty of time to make the journey there and back with a few hours to spare in between to spend with the doctor. Towards the end of that shift there was a large disturbance on the Souk, involving drug fuelled, knife armed violence. I had to empty the station of officers to bring it under control. I arrived home about five and after listening to Anna going on about our being unable to catch the bus she had expected to, I had a wash and rolled into bed. I never liked losing any sleep so when I was awakened by Anna telling me to get up or it would be too late altogether for us to go to Nazareth I wasn't very pleased at all. It was ten o'clock, we caught a ramshackle bus at about 11 pm and made the journey. The roads were awful and the bus gave the impresssion it was only just managing to hold itself together. The bus was full of goats, hens, screaming children, men smoking pipes that gave off foul fumes, and pregnant women who shuddered every time the bus went over one of the innumerable pot holes that punctuated our journey. There were heaps of goods tied on top of the bus and inside, pushed and squashed into every available space, were more bundles tied insecurely with bits of rope. It was very hot, dusty, noisy, and smelly, and I wished I was at home enjoying my day off. However I could not complain as it was my fault that we had not caught the better class type of transport we had intended. We, unfortunately, were making the journey in one that catered for the people who used them to carry all their worldly goods, including livestock.

After what seemed to be an eternity I was put out of my misery by the arrival of the bus at the dropping off point in the centre of Nazareth. Anna led the way, and when we had negotiated a rather steep climb through a number of fairly narrow alleyways with wide stone steps, we came to a house where we were met by a distinguished looking man who invited us inside. He was a Christian Arab. He showed us round his facilities and gave her plenty of advice. Afterwards we went into the dining room where some food and drink was brought to us by a servant. When we were finished the doctor accompanied us to the picking up point and we boarded a bus bound for Haifa. This time we were lucky in that it was one of the better class type, with a lot more room and was much cleaner. It wasn't very late when we arrived home and it seemed as if Anna was very happy we had made the trip and was more settled now. Nevertheless, I was to be reminded of my "inconsiderate behaviour" for a great many years. Somehow I don't think Anna ever came to terms with the uncertainty of the kind of job I was doing, if I should have been home at a certain time at the end of my normal shift, she fully expected me to be there at that time, and despite all my explanations as to why it sometimes was impossible, she always seemed to think it was my fault entirely.

One afternoon I arrived home at around 2.30 after completing my day shift. Anna was there doing some dressmaking. To reach home I had made my way as usual through the Souk, past the shops, cafe bars, market stalls, and the well populated Khamra Square. On the afternoon in question I had no sooner set foot in the door than Anna said she fancied some fish for lunch and would I go and get some. I did a smart about turn and as the wet fish shop was inside the Souk I made my way back using the same route I had just taken to get home. It was a very busy time of the day and it appeared to have got much busier since I had come through that narrow street about half an hour earlier. I was about halfway to the fish shop when I heard a police whistle being blown, it was coming from a short distance in front of me. I could just see through the crowd a Ghaffir attempting to run towards me, waving his arms about and blowing furiously upon his whistle. I quickened up a bit and when I reached him he told me there was trouble in Khamra Square, where a lot of men were fighting. Someone had called out to him as he was passing and told him that knives were being used. and some men were bleeding badly. I immediately headed for the square, and remember thinking that this was something I could have done without. When I arrived at the entrance I was somewhat taken aback by the number of men there; it was absolutely full. I took a very quick look around weighing up the situation. All the fighting appeared to be going on in the very centre of the crowd and a number of men, how many I didn't know, looked to be having a right go at each other. I reached a decision, but I can assure you it is not a very comforting thought when you know that you alone are going to have to make your way into the middle of such a heaving mass to break up a fight between knife wielding adversaries who were intent on killing each other. I asked the Ghaffir to call an ambulance, and told him to stay outside the square. I fastened the two safety straps on my revolver holster, just in case someone decided to help themselves. I also tucked the strap from the truncheon under my waist belt, underneath my tunic, not relishing a crack on the head from that thing. I "walked" up to the edge of the jostling crowd, there was no point in running, let them see I was in no way concerned about their antics, and with a few choice words in Arabic, and a few flicks of my old army stick, I was inside them and making my way towards the middle. I was in the middle sorting them out in no time at all. There were three who had been going at it hammer and tongs, but as soon as I reached them all the fight seemed to go out of them, they were probably tired anyway. I didn't have to demand that they give me the knives that each one of them had been using, they simply handed them to me. They were all suffering from their exertions, one had a nasty looking neck wound, blood was literally pouring from it. Another had blood all over the chest part of his gallabia, and as I looked at it the colour was getting much darker by the second which meant the wound was pretty severe. He needed medical attention as quickly as possible. The third fellow had a long gaping wound stretching down from the top of his arm all the way to his wrist. As I endeavoured to manoeuvre them into position ready to make our exit from the melee, the attitude of the hitherto pretty docile and surprisingly co-operative crowd changed dramatically. I was pushed and jostled to such an extent that I had difficulty keeping my feet, attempts were being made to separate me from the three men. Dozens of voices were raised proclaiming which party had started the fracas and more fist fights developed between those offering this information and those who disagreed. For a time it appeared as if things were going beyond my control, that is until I raised my voice, much louder than their's, and returned the pushes with even more forceful vigour. Using my stick to greater effect, some form of stability returned.

We reached the entrance to the square, and although it had only been a short walk from the centre, about sixty yards, it had been like "running the gauntlet". We didn't have to wait long before the ambulance arrived, manned by two police constables. The driver turned it round and parked alongside the footpath in the street opposite the square, quite a long way from where we were standing. I waved him back towards us but he seemed reluctant to get any nearer the crowd which was still hanging around gesticulating and voicing their opinions. I suppose they appeared to be in an ominous mood and he must have thought it safer to keep well away from them. I marched across to where he was seated behind the steering wheel, tapping my leg with the stick in an agitated manner until he realised that I wanted him closer to the injured men. The men were seated inside the ambulance and made as comfortable as possible. I had waisted too much time already and as it was not necessary for me to go to the station at this time I asked him to see that an entry was made in the diary stating that I had made the arrests, but that there was no need for him to go into further details as I would make out my report later that evening. Right now though I was going to get that fish. The fish shopkeeper was very obliging, helping me to choose one of the best fish swimming around in one of the large tanks, he netted the exact one, killed and boned it, before wrapping it up sufficiently to avoid any leakage, and once more I was on my way home.

As I walked towards the scene of yet another of my many "triumphs" I was feeling quite pleased with myself. That pleasant feeling was soon to evaporate however because as I neared the entrance to the square I saw an ambulance driving away. The Ghaffir was still there and when he saw me he came across and told me some disturbing news. The ambulance had just taken away another very seriously injured man, apparently he had been on the ground, under the feet of the jostling crowd. The driver of the ambulance had said that he considered the fellow to be already dead. Now, what was there for me to be feeling so pleased about? Although I could still feel satisfied that I had prevented the situation escalating into a riot I had failed to notice the fourth man lying on the ground. I did not check thoroughly and had taken it for granted there were only three men involved. I must admit that when I had reached the middle and was confronted by so many of those idiots at such close quarters I did have serious doubts as to whether I should have waited for assistance and not gone in alone.

I was less than five minutes walk away from the station, and deemed it necessary to go there straight away. At this time no entry had been made in the desk diary, as the constable who was to have made it would have still been at the hospital. Having made it, including that unfortunate outcome, I phoned the hospital and was told the fourth man was dead when he arrived. The three others were having their injuries attended to and that one of them was in a critical condition. It was important to hear their side of the story as soon as possible before they had too much time in which to think and prepare something to suit their purpose. I detailed two Arab constables to go and take statements from them. Even though the incident had been entered in the desk diary, there was still my own report to be written out, and it was almost five thirty when I had it completed. There was very little more I could do, so I went home. It had taken me more than three hours to do something that should have only required forty five minutes at the outside. It wasn't too late to prepare it for an "evening " meal, as lunch time had gone, hours ago. My account of the afternoon's happenings did nothing to alleviate the strained atmosphere, an atmosphere that was to remain for quite some time.

When I had been given the post of station Sgt it had been explained to me that there would possibly be occasions when I would be required to return to the depot, probably staying overnight. The terrorists were stepping up their campaign of bombings, murders, and other atrocities. One morning when I went there the depot had received a visit from them, and despite the two very high tiers of coiled barbed wire all the way round the building the terrorists had managed to place a bomb at the bottom of the observation tower, alongside the only entrance to the building. It had exploded and blown a large hole in the tower, but only on the outside, and thankfully there were no casualties.

There was also another time when I was late arriving home, it happened when I was coming off the night shift, and expected to be there around six thirty. It was to annoy Anna as usual, but I was to find myself in a predicament, the outcome of which, I had no control over. It could have resulted in someone getting seriously hurt.

That particular night duty started well enough, only the normal small problems arose and were dealt with satisfactorily. It would have been well after midnight when someone came into the station and complained about a British soldier who was causing trouble in one of the cafe bars. I think it must have been a real pleasure for some members of the local community to be able to bring something like this to our attention. As it was a British soldier I decided to take a walk to the cafe myself, sometimes these complaints were unfounded and the wrong approach to a soldier could cause trouble.

Upon entering the cafe I saw a British soldier, a Sgt, laying down the law to everyone around him and adopting a very threatening stance. He was unsteady on his feet and had obviously partaken of a fair quantity of alcohol. I noticed he was carrying a revolver, he hadn't removed it from it's holster but his hand was hovering over the butt in readiness to do so. He had turned to face me as I entered and I immediately recognised him as being a member of my old A/A battery. As a matter of fact he was one of the few men I liked, a really nice unassuming fellow, and we had been good friends. I found it strange to see him in such a position being objectionable, he had always been a solid chap and this type of behaviour was out of character. Nevertheless, he was drunk and carrying a weapon. With some trepidation I began to walk towards him. Despite his bleary eyes and vacant stare he looked straight at me and much to my relief, his face broke into a broad smile, he had recognised me straight away. There were other soldiers sitting around the tables but none that I knew. I am sure that if any of them had been from his lot they would have been alongside him offering their support, as it was they just sat there apparently unconcerned. The expected shaking of hands ritual completed, he spoke, and in a very loud voice proclaimed that he had been threatened and definitely overcharged, all night, insisting that I do something about it. here, and now. I noticed the proprietor was making his way towards us, presumably to add his "four pennyworth". I waved him away as I knew this particular proprietor and wouldn't put anything past him, although threatening anyone was out of his league. I had no intention of becoming involved, my job was to remove the cause of the trouble without further incident so I did that by gently but firmly taking hold of the Sgts right arm, removing his hand away from the butt of his revolver, and keeping my right arm free, just in case. We moved towards the door in a most ungainly manner, I endeavouring to keep him on the move. After staggering along we entered the station, where a large mug of Arabic coffee was prepared to hasten the sobering up process. At my request he handed me his revolver, I took note of it's number, and put it in the arms rack under lock and key. He was then deposited inside a clean, empty cell, presented with two regulation blankets and the mug of piping hot coffee, and invited to "sleep it off". I made frequent visits to the cell ensuring he was all right. There were occupants in most of the other cells, some quite noisy too, but he slept like a log, without making a sound. There had been no entry made in the desk diary when the complaint had initially been made, and I saw no reason for an entry to be made now, after all no harm had been done, no charges would be brought and hopefully he could be sent on his way early in the morning.

About 1.30 the interior of the station was running on an even keel and I was preparing to go out and make my presence known around the area when one of the P.M.F. patrols brought in two R.A.F. officers who they had seen driving a jeep along the high street in a dangerous manner. When they were stopped they jumped out and ran to the side of the street. No one in the patrol could be sure which of them had been driving at the time they were stopped. They were both obviously under the influence of alcohol. Two cells were finally emptied and put at their disposal. The coffee pot was employed again and eventually they fell to sleep. I asked the PMF patrol to bring the jeep back to the station before the end of their shift.

I decided to go out to see what was happening in the rest of the district, but not before telling the desk officer that he must not sign out any of our three British residents until I returned. Thankfully there were no problems anywhere and I was back in the station just before 5.30. The Sgt was awake when I went to call him, he had a quick wash before coming into the front office. It would have been about five fifty when we left the station together. I knew the transport from his camp brought the men on day leave to a certain place not far from where we were at around six every morning. I told him to make sure he told the truck driver that he had missed the previous night's truck and spent the night walking around and assured him that his misdemeanour would not be reported.

Upon my arrival back at the station I was informed that the jeep had been delivered and had been put in a safe place. I had an entry made in the diary of the facts appertaining to the two R.A.F. officers. Their situation was somewhat different in that the P.M.F. patrol Sgt would have to report it, as his time away from the area designated to them, had to be accounted for. Those two officers were still asleep when I left for home, the new duty officer had been told they must not be allowed to leave until he was satisfied they were absolutely sober, and had been formally charged. There had been so much to do it had made me almost two hours late before I felt able to leave.

I found myself wending my way home through the early morning hubbub of the Souk. As I passed all the shops and stalls etc; I had no idea how much I was to be affected by the going's on during that night. It would have been somewhere around 8.45 when I arrived at the beginning of the spare ground which was approximately two hundred yards from home. It was an almost empty piece of land, slightly uphill, consisting of dry soil and sand, practically barren, but dotted about were a number of small evergreen shrubs. The top side of the incline ran parallel with the street adjoining the Carmelia Court Hotel, the longest sloping side stopped at the Mount Carmel road, here this road went up the hill to Mount Carmel and the other way, downwards, to a very sharp left hand bend. Exactly opposite this bend was a "no entry" sign at the top of Mountain road. I was halfway across this ground and could see the gates at the entrance to our flat in Abbass street. I had a good open view with no obstructions, apart from the small shrubs, but I was having to watch my step as the ground was very uneven. At the front of the Carmelia Court Hotel, and running alongside a footpath, was a wall approximately three feet high. Opposite this, separated by Mount Carmel road, was another stone wall but this one was probably twelve feet high, it extended from the end of Abbass street up the road for about eighty yards, culminating ten to fifteen yards before the uphill bend. At it's bottom was a footpath, at it's top was a large garden, on a slope and stretching back quite some way to the house it belonged to. I would have been about twenty yards from the road when I noticed something peculiar about fifty yards up on the opposite side of the road. It was a farmer's type dray, full of straw, the back of it was pressed hard against the bottom of the high wall, leaving no room for anyone to walk past on the footpath. This was a very unusual position for this type of transport, and the position it was in suggested it had been pushed and man handled there as there was no horse. I must have walked about another ten yards or so when suddenly the dray began to move quickly across the road, someone was pushing it but I couldn't see who. At the same time I heard the sound of a car's engine as it came down the hill towards the sharp bend which was about thirty five yards higher up from the dray. The nose of the car appeared as it took the bend and came down towards the dray, which by this time was completely blocking the road. I had carried on walking but suddenly dived for cover as automatic gunfire poured out from the garden at the top of the high wall. I couldn't see who was doing the firing, they must have been laid down, but I could see it was all being directed at the car approaching from their right. Then I heard the car accelerating and it's radiator came into view between the dray shafts and the hotel wall. It was then that I noticed the flag attached to the bonnet and immediately recognised it as the one on the Chief Superintendent's Humber. I didn't have a lot of time in which to decide what I could do to help. If I used my revolver and fired at the persons doing the shooting I would most certainly give my position away and be cut down by their more powerful weapons. I therefore decided that "discretion was the better part of valour", and rolled over to the nearest shrub in an attempt to make my precarious position slightly better. Meanwhile the car had managed to get through the very small gap between the hotel wall and the dray shafts, scraping it's side on the wall and smashing the dray shafts, and then running onto the ground I was on. It then returned to the road for a short distance before driving down the one way street against the traffic, it would then end up in Kingsway, close to police headquarters. So much for the car and it's occupants; I couldn't know whether anyone inside it had been injured, but at least they were away from any further contact with their attackers. The dray was still all the way across the road, the firing had stopped, there was a deathly silence. This was a predominantly Jewish area and the idea of a warning hav-ing been issued could not be ruled out. I remained flat on the ground behind the shrub but managed to take a look around hoping to see some sign of the attackers. After what seemed like an age I got up slowly, looking around as I did so, and ran across the road towards Abbas street, then up and into the small courtyard of the house in which our ground floor flat was situated. I had to hope that my departure from the scene had not been noticed. I entered the flat where I was confronted by a very irate Anna wanting to know where I had been as I was more than three hours late. I was tired, and not a little up tight under the circumstances, so I said I would explain everything when we were together that evening. I washed, ate a light breakfast, and dropped into bed. I didn't sleep for quite a long time as I lay wondering if I had done everything possible.

I was up and dressed by the time she came home, and after we had settled down with a cup of tea I explained the whys and wherefores of that night and the early morning fracas. She was upset but there was nothing else I could say to help matters. I did promised to obtain all the information about the state of his health when I arrived at work that evening and to phone her as soon as I knew exactly what did happen. I made the necessary enquiries as soon as I got to the station at ten o clock and I was told the Supt had been driving the car, which he did often, the chauffeur was seated in the back. The car had suffered a few dents and scratches on it's right hand side, and as it turned out neither of the occupants received any injuries whatsoever. If the gunmen had managed to stop the Humber then it would most certainly have been a different outcome.

I passed all the relevant information on to Anna and then got down to the serious business of running the station. It was then I discovered that the two R.A.F. officers had been released from custody almost as soon as I had left that morning after they had started complaining to the desk diary officer. I had checked them before I left and they were both still in no way fit to be let out onto the streets for their own safety never mind driving. My orders had been ignored completely, but as I read the diary entries for the rest of the day it gave some very disturbing news. About one and a half hours after the two officers had left in their jeep an accident was reported to have taken place at a notorious cross roads on the outskirts of town. An eye witness had stated that an R.A.F. jeep, travelling very fast, had collided with a large lorry and both occupants of the jeep had been killed. I made further enquiries and my suspicions were confirmed; it had been the two officers who had been in our cells. Words cannot describe how I felt.

Anna and I went out almost every evening visiting friends but there were ocassions when we would go out alone, to see a film at the cinema in the Jewish district and have a meal somewhere. There were many good restaurants in various parts of the town (although we never went into the Souk area) there were some good Arab ones in Kingsway, together with Greek, Italian, and others, but our favourite place was Hertzlia street in the Jewish district. We would select a restaurant where there was an empty table in a nice position on the footpath, one that had a good view of all that was going on at both sides of the street, and order a meal from an immaculately dressed and very attentive waiter, the service was excellent in every way. Although I was dressed in civvies, not drawing attention to myself, I couldn't help feeling like a fish in a goldfish bowl. Added to this was knowing that I didn't just have myself to think of as Anna was seated alongside me. Nevertheless I enjoyed those evenings out, brushing shoulders with people who I knew would rather see me dead than serve me a nice juicy steak!

Everything went on as normal during the following few weeks, we were both kept busy with the work we had to do, Anna with her dress making, and I with the station. Anna had about two weeks to go before the baby was due when things started to go wrong, she began to feel that all was not quite as it should be and made frequent visits to the doctor. He tried to assure her that everything was normal and that she had no reason to worry, but after a number of visits and not being able to convince her, he suggested a spell in hospital would help to calm all her fears. I went to visit her as often as possible, thinking that everything would be all right and that she would soon be home again. During those visits I was told by the doctor attending her that she was complaining about having severe pains and because of this they were giving her Morphia every time she said she was getting these pains. Two days later the baby, a boy, decided to arrive, but he was still-born. There have been a great many reasons put forward as to why this tragedy occurred, and over the years many bitter arguments have ensued. The baby was born during the early hours of one day, all the arrangements were made within the next few hours, and at two p.m. I was driven to the cemetery in an undertaker's car with the baby in his tiny wooden coffin on the back seat. We were accompanied by a vicar and one of the undertakers as I carried the coffin to a spot where a little oblong grave had been prepared.

The vicar said prayers and our first born son was laid to rest in the British cemetery in Haifa, Palestine. Unfortunately Anna had been too ill to attend the ceremony.

Anna returned home after about four days, understandably she was very upset and it was to take her quite a long time before she could come to terms with what had happened. I did my best to console her but words at such a time were of very little comfort to her. We spent a lot of hours at home together, as she could not bring herself to go out working. I organised my duties to enable me to be at home during the days and evenings, and not doing any of the usual off duty inspections or impromptu patrols of the area. The flat was on the first floor of a very large house, this house had a wide footpath running all around it, extending from large double cast iron gates at the front. At the sides of this path were walls about four feet high and on top of these were sloping gardens stretching back almost six feet and up to a height of at least twelve feet, lovingly tended by the landlord. There were plants and shrubs of every description, beautiful colours and some giving off a nose tingling aroma. These gardens, walls and footpaths, started at the entrance to the property and ended at the entrance, completing a full circle of different scents and colours. It was ideal for Anna to sit at the door recuperating.

Our stay in these pleasant surroundings was very peaceful indeed, but that peace was nearly shattered one evening. We were both at home, Anna making some dress or other, and I was seated at a table opposite the living room window. It was a balmy night, about seven o clock, the window was wide open and the shutters closed and locked, what air there was filtered into the room through the shutters but it was still uncomfortably hot. I was facing the window and writing a letter to my Mother, intending to have it ready to post early the next day. The writing had come easy to me and I must have completed two pages when I became aware of a scratching sound, it wasn't continuous and so faint it could barely be heard. I carried on writing and listening until one such noise was quite distinct, and it came from the shutter directly in front of me. I ran to the front door, opened it, and went quickly round the corner of the house towards the shutter and came face to face with a person dressed in dark clothing. It was impossible to see a face, but it appeared to be a man. He was startled when he saw me and seemed to panic, turning one way then the other before running away along the end of the building and round the corner. I followed, round one blind corner, then another blind corner, and out through the open gates into the street. He had certainly beaten me in my floppy slippers. I looked up and down the street but nothing was moving, he had gone. It was then I realised I had come out of the flat leaving my revolver reclining peacefully on the table where I had put it, in front of me. Then there was the little matter of my having run round two blind corners, where he could have been waiting for me to appear, and to complete my stupidity I had run out into the street, and calmly stood under a brilliant light from the street lamp, in full view of everyone.

I went back inside the flat and picked up my gun, took a torch, told Anna to stay in the flat with the door locked, then went back to the shutter. Immediately underneath it, on the ground, were a few wood shavings, and a single sided razor blade. On inspecting the shutter I found that at approximately eye level one of the slats had been cut away almost forming a semi-circle. Had another thirty secondth of an inch been cut away this semi-circle would have fallen onto the floor leaving a perfect view into the room. I had been sitting at the table about five feet from the shutter, it would have been simplicity itself for him to line up a shot and fire through the shutter. I phoned security headquarters, and in less than half an hour an Army officer arrived bringing with him three heavily armed Arab soldiers. He told me they were

177

the first of a twenty four hour guard to be placed on the flat. They were there right up to, and including, the day we left the country. It was re-assuring to know they were there, but even so I knew I would have to be even more attentive in everything I was to do.

Anna had the baby in June, it was now two months later, August 1946, and she had almost returned to normal. When Anna seemed to have come to terms with the awful events of the past months we started to go out and spend some time with our friends again. Meeting them for the first time after our baby was born must have been very painful for Anna and consequently those first few meetings were somewhat subdued.

It was now the middle of summer, and the daytime heat was almost unbearable, simply drinking a cup of tea had streams of perspiration running down your face and body. These were the kind of days when night shifts were the much better duty; the patrols were done at a more leisurely pace, without the hordes of pedestrians cluttering the footpaths, and the temperature had dropped considerably. It was a definite improvement from being on the daytime shifts. The cafe bars still had their fair share of customers although when it got to around one a.m., a large number of them could be seen sleeping it off, sitting on chairs and sprawled across the tables. Most of the shops were open but the stall holders were most probably fast asleep in their beds. Despite all the problems I had a feeling of contentment as I toured the Souk and the other parts of the district, I felt in total control. During this period I decided it was necessary for me to make my presence felt on a few early turns instead of doing nights. I was agreeably surprised and felt as if my efforts were beginning to pay off.

I arrived back at the station around ten o'clock and was told that my wife had phoned asking for me to call her as soon as I returned. I phoned Anna, she told me that her friend, the one whose husband was the detective, had phoned her just after eight fifteen telling her that her husband had been shot, and that it had happened in the street outside their home as he set off to go to work. Anna asked me if I could go home and pick her up so that we could both go to see her friend as quickly as possible. That devastating news threw me off balance for a minute or two, but after regaining my composure I told the officer in charge of the desk to look after things as I was going home, but would return sometime later in the day.

On the way to her friend's home I asked Anna if the Sgt was all right. She said she didn't know as her friend had been hysterical on the phone. All she could make out was that he had been shot. We arrived and were met by a very distraught young woman, when she had calmed down a bit she told us what had happened. Her husband had left for work at 8 o'clock, she had gone onto the balcony to wave to him, as she did every morning. He had only walked a few yards when a taxi cab drove up the street towards him, he took a good look at it as it drove past him. A few yards further up the street it stopped and three men dressed as if they were going to play tennis, carrying tennis racquets got out. Suddenly all three of them took revolvers from inside their white shirts and started to fire at him. He fell to the ground, with that one of the men walked up to him and fired two shots into his head at close range, then all three walked back to the taxi, got in, and it drove off. She said she was screaming all the time this was taking place. She then ran down the stairs and went to him lying on the ground, he wasn't moving and she knew he was dead. She went back and phoned police headquarters, they sent an ambulance which took him to hospital but he had died instantly. We did our best to console her, but there is very little that can be said at such a time to be of any real help. We arranged for a doctor to come and see her, and Anna stayed to keep her company. I went home and informed my superior, and he gave me permission to attend his funeral which took place at two p.m. that same day, at the British cemetery in Haifa with full military honours.

The lives of Anna and myself had been affected by two very sad events during the last two months. When we were alone at home we talked about what had happened, and it made us think how suddenly life could change; first the baby, and then our friend. It was about this time that we began to consider our future, and if we would have one at all if we stayed in this country. At present my time was fully occupied with the station and the area. I liked my work, knowing that I was doing valuable work. Many things were a challenge, and I liked nothing better than a challenge. I would be very sorry indeed if I had to leave all this, but it was a fore-gone conclusion that I, along with all the other British policemen, would have to leave in the not too distant future, when one of the two dominant nationalities would take over the running of the country. It was a beautiful country, we had a good lifestyle and I liked the people but more problems were arising every day as throughout the country the Jewish terrorist organisa-tions were committing more and more atrocities.

Anna and I held frequent discussions, and from these I got the impression that she fa-voured leaving the land of her birth and going elsewhere. We did have options; I could transfer to the Hong Kong police force, and could expect a suitable promotion when, doing so; There was also Southern Rhodesia and Kenya. When I had told Anna about this before we were married she had refused to consider a move to Hong Kong, but said the other two sounded much more to her liking. One day I had reason to go to Shafa Amr, and whilst I was there I had an interview with the Deputy Supt. During the interview I asked about a move to either Southern Rhodesia or Kenya, he said that neither place was any use to me as both would be handed over to their respective local communities not long after the handover of Palestine. The discussions continued between Anna and myself without reaching any concrete decision, then one day she came home after talking to her Godfather, the one of the Mount Carmel road incident, and he had told her that the country was going to be handed over to the Jews at some-time in the very near future. He strongly advised that we should leave and sooner rather than later, as it would be impossible for anyone British to stay after the handover. He also told her that he had already made arrangements for his wife and family to return to England and that they were already preparing to go, adding that it was his intention to follow them very soon. That seemed to be the answer to all our deliberations, so acting on his advice, we decided to leave also and there was only one place we could go, and that was England.

We had finally reached a decision, I informed the necessary authority and reluctantly tendered my resignation, on the grounds that I wished to return to England. It was accepted, and the work commenced making all the required arrangements. I was not overjoyed at the prospect of leaving, but there was one aspect of it that cheered me up immensely; I would be going to see my Mother, sister Jacqueline and brother Peter, all of whom I hadn't seen for more than three and a half years, and my Father who I hadn't seen for much longer than that.

It was a hectic time with all the packing that had to be done and the unenviable tour of the homes of our friends began with tearful exchanges from them and Anna. The friends we left behind, have been in my thoughts wondering what happened to them during those horrendous troubles that were to envelope their country.

I was still doing the job of station Sgt and putting as much effort into it as before. I made one last visit to the depot, Shafa Amr, and saw Peter and the others. Peter hadn't decided what he was going to do at that stage. When I did see him at his home after his return, he told me he had stayed on and that they had an awful time just prior to, and after, the official handover. He spoke of one officer, a happy go lucky type of chap, who at theheight of the troubles was caught in an explosion and lost an arm. As Peter was unfolding the many stories about the rotten time they had endured I got the terrible feeling of having let them all down by not being with them when they could have done with my support. I left eighteen months before the handover and was safely ensconced in civvy street at that time, something of which I am still not proud.

Eventually our three crates and portmanteau were packed to bursting, and collected to be transported to England. At this time I made a big mistake. For many weeks Anna had been trying to get me to collect a large box of long playing records she had stored in an Armenian families home about two years ago. Even at that time some of them would have been quite valuable but due to pressure of work and maybe no inclination to do such a menial task, I never got round to doing it. However, one day the son of the family, a young chap about eighteen years of age, came to the flat. I noticed he was becoming rather stroppy with Anna, practically demanding she go with him immediately and remove this box of records. I was then a very placid person, but hearing him speak to Anna in that tone of voice made me propel him to the door and forcibly eject him out into the courtyard. The outcome was that Anna never got her records, as the family took umbrage at having their son manhandled in this manner, and when asked for them, refused to hand them over. It was a very sore point with Anna for many years to come, and I knew it, having it thrust down my throat on more ocassions than I care to recall.

Four days before our impending departure I was informed that a Sgt from the regular force would be taking over the Central station, and I was told to give him every assistance to do so for twenty four hours and then present myself to the Inspector at Western police station where I would spend the next two days, prior to my departure. Handing over the station and my responsibilities was bad enough, but knowing I was to spend the last two days of my, hitherto enjoyable, career in the company of that same objectionable Inspector who had been in charge of that station when I had done those first foot patrols, was something I was not looking forward to. I had heard that resignations, in some cases, were not appreciated by the British Foreign and Colonial offices. One instance comes to mind of which I had first hand knowledge where a young constable who served with me in the Nablus, Jenin, and Shafa Amr depots, did resign and went home to England, only to return a few months later having been trained as a store manager for Spinneys, and took over that position in one of their stores. He had no sooner taken over than a vendetta was started against him by the police. I heard he was constantly being hounded and of one instance where he was actually arrested. The decision for this must have come from the upper echelons of power. When he was in the P.M.F., I had found him to be a decent fellow, reliable, good natured and unassuming. Now I had resigned and also done something that had not been appreciated, I had married a member of the local community, and although Anna had a British passport, she was still of a different nationality. Only time would tell whether I would be regarded in the same light as some of my predecessors. How they could do anything that was to affect me though, back in England and once more in civvy street, is something I am unable to answer for the time being, but, wait for it, there is a sting in the tail.

However, those two days at Central Station, were nowhere near as bad as I had anticipated, probably because I kept myself to myself. I worked inside the station doing the jobs that were necessary there. I was told to bring all my police uniform and equipment with me to hand in at the end of my final shift. I attempted to hang on to one cap badge but the Inspector was having none of it, insisting that it must be included. The notebook I considered to be my personal property, it stayed with me along with the truncheon and the leg holster I had purchased. I was going to miss the feeling of the Smith and Wessen swinging against my thigh, and the thought had crossed my mind that when I did leave the station that evening I wouldn't have the usual comforting bulge under my civilian jacket. I had to walk quite a long way home, and it would be the first time I had walked those streets without the company of my 'friend'. However, at five o'clock I walked out of that station, a civilian, but not before that Inspector had informed me that my resignation had been put on hold. I was officially on three months leave, at the end of which I would be given two options, to withdraw it and return to Palestine, or confirm it, and that I would receive the appropriate papers sometime during the next three months. The journey back to the flat was without incident, although eyes and ears worked overtime during the trip. That evening was spent doing all the little jobs necessary in preparation for the following day, which was certainly going to be hectic. A taxi had been booked and duly arrived about ten o'clock. A last look around the flat to ensure we had got everything, then it was just a case of picking up the hand luggage, locking the door for the last time, and Anna taking the keys to the landlord. He and his wife and sister came to see us off at the gates amid tearful goodbyes. I was very sorry to leave knowing I would never see them again. The taxi took us to Haifa railway station, where we boarded a train to the port of Alexandria, in Egypt.

Eighteen months after we left, the Jewish nation became the owners of the greater part of Palestine and re-named it Israel. In contrast to the other countries I had visited this was an experience I thoroughly enjoyed and was very sorry to leave. The people on the whole were very easy to get on with making it a pleasure to have known them, although there were of course some that were anything but friendly. I had a job that is never the kind of work that is conducive to making a great many friends and yet I did; really good friends too. I took a great interest in all that I did, hopefully contributing towards the task of keeping the peace.

The members of the civilian population, of all nationalities, have been in my thoughts over the many years I have lived, wondering where they are and how they have coped with the serious problems that have engulfed them during these years. There were some wonderful people amongst them, and I shall never forget them or the kindness they showed towards me. This particular episode in my life is one that I shall always look back on and say in all sincerity that it was great to have experienced almost all aspects of it.

CHAPTER 10

The train journey from Haifa to Alexandria, although it was hot and sticky for most of the time, was made without incident, and we soon found ourselves on board a ship bound for southern France. It was late October 1946, the war in europe had been over for more than sixteen months. The sea trip found the Mediterranean in an uncharacteristically unsettled state, the ship rose and fell with the swell and Anna spent the time largely below deck feeling ill. Eventually we docked and after waiting around a while caught a train to Paris where we spent three days before going on to Calais. Upon our arrival there we had to hang about for quite some time before we went on board the channel ferry which took us across to Dover. The Channel was choppy and Anna was ill again. It was late afternoon when we caught the train to London, and then changed at Waterloo station to the underground tube line to reach King's Cross main line station. From now on things only got worse. We had to wait for a connection that would, after many changes, eventually see us deposited in the station of my home town Barnsley. Having to wait around for the connections on cold, dark, dank, station platforms was no way to introduce Anna to Britain. Only a few days ago we had left a beautifully clean, warm country, and here we were almost freezing on station platforms, looking out on a dull smoky atmosphere. When asking questions of the railway staff we were treated with complete indifference. We had left a place that was supposedly inferior to the one we were now in. At least there it had been possible to receive a civil reply to a civil question. We were cold and hungry, the passengers' waiting rooms were locked, the platform buffets were closed for the night, and on most of the stations there was a gale belting from one end of the platform to the other. I still feel very ashamed to have allowed myself to forget what my own country was really like, and to have brought my wife here. I just cannot imagine how she must have felt, I do know she had expressed a wish to see this country. I arrived at the conclusion that I was entirely to blame for this state of affairs in not having thought things out a lot more thoroughly. I could have decided upon somewhere much more suitable, I had the right background and the right connections to have been able to do this, instead I had brought Anna here to a country I knew would have the kind of difficulties that could not be conducive to her. Also knowing that her previous lifestyle could in no way be compared to anything there was to offer here, I should have made more of an effort to find some other place that would have been more conducive. As I stood brooding I couldn't have known, but could have predicted that in the next few years I was going to have a lot to answer for.

After all the problems of the train journey we eventually arrived at my home in the coal mining village of Worsbrough Dale, situated about three miles from the market town of Barnsley. My Mother, sister Jacqueline, and brother Peter, gave us a warm welcome. Jacqueline had grown into quite a young lady, she had been a mere eight year old when I first left just before the war started. I had seen her on occasions before I went abroad but she was now fifteen and the change in her was quite remarkable. Peter had grown considerably and was now a strapping ten year old, and bombarded me with questions about my time abroad, "had I killed many Germans and Italians, had I been shot or injured in any way ? I relieved him on all counts, saying I had kept well away from places where anything such as he was asking could have taken place, but he listened intently when told of some of the funny things I had come across in my travels. Mother hadn't changed much, although I did think she appeared to have lost some weight. My Father was back working for the G.P.O. in Barnsley, and was expected home around tea time, five thirty. He had been promoted and was having to travel quite a long distance to reach the office in which he now worked. When he did arrive home the conversation turned to what he had done for the past four years. He had left my AA. battery during 1942 and we hadn't seen each other since then. Everyone had plenty to talk about in the following days, and Anna seemed to be settling in quite nicely although just what exactly she was feeling I had no way of knowing. At the time she appeared to be happy enough, although when Mother brought up the subject of the girlfriend or two of mine who had been to see her on occasions during my absence I did notice a narrowing of her eyes and could almost feel the annoyance she was doing her very best not to show. The house here had three bedrooms and Jacqueline and Peter had one each. Which one of them was cajoled into vacating their's and giving it to Anna and myself I cannot remember, although it must have made things rather awkward for them at the time.

After a couple of days my Mother, Anna, and I, went to see my Grandmother at the new farm my uncle Harold had taken over during the war. We found her to be in good spirits, despite the fact that she was still completely paralysed from the waist down and had to be carried everywhere. It was so good to see her after being away for what seemed such a long time and she was still the same sweet lady. Harold and his wife, my aunt Annie, were in the best of health and were obviously enjoying life on their new farm. It was a big improvement on their first one; it had more land, and the fields were adjoining the farm. There was no more bringing the cows along busy roads to reach their milking quarters. The buildings were more in keeping with a dairy farm, the cow byre, (milking shed), was larger and with it being all in one place it made things much easier. I was very pleased to see they were doing so well, they thoroughly deserved it.

Eventually all our worldly goods arrived. I had had to go back to King's Cross to witness a Customs check, and then endure a hair raising ride in Uncle Harold's ramshackle truck to collect them from Barnsley station, but we now had those three crates and a portmanteau with us in our one room! We set to work unpacking them. A great many things were on ration still and we had brought as much of this kind of stuff as we thought would come in handy. It was much appreciated by Mother. I had one or two personal things which I gave to Peter, the truncheon, the leg holster, and one or two other bits and pieces including an exceptionally good pair of binoculars in a leather case with long carrying straps. It took quite a long time to get everything out and into drawers and cupboards but eventually it was all put away. Everything we possessed on earth had been incorporated into such a few items of furniture, out of sight, and making it almost impossible to believe that was all we had in the whole wide world.

For the next few weeks we made more visits and toured the shopping areas of Barnsley.

This brought home to us how different everything was here. Gone were the brightly lit streets, the shops with their doors wide open and the inviting window displays. Everything here was so dull, and apart from the greengrocery stall holders in the market place raucously voicing the assets of their wares, it was so quiet and lifeless. I know it was cold and damp with most people walking around with their shoulders hunched and heads receding into their coat collars, but it all looked so miserable and depressing. At the time Anna made no complaints to me but I saw her looking at everything and knew what she must have been thinking; the same as myself I suppose.

One day I called upon my employers, the firm where I had been taken on to train as a warehouse manager, from where I had been called up in August 1939. They were pleased to see me and asked when I would be returning to work at the warehouse. To be quite honest I didn't feel like going back, but they had been good enough to keep the position open for me, so I started the following week. There was a great deal I would have to learn having lost all that time during the war years but I had seen and done so many things since I left there that I couldn't settle down to the work I was required to do. I did try, but only half heartedly, and I could never work like that so after three weeks I left. Maybe I was wrong but it wasn't what I had in mind for myself at that time. The employment situation was very much on my mind, but not knowing what I wanted to do made things difficult. During the time we spent living with my family I considered many things which may have been suitable for me. There was work in other countries, some under Arab control and to these I gave considerable thought, but it would have meant another upheaval and neither Anna or myself would have appreciated that coming so soon after the last one. I was like a "fish out of water" but I decided that we would stay here, and sink, or swim.

After I had been doing the warehouse work for about three days I came home one evening and became aware of a decidedly uncomfortable atmosphere, there appeared to be some kind of tension in the air. Each evening things were getting progressively worse and after about two weeks the atmosphere got to such a stage I thought I should do something about it. That night I asked Anna if she was having some kind of problem when I was at work. My enquiry brought on a tirade of abuse deriding me for bringing her to this country and to this house and for agreeing to go back to doing such a menial type of work. I listened intently and, after thinking about it, came to the conclusion that Anna had somehow made herself unwelcome. How this had come about was difficult to ascertain, but I was fully aware of her aptitude to cause problems. I had a serious dilemma, on the one hand was my wife, and on the other my family. My Mother was a very timid person and would have walked miles to avoid even the slightest hint of a confrontation. My Father, I feel sure would have kept his own counsel, and as for Jacqueline and Peter they would not dream of saying or doing anything to upset the applecart in case they incurred the wrath of their Father. I found it to be a very uneasy and uncomfortable situation and my mind worked overtime hoping to find a satisfactory solution. Then something was to happen that relieved me of many problems all at once.

Anna and I went to the farm one day and Harold gave us some good news. Apparently the farm he used to occupy was soon to become vacant. Harold thought I would be interested so he had spoken to the landlord. This landlord was William Elmhirst and I met him with a view to taking over the farm. Anna and I talked it over and it was agreed that I take over the tenancy. It could no longer be used as a dairy farm because the local council had taken almost all the land for building purposes. The fields where cows used to graze now sported semi-detached houses, bungalows, clubs, and pubs. There was one field opposite the farm house and the land alongside the house, also the farm buildings with the stack yard at the rear of them. At that time I hadn't the faintest idea what I intended to do with it, but it meant we would have a house of our own and with the amount of work that was necessary to make the buildings in some small way serviceable, I would be fully occupied for a while at least. The land at the side and front of the house was substantial and with a lot of hard work should make an ideal vegetable garden. So we had a house and I had work to do.

When we moved in it was three weeks before Christmas and we had not one item of furniture. A trip to the appropriate shops gave us the bare essentials. Other bits and pieces were provided by relatives and friends. It was a very large house and it was to take many years before it even looked as if it had enough furniture to cater for a family. I couldn't help thinking how things had turned full circle. Here I was, living in the house where almost ten years ago I had stayed, trying to learn all there was to know about farming. I had done an awful lot of travelling since then, and seen and done things that now seemed so remote as to be almost like a dream. Except for the fact that I now had a wife who I had brought with me out of that dream.

"Elm House Farm", 68 West street, Worsbrough Bridge had been left to it's own devices for far too many years. It had low brick walls on two sides, a wooden fence that separated it from a railway line on the top end, and the next door neighbours garden taking up the rest. There was a small gate leading into a decent sized front garden that had a low brick wall across the front and down one side opposite the footpath that came from the gate. This stone flagged footpath ran all the way to the back door with a side piece which gave access to the front door. The buildings needed some minor re-pointing work but I wasn't too disappointed at what I had seen, ideas had begun to form in my mind as to it's potential. The first couple of days in the house meant an awful lot of cleaning had to be done, we were helped to do this by my aunt Jane and her sister Ada.

The residence we had taken over was a semi detached, three bedroomed house and was very big. Downstairs was a large oblong shaped kitchen, a door at one end led to an outside small yard from where it was possible to gain access to the farm buildings, the garden and to the road. Another door from this kitchen opened out into the living room come diner, it had a large Yorkshire range standing on a tiled hearth. Exactly opposite the range was a door to a hallway, at one end of which was a solid door that opened out into the yard at the rear of the house. At the other end were about twelve wide stone steps down to a cellar. This was a magnificent place with a fairly high ceiling and solid oak beams to which were attached large brass hooks. The floor was stone flagged and there were about five solid stone tables built on top of it spaced about two yards apart. All the surrounding walls had strong wide shelves fitted, but there were no windows and it meant having to carry a lighted candle or a paraffin lamp when entering or working in the place. The hooks on the beams were obviously used to hang meat. The stone tables were for placing sides of bacon on them in order to cure them before they could be used. I remember the shelves had contained many of Grandma's home made wines and cordials before she had become paralysed and was unable to make them anymore.

There was another door in the living room, it opened out into a spacious hallway, and just inside it was another door, this lead into the most prestigious front room you could ever wish to see. It had a very large bay window which looked out onto the reasonably sized front garden. The ceiling was very high and it made the whole room light and airy. Another striking thing was the highly polished wooden floor, it was stained in a mahogany colour and shone and glistened so much it seemed a shame to walk on it. In the middle of the outside wall was an open fireplace incorporated into an attractive surround with a wide mantelpiece. The hallway was wide and long with an exceptionally large solid looking front door, above which was a skylight so big that in the summer time the entire hall was bathed in sunshine. A staircase led to the upstairs rooms with a beautiful mahogany coloured bannister, it was varnished and glistened and gleamed in the early morning sunlight. The stairs were wide and rather steep. There was one landing on a tight bend, then a few more stairs up to another longer landing, here there were three doors, the first opened into the smallest bedroom, this had a large window looking out onto the rear garden and the farm buildings. It was the smallest but large enough to accommodate a double bed, wardrobes, cupboards and a dressing table. The second room was much larger, it had a window that looked out onto the front garden and had spectacular views of the countryside beyond the field and the canal. There was an open fireplace with a small hearth and mantelpiece. The third room was almost as large as both of the other two put together. The window looked out onto the side garden. An open fireplace adorned one wall and alongside this was another door leading into the bathroom. It contained a gigantic white enamelled bath, a white wash hand basin and a toilet. The two hallways, the cellar, the living room-diner, and the kitchen all had stone slabbed floors. The rest were made of wood. The Yorkshire Range had a back boiler that provided hot water for the kitchen and bathroom, the fire in it was quite easy to light and all it required was a well stocked coal shed. The house seemed huge but neither of us were complaining, It was a house of our own and I could see it's potential for supplementing our income.

Before we realised it Christmas was upon us, and we spent it largely with relatives. We had only been in the house just over two weeks and weren't prepared ourselves. When we moved Anna told me her version of the events that took place at my parents home, during and after, those first three days I was at work. There are two sides to most stories and Anna and I had been married for only a few short weeks when I became very much aware that everything she said was not always the truth. I had been led to believe many things that I was later to find out were incorrect. Some of these things were of paramount importance, not only for myself but for others with whom we were to come into contact with during our life together. In a very short time I realised our life together was not destined to become one of harmony and tranquillity. Not wishing to create the impression that I was entirely blameless for the unfortunate things that were to occur in the years that followed, I think it only fair that I should quote another saying, "It takes two to make an argument".

Having said all that I will return to the time I listened to Anna's version of what happened when we were staying with my family. The actual details were taken by me with the proverbial "pinch of salt", but it was what she came out with at the end of it all that caused me most problems. It was a statement to the effect that if I went to my parent's home and spoke with them, she would cause me untold problems until I agreed that I wouldn't go there again. Now that kind of threat always had the effect upon me to do just the opposite and that is what I fully intended to do, but I hadn't taken into account the determination of my spouse to see to it that I never got the opportunity to go against her wishes. Every time I had to leave the house she made some excuse to accompany me. It was to be a very long time before I went to see them, months in fact, and even then it was without her knowledge. I didn't have the guts to defy her openly, and that was not like me at all. It was many months before my Mother, sister and brother, eventually came to see us, although my Father did pay us a visit occasionally from when we had first moved into the house.

It was wintertime and the weather determined where I could work. The garden was my first priority. It had to be dug over as soon as possible in order to plant the vegetables we would need. Every day when the weather was kind to me I had the spade working overtime. There was a lovely pile of well rotted cow and horse manure in the yard which was incorporated into each row as it was turned over. When the weather wasn't suitable for digging I transferred my energies to the inside of the buildings. The side garden was dug from one end to the other and made ready for planting, the front garden was dug and tidied up ready to take some flower plants, the buildings were cleaned and scrubbed down making them available for what I had in mind.

Very early one Thursday morning I caught a bus from home to Barnsley and then another from there to Penistone where I knew there would be a cattle market in progress. I had been there many times before with Harold. In the ring where the pigs were auctioned I purchased one pig; a sow, due to have her piglets in five weeks. Then onto the miscellaneous ring where I bought two nanny goats, both of them had kids recently and were in full milk. In the same place four belgian hares were knocked down to me; three doe's and one buck, my intention being that they would breed. When I was in the pig department I noticed that an exceptionally large sow had been withdrawn from the sale as it didn't reach it's reserved selling price, apparently it had been unsuccessful in attempts to use it for breeding and the farmers present showed no interest in it at all, I found out where it's owner was, had a chat with him and bought it at a decent price. At the farmers store I arranged for some pig meal, pig potatoes, and cow cake, to be delivered at the same time and in the same transport as the livestock I had bought, I also obtained a lift back home in the same vehicle. There was plenty of straw and sawdust in the dilapidated horse stable. The largest of the cow byres made a nice warm pig sty for the expectant mother when these two commodities had been spread around. The two nannies were put into one of the two smaller byres. Then after I had barrowed some clean dry soil from the garden and spread it all over the floor of the other small byre to a depth of two feet, I deposited the four rabbits inside and was pleased to see them do as I had expected them to do, and that was start to burrow deep into it straight away. I would only see them again at feeding times. The barren Sow was put into the old bull pen which was suitably furnished with sawdust and straw. It took me ages to get the hang of milking the goats, until I realised I was making the mistake of squeezing, as with cows, when instead I should have been pulling. .

It would have been late January when all this took place, I was still receiving full pay from the police force and it was taking care of the immediate financial requirements. I had received a letter from the War Office asking if I had decided to withdraw my resignation and return to Palestine under the same circumstances in which I had left. It was very tempting but I was now entirely committed to what I was doing. I was giving the impression I was happy and settling down, but it was a completely false impression. My mind and thoughts were still in the land Anna and I had so recently vacated. Nothing I was doing here could compare with, or compensate for, those interesting and compelling duties at Central police station in Haifa or those warm days when the air was fresh and clean, a cloudless sky with unlimited visibility, and the balmy nights when we would meet friends for a meal in stupendously beautiful and pleasant surroundings. However, I also remembered the reasons why we had chosen to leave that beautiful land. It was with great sadness that I replied expressing my regrets at not wishing to withdraw my original resignation. I knew I had made the right decision but I also knew that I was going to find it extremely hard to remove from my mind altogether from those years I had spent doing a job I had found to be something I really enjoyed, and one at which I considered myself to have been really good. It was to be a great many years before I eventually did find work that gave me a similar sense of satisfaction.

At the beginning of February I received my discharge papers from the police force and at the same time those from the army. Everyone who had been in the armed forces during the war were given their discharge papers together with cash to enable them to purchase and fit themselves out with a complete set of civilian clothing. This was certainly a good idea and one that was appreciated by all who had received this payment. I had not returned when most were demobbed, having been in the police force, it was more than a year before I came back. I had been on three months paid leave and that leave ended at the beginning of February. So you can imagine my feelings when along with the army papers I received a postal order for the princely sum of seven shillings and sixpence. At that time it could have bought me a really nice Neck Tie! So much for serving your country!

That insult was bad enough but the papers from the police force contained an even greater insult in the form of errors in my information. This included getting my rank wrong, spelling my name incorrectly, getting my branch of service wrong, my date of leaving wrong. There were also comments on these papers, and although it recorded my conduct as being 'good', and stated my general efficiency as "Carried out his duties in a satisfactory manner", under General Remarks it recorded, "Reliable and trustworthy, but lost interest towards the end of his service". A Certificate of Discharge is in fact a reference, every detail upon the certificate should be absolutely correct. I can only assume that the person given the job of compiling this report either did not know me well enough to do so, or were told what to say by someone in authority. Do you remember the remarks I made previously about the way a police officer was treated and regarded by some high ranking officers and the Foreign and Colonial offices,if he chose to marry a person from the local community. Also, if an officer. chose to resign from the force. Well, I had done both of these, so it was only to be expected that I should be given a reference of this calibre. The Superintendent in charge of Shafa Amr told me personally that he held me in high regard, that was until I had chosen not to take the advice of the senior officers he told to get me to change my mind about getting married, then his attitude changed completely.

I had been back home almost four months when my Grandmother died. She had confided in someone that she had only been waiting for my Father and I to return home safely. As I have said many times before, she was a wonderful person. She had been paralysed from a stroke at the age of seventy two and had suffered for ten years, the helplessness she must have felt at having to rely on others to do practically everything for her must have been very upsetting as she had been such an active person and doing so many things apart from just being an excellent wife and Mother. As a boy I had spent many happy hours in her company and my whole life was very much the better for having known her. I remember the day of her funeral

THE PALESTINE POLICE FORCE   Serial No. **552/46.**

CERTIFICATE OF DISCHARGE — BRITISH SECTION

Number **3883**   Rank **Constable.**   Conduct **Good.**

Name (in full) **WOOD,**

Jack Lawrence.

Branch of service **Foot.**

Period of service **30.9.44.** **26 AUG. 1946**
(and leave) 90

Reason for discharge **Resignation.**

General efficiency **Carried out his duties in a satisfactory manner.**

General remarks **Reliable and trustworthy, but lost interest towards the end of his service.**

Jerusalem.
Date **23.8.46.**
INSPECTOR-GENERAL

Certificate of discharge

vividly; it had been snowing heavily for at least two days, the streets were barely passable and the cortege travelled along making a distinct cracking sound as the vehicles tyres crunched over the hard packed snow. She was laid to rest in the family grave with her husband, in the large cemetery in Worsbrough village. A pathway to the graveside had been cleared of snow and everyone present was shivering in the icy cold wind. It was an awful day and one which I shall never forget.

Things were progressing nicely in our animal kingdom, the sow had given birth to ten piglets and surprisingly all ten were doing well. Both goats were giving of their best and producing plenty of milk. When I entered the rabbit shed to deliver their twice daily ration of food, all the scurrying to reach the sanctuary of their underground burrows told me that the four original occupants had been active and we now had considerably more than just those four. The barren sow was eating well, in fact too well, so I put my plans for it into operation. I had spoken to a butcher I knew and we reached an agreement whereby we would both benefit. There had been no records kept of it's existence and one day he came and took it away. The next day he brought a complete half of it back, and paid me the agreed price for the half he had kept for himself. I now manipulated it down into the cellar and onto one of the stone slabs where a special salt was rubbed all over it, and salt peter vigorously rubbed around all the bone parts. Later the rump and shoulder were removed, the excess salt washed off them, a strong piece of string attached to each and then they were hung up on the hooks on the overhead beams to remain there until a rump steak or slice of ham was needed. The side itself was then thoroughly washed to remove the salt and it was then bacon. This kept us supplied with meat for some time.

I didn't have an awful lot of travelling around to do but whenever I did wasting time catching a bus was proving to be a nuisance, so I bought a small van. I had to write to the war office to get my driving licence in order to enable me to drive it, as by this time driving tests had been introduced. At that time there was strict rationing of many things, mostly foods, but petrol was also rationed. I was issued with a book of petrol coupons, I cannot remember exactly for how many gallons but I know it wasn't a lot.

I had almost completed digging the garden despite all the bad weather we had at that time. There had been a chicken run complete with a wire netting fence and a shed at the top of the garden. Both shed and wire were in need of repair but in a very short while they were made suitable to house a few hens. One morning, bright and early, saw me taking a trip in my newly acquired transport to the cattle market, where I successfully bargained for a dozen pullets, "young hens that had not yet started to lay eggs", and one very attractive young cockerill with a large bright red healthy looking comb which stood tall adorning the top of his head.

So far only money had been going out, except for the three months leave payments I had been receiving, which were now ended. Anna had informed me just after Christmas that she was expecting again. I had immediately thought of the last time she told me that and fervently hoped this time would not have the same ending. There appeared to be plenty of work around but I had no idea what type to look for, then I heard that a transport firm required heavy goods lorry drivers. I held a licence for the Bedford three tonners and the Matadors I had been trained on in the army. I didn't think there would be many Matadors used to transport goods but it was more than likely there were three tonners, and the haulage firm turned out to be the one opposite to where I had lived with my parents just outside Barnsley. I went to see the owner and started work that same week. The job entailed loading the lorry with glass bottles in cartons from the manufacturer and delivering them to the customers who could be quite a considerable distance away. It meant having to start fairly early and probably return late at night. The feeding and caring for the animals was arranged so that every night I would prepare the feed for the next day, in this way Anna had no difficulty doing the feeding if I was late home.

I had only been doing this job a few weeks when Anna came up with the idea that it wasn't the kind of work I should be doing. At that time I was open to suggestions because I couldn't decide for myself what would be suitable for me. There was nothing I had done so far in my life outside the police, apart from farming, that could be regarded as a vocation. Anna didn't complain about doing the feeding work but said she thought I should try for something better, so armed with my "discharge certificate" I went to the local Borough Police Station, where I made my intentions known. The Sergeant in charge helped me fill in an application form and when it was completed he said, "I suppose I had better check your discharge papers". He read it, paused for a while and then said, "not much of a recommendation that, is it ?". I couldn't disagree with him on that score. Anyway the forms were sent off, minus certificate, and some days later I received a letter regretting that my application had not been successful. There was no explanation as to why, and I didn't bother to ask. I was told by someone that I shouldn't have applied to the Borough force as they were sure I would have been accepted into the County force, their work was carried out in the rural areas. I didn't apply because I wasn't really interested, the Borough work would have been more like the kind of job I had been used to. So, I carried on driving, thinking that something with better prospects could be just around the corner.

During that first year, 1947, I drove lorries for the firm I first went to. The menagerie was increased by additions to the pig and it's piglets, two more "in pig" sows, a further two "in kid" nanny goats, and one "Tup", the male of the species, he had magnificent horns and his overall appearance was truly frightening. A few more laying hens were introduced to the young pullets and their master. The reason for this being the pullets were slow in reaching the point when they would start to lay, consequently no eggs had been forthcoming. When the ten piglets reached the age of eight weeks they were sent to market and sold at a very good price to someone who intended to grow them on to reach "porker" size.

The two nanny goats were put in with the others in the top shed, the Billy goat "tup", was housed in the barn stable in the stack yard. When I was working in the buildings I would allow him to have a little exercise by opening the door from where he had access to the whole of the stack yard. His idea of exercise was to tear around the yard at a breakneck speed until he obviously became too exhausted to continue, then he would stand near the stack of straw in the open sides of the barn and rip chunks out of it for a while. I would watch him during these "speed trials" and marvelled at the way he would put the brakes on at the last second as the wall loomed up in front of him, both his forelegs stretched out in front and the back one's taking the weight of his rump as they strove to maintain a foothold.

After a few weeks both nanny goats had their kids, two each, and milk puddings became the order of the day at meal times in order to make good use of their produce. About this time the sow, who's offspring had gone to market, required the attentions of a boar. A man at the top end of the village had one, and so it was with some trepidation that I fastened a stout piece of rope around the shoulders of the sow and holding one end of this rope, we; the pig and I, set off to make the journey to the boar. Most of the route would be taken by using the pedestrian footpaths, and as the shops were situated at the side of these footpaths, a great deal of interest was shown by the proprietors and their customers at the sight of the pig and I making our way up the hill. Now pigs are not like dogs and horses, they do not take kindly to being tethered and manoeuvred along, their sense of direction is such that they can go any way at any time, and change direction very suddenly indeed. This particular one had the edge over me as it was very much heavier than me, and any attempt I made to hold it back was a lost cause even before it began. It's large head would swing from side to side giving me no idea of what it might do next. After many attempts to run into the middle of the road, or trespass into someone's garden, I got the hang of it. If I kept as close to it's head as possible any signs of an intended change of direction could be detected and curtailed before it gained momentum by simply pulling on the rope and digging both my knees into it's midriff. Not a dignified method by any means, but it worked.

Anna was now in the later stages of her pregnancy, it had been her decision not to go into hospital this time. For the past few weeks she was attended by the local midwife, an exceptionally pleasant woman. She used to enter the house her face wreathed in smiles accompanied by some cryptic comment about something or other. It was obvious that Anna looked forward to her visits and they appeared to get on very well together. My presence at these sessions was not welcomed but I gathered that all was going well and no problems were envisaged. The unhappy outcome1 to Anna's pregnancy in Haifa was very much in both our minds and it must have been an especially trying time for Anna. As the day drew near the midwife gave me explicit instructions as to what would be expected of me. I must have plenty

191

of hot water to hand and take it up to the bedroom when it was requested. Various articles of clothing and clean white linen were placed on a chair in the front room ready for me to take up when they were called for. I was lorry driving at the time and knowing I would have to take some time off I informed my boss of the situation. I only had one problem and that was to hope I was not away on some journey when the time arrived. Well, as luck would have it, I was at home when Anna told me to call the midwife. She duly arrived and got on with the job in hand. It was late one afternoon and I soon had things under control, two kettles boiling on the stove, a large clean enamel bowl on the table, and a good supply of Players cigarettes and matches at my elbow. I was ready, and hoping everyone else concerned were also!

Now I hadn't been present at the hospital in Haifa but had been told of the large amount of screaming, shouting, and yelling from Anna. So I, seated in a comfortable armchair, waited for the commotion to begin. I didn't have to wait long. The screams, the shouts, the yells, all combined to make me think that people walking past in the street would surely hear everything that was going on. Also at that time I began to think that what the midwife had said about everything going well was proving not to be the case, there was so much noise and screams of anguish that surely something must be wrong. It seemed to go on for an eternity, but gradually the hubbub subsided, only a faint cry was heard, and that was Michael arriving on the scene. It was the 9th of July 1947.

It was sometime later when the midwife came downstairs to inform me that I had a son, and invited me to go with her to the bedroom to take a peek at the end product of all the preceding commotion. Anna was sitting up in bed holding him and she looked remarkably composed. The midwife accompanied me downstairs and I asked her if all was well. She said everything was fine. She went on to say that some of her patients did tend to scream and shout a lot, but that Anna had surprised even her with the volume she had produced and at the length of time it had gone on for. However, "all's well that ends well".

Michael was soon to let us know he had a sound pair of lungs, and put them to good use, usually at night when we were trying to sleep. I paced the bedroom floor with him for hours on end and he got so bad that the doctor thought there must be something wrong with him and made arrangements for him to go into the local hospital for an examination. We visited him every day in the mornings, afternoons, and evenings and it was on the morning of the fifth day when we were told to take him home as all the tests had shown there was nothing wrong with him. The conclusion the doctors had reached was that he was simply a very miserable baby and a very noisy one at that.

Things eventually returned to something like normality but Anna was still expressing her wish for something better. It was then I decided to apply for permission to emigrate to Australia. At that time people were being invited to do this by the Australian authorities. A large amount of paperwork was consulted and filled in, and two visits to Australia House in London were made for interviews. It all took time but then we were told our application had been successful and to return there for the third time to sign the necessary papers. There were quite a lot of people in the room where we were waiting to be called in to finalise everything. There were one or two amongst them who had recently returned from that country. Why they were there I had no idea but we had been waiting for quite a long time when I noticed Anna having a conversation with a woman, who it turned out, had just returned. At the cessation of this conversation Anna informed me that we wouldn't be emigrating, at least not to Australia.

This woman she had been talking to had told her that no matter where you went in the country there were always very strong winds and that was why she and her family had returned. Now, Anna had a thing about strong winds, she really hated them, so it put paid to our becoming Aussie's, not that it worried me unduly, except for all the time we had wasted.

As I was now lorry driving and somewhat free from the "ties that bound me", I was able to make frequent visits to my parents. I could do this in the knowledge that "what the eye doesn't see, the heart doesn't grieve for". When I was with them I refrained from burdening them with my problems, even though it must have been obvious to all of them at a very early stage that problems were almost certain to arise. The saying "a trouble shared, is a trouble halved", would not have applied in my case, it would have caused then unnecessary distress, especially as they would know they couldn't do anything to help.

At this time I was very much on the lookout for anything that could be incorporated into the things I was doing at present. I heard of a sale where a number of greenhouses were to be auctioned so I went along to take a look. There were three of them, one 24' by 16', another 20' by 16', and another 18' by 12'. The framework of each one was made of solid timber and bolted together. Each one contained a fireplace and iron pipes running all around the inside of them. The auctioneer announced that the purchaser would have to dismantle the houses but the vendor would deliver them for a reasonable charge. There were not many bidders, as it involved a considerable amount of work, so I obtained all of them, and four strong cold frames at a very reasonable price. It took the vendor, a friend of his and I, the best part of a day to have everything down and laid out ready to load onto a truck. It was November 1947, I had gone through all the nice warm days of that summer wanting some greenhouses, I had now got them and it was now almost the middle of winter. The frosts were hard and developed practically every night with much of it remaining throughout the day. These types of greenhouse had to be erected upon a solid foundation, and this was to be built of bricks and mortar. This was going to make things difficult as the winter of '47 was to be the worst on record. I made a start on the largest greenhouse. The first job was to dig out the foundations, it wasn't easy as the ground was hard and very stony, but they were completed in about a week, using the hours I was away from the lorry driving. Some old bricks were used on top of the foundations to form a wall about two feet in height upon which the wooden frames of the greenhouses would be placed. The frosts were heavy and prolonged so in order to give all the concrete and mortar some kind of protection I erected three tarpaulin sheets across the area in which I would be working. It was a large area to cover completely and because of this there was very little room in which to work. At the highest point it would only have been about three feet high, therefore the brick laying had to be carried out on my knees and with the ground being so hard my poor old knees were to suffer. The digging and concreting took weeks as I could only work when not driving my lorry. It was usually dark during the hours I could work and working under the sheets with two "Tilley lamps" for illumination was not ideal. The standard of brick laying would not have passed any inspection, but at least the top was level. After much hard work, frustrated by some heavy snow, and interrupted by an all too short Christmas break, I had got the brickwork for the large greenhouse completed. I decided to concentrate on finishing that one first.

I got down to the job of putting the fireplace into the finished base and attaching the cast iron pipe to the back of it. This pipe was then laid along the ground inside the base, at the bottom of the brick wall, the sections and bends of it were attached and it was placed all around the wall until the end came out at another gap that had been left at the other side of the door, another bend and a length of pipe was attached to this end making it stick up in the air about four feet. From now on a shovel full of coal put onto the fire every now and again would ensure there were no more cold hands and feet. Next I replaced a few broken panes of glass and then assembled the greenhouse. The sides were in sections of six feet wide and three feet high, using long timbers to hold two sections steady while I fastened the bolts, proved to be rather difficult , but eventually the sides and ends were all in position and securely bolted. After all the time and trouble that had caused me I was pleasantly surprised at the comparative ease with which I was able to fit the roof sections. When it was all completed, I stood well back and admired my handiwork. It was a sight for sore eyes, this massive piece of timber and glass, standing out in the confines of that scruffy stack yard.

It was now time to work on the inside, more two feet high brick walls had to be built to separate the plant beds from the walkway down the middle. Then I hammered about a dozen pieces of two inch piping into the floor of the beds, spacing them out to ensure good drainage, and then filled the three beds with a mixture of good soil and well rotted cow manure. Something temporary was required upon which to prepare and stand some seed boxes, so a timber bench was concocted and laid across the top of one of the side beds. I obtained about twenty empty tomato boxes from a greengrocers which were ideal for use as seed trays. A mixture of fine soil and manure was put into two of them, both were popped into a metal tray containing about two inches of water and not removed until they had soaked up enough of this water to wet all the soil and manure that was in them, then in one, tomato seeds were placed, in the other, a sprinkling of lettuce seeds. Both were left on the makeshift bench to commence the growing process for my first crop in the fabulous greenhouse. The fire had to be kept burning from now on, it couldn't be allowed to go out at any time.

Getting the largest of the greenhouses in full operation had taken a lot out of me, both physically and in terms of enthusiasm. It was to take many months before the second largest greenhouse was completed, and the smallest one never did get done. The cold frames were eventually put together and positioned down one side of both houses. It looked good when it was all finished and those greenhouses and cold frames were in operation all the years we were to live at the smallholding. Every year at the appropriate time, they were to produce, tomatoes, grapes, cucumbers, aubergines, red and green peppers, sugar melons, and many thousands of plants from seed. I have made many investments, some of which have been profitable, others have not, but I regard the purchase of those greenhouses to have been one of the best, if not the best. The things they produced were helpful in so many ways as they gave me all the plants I required to put in the garden; flowers of all descriptions, vegetables like cauliflower, cabbage, lettuce, sprouts, broccoli. Over the years the product of the greenhouses and garden supplied not only my family but also large numbers of people who liked to buy my fresh produce.

Anna regarded the time I spent in the garden as unneccessary and harmful for me, partly encouraged by the local gossips. These particular women lived close by and almost as soon as we had moved in were frequent visitors to our home. They grasped eagerly at anything that could be used to undermine my credibility in the community, although here I must say they didn't have to probe as Anna was only too pleased to have someone to whom she could pour out her tales of woe. Not that I allowed this dubious state of affairs to worry me unduly,

I had long since been made aware of Anna's aptitude for causing trouble. These tales were not always about me, others came under the hammer as well. I did spend the greater part of my waking hours out in the buildings or garden when not at work as there were things that required doing in order to keep everything running. In doing so I obtained a feeling of great contentment.

Our Son, Michael, was growing nicely, his habit of continually crying had gradually petered out and Anna had told me she was expecting another baby. The day arrived, again I was at home. Everything was exactly the same as when Michael was born. Michael was with me in the dining room in his cot, and as it was very late in the evening he was fast asleep. My pack of Players' cigarettes dwindled as I waited for the screaming subside and when it did, as before, a faint cry was heard and this was Phillip. It was the 9th of August, 1948. He was to have the usual problems all baby boys seem to have, namely excessive bouts of "wind" which obviously made him cry, but there were very few times when it became necessary to pace the bedroom floor with him, much to the relief of all concerned. The memories of those nights with Michael were still very fresh in our minds.

Shortly after he was born the time taken up with the lorry driving became a bit of a bind as it wasn't allowing me sufficient hours at either end of the day to do all the jobs at home. The weather at that time was very nice so I reluctantly gave up the driving and decided to use the van I had for selling ice cream. It was thoroughly cleaned and given a face lift, the decorative attractive paintwork on the outside was renewed, it's wheels, and tyres, painted white, and it's chimes given a complete overhaul. The chap from whom I had bought the van was an ice cream manufacturer, and arrangements were made for him to supply me with a particular kind of ice cream. I didn't fancy delving into a tub, making cornets and sandwiches, and buying all the equipment needed to go with it. He loaned me one freezer, it was simply a large, oblong, white enamelled, insulated, metal box, with a lid, and several partitions inside it. For it to function as a freezer packets of "dry ice" were placed inside it. One particular kind of ice cream I bought was plain and came in paper packs, in which there were forty eight individually wrapped oblong blocks. They sold for two old pennies each, and when asked for one by a customer all that had to be done was take one of the oblong blocks out of the box and hand it over. I also carried larger brickettes, at four pennies each, chocolate coated blocks, tubs, and Snowfrute's. These Snowfrutes were similar to lollipops and were sold in a cellophane wrapper. I wore a "Rinso white" smock, it had two large pockets which were used in place of a cash till (Rinso being the washing powder of the time). The job was interesting and on a good day a reasonable profit could be assured. My brother Peter liked to accompany me whenever he was off school, we had some really good happy journeys together. There were the odd ocassions when my sister Jacqueline or my Mother had the experience of ice cream selling for an hour or two, they enjoyed it and were good company for me. I used to fit in the work at home with the times I needed to be out on the road, and it worked very well for a while.

Somewhere around the beginning of October sales began to drop, they were bound to drop further as the weather deteriorated, and as it was necessary to have a decent turnover in order to make a reasonable profit, I returned the freezer and looked around for something else of a similar nature. I had become quite used to being able to have plenty of time to look after the menagerie and garden work and still do a job that brought in enough money to take care of things. When I worked on the farm I delivered milk to a bakery in the village, the owner used to talk about the days when he went round the streets near the bakery selling bread and cakes from a four wheeled box barrow. He always maintained that there was a good business to be had for anyone willing to do the same on a larger scale. I paid him a visit and he said he would be pleased to provide me with the appropriate goods at a competitive price, and help in any way he could.

The set-up appealed to me so I made some shelves and runners for inside the van so that the trays of buns, bread, teacakes, and cakes could be positioned around the sides. I started on a very small scale as I knew a round would have to be established before things could start to move. I concentrated upon the outlying districts, and tried to be in the same vicinity about the same time every day. People soon got used to this and began to expect me, and I started to do quite well. At that time eggs were on ration, so selling one or two to the good customers helped with the sale of the other items. After Christmas, when everything sold like "hot cakes", things were quieter, and the weather was causing problems. There were days when it was impossible to do the round because of the deep snow. The van was only light and the tyres found it difficult to get a grip with very little weight to hold them down. More and more days were missed and not only was I letting the customers down, I wasn't selling enough to make a decent profit. The baker and I had a chat, he realised the difficulties I was facing, and agreed that we should leave things for a while, at least until the bad weather subsided. The van was parked in the yard in front of the buildings and I answered a newspaper advert for an early morning Milk roundsman, had an interview, and started that same week.

So I became a Milkman for the second time, but this time it was already in bottles. The transport was an open sided van with a roof and flat body. Other things apart from milk were also delivered, like cream, butter, eggs, and potatoes. I had chosen a bad time of the year for this job, as early mornings could be cold. There were two of us to do the round, it was quite a large one, mostly out in the country. There were a lot of villages, and quite long distances between them. My day commenced usually around four in the morning, the animals and birds were fed, two goats milked, both fires in the greenhouses were raked and banked up, a wash and a hastily taken breakfast were all completed before driving to the dairy just after five. My partner was usually there. It hadn't taken me long to get into the routine of checking over the milk float then reversing it into a loading bay where there would be crates of milk waiting on the landing ready to be loaded onto the truck. The platform of the truck on the driver's side was mine, the other, my partners. We each had our own complement of customers and our own individual delivery and account books. We would put on our sides the amount of milk and other goods we personally required for that day, in the event of more milk being needed, two crates, one containing pints, the other half pints, would be added to the load. When the loading had been completed it was checked by an inspector to see that it had the correct amount on board for each of our two designated rounds, we would then both sign his check sheet.

There were two colliery canteens on the round, delivering to them was a doddle; two, sometimes three, crates with twenty four bottles in each, were carried into the kitchen, and the empties put back on the truck. At one of these the woman in charge would invite us to sit down and bring over two large mugs of tea and four warm buttered tea cakes which had just been baked on the premises! On cold mornings it not only gave us a much needed rest, we got thoroughly warmed through as well. It was a steady job, reasonably well paid, and suited me with the early afternoon finishes, except Fridays, these were cash collection days. My partner and I seemed to get on well together but I did find him to be rather erratic at times. We soon got into a routine doing the round, which suited us both. When we were working a row of houses in some village we would split the deliveries, he starting from one end while I did the other. On Friday afternoons and evenings doing the collections it did happen occasionally that where one of us had collected from his customers in one of the rows, there would probably have been one of them out and consequently unable to pay. If the other one of us had still not completed that particular row, and in the meantime the customer had returned, it wasn't unusual for that customer to pay him and not their regular man.

We worked seven days every week and on six of those I was usually home around one-o-clock in the afternoon giving me plenty of time to do the things in the garden. I was happy but then one Monday afternoon, as we were preparing to go home, I was called into the Inspector's office. He asked me if I knew of any reason why the cost of my outgoings did not tally with the cash brought in. He was very polite and stressed that he was not at this stage accusing me of anything. That didn't stop my blood from rising, my honesty was being questioned, and with great difficulty I controlled my temper. Apparently this situation had been going on for the past few weeks and nothing had been said in the hope that it would sort itself out. I spent the whole of that evening going through my book looking for any discepencies but there were none. On the Tuesday afternoon we were both called into the managers office, I had the honour of going in to see him first, where I found him to be full of apologies for what had taken place the previous day. He explained that the office staff had found that all the cash my partner was collecting from my customers was not being paid in. The next day I had a new partner, pity really, because he had been very pleasant to work with. "Ah Well", such is life.

I took on the milk job when the weather was anything but pleasant for working out of doors but ideal for doing the work necessary in the greenhouses. By the time the days began to get a bit warmer it was all completed and ready for planting. I did make time in the afternoons and evenings for Anna and I to take the two boys out, we usually paid my relatives a visit, nothing exciting but it was nice to see them all occasionally. It was at these times I couldn't help remembering the evenings we had spent calling upon our friends, the pleasant walks along the brightly lit streets, and the scents from the flowering trees lining the footpaths and in the adjoining gardens. The clean atmosphere and fresh healthy air. Compared to the dingy, lifeless houses and the dull, very badly lit streets and the grey polluted skies it seemed like an image of perfection. I worked on the milk deliveries for a few more months, the job had suited me in many ways but I wasn't pleased that they believed me to be capable of dishonesty. It was this that had me looking for something else, that would give me a similar kind of freedom so I settled for a job on nights in one of the wholesale newsagents' warehouses.

The shift began at ten-o-clock doing things like, sorting out yesterdays unsold newspapers and tying them in bundles, preparing magazines ready for next day's deliveries, and various other jobs until about four in the morning when we (two or three others doing the same job, and myself) would go with a small enclosed truck to one of the two local railway stations and collect that day's newspapers, then take these back to the warehouse and sort them out into specific bundles ready for delivery to newspaper shops. At six o'clock I went home and did what was necessary, the feeding and milking etc, and then had a few hours sleep before doing things in the buildings and greenhouses. This night job gave me all the daylight hours I needed and I found time to go to the cattle markets again. It was great to have the freedom and the time to do all this.

A few months earlier I had been informed that Anna was pregnant again. I did wonder at what time of the day or night the event was likely to take place but she must have arranged things so that I would be at home when required, consequently she was to disturb my usual few hours sleep one morning, almost as soon as my head hit the pillow, by telling me she 'thought it was time for the midwife to put in an appearance. She was notified and arrived about nine thirty carrying her necessary bag of tricks and wearing her usual broad smile. I had already got my job underway, the kettles were boiling, the enamel bowl was in it's position on the table, and all the other things that would be needed were residing on an armchair in the front room. Michael and Phillip were ensconced in their double pram. With it being mid morning I couldn't expect either of them to sleep, so in between checking the kettles I did my best to keep them both amused. As it happened they were as good as gold, much to my relief. There was the now customary outpouring of screaming and shouting, but this time with a difference. After about an hour I heard heavy footsteps on the stairs and loud argumentative voices. I went into the hallway and saw, much to my annoyance, two women clumping down the stairs; one was the woman from across the garden, the village gossip, the other, her Mother. Before they arrived at the bottom of the stairs both of them started to berate me, saying "you are a pig, you should be thoroughly ashamed of yourself for putting your wife through all this every thirteen months, you should be put away and then she would get some rest from you". For a few moments I was so startled by their unexpected appearance I just stood there, then the real me took charge. I opened the front door wide and unceremoniously bundled the pair of them outside. Maybe I did make a polite request for them to leave, amidst all the mayhem I might have done, but I cannot be sure. However, I saw them off the premises and closed the front garden gate behind them.

The problem solved I returned to Michael and Phillip, surprisingly they were sitting comfortably in the pram, obviously unconcerned at what had been going on. The disturbing noises from upstairs continued for quite some time, but eventually ceased abruptly, and peace descended upon the house once more, the sole reason for all that noise had finally arrived, another boy, Robert. It was the 7th of August 1949.

From then on Anna was to have her work cut out caring for the boys, Michael was two years and two months old, Phillip one year and one month old, and Robert just starting out. It was hard work for her, very hard, I knew this and helped where and when I could. Seeing the way Anna had to work with the boys and in the house in general, I began to feel that maybe the two busybodys did have a point in some of the things they had said. However, I did fail to see how anyone could arrive at the conclusion that I was solely responsible for the way things had turned out! All this work resting upon Anna's shoulders did put a great strain on our relationship, it was bound to.

The month of August was a very busy time in the garden as there were jobs that had to be done. If they weren't done at that specific time the plants could have serious problems growing in the manner in which they should. Dividing my time between the house and the garden did cause me many headaches, I needed to pull my weight in the house but I saw no sense in allowing things to go to waste, losing things I had worked hard for during the year, after all we would need these things in the very near future. Fruits and vegetables played a very big part in the food we consumed, and were of great importance, being necessary to keep our larder well stocked. I couldn't afford to neglect either the greenhouses or the garden, and I didn't. Therefore there would have been many occasions when I should have been helping in the home instead of working outside.

One morning when we were waiting on the station platform for the newspaper train to arrive I was talking to a member of the station staff and he happened to mention that someone was required to work in the shunting depot adjoining the station, and that it was a well paid job. The wage I was receiving from the paper job was not very good so I made further enquiries, had an interview, and started working as a Shunter in the Court House station goods yard, on regular nights. I started at ten and finished at six, just the same as with the newspaper job. I had worked on the papers for about five months.

The goods yard was a massive place, containing numerous lines of railway track running parallel to each other, these lines were fixed on wooden sleepers which protruded at either side of the track and were to cause me untold problems until I got used to knowing that they made perfect stumbling blocks for the unwary. The fact that it was night time didn't help matters. Carrying a railwayman's lamp had it's drawbacks, only having one hand free to do all the work required was awkward and hazardous at times. There was only one man working in the yard apart from myself, he was in charge and responsible for everything that went on there, he had worked in that same yard for such a long time he was almost part of the yard's fixtures and fittings. At first it wasn't easy for me to take in all that was to be done in this wide open space, with it's railway lines criss crossing at varying intervals, but his knowledge and expertise soon had me wielding the shunter's most important tool as if I had been doing the job for years. The tool was simply a long pole with a type of hook on the end. It's main use was for unhooking one chain that connected two wagons allowing them to separate. The only difficult part to this operation was that it was usually done when the wagons were moving; one slip on the pole handler's part could result in him falling under the large, heavy, cast iron wheels of the wagon. We had the services of a shunting engine, a smaller version of the main line engines. There was also a manned signal box at the junction of the yard and the main line. The services of the man and his box were only required when wagons were either being brought into the yard from the main line or moving from the yard into the main line. Very rarely were any wagons brought into the yard during the hours we were working.

Our role, essentially, was to arrange all the trucks and goods wagons in the yard into their respective sidings for collection by the engines that would pull them to their intended destinations. Once arranged all the wagons on each of the tracks had to be coupled together by putting their chains onto an opposite hook. They were long nights, and I must confess I disliked the job intensely. Still, not bad pay, and it gave me time to do all the other jobs around home. I had been meaning to sort out the stack yard ever since I had finished working on the greenhouses, now I had the time and enough daylight in which to do something about it. There was practically no soil at all, it was made up of what seemed to be burned coke and ashes interspersed with large stones, bits of glass, and other rubbish. After a great deal of work clearing the surface and then utilising a pick axe it was done and I purchased some fruit bushes which I planted up which gave bountiful supplies of raspberries, redcurrant, blackcurrant, blackberries and gooseberries. At the same time the menagerie had to be taken care of and the greenhouses were full of trays of plants that had to be pricked out into separate trays before they grew too big. There were never enough hours in the day to do everything, but having said that, I enjoyed every minute of it.

Unfortunately all the time I had at home being able to fit in so much work in daylight wasn't reason enough for me to endure any more nights in the shunting yard, so I took another driving job with better pay and conditions. I was to find it very awkward not having so much time for the jobs at home as I started early in the mornings and was away until late in the evenings but I always had Saturday afternoons and all day Sunday off, and this helped me to get most things done. They were hectic weekends rushing around doing the work that couldn't wait another seven days before being seen to. The menagerie's meal times were altered again, the goats were milked earlier in the mornings and later in the evenings. The pigs, goats, and chicks, had lighting, and the rabbits could eat at anytime, but the hens stayed on their perches when it was dark so Anna gave them their mash and corn at their usual times.

The driving job had it's drawbacks and after doing it for about five months I decided to give it up, purchased a pair of wooden ladders, a bucket, and using my dilapidated push bike, I made my way to the largest Council house estate about three miles from home, and trying to look very efficient, asked the occupiers if they would engage me as their permanent "window cleaner". I had been told this particular estate was in need of such a person and that once a round had been established it could prove to be a lucrative form of employment. Some of the answers I got were pleasant, others not so pleasant, but by the end of that day I had cleaned enough windows to convince me that the job had great potential. It took no more than three weeks of door knocking in a number of streets, to obtain a round of sufficient proportions to give me a very reasonable return for my labours.

There were times when I was unable to put in a good days work when it was raining. I made no attempt to do the job when this happened as I regarded it to be a complete waste of money for the customers. One morning I had done well and then it rained and looked as if it was going to do so for the rest of the day, so I went home. As I entered through the kitchen I heard loud voices coming from the dining room. I investigated, and to my extreme annoyance I saw Anna seated at the table, and sitting opposite her were the mother and daughter from across the way. I "invited" them to leave at once, saying they were not welcome in my home and was immediately subjected to a tirade of abuse from Anna, informing me that it was her house and she would invite who she pleased. She was well aware of how much I loathed these two women but my feelings never seemed to matter.

Somewhere around this time I got in touch with Peter, my policeman pal. He had returned home in 1948 after the handover of the country to the Jews. I wanted to see him so we; Anna, the three boys and myself, went to his parent's home in Penge, south London, where he was staying. We were made very welcome and stayed a couple of days. When we were alone he told me of some of the things that had taken place after I had left, one of our closest friends, a constable, was caught in a bomb explosion and lost an arm, others he mentioned were even less fortunate. He appeared to have settled down and was getting on with his life doing a collar and tie job in the city, but seeing him brought back memories of what used to be.

After we had returned home Anna persisted in making comments upon the much cleaner aspect of the area where we had just been, and I had to agree with her. It was much nicer all round and it had made her even more dissatisfied with her lot in Worsbrough Bridge. In an effort to do something about it I bought newspapers containing advertisements dealing with houses for sale. After looking through dozens of such papers I eventually found one in Colchester in Essex. I knew it was a nice clean place in most parts and arrangements were made for us to go and see it. The house was gorgeous, with wonderful amenities. The gardens front and rear were immaculate, slightly smaller than I had now, but with two reasonable sized greenhouses, a work shed, innumerable fruit trees, with flower, and vegetable patches. It was situated in an area that was bright and pleasing to the eye, and the front garden overlooked a wide tree lined street. The price was right, £395, which we could easily afford, and I thought it would be just what we were looking for until Anna pointed out how difficult it would be for her negotiating the approach to the house with the double pram. There were at least twenty stone steps weaving their way between the flowers and plants on either side, and going upwards all the time at a very steep angle leading up from the street to reach either the front or back doors. It was with deep regret we were forced to turn the offer down as it would not have been suitable for us under the circumstances. We were both disappointed.

When I went on the window cleaning job it was good, but because I was my own boss, and could take time off whenever I pleased, I seemed to allow too many things to interfere with my work. I had built up a really good round and enjoyed doing it but the temptation to have time off was too great and consequently resulted in there being an inadequate amount of cash return at the end of the week so reluctantly gave it up.

I had already been offered work in an iron foundry and arranged to start work as a labourer the following week. It was a five and a half day week, starting at seven thirty a.m., and finishing at four thirty p.m., giving me plenty of time in the mornings and evenings to do what I had to do at home. It soon became clear to me that I would not be working there very long, the smell from the "Cores", (sand that was moulded into shapes, around which the melted iron was poured to produce a casting of that particular shape), was very objectionable and it penetrated everywhere, it got into your throat, your eyes and hair, but the worst thing was how it enveloped your clothing.

I am not sure how long I worked at the foundry but I know it wasn't more than a few months. There was one very dubious practice performed almost daily. When the "cores" were ready to have hot metal poured around them the pouring was usually done by two men holding the handles of the ladle containing the hot molten metal, they would go round pouring the required amount into each core and when the ladle was nearly empty they would return to the kiln for more. It was impossible to judge the correct amount needed for the last few cores, and when the last had been done there was always some still left in the ladle and it had to be got rid of. The first day I was there I noticed what they did, they used a small spade and dug a "V" shaped trench in the sand about six feet in length, and about one foot deep, and then proceeded to empty the hot metal into it. I couldn't believe my eyes, they kicked loose sand all over it until the red hot metal, in it's liquid state, could no longer be seen. There were no footpaths as such, everything was done by walking across the floor. The cores were made in holes dug into it, and when the castings had been completed they were removed from these holes, so not only was it the means of going about inside the foundry it was also the main "work bench". On my first day I was told to be careful not to stand on this trench as it could possibly result in my losing a foot, and that I wouldn't be the first person to do so. It was all regarded as being one big joke, but I failed to see anything funny about it at all. How was anyone to know exactly where the trench had been made?

Suffice to say that I was not enthralled with the place and soon took myself off to fresh fields. Since returning to England I had not dallied long in any form of employment, but this next port of call for my services must surely be the shortest term of all. In most cases it hadn't been the fault of the actual employment, the blame could be firmly placed at my door, and I accept that. The trouble was that I had not yet been able to come to terms with the sudden dramatic change in my circumstances. and at this time I was not to know that I never would; my time in Palestine has always had precedence over everything.

The job in question was making "hot water bottles". On the first day I clocked in and was put in the capable hands of a young chap who proceeded to show me what to do. There were a lot of benches spread around a room at which people were intently working. He took me to one such bench upon which was a type of press and two piles of coloured and shaped thick rubber, he took one piece from each pile and placed them together, they formed the shape of a hot water bottle, one pile being the top half the other the bottom. He positioned them so that they formed a perfect shape, put them onto the press, and pulled down on the lever. This put heated pressure onto the outside edges of both pieces of rubber and in so doing sealed them together. It was then a bottle, and was placed on a table at the side of the press ready to be taken away by someone to be finished.

So this picking up of two pieces of rubber, placing them on the press, and pulling down on that lever was to be my job each working day. As those two pieces of rubber were sealed together a cloud of choking, horrible smelling steam rose up and enveloped the press, the chap, and me. It is quite possible that I paired, placed, and pulled some twenty times before reaching the conclusion that enough was enough. I switched off the press and went in search of the foreman who directed me to the manager's office where a very amicable conversation took place. I, pointing out that the smell was making me feel sick, he, stating that it did have that effect on some people and although some had tried to stick it out, in the hope that they would eventually get used to it, they never did and had to leave. I appreciated his honesty, and with a firm handshake and mutual feeling of regret, we parted company. I picked up my coat, said cheerio to my puzzled looking instructor, and walked out of the factory door, unemployed. Approximately one hour after clocking in.

There were a number of things I had been unable to do around home because of my daily commitments, but being temporarily unemployed allowed me to sort them out. A larger hen run was needed owing to the increase in the number of chicks reaching the pullet stage, making that and another smaller hen house took a couple of days. Two litters of piglets, one of ten and another of nine, had reached the time for them to move on. I made arrangements for them to be picked up by cattle truck and delivered to Doncaster cattle market, along with two young nanny goats and two young billy goats. They all sold for a good price and although I never intended to buy anything that day, two Berkshire Black pigs caught my eye. They were about twelve weeks old, short and stocky and as they were both sows I bought them with the intention of using them for breeding. I never did, but that is beside the point. They were a change of colour to the other pigs we had and sometime later were to be sold at a large profit upon my initial investment.

Two of the milking nannies were in full milk and another was coming towards the end of her lactation period and already "in kid", that would mean quite possibly another two kids arriving on the scene, and as we already had four young nannies coming along nicely the expected new arrivals would be on their way to market shortly after they had been weaned off the milk. So I was pleased to have sent the four to market with the pigs as we were becoming rather over crowded. Every shed in all the buildings was given a face lift, all except the rabbit warren, that could not be disturbed. The floors were cleaned out right down to the concrete floors and new bedding distributed.

The garden was worked on and brought up to scratch, my being away five and a half days in the previous weeks had encouraged the weeds to take advantage of the situation. The greenhouses were always needing some kind of attention and it was nice to have a few hours of uninterrupted work doing the jobs I couldn't start on before, knowing that I wouldn't have to break off to go to bed or get ready to go to work.

Working as I had been doing for the six or seven days after my self induced unemployment, had given me plenty of time to think, and consider what kind of job I should take up next. At that time, shortly after the war, there was no shortage of varying types of work, industry was in full swing and most firms appeared to have plenty of orders on their books. Even though I was spoilt for choice, some types of employment were out of the question as I just didn't have the necessary qualifications. I suppose now, I should have given the matter more careful consideration and trained, or studied to give myself the chance of a long term permanent job. Unfortunately at that time, I was more concerned with the rapid deterioration of things on the domestic front. I took what may only be considered as the easy way out. I decided not to start any kind of employment which would include bringing some sort of work home with me.

There are times in life when the unexpected occurs, some of course are not welcome, others are good. One of the latter was delivered to me on a plate, so to speak. When the garden supply of potatoes began to get low it was necessary to buy in some pig potatoes, leaving ours for domestic use, and every two weeks a potato merchant would deliver half a ton. One morning I was doing some sort of job around the yard and as usual giving the matter of where, and when, I should take positive steps to secure paid employment some thought, when the potato truck drove into the yard. The merchant had two sons and it was the younger of the two that was delivering that day. The potatoes were unloaded and during the general conversation that followed he casually mentioned that his Father required a new driver for a six ton truck which was used for collecting potatoes from farmers in various parts of the country. It appeared to be the answer to my dilemma, I went to see his Father, and started the next day. I was to find it to be a nice steady job, and having to start usually around seven a.m., and finishing about seven in the evenings, made it possible to fit in the necessary work at home without putting too much strain on me or the animal's feeding times.

Somewhere around this time, I cannot remember exactly when, the house was turned upside down for a few days with workmen installing electricity. Gone were the unsightly gas lamps, no further need to carry a lighted candle about when going upstairs, or purchase any more of those flimsy gas mantles. Now we could buy some electrical gadgets, priority being given to a washing machine, this being a great asset to Anna with the mounds of washing she had to do every day. Other electrical goods were to follow but the next thing to be obtained was a radio. We did have one, but it was powered by an accumulator.

When the days began to shorten it made things awkward for me to do any jobs at home apart from the feeding and cleaning. It was necessary for me to have more hours of daylight for the work required on the garden and greenhouses, so the potato job was relinquished. I had been there about seven months and would have stayed for much longer had it not been for my other commitments. This time though I found another job before I left. I had heard so many stories of how much money men were taking home from this job that I decided to have a go and follow in the footsteps of my Grandfather, my uncles, and my Father. The sole reason I was lured was the promise of a hefty pay packet, and even now I think I must have been quite mad to even consider what I was about to let myself in for. I underwent four weeks of rigorous underground training, after which I became a "Coal Miner".

Chapter 11

My first introduction to actually working underground was doing the lowest paid job in the mine, a "Trammer". This meant pushing "Tubs" on lines throughout parts of the underground workings of the mine.

These tubs were the means by which most of the equipment required by the men working at the coal face was transported. They were either made of steel or strong timber, and were extremely heavy even when they were empty. They had strong iron wheels, the same design as the engines', carriages', and wagons', on a normal railway line, and the lines (track) upon which they ran were similar, but of a much smaller gauge. If, as did happen occasionally, the wheels came off the track, it was one almighty struggle to put them back on again.

To describe everything that went on in a coal mine (Pit) is a job for an expert. I know very little about anything that didn't actually concern me at the time, therefore I shall endeavour to give you an insight into those things that did, and hopefully depict them in such a manner as to enable you to understand why, and how, I did them.

I feel it necessary at this stage to explain how it was possible to get underground in the first place. The surface of the pit top was known as the pit head, and it was from here that men and equipment ware sent underground by means of this shaft dug deep into the ground. The depth of the shaft varied from one coal mine to another but here where I was working it was approximately three hundred feet deep. A kind of lift operated inside this shaft called the "chair", or "cage", and at shift times it was used to take men starting their shift down to the pit bottom, and for those who had just finished their shift to bring them back up to the top. At other times it was used for taking equipment down or bringing the tubs of coal up. The chair was operated by one highly skilled man on each shift, he was known as the "Banksman". It was his responsibility to see the chair was loaded correctly, and when it was done to his satisfaction he used a type of bell signal to inform the wheel house man, who would then lower the chair. Each commodity carried had a special number of bell rings, for men it was, three, for equipment and coal, two. Depending upon the number of rings the wheel house man heard determined the speed at which the chair would be allowed to travel down the shaft, for goods it would drop down at one heck of a lick, but for men it travelled more slowly, but I always left my stomach behind at the top of the shaft as we hurtled downwards.

I had done my training at another pit which was geared up specially for this, it also provided the equipment I needed to do the training and take with me when I was assigned to my job at Barrow Colliery, Worsbrough. It consisted of one pair of leather, steel toe and heel capped, heavy duty working boots. One pair of knee pads, strong leather, shaped to enclose the front of the knee, with two straps to fasten one above and one below the knee, one miner's steel helmet, and one pair of industrial gloves. All provided, but charged for out of my first pay packet.

I started work on the day shift and this did cause problems having to feed the animals and do the milking very early in the mornings, which meant Anna feeding the hens and chicks at the usual time. I did the job of "trammer" for four or five months on this shift, and soon got into a daily routine of getting up at four, and completing the jobs by five, then having a cup of tea and a light breakfast before picking up my shoulder bag with my heavily laden snap tin inside

The pit was almost opposite our home, over a hill, and would have been about one mile away, as the crow flys, but not being blessed with a pair of wings I had to walk about one and a half miles, much of it over uneven ground. My first port of call when I arrived was the "lamp room", a building which housed the lockers, and -as it's name implies- the lamps, which every man had to collect before going underground. The first morning I was allocated a locker. This was where I could deposit items of clothing I would not require until the end of the shift. I put on my boots and placed the shoes I was wearing in the carrier bag and put them in the locker, along with the raincoat I had worn. The next thing was the knee pads, I had practiced putting them on just to get the hang of it, therefore I was to experience no difficulty attaching them to both knees it was easy, the awkward part was walking in them, it was necessary to adopt a slight "knees bendy" posture which made the walk look similar to that of a flat footed penguin. The next thing to be done was go to the enclosed counter at one end of the room and collect a lamp, it was small, and round, with a metal attachment to fit it onto the front of the helmet, and looked very similar to a cycle front light. A rubber cable at the back of it extended to an oblong metal box (the battery) and this battery was strapped around the waist with a thick leather belt allowing it to rest between the small of the back and the rump. When the lamp was handed over I was also given a small metal disc with a number on it, this was to be my number for that day, my identification, as it were.

I had all the necessary gear and the next thing was to follow the other men making their way to the pit head and the "chair". It wasn't far but as we neared the "bank", a flat timber platform about ten yards square that formed the waiting area on the approaches to the chair, an orderly queue formed from the top of the shaft by men standing in pairs, extending almost to the rear end of the platform. It got shorter as they were loaded onto the chair and taken down to the pit bottom, there was then a short wait until the chair returned to the top for more passengers. It was a double decker chair and I cannot say for sure how many men were loaded onto each deck but it would have been somewhere around eight, quite possibly more. The deputy (man in charge of that shift) came and stood nearby and entered the chair with me, as we did so the banksman held out his hand and asked for my disc, this was taken by him from every man going down on the chair and given back to them when they returned at the end of the shift, it was the means by which each man was checked down and back up, a record of who was down and who had returned. We were on the top deck, I felt the chair rise, (to clear the brake chocks as they were withdrawn), then we were off, but not as fast as the ones I had been on during the training.

The pit bottom was a huge place, very brightly lit, and a hive of activity. The deputy took my arm and guided me away from all the hustle and bustle to where there were a number of tubs filled with all kinds of materials; iron rings, different sizes and lengths of timber, a couple of shovels, a pick, and other things dropped in the bottom. He directed me to the end one where another chap was standing, and told me to work with him for that shift. It turned out that I was to do this other fellow's job of trammer, as he was going to work in another part of the pit on an entirely different type of job, but first he had to show me the ropes. He kept up a running commentary as we pushed the first tub along the track, away from the well lit area of the pit bottom and out into a narrow roadway, a kind of tunnel, with horse shoe shaped steel rings every few yards holding up the roof, to prevent it from falling in on top of anyone passing underneath. These so called "rings" were actually girders and were possibly eight or nine feet tall, their shape allowed their two legs to rest on the ground with the bow at the top. They were held in position by means of "chocks" (wedge shaped pieces of timber), which were hammered in, jamming them tight up to the roof and the sides, lengths of timber were trapped between the tops of each two rings to prevent any loose stones or soil from falling through, there were some fairly large stones on the ground which had somehow managed to find their way through. As soon as we entered this tunnel we were in total darkness except for the light from our two helmet lamps. Having these placed on the helmet at the front meant that whichever way you turned your head it was possible to see directly in front of you. However, both sides and the rear gave the impression of being just one big black empty space and that caused problems, because it wasn't empty. An unguarded sideways step could have painful results for many parts of the body and consequently I was guilty of an awful lot of head turning for those first few weeks.

The tunnel was known as the "return air road", and I think the best way to explain it's particular role in the mine is to tell you, very briefly, how it is possible to breathe underground. There are two shafts drilled into the ground, one housing the chair, the other quite some distance away, this has large fans installed inside it, and when they are in operation they don't blow like an ordinary fan they pull, withdrawing air from around it's base. The main one, even though it contains the chair, is still wide enough to allow a large amount of air to travel down it. If you can imagine for a moment, a long length of "U" shaped tubing, open at both ends, and you put your mouth over one end and breathe in you would pull air through from the other end. That principal applies to the two shafts, one lets air in, the other draws it out. At the pit bottom, a road, the "air intake road", leads off to the main workings, where men are digging coal out from a seam. This area is known as the "coal face", everything else done in the mine and on the pit top, is geared solely for this mining operation. Using the principal again of the "U" shaped tubing, the coal face is at the top of the "U", and at the end of the air intake road, therefore the men working at the face receive the cleanest, coolest, and freshest, air available. We on the other hand were in another road, the other leg of the "U" as it were, and in the return air road; here it was stiflingly hot, and the air was foul as it had travelled through the workings gathering all the pre-used air as it made it's way out towards the other shaft. Working conditions down a mine are completely different to almost all other types of employment; there are no canteens, no washing facilities and, worst of all, no toilets. This, together with the large amounts of perspiration produced, did much to ensure the returning air was thick and putrid. Breathing became laboured, inducing a feeling of unpleasant restricted confinement. My first impressions lead me to believe I was working in a dirty uncompromising place, and I am afraid those impressions were to remain with me throughout the whole of my time spent in that environment.

The 'road' in which we were travelling and pushing the tub along in front of us was not a road as such, it had most likely been where coal had been extracted at one time and the ground underfoot was very uneven, to such an extent that the height of the roof in some places was as low as three or four feet and with the tub running on raised lines there were times when there was only an inch or two to spare. There was also stagnant water in the deepest of the dips making the 'slag' floor slippery. The road twisted and turned at an alarming rate, producing sharp turns and narrow bends. Not only had the floor risen or lowered in places, the sides also closed in at points making the road very narrow indeed. I was given the benefit of my companion's experience and learned the best way to combat all these obstacles. Another thing that made the journey even more laborious was the number of doors that had to be opened and closed. These were made from lengths of steel impregnated rubber, pieces cut from the belts which at one time had been used for transporting the coal from the face to the pit bottom, but were now old and had been replaced. They did make good solid doors though, one piece was attached to a post at one side and another at the other side, and made in such a way as to overlap in the middle. They were heavy and took a lot of pulling or pushing. These doors could never be left open as they were the only means of controlling the amount of air allowed to circulate through the mine. If they were left open the speed at which it would travel through the roads could reach gale force proportions making it impossible to even stand up. Eventually we arrived at the face and left the tub and it's contents in the capable hands of the overman, then collected an empty tub and returned it to the pit bottom. How many trips were made during one shift I don't know. At the end of the shift I collected my tab (identity disc) from the banksman and went to the lamp room, handed in the lamp, and tab, and put my helmet and knee pads in the locker, put my shoes in the carrier bag and went home wearing my boots having considered them to be more suitable for negotiating the precarious terrain I had to travel twice each working day. I was to follow this same routine for almost five months. One thing did cause me some concern however, at that time I was a heavy smoker and I would light a cigarette as I left home in the mornings, smoke it on the way, but was unable to have another until I returned home around two thirty in the afternoon. Then someone told me how that he had a small tin which held one cigarette and two matches and before he got onto the chair he found a suitable spot on the bank (platform) where he could hide this tin until he came up at the end of the shift. So, I obtained a similar time and began to secrete it underneath the bank timbers, well out of sight, and eagerly collect it as soon as I got off the chair, and light up. I went one better than most of the other men by putting two cigarettes in the tin. Having been gasping for a smoke for the past eight hours, that one extra fag, plus matches, placed in that tiny tin, had me singing joyfully as I travelled home.

One pay day I was asked to go to the personnel office where I was told I would be changing jobs. From the following Monday night I would be working as a "Ripper" in a "Z" type gate on the back shift. The tramming job had been reasonably well paid but this was one of the best paid jobs in the mine, I knew nothing about it and could only hope I would be able to do it to everyone's satisfaction. I have vivid memories of that first shift, having to be at the pit bottom for nine thirty, then, along with six other men, walking for a good half an hour to reach the end of the main gate (the face), where we all sat on the ground for a few minutes. The Overman, went through what was expected of me, along with an all too brief summary of what was about to take place. The gate (tunnel) was about four times as wide as the one

I had been working in, and some twelve feet high. The roof supports were bigger and much stronger; there were no tub lines but it was the same dark, foreboding place. We had walked up the gate and were now faced with a dead end, almost straight at the sides and round at the top. There was a gap at the bottom about three feet high, and about three feet deep, and on closer inspection I could see that this gap extended to either side of the gate, like a small tunnel into the side walls. This was from where the coal had already been extracted. Above this gap, up to a height of eleven feet or so, was a solid mass of stone and dirt. This had to be removed, and our job for the next seven hours or so, was to do just that. It wasn't going to be loaded onto tubs and taken out of the mine, it was to be used as packing for the gap created by the removal of the coal, if this gap was not filled in and packed tightly all the earth above it could sink causing subsidence. The first thing to be done was for one man, using an air pick, to drill a number of deep holes into this mass. As soon as all the holes were drilled, another man, a deputy, came and put dynamite into each one, and all were connected by wires to a detonator. This man was a very skilled person. Dealing with dynamite in such a volatile area as a coal mine where even a tiny spark in the wrong place could cause an explosion did require a person with a full understanding of the very important work he was undertaking. He carried the box very carefully as he walked backwards away from the face, unrolling the wires in a deliberate but painstaking manner as he did so. We all found spots close to the side walls, and adopted crouching positions, head's bowed, holding the helmets with both hands. The deputy retired from the face almost as far away as we were, he then placed the box on the ground, and with a shouted warning he pressed the plunger. There followed an almighty explosion with dust and stones flying everywhere and it was quite some time before the dust settled and we were able to see. I looked up and what a sight it was. Before the explosion the mass of stones and dirt above the gap was big, but now it was on the ground it looked massive and we, the seven of us, were going to have to move it before we went home. The method we were about to use to get rid of it seemed to me to be be an impossibility, just looking at that heap made me wonder how on earth we could do it in the time we had, but remove it we did, every night.

Three men began working at the bottom of each corner of the heap making an inroad towards the gap on their side, the overman helping at both sides, as and when his services were required . When enough space had been obtained it became possible to look along the gap that extended outwards from the gate, and it was then that one of the men I was working with, the Overman, and myself, crawled under the very low roof and made our way along the gap. This would have been about twenty yards or so, in length, about three yards wide, and approximately two and a half feet high at best. The Overman and I stopped about halfway along and the other man continued to some six yards from the end. The first man, at the entrance, whilst laying flat on the slate bed floor, would then obtain a shovel full of dust and stones from the heap, and would turn and throw it towards the second man, he would stretch to retrieve it and throw it on to the third. The floor, "bed", was hard, shiny, slippery, slate, "slag", which enabled the shovel full to slide for quite some way, especially the stones, they skidded across the surface at above average speed and didn't always come to rest before striking some part of the body, the dust however, seemed to come to a sudden stop almost as soon as it left the shovel which meant having to stretch out considerably to retrieve it. I had been allocated the job of "piggy in the middle", and after the overman had shown me what to do he left and went back to the gate, leaving the three of us to get on with the job.

Every so often the third man, the one at the end, would call out that he was about to do some packing. This was the signal for me to do the same by bringing a number of shovels full towards me making a pile at my side, and throwing most of it into the "gob" (the farthest point in the gap, opposite to where we were working). All the dust and small stones were shovelled into this "gob" but the larger stones had to be used to pack it all in very tightly up to the roof. Sometime around two a.m. we scrambled our way out of the gap into the gate for a much needed break and refreshments. Just being able to stand up straight and stretch was a great feeling.

When I had been doing the tramming job I made my own break times, and my snap tin was always full to overflowing with six or seven thick bread sandwiches containing, cheese, or lard, complemented by a couple of buns or a piece of cake. It being common knowledge that ripping was a hard job, I considered that I would be in need of sustenance so I arrived for that first shift with a heavily laden snap tin. I was holding the first of my sandwiches in both hands ready to take a large bite when the Overman came and sat beside me and said, "if you eat any of that now you won't be able to go back underneath". He went on to explain that it would cause me to have such a terrible stomach cramp it could kill me, and the only thing to pass through the lips was water. Apparently all the men brought at least four pints of it every shift. There is no doubt about it being a hard, uncomfortable job, but there was the nice fat wage packet at the end of each week, and all that swivelling and confined turning and twisting helped keep my waistline down to a steady thirty two inches!

Working in the mine had given me plenty of time to do the jobs at home as I was free all day which made everything much easier, although Anna kept complaining about hearing noises in the yard during the nights I was away. To pacify her I bought a young dog, a "Border Collie", and named him "Bobby". I didn't think it would be much of a deterent; it's bark being much worse than it's bite, but the row it kicked up when anyone approached would certainly help. Robert was three at the time and he made a friend of the dog straight away, they were almost inseparable, and one day we decided to take some photographs when the boys were playing under the apple trees. I had the "Brownie Box Camera", and Robert was sitting alongside the dog, then he must have decided that if he sat on it he would be more comfortable than sitting on the hard ground, the dog was laid down and he sat astride it holding the thick hair around it's neck, he looked so comical I took a photo, just as I did so the dog stood up and started to run round the garden with Robert hanging on, they made one complete circuit, which was quite a distance then stopped at the trees, suddenly, dislodging Robert. I have that photo with him sitting comfortably on the dog's back just before it took off, but not the journey they made together.

I was speaking to our next door neighbour one day when he told me that he had seen the local policeman, on more than one occasion, walking about in the yard at night shining his torch into the buildings. There had been a number of instances when that particular policeman and I had not seen eye to eye, although in fairness to him I must state that most of them took place when he had been given the job of officiating in the few domestic disputes that got out of hand between Anna and myself. .

Apart from the many other things she found to complain about, Anna still persisted with her demands to move from where we were living. I was of the same opinion, but we found it difficult to locate anything suitable until one day I saw an advert in one of the national newspapers. It stated that for £250 deposit and then monthly payments for the balance of £2500- arranged to suit each buyer's circumstances- a brand new executive five bedroomed detached house, situated in forty five acres of land, in Alton, Hants, could be ours to occupy in a few months time. I wrote off for further particulars and was invited to see the area in which these houses were being built. I met one of their representatives on the site one Saturday morning, where I was shown round the area by a very enthusiastic fellow singing the praises of the deal he hoped we were about to make. It was a very extensive area of woodland, a great deal of which had been cleared of trees and grubbed, there were a number of houses in various stages of construction and some looked almost ready to be occupied. He showed me where one plot had been marked out and said this would be ours if we wanted it. The whole area was idyllic with wide open spaces where the trees had been, and very much a countryside atmosphere. I liked the look of it but without making any decision I agreed to think it over for a few days and then if I did want it I would contact the office again and arrange to pay the deposit.

Anna and I discussed the purchase of the house and it's implications and decided we would have it. One of the partners came to see us and we handed over a cheque for the deposit and obtained a receipt together with the appropriate papers appertaining to the sale when it was ready. A few weeks later I took a friend down to see the place again. Progress had been made on all the existing buildings and we went to the site office and spoke to the same fellow I had seen before. He told me we would be able to take possession in about two to three months. Anna and I settled down eagerly awaiting the day when we could move in to our new, presti- gious property in the clean area of the south of England. A number of letters were exchanged during the next three months until we received one that was very disturbing. It stated that they were having financial difficulties and were we prepared to advance more of the purchase price. Before we could make up our minds whether to do so another letter arrived, this one was from the "Old Bailey" court in London, informing us that the people we had been dealing with were accused of fraud, and giving us a date upon which we were told to appear in that court to give evidence. On the day, Anna, the three boys, and myself, drove down to London in the early hours of the morning arriving in good time for the ten o'clock session.

There were two men on trial, the one that had collected the cheque, the other one I hadn't seen before; he was apparently the main man doing all the dealings behind the scenes. They had chosen to be tried by jury and we had to stay outside the courtroom for the best part of three hours before I was called. The case for the prosecution was that these two men had sold land that had not been their's to sell. The defence was based on the fact that they had been loaned money by a bank to proceed with the purchase of this land on the understanding that the loan be repaid when all the properties had been sold, but that the bank had asked for a return of the loan before this had time to be done and consequently the building of the houses and the clearing of the land was delayed because of the lack of funds with which to pay the contrac- tors.

I gave evidence for the prosecution by simply stating my involvement, saying that I had been to the site on two occasions and seen some houses in varying stages of construction, and on my second visit had noted the plot number as being the one on the receipt I had been given when handing over the cheque for the deposit. The prosecuting counsel asked me a lot of questions, most of which I had no answers for, at one stage getting frustrated and saying that I had been duped into handing over a considerable amount of money by these men and that

I should want to see justice done. I only knew what I had told the court, nothing more and nothing less. As the case went on it became apparent why it had been brought, some of the would be purchasers were not satisfied with the explanations they were given, so they notified the police. After hearing most of the evidence for and against I couldn't make up my mind one way or the other, but I did think the defence seemed to be very feasible and it could have happened that way. Nevertheless the case went against them and both men were sentenced to three years in prison. During the summing up by the judge it came out that one of the men had been convicted of fraud once before, not the doctor, the other one.

Somewhere about this time I decided to broaden my outlook by using some of the hours I could spare to go to a car auction that was held every week in Conisbrough, a small place about ten miles away. The night shift in the mine gave me enough time to do other things, even though it did mean going short of sleep occasionally. The auction was situated in a large plot of land which was used to accommodate all the vehicles that were to be offered for sale that day, there were hundreds of them placed in rows and all displaying a "lot" number making it easy for prospective buyers to walk around and inspect them before the sale began. I had heard of this sale but had no idea so many people attended it and the first time I went I arrived when the auction was already in progress, the massive building was crammed with people standing on both sides, with a wide gap running through the middle. I was amazed at the speed with which each vehicle was sold and driven straight out of the other end of the building.

That first time I made no bids as I hadn't looked around the vehicles in the viewing area beforehand. Having every intention of buying one the next time, I went there on a bus so that I could drive my purchase home. There were one or two occasions when I was inspecting one of my purchases in the viewing area when someone would come up and offer me quite a bit more than I had paid for it, making me a nice profit from having done nothing. It was possible to purchase a vehicle in good running order for as little as twelve pounds, although some were in need of a complete overhaul and when dealt with were either sold privately or taken back to the auction.

I do have fond memories of two cars in particular, one was a Lanchester 18, a magnificent beast, built on the lines of a Rolls Royce. It had a long beautiful bonnet which lifted up from both sides, being hinged in the middle, an enormous chromium plated radiator surround which stood out from the immaculate dark blue finish of the bodywork. The dash board and the in-sides of the doors had large amounts of highly polished woodwork which, surprisingly enough taking the car's age into consideration, had no scratch marks anywhere. The wheels and tyres were much bigger than normal which made the body higher off the road, but this was com-pensated by two running boards along both sides enabling passengers to stand on them when getting in and out therefore reducing the height considerably. Overall it was a very attractive sight to behold and after filling it with petrol I drove it home, the power and the comfort were really something, I hadn't experienced anything like it before and felt quite proud of my new acquisition.

The other one was an Austin 12, it was much smaller but it did have nineteen inch wire wheels, it's appearance was reasonable, no rust or damage anywhere but there was nothing prepossessing about it and when it was parked alongside the Lanchester it looked like a tiny toy. At the time it was just another car to be worked on and then sold. I did some work on it and began to use it for running around in, it was reliable and comfortable so consequently I didn't sell it for many years and that "toy" was to give me far better service than I could ever have imagined.

After a couple of months and many visits to the auction the farm yard took on the appearance of a car park, with so many of my recent purchases taking up all the available space. Some were standing there with their wheels off and solid blocks of timber supporting the chassis, others had their bonnets up and on closer inspection were seen to be minus the engine. It didn't look very nice and caused some problems having to find a way round them during the animal feeding times, but I enjoyed what I was doing and regarded it all as somewhat of a light relief from my work underground. I have learned only during the past years that the boys; Michael, Phillip, and Robert, also obtained pleasure from the conglomeration of cars in the yard, apparently they spent many happy hours sitting behind the steering wheels pretending to be Stirling Moss at Silverstone race track. It was many years before that yard returned to normal but I have no regrets as my inauguration into the realms of second hand car dealing had been fairly profitable and extremely interesting.

The fat pay packet and the many hours of daylight in which I could do the necessary chores at home began to seem irrelevant when compared with the unhealthy hard work I was doing in the mine, so I left and went back to lorry driving. This time to doing long distance jobs which meant that I was away from home for two or three days at a time. During the previous two months the menagerie had been reduced considerably, the rabbits were still thriving in the bottom shed and one sow was due to have little ones in the next few weeks, but the two Berkshire Black sows had been sold to a local pig breeder. The billy goat and three of the older nannies (the ones which had been giving milk but had now stopped, which meant that we no longer had any milkers), and two barren sows and their seventeen offspring (all eight weeks old), had been sent to Doncaster market and sold. The reason for this dramatic reduction was a sudden leap in feed prices. When the last batch of eggs had hatched in the incubator we had enough chicks to be going on with so I didn't use it again. Now feeding time was not the hectic operation it used to be. Having reduced the livestock to an easily manageable number I was able to go away on those long trips knowing that Anna would have no difficulty keeping them well fed.

The long distance driving took me to many different places of business, some large some small, and it was at one of these small one's where I was offered, and bought, a toy train. It consisted of an engine and one carriage, both made of wood with a cast iron chassis and wheels and approximately three feet long, two feet wide and two feet in depth, with a set of straight and curved iron rails which when connected extended for about twenty yards. I fixed them up in an oblong shape under the fruit trees in the side garden near the back door, ensuring they were fairly level so that when the engine and carriage were placed on them they would run, but only when pushed. The three boys found them to be great fun, and they were to provide them with hours of amusement, but although there was enough room in both the engine and the carriage for them all to be seated, one had to push, and taking it in turns to perform this task often developed into furious arguments as to whose turn it was to ride, and whose to push, but the amount of pleasure they had outweighed all the arguments.

They all took a great interest in the garden with Michael and Phillip helping a great deal where possible, but Robert took more than just an interest, his idea of helping was to dig in places where there weren't any plants. He would make a hole in the softest soil and collect anything that crawled, ran, or wriggled, and deposit them in his trouser pockets. When this peculiar habit of his became known to everyone he was usually searched, and his pockets emptied of any foreign bodies, before he entered the house. One day security must have been lax because when Anna was doing the washing that night, (as she had to do almost every night), she just dropped his shorts into the washer along with all the other clothes and closed the lid, allowing it to wash for quite some time before taking a look to see how things were progressing only to be faced with all the surface water heaving and thrashing about as if it were alive, which it was. There were dozens of wet, rather warm, sparklingly clean worms, all trying to escape from the predicament they found themselves in.

Robert was no different to any other little boy, apart from his fascination for worms that is, and he liked nothing better than to follow me around hoping I would give him some little job to do, but he was in his element when people came to the house to buy vegetables, eggs, and flowers. Under supervision from his mother, deriving great pleasure from handing them over and collecting the money. There was a factory two or three hundred yards from the house where women worked making some kind of clothing and it became something of a regular ritual that many of these women would call every Friday evening on their way home from work to buy bunches of flowers and the odd vegetable or a few eggs. It was then Robert came into his own being hard at it for a good half hour or so, Anna making up the bunches of flowers for him to hand over, along with any eggs that were required, and he collecting the cash. Michael and Phillip had done the same thing on previous occasion's but being a bit older they seemed quite prepared to allow him to do the honours.

During the times when I worked on the lorry driving jobs and down the mine it was possible to make good use of the Sundays I was off by taking the family out to various places of interest. Any prearranged trip to the seaside was always looked upon with great anticipation, and as the east coast, just north of Hull, was the nearest we invariably ended up at a spot known as "Primrose Valley", between Filey and Scarborough. We did make others to Bridlington, Whitby, Robin Hoods Bay, and south of the Humber to Cleethorpes, Mablethorpe, and Skegness, with the odd visit to Blackpool at Illumination time, but we seemed to favour Primrose Valley and went there more often. One time in particular stands out for two reasons. We had arrived just before lunch and had parked the car in the usual place, a stretch of grass which sloped down to the cliff edge. We had made the journey in style, and the Lanchester 18 looked magnificent, glistening and gleaming in the sunlight as it stood on the grass high above the cliffs. It was the first long journey it had made since it's purchase and we had travelled in exquisite comfort, the three boys were seated in the back and able to admire the scenery without having to kneel on the cushions. Anna sitting alongside me in the roomy leather seat must have felt more at ease than usual, but she made no comment. I was driving a truly magnificent car and I knew it, enjoying the feel of it's undoubted power and performance, therefore there was no need for anyone to tell me anything, just sitting behind the steering wheel of such an imposing vehicle was all that I required to feel on top of the world.

It was quite a long walk down an uneven footpath to the beach but once there it didn't take long for the buckets and spades to be put to good use, it was an exceptionally nice day and there were a great many people about sitting on the sand in what appeared to be family groups. The drinks and sandwiches we had brought were demolished and at sometime later on in the afternoon we were approached by two men from one of the groups, they apologised for imposing themselves upon us and went on to say that the grown up members of their party had been watching our three children playing in the sand and a difference of opinion had arisen and they had come over to ask us to settle the argument. Our boys would have been about three, four, and five years of age, and each one of them had long blonde curly hair. Anna, as you know, was a dressmaker and when the children were small she made most of their clothes and dressed them in an almost identical manner, and this -together with the blonde hair- made it obvious to anyone that they were related. Defining their gender was at that time difficult if you didn't know them and we had been asked whether they were boys or girls before. This particular group had complicated matters still further because a certain number had deduced that there were two boys and one girl, whereas the rest were convinced there were two girls and one boy. The looks of disgust on the faces of Michael, Phillip, and Robert, were sufficient to dissuade me from bursting out laughing, but I derived great pleasure in announcing to the two men, that all bets were off, as they were all wrong. That was one reason for remembering that day, the other was yet to come.

We had to make quite a long journey home and somewhere around seven thirty in the evening a few small buckets of water were collected from the sea and used in an effort to remove the clinging sand from tiny hands and feet. Clothes were brushed or shaken, and the three buckets which now contained various interesting shells, glistening pebbles, and the like, were all carefully carried by each one of the boys as we left the golden sands and climbed back up the fairly steep winding track to the car. They were all seated in the car and with one swift turn of the handle the engine burst into life. A few miles down the road a small cafe provided relief in more ways than one; the beach had no toilet facilities whatsoever, and no place from which to obtain a drink. These problems were quickly solved and the journey was resumed. We had only travelled a few more miles when the engine spluttered and we came to a stop. That type of splutter indicated that we were out of petrol, but I firmly believed we couldn't be. I had filled up before we left home and worked out the mileage but a gentle kick at the petrol tank assured me that my beliefs and calculations were incorrect, it was definitely empty. Where we had stopped to take refreshments there was a petrol station, so I retrieved my petrol can from the boot, and not knowing how far the next station would be ahead, I thought it wiser to go back to the one I knew was there. It took a lot longer than I expected even though I did a brisk trot for most of the way there and back, but as was to be expected my passenger's tempers had begun to fray by the time I returned. The boys soon calmed down but not so Anna and she gave me the benefit of her tongue for the rest of the drive home, especially when we resumed our journey looking for a filling station and came to one just over a mile from where we had stopped. Trust me to have chosen the wrong way, having walked about four miles instead of just over two to the nearest one. Anyway I filled the tank up once more and without further mishap we arrived home, everyone rather tired. Despite the "hiccups" I think it had been quite a pleasant day.

The long distance lorry driving meant that there was a good pay packet at the end of the week as it wasn't a nine to five job and there was inevitably a lot of overtime, but I had been doing it for quite a few months and Spring was just around the corner; the time for sowing seeds in the greenhouses and preparing the soil in the garden ready for sowing and planting. Being away from home for the greater part of the week, day and night, made it impossible to do these things. Saturday afternoons and all day Sunday allowed me to do some of them but it wasn't enough so I again began to consider alternative employment.

There were times when I was working in and around the farm yard someone would call in for a chat about something or other, with the five barred gate entrance to the yard being only some forty yards from the street quite a few people would walk down the short road and lean on the gate to have a word or two with me. Usually I didn't mind as it gave me an excuse to lean on whichever implement I was using at the time. There was one young fellow, Alf, who lived opposite the pub who popped in regularly and we became quite good friends. He worked as a bus driver for the Yorkshire Traction Bus Company, and frequently spoke about his desire to work for himself. One day he was looking at one of the cars in the yard, all four of it's wheels were off and it was minus it's engine, it didn't look very prepossessing which was probably the reason why he began to talk about the high cost of scrap metal and informing me that the car would fetch a good price. We went on to discuss the price of scrap metal and what it could mean to us, and the more we talked the more I began to like the idea of scrap dealing. The outcome was that he left his job, I left mine, and we agreed to work as partners in what we hoped would be the lucrative business of scrap dealing. My decision to do so did not go down well with my other half, but then, any decision I made never did.

We had made our intentions clear to one of the larger dealers in the area and he had agreed to help us in any way he could, offering to take any metal we wished to sell, and give us a reasonable price. He also sold us a small flat truck which would be suitable for us to begin with. For the first two weeks we went round the housing estates picking up anything we could from the householders, we managed to get a couple of decent loads which we sold to the dealer, but realising we weren't going to get rich doing the job in this manner we decided to call upon the farms in the outlying districts. This proved to be much better, there was plenty of scrap in almost every one we went to. The farmers always needed convincing that we were giving them good prices, and that often took some doing. We travelled quite long distances from one farm to another but managed to come home with a load of decent stuff every day and did well out of the sales.

One morning we were on our way out to a farm when we noticed a very large gas tank in the process of being demolished. There were a lot of men working on it so we drove up a small road and spoke to one chap who looked to be directing operations and asked him if we could buy any spare pieces they had laying around. He said, "I can do better than that, if you think you can handle it you can have the lot". There were large pieces of steel that had already been cut away from the massive frame, they were about two yards square and some two inches thick, solid steel. I told him we had no idea what a piece of that size was worth. He suggested that we to put as much weight on our truck as it could carry, then take it away and have it weighed and at the same time find out what it was worth then come back and tell him. Our truck was solid and strong and had a powerful engine but the body was only small and we only managed to get four of the pieces on. We had to use two pieces of strong timber to slide each one up onto the truck as they were much too heavy for us to lift, but it was thought there would be about half a ton when all four were loaded. As we were leaving the site the man did come up with a price he thought the load would be worth.

It was quite a long way to the scrap dealer we were using and as there were a number of steel works a lot nearer we decided, after some discussion, to drive to the nearest one. At that time steel was very much in demand and in short supply. At the steelworks we spoke to a man in the office and he asked how much could we get for him, because he would take all we could bring. He directed us to a weighbridge in the yard where it was weighed, and taken off our truck by stacatruck, our truck was weighed again to verify the tare (unladen weight). The load was as we had thought, just under half a ton. Up to this point there had been no mention of price but when we got back to the office he handed me some cash. After telling him we would bring more later on that day we set off back to the gas tank. The amount we had just been paid for that half a ton was four times higher than that suggested by the man in charge at the gas tank site, which meant we were about to make an extremely large profit on the whole transaction. We decided to give the man a bit more than he had suggested to ensure his boss would find it acceptable. We returned to the site and showed him the two weighbridge tickets and informed him of the price we would pay for any further loads. He was very pleased, and on the strength of this told us we could take all the sheets as they were removed from the tank. The farm touring was put on hold as we concentrated on collecting and delivering each load. It took several weeks, then it was back to the farm routine, for a short while at least.

The area where the steelworks were had a lot of other mills and factories dotted around it, and when we were unloading one day we were approached by a chap who asked if we ever came across any non-ferrous metals, brass, or copper, etc. He had a smelting plant nearby and would pay us well if we could get him some. At that time we didn't have any but kept his enquiry in mind, and it was on one journey to a farm when we came across just what he required. We were travelling along a fairly busy back road when we saw what appeared to be a general contractors yard, it seemed to stretch for miles and was full of all kinds of metal objects. We drove inside and spoke to a fellow who told us they did almost any kind of work that concerned water and pipe laying, and everything here was equipment no longer considered to be suitable for it's job. He told us we were welcome to have a look round to see if we could use anything for our business. It took us ages to meander around the field taking stock of everything we saw. There were a lot of cast iron pieces, which like steel was very much in demand. We knew we could find a good home for most of it. At one side of a muddy path were some round objects dumped in a large untidy heap, each one covered in a greyish furry matter. They looked queer so I gave one of them a swift kick and where my boot had knocked some of the stuff off underneath it glistened, and on closer inspection it turned out to be copper and was worth a lot more than cast iron or steel. We took our time having a good look round and then went back to the office. Now we had to find out what exactly he would let us have, and how he would go about pricing the different kinds of metal. His answer to both questions was very simple and to the point, he said, "You can take anything out there, just name your price per ton, take a load, have it weighed and bring me the ticket". I thought of the price we had been paid for a ton of steel from the gas tank job and offered him half that amount, he seemed satisfied and we arranged to come in early the next morning to pick up the first load. Alf and I agreed that we would take the first few loads back home and dump them in the yard after they had been weighed, just to clean them up a bit as they were very dirty and covered in that grey furry matter.

The next morning we arrived at the field about eight and after having a chat with the man we drove to the untidy heap and loaded up with the objects, they probably weighed about twenty eight pounds and were soon humped onto the flat body of the truck, forming a pile about two feet high in the middle. As they were rather unstable it was necessary to cover them with a tarpaulin sheet which we tied down with ropes. Then we made the journey to the corporation weighbridge in Barnsley where it was weighed and an official ticket obtained, before driving home and unloading in the yard. With the pieces being smaller we had been able to get more on than the awkward cumbersome gas tank sheets, and the load weighed just under one ton.

We hadn't crept into the yard in our stocking feet therefore our presence was duly noted as was the pile of "rubbish" we had just deposited in the yard. However, the commotion eventually subsided and we set off back to the field, arriving slightly later than the two hours we had said and gave the man the ticket along with the cash for a full ton. He did make some comment about being overpaid and went on to say that he had told his superiors about the transaction and they were quite happy for us to take whatever we wanted. We delivered two more loads to the yard that day, which just about cleared the heap and arranged to return in a couple of days to sort out something else. There was plenty for us to go at as we had seen on our first tour round the field but first we had to clean up what was in the yard so we spent the next day removing all the grey furry stuff to reveal the bright shiny copper. It was an arduous task but one we both relished, anticipating the large monetary return we were about to receive. At the end of that day we had cleaned them all and loaded the truck with what we considered to be a good ton.

The next morning we drove to the steelworks. On the way there the conversation was bright and cheerful but if Alf's thoughts were anything like mine he would have been wondering if our gamble was about to succeed. It was with some feelings of trepidation that I got out of the truck in the yard of the chap who had spoken to me about non-ferrous metals those few weeks ago, and walked into his office. I told him what we had brought and he came straight out of the office, took one look and pointed to the weighbridge, saying, "weigh it, and then I will show you where to unload". It was weighed and he hung onto the door of the truck as it was driven to an empty concrete bay and unloaded. Throughout these proceedings there was never any mention of price, all he seemed concerned about was how much we would be able bring him. We expected a payment of around one and a quarter times that we received for steel for a ton of copper but were completely taken aback when he quoted a price which was almost double and paid us for the exact weight. We collected the remaining two loads from home and delivered them to him that day and promised to let him have more of the same when we could get hold of it.

Feeling on top of the world at our good fortune we returned to our "pot of gold" in the field and set to work compiling another suitable load. We spent the next few days taking cast iron pieces with brass and copper fittings back home, and then had a day or two there removing the fittings and placing the different materials in their respective piles ready to make up a load. Alf's wife and child came across the street from their home and settled down to watch, and my three boys were in attendance most of the time.

Working close to home had it's compensations. Instead of taking a few sandwiches and eating them on the way round we were able to sit down at our respective tables and have proper meals. When a good day's work was satisfactorily completed Alf tootled off home and I was able to do the jobs in the buildings, the greenhouses and the garden.

We spent the next few weeks bringing similar loads and working on them until we had a large heap of cast iron, some six or seven sacks of copper and the same of brass, and it took two or three days to take it all to the smelting plant. We got slightly more than the price of steel for the cast iron and each one of the brass and copper sacks weighed almost one hundredweight. The rustle of the pound notes as they were handed over was sweet music to our ears, making us even more convinced that this scrap dealing lark was a real money spinner, especially the non-ferrous side of it as the brass and copper had been the icing on the cake. We were soon to discover something even more valuable.

When the yard at home was cleared and empty we went to pick up more of the same, there was still a lot to go at and as we began to sort out the next load we came across some much larger objects which had been covered by the pieces we were taking. They were cast iron and each one had a large wheel attached to what was obviously the top part of it, they were much too heavy to lift so we dragged one clear and examined it. There were a number of bolts around it's middle and some just below the wheel securing a round plate to the main body, the wheel was attached to this plate and after using a few strong arm tactics on it this wheel turned. We knew we wouldn't be able to lift them onto the truck before removing the bolts from the round plate first, and then the middle afterwards, thereby splitting the whole piece in half. The ones around the plate required a much larger amount of "elbow grease" than normal, but they were all eventually removed. Alf took hold of the wheel and began to ease it from the frame bringing the round plate with it, as he did so I became aware of a very distinct smell which my nostrils hadn't been assailed by since my days in the army. It was a certain type of oil which was used to cover and lubricate the moving parts of a very precious metal known as "Phosphor Bronze". I couldn't wait to plunge both my hands into that slippery golden coloured mess to find out exactly what it contained, and having done so I wasn't to be disappointed as I withdrew a large valve type component made solely of Phosphor Bronze. Having removed that weight we managed to lift the complete casting onto the truck without taking the bolts out around it's middle, and once this was on board the bronze component was put back inside and the round plate with the wheel attached was secured by hand tightening a couple of bolts. Finding this most welcome addition to our non-ferrous materials, and in anticipation of the amount of cash it would bring, we began to look around for more and spent the next couple of hours searching. They were bulky objects but a large amount of the smaller castings had been piled on top of them and it meant moving these to one side in order to find what we were looking for. It was hard work and I must admit it was done in rather feverish haste but we knew it was worth it when our efforts began to expose quite a few. By the time we had sorted out all the heaps there were fourteen or fifteen. Opening them up and transporting them home to the yard took three or four trips in two days. Another day was spent removing and putting the bronze parts into sacks before taking them to the smelting plant the next day where a highly delighted man took possession. The total weight of the sacks was just under three hundredweight and he paid us more for those than one ton of copper. Whenever we took him any further loads of cast iron, brass, or copper, his first words were always, "have you brought some more bronze?", unfortunately we hadn't, that little lot was all we ever got, more's the pity.

During the time spent on the scrap job I made a few of the all too infrequent visits to my parents. They were infrequent as I had no wish to run the risk of incurring the wrath of Anna. When I did see my Mother she said she hadn't been well for quite some time but said she was hoping to get out more now that Harold had agreed to let my Father use half his front garden to grow flowers and vegetables. The farm was out in the country and she was hoping the fresh air would do her good, even though it meant quite a long walk to the farm. One nice warm sunny afternoon I went to see them both in the garden and during a conversation my Father said he wished he had a caravan or something where they could stay overnight sometimes instead of making the long walk home and back every day. I immediately thought of a Gipsy caravan a farmer had wanted to sell us, and took him to see if it would be suitable, he said it would, so the next day Alf and I went and picked it up. It was a proper Romany horse drawn caravan so we tied the shafts to the bodywork and fastened a nine foot stout rope to the front timber chassis and secured it to the rear of the truck, and set off, not for one moment realising how uncomfortable that journey of four or five miles along narrow undulating country lanes was to be. As we drove along the road, even though it was at a snails pace, it kept swinging from side to side in an alarming fashion, at one point on a tight right hand bend we turned, it didn't. I stopped just in time to prevent it from taking a nosedive into a ditch. We made progress at an even slower pace for the rest of the journey, going straight wasn't too bad but the towing method was very unstable and couldn't prevent the caravan's front wheels from turning which resulted in it's weaving from side to side. We had realised the moment we set off that we should have used a rigid tow bar. However, apart from having to struggle bringing the contrary article into line once more after it had refused to follow the truck into the farm entrance we finally brought it to rest in a field behind the farm buildings. My Father meticulously cleaned it, inside and out, and installed suitable furnishings, and for the remainder of that summer both he and my Mother made good use of it. Sadly, I think that this task was the first time I did anything in the way of helping my parents since my return from Palestine.

When I did go to see my parents at their home I also saw Jacqueline and Peter, when they were there, and remember on one occasion being introduced to Jacqueline's boyfriend, Harry, who I took an instant liking to. It was obvious they were very happy in each other's company, but it was not so with Anna and myself. At some time during 1951 the constant bickering and nagging took a decided turn for the worse in that they were also accompanied by various degrees of physical violence which resulted in the "Law" being called in on a number of ocassions to calm the situation. It cannot be said that I was blameless for what took place, although I did take exception to the way I was deemed to be the one wholly responsible. I do maintain that I must take the blame for allowing things to get under my skin, especially the incessant accusations of infidelity and disregard for the welfare of our family. On the other hand, she was a perfect mother, an excellent cook, and kept the home and it's contents meticulously clean, along with helping me out with the animals in the yard when I was away. I never had the slightest reason to complain about that, but as with all families there were the usual arguments and differences of opinion from time to time. My presence in the home was one long round of screaming arguments and quarrels, but I have no wish to go into any details except to say that those visits by the "Law", always at Anna's request, culminated in my suffering the ignominy of appearing in court at the Leeds Assizes, charged with Grievous Bodily Harm. The outcome, a three year suspended sentence. I have vague memories of the actual court proceedings which extended over a period of three days, but as Anna and I walked through Leeds to the bus station I have vivid recollections of seeing the evening newspaper placards which stated, Palestine Police Sgt convicted of G.B.H. charge, with the whole of one side of the placard displaying a full length photograph of myself in Police uniform. This photograph could only have been made available by Anna as no-one else, apart from myself, had access to it.

The situation at home didn't improve, and Anna's belligerence was only strengthened by my conviction. However, I took the sensible way out, and when things reached the stage of threatening to cloud my judgement I walked away, anywhere, another room, out into the yard, or away from the house altogether into the street, sometimes even that did not defuse the situation as she would follow me. This was, and remains, a regrettable part of my life. I am thoroughly ashamed of myself for stooping so low instead of showing a more positive and sensible attitude throughout all the trials and tribulations.

Throughout everything that transpired Alf remained a staunch friend, he was in a better position than most as he had been present when Anna had shown her unpleasant side on more than one occasion. He had carried on doing the job as best he could when I was otherwise engaged and we soon got back into the swing of things. Everything of use was removed from the field and sold, and it became necessary to find another source of good saleable material. It didn't prove to be easy, in fact our supply completely dried up except for the poor stuff we got from our resumed farm tours. The we heard there was some heavy stuff available at an open-cast mining site a few miles out of town, so one morning we drove into the site to take a look, and after contacting the site foreman we found ourselves examining two or three giant pieces of machinery which had obviously reached the end of their working life. We were told we could have them for a certain price per ton which on the face of it would be an attractive proposition, but there was one big drawback, it was going to be necessary to make them easy to handle in sizes suitable for lifting onto our truck, some parts could be made reasonably suitable by simply unfastening the bolts holding them to the main structure, but the bulk of the weight was in this structure. Nevertheless, we needed this type of steel so we set to work removing the bolts from the parts we could handle, it was a slow tedious job and not done under the best of conditions, large noisy dumper trucks were driving around at ridiculous speeds, slipping and sliding about as they passed within a yard or so of where we were working. Two days of stripping down gave us two decent sized loads of solid steel which we delivered to the steelworks, and Alf came up with a suggestion which would overcome the problem with the larger objects, he said he could borrow an acetylene cutting tool and cut them into workable sizes, he borrowed the tool and set to work, but it soon became obvious that the time it was going to take would make the job unprofitable, so the pieces he had managed to cut in one whole day, were made into two loads, delivered, and the cutting tool returned to it's owner. The scrap dealing had been interesting and very profitable but it was now time to look for an alternative occupation but not before we had taken up the site foreman's offer of driving two of his dumper trucks for a few weeks, as he was short of drivers.

Neither of us stayed out of work; Alf went back to bus driving and I took a training course with the same bus company and went to work for the Yorkshire Traction Company Ltd. Just two weeks after Alf had returned for his second spell we were back working together, so to speak. I had experienced some very uncomfortable journeys on buses, as a consequence, that first day as the passengers began to board I made a vow that if it was at all possible no passenger of mine would suffer from that same style of driving.

In those days all passenger service vehicles had a driver and a conductor, or a conductress. Both of these were affectionately known as "Duckies". They were there to collect fares and assist the passengers, and also to perform one important role whereby they would go out onto the road at the rear of the bus when the driver was reversing.

It was a nice, steady job and I took great pleasure in driving to the best of my ability, therefore ensuring that my passengers had a comfortable ride. One thing didn't go down very well with Anna, and that was, almost every weekend my services were required driving. Some of the shifts left much to be desired in that they commenced early, then had a five or six hour break, culminating in another few hours behind the wheel later in the evening. Unfortunately I was to have something that gave me cause for concern and it had nothing to do with the actual job. After I had been there about six months Anna took it upon herself to go to the companies head office and lodge a complaint about me, to the effect that she was firmly convinced that I was having affairs with some of the conductresses. The recipient of the complaint told me about it and assured me that he didn't believe a word Anna had said, which was something, but the fact that she had brought our difficulties at home into my workplace was not very nice at all.

The duckie's were responsible for the bell instructions to the driver, one ring for stop, two for go, the press buttons were placed in various overhead positions throughout the bus and it said on them "push once", and this instruction was to the passengers who could, and did, use them when their stop was coming up. Used sensibly they were a great help to the duckie, but there were many young "jokers", who thought it funny to have the occasional stab at a bell push and roar with laughter when the driver came to a stop for no apparent reason. There were also times when a couple of ear plugs would have come in handy, if quite a few wanted to get off at the same stop and all took the push once advice literally.

The bus job, with it's unsociable hours, didn't allow much time for visiting but I did go to see my parents occasionally and sometimes when I went in the evenings or week ends Jacqueline and her boy friend Harry would be there. It seemed as if a wedding was soon to take place, but about this time Mother became very ill. She had suffered from breathing problems for the past few years, but these problems suddenly became much worse and she had to go into hospital. I went to see her on two evenings and on the second I thought I saw some improvement, but I was devastated when my Father came to see me the next morning and told me she had died during the night. I was convinced she was getting better and hadn't realised just how ill she was. She had been looking forward to seeing the coronation of Queen Elizabeth II on television the following year. It was August 1952 when she died, and comparatively young taking into account the expected lifespan at that time, although she had

Jessie Lillian 1952 - taken at 22 Clarkeson Street, Worsborough, Dale Barnsley. Taken shortly before she became ill and died

rarely been in the best of health. I firmly believe the area we lived in and the stress and strain of being alone during the war played no small part in making things much worse.

That tragic event was a devastating blow to all the family, but none more so than Jacqueline. She had been Mother's constant companion since the day she was born. Peter, on the other hand, had chosen to join the army at the age of sixteen and had been in for four years when Mother died. The empty feelings at such a great loss would be there for him, but companionship and the work would help to take his mind off things, not completely or immediately, but they would certainly help.

Jacqueline and Harry had decisions to make regarding their future, and as they had previously considered getting married in July the following year it now seemed to be appropriate to bring it forward to a much earlier date. Arrangements were made and they were married in December 1952, in St; Thomas's church Worsbrough Dale. Anna, our three boys, and myself, attended the reception, which was held in the Cooperative societies Arcadian restaurant banqueting room in Barnsley. It was a grand "do", with some fifty or so guests. For some reason or another we didn't attend the church ceremony? My uncle Harold was present at the reception and he had also attended Mother's funeral, on both occasions we had spoken but only briefly. I made no reference to the problem which had turned everyone against me, maybe I should have done, but I was of the opinion that if any one of them had shown any inclination to hear my side of things they would have asked, and besides, neither occasion was a suitable time for such a discussion.

Even though I thought about it then and have done so ever since, I have not been able to convince myself that I could have done anything different to change the situation. Prior to the reception I had been in Harold's company twice since the court case, once when his hay and straw barn had burned down and I went to see him to see if I could be of help; it wasn't required and my reception was very cool. The second time was at Annie's funeral, apparently she had been ill for a few months, and as I wasn't in touch, I knew nothing about it. Other relatives were there, but apart from Harold, who spoke, but only just, I was given the cold shoulder. Not very nice especially when I thought a great deal of all of them, and had fond memories of being in their company many times during my life.

The bus driving job was suiting me, we had fewer animals, there were only three cars in the yard, and all the hard work I had put into the garden and greenhouses was paying off handsomely, but my home life had not changed for the better. It was about this time when something I had never expected took place and it disrupted everything for quite a few days.

I had started to have some discomfort from the tooth which had given me trouble in North Africa. It had gone black and although not painful, was just not feeling right. I went to a dentist at the other side of town, and he removed it, then told me that all my teeth should be removed as soon as possible. I couldn't understand this as I wasn't having any trouble with the rest. He insisted that I had a disease in the gums and only the removal of all the teeth would prevent it from getting worse. I had noticed that sometimes my gums were inclined to bleed a little after I had cleaned them, but I hadn't thought it was anything to worry about. Nevertheless, I found myself back their, awaiting the anaesthetic.

I was told I should try to relax as the anaesthetic was administered. I had the gas, and relaxed. When I came round the dentist and his assistant were looking flustered and exhausted. Apparently I had relaxed, totally, and I had slithered down the chair, ending up on the floor in a twisted heap. They had somehow managed to get me back onto the chair and continued with the operation. I had a few minutes in the chair just to get my bearings then the nurse took me to the waiting room and asked me to stay there until I had recovered from the effects of the gas. I had developed an attitude of "I am not waiting around for anyone", I had done far too much of that in the army, the sooner I could get out the better. I had a large white gauze pad covering my mouth and a thick scarf, which I had somehow remembered to bring, wrapped around my face head and neck. I made my way out to my Austin, which was standing alongside the kerb, got in, and started it up. I was just about to drive off when I found that my vision was somewhat impaired. In spite of this, my desire to go home led me to throw all caution to the wind, and I drove off. That three mile journey home through the centre of town, negotiating the other many hazards along the way was a nightmare and one I shall never forget. I was woozy, not in control of any of my senses. It was a recipe for disaster and possibly the most stupid act of irresponsible driving that anyone can imagine. I was very lucky not to have been the cause of a serious accident.

My troubles were not to end there as in the months that followed I had to make many return visits to that dentist to have roots dug out where he had broken them off in his haste to get the job done before I came round. I have had a number of sets of false teeth, none of which have been satisfactory, despite the efforts of some really good dentists. All of them have told me the same thing, that so much damage had been done to the gums that they were unable to hold a palate in place. Quite naturally I have discussed my problem with people and some of them have said that around the time I made that first appointment there seemed to be unusually large numbers having all their teeth extracted under the National Health scheme. Rumour had it that dentists were removing full sets of teeth because they were paid per extraction. I don't know if there was any truth in that but it did leave me room for speculation as to whether I had been the unwitting victim of a "Con".

I had done two years on the buses, which according to my usual practice meant it was time for a change, so I went back to long distance lorry driving. Then, in 1954, Anna announced that she was expecting another baby and on August 7th Laurice was born, breaking the previous trend of boys. Michael, Phillip, and Robert, were all going to school, Robert having only just started. My boss took pity on me and gave me local pick-ups and deliveries for the next couple of months, which allowed me to be at home in the early mornings and evenings to do the relevant chores at the correct times, and although I didn't relish the thought of being in the house more than was absolutely necessary I was at home at night and in the evenings should my services, or assistance, be required.

The festive season of Christmas was a very special time in the Middle East, for the Christian Arabs, they had their own way of doing things. No trimmings or trees were put up until late on Christmas eve, the children would go to bed as usual and when they came down in the morning everything had been transformed overnight. So, we had to do the same. Every downstairs room had more than it's fair share of trimmings, a tree decorated with baubles and crackers and small wax candles fitted into holders at the ends of quite a few of the stronger branches, and presents, fastidiously name-tagged, were strategically placed around the front room . This elaborate way of doing things was not introduced into our home until the children were old enough to understand

Those Christmas Eves were very hectic, it was all far too "fiddly" for me and it all seemed to be done in such a frenzied rush. I was usually left to my own devices to sort it out the best way I could as Anna would be baking and preparing other tasty morsels for consumption during the days to come. It was vital for me to get everything done as quickly as possible as I had an important chore to perform immediately afterwards. At sometime during the preceding week or so I would have reconnoitred the woods about two miles away, in daylight, for a suitable Christmas tree, and marked it and the easiest route to get to it. When I had pushed the final drawing pin into the ceiling, somewhere around ten thirty, I would set off along Haverlands lane to the wood in search of my quarry, armed with a razor sharp axe and a length of rope. Once I had found the target it was a simple job to chop it down and I had a tree ready to be taken home. This method of obtaining a tree was commonplace in those days and it was many years before it became regarded as a serious offence to do so.

The Lanchester's love for large amounts of petrol made it extremely expensive for it to be used as an every day runabout. The Austin was reliable, and as I had one weeks holiday to come during the forthcoming summer, arrangements were made for us to go and stay with uncle Ted and his wife -aunt Gladys- in Norwich. They both had to go out to work during the daytime, Monday to Friday, and it was our intention to go out also and see as much of the surrounding area as possible, including a trip to the nearest seaside, weather permitting. They had moved from their bungalow shop where I had stayed with them for a year in 1936 and were now living in a terrace house much nearer to the city centre. It was a smaller house but big enough to accommodate all of us quite comfortably.

We arrived in Norwich one Saturday afternoon and Ted and Gladys were there to greet us. It had been an uneventful journey in bright warm sunshine for most of the way and we were all looking forward to our holiday, the boys were excited but Laurice was a little too young to express her feelings as she was only a baby about one year old. Everything had been sorted out at home as one of our neighbours had agreed to feed and take care of the animals. The rest of the weekend we spent with Ted and Gladys and went with them to see my relatives who lived in the area, including a tour of their beautiful city.

We kept ourselves pleasantly occupied until the Thursday, and it had been decided that we should go to Yarmouth on that day. The weather was being kind to us and a trip out to

Uncle Ted & Auntie Gladys and Mrs Woods (Gladys' mum) Taken at Great Yarmouth in 1952 enjoying a day at the seaside

the seaside would make a nice change. There was plenty of room in the car so we took Gladys' Mother along with us. She was an exceedingly jovial person and brightened up our day considerably. Almost all our time was spent on the wide clean beach, with a couple of necessary visits to the nearest cafe' for a cup of tea and the use of their facilities. Somewhere around five in the afternoon the paddling and the sand castle making had begun to wear a bit thin, so we set off to make the return journey. It had been quite an exhausting day for the boys and they would need no rocking to sleep. We had passed the small town of Acle, which was about seven miles from Yarmouth, and approximately seven to Norwich, when there was an awful bang and a clatter, giving the impression the engine had shattered into small pieces; it hadn't, but it did stop. I got out and looked under the bonnet and to my dismay I saw oil running out onto the road. I crawled underneath and my worst fears were confirmed, the sump (a metal cover on the bottom of the engine holding the oil in) had a gaping five inch hole in it, and one of the conrods was protruding through it. That meant that one of the pistons had broken loose somehow. There was no way that engine was going to run again without first undergoing major repairs. It was a calamity of great proportions, and for a few fleeting seconds I was thrown completely off balance. Then, I knew what had to be done. First my passengers had to be taken care of, they needed to go on to Norwich and back to Ted's. Trying my best not to give the impression that I was at all worried, I helped them out of the car along with the pram and other things they would need, and with a minimum amount of fuss we all put our backs into it and pushed the car off the road onto a small area of rough tarmacadam a short distance away from where we had come to a stop. It wasn't very wide, but big enough for the side of the car nearest the road to be clear. Then I looked down the long straight road for something suitable to stop and pick them up, and what did I see?, a bus! In answer to my vigorous arm waving the bus stopped and they were assisted aboard, fortunately there was plenty of room for them all to be seated comfortably. I had explained to Anna what I intended to do, she wasn't happy, but then they were off and I was left to sort out the car.

I got my tools out of the boot, and a pair of scruffy overalls I always carried. I had to know exactly what had happened so I crawled underneath the engine and removed the sump, narrowly avoiding the rest of the oil as it covered the ground where I needed to lay down to work. I pushed the car another five or six yards further along before I got underneath again to check the full extent of the damage. It was a very depressing sight. Two con rods (steel rods connecting the crank shaft to the piston, there were four of these in a four cylinder engine such as this one in the Austin) had broken clear from the crank shaft and were hanging loose suspended from their respective pistons. From the position I was in I couldn't see any other damage, but in order to ascertain just what had taken place the cylinder head had to come off. I lifted the bonnet and set to work on the top part of the engine. When the head was off I withdrew the two loose pistons with the conrods attached, both of these conrods were badly damaged as one of the two bolts securing them to the crank shaft had severed. They were both useless and would have to be replaced. The big-ends (a type of thick moulded washer) at the crank shaft end of both of these were also damaged beyond repair, but the pistons themselves didn't appear to be too bad, one scraper ring was twisted, and may have marked the cylinder but at that stage I had no way of knowing. I wrapped one conrod and one piston in a fairly clean piece of rag, put all the other spare parts and both tool boxes in the boot, locked it, and all the doors, and went to catch a bus. Time had not stood still, and the shades of night were falling fast. Surprisingly there was very little traffic on the road and my eagerly awaited bus was noticeable only by it's absence. I stood at the side of the road for quite a long time and by now it was really dark, I had despaired of being picked up by bus and although I knew it was a heck of a long way I started to walk, occasionally turning round at the sound of an approaching vehicle in the hope that some driver may take pity on me and give me a lift. Hitch-hiking during the war had been easy, especially if you were in uniform, but nowadays it seemed to be a thing of the past. Eventually a motorbike stopped and it's rider said that if I was waiting for a bus I was in for a long wait as it was almost ten thirty and the last one had gone. He asked where I was heading and told me to hop aboard. I did so, and at the same time thinking what an extraordinary bit of luck. Unfortunately the rider was a little the worse for wear as he had obviously partaken of no small amount of alcohol. He also had a hip flask from which he took frequent "sips", and kept talking as he rode, each time he spoke he would turn round and look at me, consequently the bike was left to it's own devices. I made no comment as it would have given him another excuse to turn round again! I held on tightly and stuck it out. We arrived at my dropping off point, at the end of Ted's street, more by good luck than good management, but I was very grateful for the ride.

When I got in the house only Ted was up, I used some of his Swarfega to remove the oil from my hands and face and then had a bite to eat. I explained briefly the situation and he told me where to go to find a shop dealing in motor spare parts, and we both went to bed.

I awoke next morning around seven to the sound of water hitting the window. That's all I needed, it was thumping it down with rain. I washed and dressed and went downstairs, all my family were up and raring to go, Gladys had prepared breakfast. and in between mouthfuls I explained what I had to do. The boy's were disappointed at not being able to come with me. Gladys gave me one of Ted's old raincoats, an umbrella, a flask of tea and a few cheese sandwiches. Amid moans and groans I made my apologies to all and went to the bottom of the street and caught a bus, which dropped me off outside the spares shop. The assistant was very obliging and I bought the parts I needed. The shop was near the bus station and after waiting for what I considered to be a long time I was on my way back to the scene of my misfortune, where I arrived somewhere around ten-o-clock. It was still raining heavily and the first thing to be done was to get the damaged sump repaired, I had seen a garage from the bus about half a mile away, so carrying the sump I set off towards it. I told the chap in charge what I required and he said he would braze it and that it would be as good as new. I left it with him and returned to the car, it had been quite a walk and I was glad for the services of the umbrella, the raincoat was wet but my head had been kept dry. I got the tools and other parts from the boot and set to work from the top of the engine and put the pistons back in their cylinders, lowering the conrod's inside first. Luckily the scraper ring tool to fix them on to the side of the pistons was in one of the tool boxes, and without knocking too much skin off my knuckles I managed to fit them both on, one on each of the pistons. It was now time to go underneath, the ground where I needed to lay down was very wet, so I placed a piece of canvas I always carried in the boot, where it was needed, under the engine. I had thought things out during the night and had decided to jack the car up on one side at the front, away from the road, then, as I was well aware that it is very dangerous to go underneath relying solely upon the jack, I took the spare wheel and placed it under the raised wheel, put the largest of my tool boxes on top of this, and lowered the jack until the raised wheel was just resting on it. I felt safe enough knowing that if the jack slipped I stood less chance of having my chest caved in. I fitted both conrods into position on the crankshaft, and manoeuvred two big ends onto the bottom of each and tightened the four retaining bolts. Then I took another walk in the rain and picked up the sump. He had made a good job of it, there was a blister where there hadn't been one before, but it looked solid enough. I fitted it, put on the new head gasket and fitted the cylinder head, topped the engine up with oil, tidied up and said a quiet prayer as I placed the starting handle into position and gave it a couple of turns. No problems, the engine started sweetlyt. I left it running for a good ten minutes listening for any tell tale knocking sounds while I took off the raincoat and the oil stained overalls and had some lunch. So, fed and watered, I put it into gear and drove to Norwich, approximately twenty three hours later than expected but at least arriving under our own steam. I felt reasonably confident about the job I had done considering the circumstances in which I had carried out the emergency operation

Our holiday ended the following day, Saturday, and we returned to Barnsley. During the return journey I had been a little worried in case I had tightened up the bolts a bit too much on the conrods, it was something that could easily be done, and would inevitably have resulted in another similar catastrophe. However, that car was to serve me well for several more years without any problems.

Another change of employment was in the offing as I had got fed up with all the hours spent travelling and with all the nights away every week. I began to feel I wasn't part of the family, just an occasional visitor, so I returned to bus driving: The same company, for a second spell.

That holiday was the first time we had all been away together. Previously it hadn't been easy to go away for such a long time as the large menagerie required our daily attention. With it being summertime the garden and greenhouses could be left for quite a few days, although it did mean getting stuck in to keep things shipshape as soon as we returned. The menagerie was to deplete even further over the next few years until we had no livestock at all, it was then we had the only other holiday, one week in the seaside resort of Rhyl, in Wales. That doesn't mean to imply that we never went out together, there were many day trips to the seaside, some to parks and other places of interest, and as the children grew there were more and more visits to the swimming pools at Barnsley and Wombwell. All of them turned out to be very good swimmers. So the children didn't have to go away to enjoy life, they had plenty to entertain them right here at home. From a very early age they took a great interest in what I was doing in the garden, and greenhouses, with the poultry, and the animals. If I was building something somewhere they liked nothing better than to take on the job of keeping me well supplied with the materials I needed at the time, using buckets, baskets, bags, anything appearing to be suit-able in which to carry things. I found it a little disturbing when one of them would come stag-gering up with two or three full sized bricks in a bag, dragging it along the floor behind him, or carrying them in an old basket that looked in danger of dropping to bits at any moment. So, I had a brainwave, we had plenty of old pieces of timber around the place and it didn't prove to be a very hard job sawing a few into sizes and nailing them together to make three trolleys , twelve sturdy metal wheels were bought from an ironmonger's shop and four fixed to each of the three knocked up frames, a bit of strong rope attached to the fronts and we were in busi-ness. I can still see one of the boys now proudly trundling his loaded trolley along behind him. To get to the back garden or the greenhouses these trolleys had to be lifted down a couple of steps, but that didn't seem to be too much of a problem to any one of them.

One year, at Christmas, when the toys we had bought them either broke or refused to operate as they should only a few days after they had begun to play with them, I decided I would do something about it. Mid way through the following year I put my plan into operation. I had given it plenty of thought and come up with, a "Rocking Cradle" for Laurice", a "Circus " for Phillip, a "Farmyard" for Robert, and a "Fort" for Michael. I was well aware of the mammoth task I had set myself, however, I had a strong resolve to make every effort to succeed in everything I was about to do. I made a list of all the things I would need, and bought them, transporting them to the place I had selected as my workshop: the cellar. It had wide stone slabs to use as benches, was well insulated to keep the noise down, and most important it was away from prying eyes. I found many aspects of the work challenging, especially getting to grips with the different materials, and the tongue and grooving of joints but eventually all the complicated work was completed.

The Cradle only required french polishing, Anna had made the pillows, sheets and blankets, and a baby doll was in a wardrobe upstairs. The Circus had been fairly straightforward except for the performing Ring, I made that from galvanised very small wire mesh. I really enjoyed doing the Farm, I copied the shape and design of the buildings we had at the present time. The Fort was simply a case of giving it a complete overhaul. It had been mine and I had given it to Peter when I went into the army. Now he was in the army and at my request it was returned to me. It had been well used, almost all of the papier-mache around the whole of the outside had to be renewed. The battlements and ramparts had been badly chipped in some places, and the camouflage paint had a face lift. It did take time but nothing had to be made from scratch like the others. During the summer I had been shopping regularly for all the accompanying things each one required to complete it. In due course the day arrived when it would soon be known if my idea, and efforts, had all been in vain, or were to be acclaimed as a roaring success.

It was Christmas Eve, the children were all in bed asleep, the trimmings were up, the tree decorated, and somewhere around one a.m., four trips were made into the cellar and my works of art were carefully carried up and taken into the front room. The many little packets and paper bags containing the various components for each present were brought out of their hiding places and also taken to the front room, where I began setting everything up using the empty spaces around the floor. The Rocking Cradle was placed on the settee, the Farm on one side of the floor, the Circus on the other, and the Fort in one corner at the side of, but well away from, the large fireplace, the opposite corner was taken up by the beautifully decorated tree. They were all set out to be eyecatching and each one had the appropriate name tag placed immediately in front of it. All the frustrating hours spent in the cellar were proved to have been worth every minute when I saw their faces that morning. The looks of sheer amazement on all their faces and the excitement in their voices did me a power of good, knowing that my idea had been an all out success.

The split shifts in Bus driving, and not knowing which shift I would be on the following week until the Friday before were drawbacks to the job. It made it impossible to organise things or plan ahead. So, when I heard of the excellent wages being paid at a steelworks a few miles away I considered making a move. I applied for a job there, and after the statutory one weeks notice had been served I found myself sitting on a bus, as a passenger, on my way to a stainless steel works in Stocksbridge to work as a general labourer in a hot rolling mill.

Chapter 12

The Iron foundry where I had worked was a big place but nothing compared to this steel works. As I walked through the wide open doors that morning I was taken aback by the size and intensity of it all: it was massive. The double doors I had just come through were both at least fifteen feet wide and some twenty five feet in height. I stood just inside them taking stock of all I could see. It was a large spacious building about twenty yards wide and sixty yards long, there was no ceiling as such but it had an inverted "V" roof about sixty feet high at it's apex. To my right there was a separate building, closed at both ends, with a very large walk through opening in the middle. There were clouds of steam rising inside which made it difficult to see exactly what was being done, but I did see at least one man working. About sixty yards away, towards the end of the place I saw something which could only be described as a hive of activity. A great deal of noise was coming from it, with a constantly irritating, and very loud, knocking sound. There appeared to be a couple of dozen men working in that area, some of them had a kind of towelling wrapped around the lower part of their faces, covering all of the nose and cheeks. I could make out that the most activity was taking place in two separate positions at either end of a long black drive shaft of some kind which was about fifteen yards long, continuously turning, and making that uncomfortably loud knocking sound I could hear. Beyond these two positions, there were sudden dazzlingly bright glares of orange coloured light which came at varying intervals from behind one or the other of these.

I stood there, engrossed in all the activity going on in front of me, and wondering just what I had let myself in for. The view was so captivating that I hadn't noticed the small wooden structure alongside me until it's door opened and I was confronted by an elderly man who asked who I was. When I told him he said he had been expecting me. He was the type of person I was able to take to immediately, having a nice quiet voice and an understanding manner. I knew straight away that I would have no difficulty getting on with him. He took me first to the other side of the wooden structure, which was apparently his office where, fixed to the wall, there was a clock and a rack containing cards. He took one from the rack, placed it in a slot at the front of the clock, took it out and handed it to me. It had my name and a number on it. He went on to explain that I had been allocated to his shift, there were three shifts working alternate days, afternoons, and nights, and this week his was on days. I had rolled up at eight-o-clock as arranged but the men already working had started at six, and that was the time I would be expected to start the next day. He asked if I had worked in a similar place before and I mentioned the foundry but saying it was nothing like this. He went on to inform me that I would need a pair of strong, steel covered heels and steel toe capped, leather boots, a pair of hard wearing trousers, and a sweat towel. He then spoke about safety and took me on a guided tour.

As we walked towards our first port of call he brought to my attention the bright, shiny, floor, saying it was made from large stainless steel sheets permanently fixed in position. They were very slippery, and covered the majority of the area in which the work was carried out. We arrived at the place which had been the nearest to my viewing position. It was known as the softening furnace, and was a vertical furnace set into the ground, usually two steel sheets were clipped onto an overhead rail and lowered into it, they were heated at a particular temperature for a certain length of time and then removed, and still connected to the rail they would take a short circular journey of some six or seven yards or so allowing them to cool.

Our next port of call was to the place I had thought was a separate building, as soon as we walked through the wide entrance the stench was overpowering, there was no doubting what it was; extremely hot acid. This was the de-scaling unit where steel sheets were lowered into vats containing acid and left there until all the accumulated scale had dropped off. This was where I had seen the steam rising.

The next place we called at was over the other side of the building. This piece of equipment was used to trim off any sharp edges or splits on thick steel plates which would then be taken to the finishing mill to be rolled to the required length and width. It was aptly named the Shearer, and was in fact a guillotine. While we were there a man delivered more plates and deposited them at the side of the machine, he was using a Stacatruck, one that was battery operated but the operator walked along behind it. This was something else I was introduced to, along with a larger one that did the same job but with the operator sitting comfortably aboard.

My tour guide, the Foreman, said I would soon learn how to handle both as these, and the three places we had been to, the Softening furnace, the De-scaling unit, and the Shearer, were the things I would be working on for the first few weeks.

About five or six paces away from the Shearer there was a small door, he opened it and we walked inside a long room, it had a number of long bare tables down one side and at the other a smaller table, above which was a tall brass urn. He explained that this was where "Snap time" would be observed during a short break taken about halfway through the shift.

We then moved on the area known as the Finishing Mill, and it did just that, it finished off the rough sheets of steel which had come from the aptly named, Roughing Mill at the other end of the driveshaft.

As we had been making our way towards the Finishing mill I suddenly became aware of the reason for the bright glare which had seemed to envelope everything at the far end of the building. The red hot sheets these men were dragging across the floor to the mill to be rolled had been inside a furnace, and each time one was required, the furnace door had to be opened to get one out. This was when the glare appeared.

We gradually made our way across the glistening steel floor to the Roughing Mill at the other end of the driveshaft. It's incessant bumping and banging was getting on my nerves.

The Roughing end was where those long wide sheets began to take shape. They had been comparatively small solid slabs until they reached this point. Here everything started off in slab form, varying in size, some two inches thick, two feet in length, and twelve inches wide. Some were smaller, others larger. They were heated in a furnace until they became hot enough and soft enough to be put through two very heavy rolls a number of times and squeezed to a certain thickness. The length and width were entirely dependant upon the thickness, once that required thickness was obtained there was no need for it to be put through the rolls again, no matter what it's length or width. The furnace door here was the same as at the Finishing end, it lifted straight up revealing the whole of the inside of the furnace. Slabs were put inside in straight rows and taken out the same way. Only one was required at any one time and when that row became empty the furnaceman replenished it with more of the same, and when he was doing this that door remained open for quite a long time leading to a much longer exposure to the glare and the heat. To me it was unbearable, and I remember thinking at the time, "how could those men work continuously in such unfavourable conditions for almost eight hours?".

We had now reached the end of the building, as far as I could see but there was more. We went through a fairly wide opening, not a door; a gap, and here there were men using "Swing Grinders". They had a kind of harness across their shoulders, to which was attached an electrically operated heavy grinder. They stood with legs apart swinging this from side to side, removing flaws from a slab which was securely positioned on a wooden bench in front of them. The smallest of flaws had to be removed before they could be rolled.

We came back through the opening which was only a few yards from the side of the roughing mill furnace and turned left into another part of the building I hadn't been able to see. It was an extension of the main one, still the same height but not quite as wide, there were all kinds of equipment on the floor, including some large shiny steel rolls with a type of blanket covering them. He said they were electric blankets and that I must always remember they were switched on, as they were used to maintain a certain temperature in the rolls. If, for instance, one of the rolls at present working on either of the mills was to break, a replacement had to be at the correct temperature, if it wasn't it would crack immediately when it came into contact with any hot type of steel in the form of a sheet or a slab. He also brought to my attention the many stacks of sheets and slabs which he said were waiting to be transported, by crane, to whichever mill needed them. Then he looked up and said "that's the crane we use in here, the "High Flyer", it runs on a track which extends from one end of this place to the Finishing mill". He then calmly announced that I would be trained to handle it at sometime during the forthcoming weeks. As I took a much closer look at this apparatus I was about to use, I concluded that it was so high I would be lucky not to suffer a nose-bleed each time I went up there.

Well, I clocked in at the correct time next morning, having caught a bus at the end of West street at five a.m. and the first job I was put on to learn was a doddle, all it entailed was attaching sheets to the overhead rail, lowering them into the vertical furnace by means of a small hand operated crane, and when they were "cooked", hauling them out and starting them off on their circular tour. There was a little more to it than that though. Furnace temperatures, and the length of time the sheets required inside the furnace, were things I had to get to know and remember, a bit like baking a cake really. During the next week or so I also worked on the Shearer, the two stacatrucks, and I made very brief visits to the De-scaling unit.

The weeks spent doing those different jobs taught me enough about them to enable me to step into the breach if one of the regular men was off. I was destined to join the ranks of the Roughing mill at the end of this learning period, which did end shortly after I had been initiated into the art of operating the crane. The fellow whose job it had been for many years was a real nice chap and the hours I spent with him in that little "box in the sky" were interesting, educational, and very pleasant. There was just about enough room inside it for the pair of us. It looked simple but the enormous weight of some of those objects, especially long floppy sheets, and the precision needed to place those ropes in the exact position where they would be lifted cleanly meant that it wasn't. I thoroughly enjoyed the instruction and whenever the opportunity and throughout the many years I was to work there I did a lot of weekend overtime on various jobs, and I was sometimes asked to handle the crane, often on really exacting work.

One Monday morning the foreman took me along to a separate building, a couple of hundred yards further up the road. He hadn't included this in our initial tour. It was known as the Cold rolling mill and was where all the sheets came to be rolled to the precise thickness before going on to be wrapped individually in sheets of brown paper ready to be packed and despatched. There were usually three men working there and I did two of the jobs but not the Roller's. He was a quiet type of person, knew his job to a "t" and was easy to work with. The sheets were not heated in any way but the constant rolling they endured sometimes made them get very warm indeed, a strong apron and a pair of thick gloves were essential. It wasn't a hard job but it was repetitive. I had quite a few shifts there learning what was required of me and soon felt capable of standing in for someone when it became necessary. That was the last of my "getting to know you " jobs, and at the end of a week on nights the foreman told me I would start work in the highly paid ranks of the Hot rolling mill hands. The first one I would go to was the Cogging mill, better known as the Roughing end.

There were eight men working there, the Furnaceman, who's job it was to look after the furnace, keeping it at the correct temperature for whichever job was being done. He loaded it with slabs, using a kind of very long handled, flat ended spade, placing them in straight rows, about six rows in all and anything between six and ten in a row if they were the smallest, and maybe only four in a row if they were the largest. When they were hot enough he would drag them one at a time to the front edge of the furnace with a long handled hook, this one would then be taken to the Cogger and rolled. The floor of the furnace was ribbed in straight lines, from front to back, and was about eight feet wide and ten feet in depth, which meant that the handles of both the spade and the hook had to be quite a bit longer than this in order to reach the back without the furnaceman's hands or arms entering the furnace. There was a steel cylinder about ten inches in diameter which stretched the full width of the front of the furnace, a type of roll bar. It only worked when pressure was put upon it. The furnaceman would place the flat end of his spade on top of it, a slab was gently placed on the spade, and he would then push forward keeping some downward pressure on the roll bar with the handle of the spade as it went into the furnace, it was a great help when loading any slab but especially when they were about two inches thick, two feet or more in length and one foot wide. When these very heavy things were being loaded he would also ask for some assistance to power them in and to drag them out. He was a very unassuming chap, cheerful and very helpful, his was a highly skilled job and one which took many years to perfect.

Another man would pick a slab up from a stack at the side of the furnace and place it carefully on the spade during the loading period, and when a slab was ready and brought to the front he would grasp it with a pair of tongs, which were about three feet long, and trundle it across the floor to the Cogger, and it would be rolled. When the heavier slabs were being worked the furnaceman would draw one to the top of the roll bar and load it onto a long handled flat steel barrow and the slab would be wheeled across, but the trundling bit could be got down to a fine art if practised regularly. Care had to be taken to get the right grip on the top and end of the slab as it protruded out on the top of the roll bar, it would be laying flat and had to be grasped with the tongs about one inch from the end nearest you, making sure the mouth of the tongs had a full grip by lifting it slightly and forcing them down. A quick pull and a twist to the left, would have the furthest edge away from you landing on the floor in an upright position, it was then very simple to drag it on it's edge to the waiting Cogger who would grip it at the opposite edge to you and chuck it in a controlled manner onto the plate in front of the rolls. Once perfected it was easy but before then serious problems could arise if the slab didn't twist and simply dropped onto it's flat side, the sudden jarring when this happened could break your wrist.

In order to squeeze the slabs between the two rolls, one turning clockwise the other anti-clockwise, it was neccesary to reduce the gap between them. This was done by a man who stood about one yard away from the front of the mill housing and slightly to the right of the rolls, alongside a round metal stand which was fixed into the floor, it was about four feet tall and on top of it was an oval shaped box with a handle and small copper studs at regular intervals in a half circle at it's top. His job was to operate this handle, in ratchet fashion, to increase or decrease the pressure between the two rolls, acting upon instructions from the Cogger. The bottom roll could turn but couldn't be raised or lowered as it was fixed, the top roll answered to the instruction it was given from this box. Apart from operating the ratchet he would assist the Cogger when required. He also had another very important job to perform. At the opposite side to where he was standing there was a large trough full of water and usually floating inside it was a Besum brush (a three foot length of a tree branch fitted inside a number of smaller heavily twigged branches). Some of the slabs had a tendency to "flake" when being heated and to leave this flake on the top of the slab as it was being rolled would seriously damage the end product, so when he saw this flaking on a slab he would grab the brush, swish it through the water, and swiftly clean off the slab. He would then quickly return to his position ready to operate the ratchet.

The Cogger, in my opinion, had the most important role to play in the whole building. When the Cogger gave that slab it's first push into the rolls, apart from it's probably having had to pay a visit to the Swing Grinder department beforehand, that was the beginning of it's journey towards becoming a sheet of high quality stainless steel. If it wasn't rolled to perfection there was no hope for it later on. He would stand at the front of the rolls waiting for a slab to be brought to him from the furnace, he would have told the "ratchet" man what pressure he required and when the slab arrived he would feed it into the rolls. In order to begin the widening and lengthening of the slab he would feed it in at an angle, probably the left hand corner in first. It would go through the rolls and be returned to him over the top of them, his next pass he would feed the left hand corner in first, this process would be repeated until the correct width was obtained and from then on it would be fed in straight. His objective was to continue rolling until it reached the required thickness and to this end the sheet would be periodically checked with a thickness gauge until it was found to be correct. During all this he would have kept giving instructions to the ratchet man who would change the pressure accordingly. The Cogger had to use all the skill and expertise he had acquired over many years to do his job effectively. From the moment the slab made it's first entry into those rolls the Cogger's mind had to be firmly concentrated and it was also hard work. The first few passes were simply slabs, there was no length or width to speak of, and each time one was passed back to him over the rolls he had to grasp it with his tongs and keeping a tight grip on it, let it drop onto the plate in front of him which jarred every bone in his body. When the length began to increase, sometimes up to ten feet, he would have to grasp it and move quickly backwards until the end reached the plate in order for it to be fed through again. The Cogger on our shift was a smashing bloke, he was a master of his job, and had a very pleasant unassuming nature.

At the other side of the rolls were four men, two known as Hookers and two Backers. It was their job to combine with each other to pass the slabs, or sheets, back over the top of the rolls to the Cogger. There was a thick strong chain attached to the end of each side of the housing, and a long heavy steel bar attached to the end link of each chain, it had a long round arm about nine feet long, and at the other end it was shaped something like a narrow spade. This spade was about twelve inches long and three inches wide, with a flat oblong shaped sloping end, about half an inch thick at this end but gradually getting thicker farther back up it's length and would have been about three inches thick at it's thickest part. It was an exceptionally long unwieldy object, very heavy, and needed great strength to manipulate it. This then was the tool of the Hooker, he would hold it as far up the arm as was possible to reach, and position the spade slightly suspended above the exit plate about twelve inches from the gap between the two rolls, and when the slab came through he would push the flat end of the spade underneath the one side of it nearest to him and bring some weight to bear on the arm, not a lot, only enough to enable the Backer to get a grip with his tongs. This was performed by both Hookers simultaneously, and as soon as the Backer had got a good grip on the slab they would pull down on their hooks and swing the slab away from the top roll, just to clear it, and then keeping it tightly under control allow it to swing back across the top of the roll towards the waiting Cogger at the other side of the rolls. All of this was done to a precise pattern with all the men working together in unison.

When the mill was rolling slabs of a reasonable weight it only required one man to do the job of Backer, he was positioned between the two Hookers, in line with the rolls, as the slab came through between the rolls the Hookers would do their job, raising it slightly and he would grasp it with his tongs, pull it towards him and it would then be lifted by the hooks and sent back over he rolls. Difficulties arose when one of the Hookers went under the slab early and lifted slightly. It would tip, and the other one wouldn't be able to get his hook under it. In that situation the Backer could only stand and wait until the Hookers sorted themselves out. When the slab had been through the rolls a few times it widened and lengthened and became a sheet, this was when things could go drastically wrong and extra care had to be taken. If the sheet had reached a length of around eight feet, it would still be glowing red hot, the backer would grasp it as it came out of the rolls and lift it straight upwards in front of his body, this was to allow the hookers to select the correct position for the hook, somewhere around the middle of the length of the sheet. At this time he would be holding about four feet of red hot steel approximately one foot away from his body, the longer he held it there the more he burned. His trousers, shirt, and sweat towel, would all start to crozzle, his forehead and the exposed top part of his nose were seconds away from blistering. This put his well being in the hands of the two men at either side of him. They had to be precise in gauging the middle of the length, if they weren't, and had more sheet at the roll end, he was in danger of being lifted clean off his feet. If on the other hand they had more at his end the sheet would simply flop onto the floor at it's middle, and the end that needed to go back over the rolls would be sticking up in the air, either way all three were in trouble but he would suffer the most. When the slabs were regarded as being too heavy for one man to do the backing on his own, a fourth man, whose job it was to stamp a number on the rolled sheets after they had been dragged clear, would step in and work as a second Backer, stamping the sheets in between. Those four men working at the back of that Roughing End certainly earned every penny they got in their pay packet's.

I was now a member of the elite Cogging mill gang and as such did the first two or three weeks on the prestigious job of "trundling" the slabs from the furnace to the rolls, and doing my bit towards loading up the furnace with slabs. I was also to become the official tea can carrier to the canteen.

When my "trundling" apprenticeship was completed, I took over the Ratchet job and made progress as a future Besum wielding champion. Concentration was required during the rolling and I took an interest in everything the Cogger did, including his use of the thickness gauge, but standing at that Ratchet for hours on end was really boring. I was very pleased when, after two or three weeks the foreman said put me at the back of the mill to do the jobs of Hooker and Backer. Now I really was, "one of the big hitters", and looking forward to the challenge immensely.

I had considered myself to be reasonable fit and strong with all the work I had done in the garden and the large amounts of lifting heavy goods on and off lorries, but it became obvious I hadn't been using the same muscles I required for this job. Every muscle in my body seemed to be stretched to it's utmost limit.

I was nearing the end of that first, back aching, month and one night I went to bed at a fairly reasonable time. The alarm was set for 4 a.m. as I was on days. I was tired and dropped off into a deep sleep, awaking with a start and it appeared to be daylight. Thinking I had over-slept I had a quick wash, got dressed, grabbed the rucksack containing my snap tin, and ran to the bus stop. I must have waited a good half hour and there was no sign of the bus. Thinking I had missed it, I set off to walk back home. Then I thought it was funny that I hadn't seen anyone at all while I had been waiting, so I decided to walk up to the signal box at the railway crossing about a hundred yards up the road, intending to call out to the signal man and ask him if the bus had gone. When I got there I could see the large clock inside the box, the little hand was on one, the big hand on ten. It was ten minutes to one. I was slightly early.

That morning I went home and made myself a cup of tea and a couple of cheese sand-wiches, and during the time I sat resting on the settee I thought about the Austin 12 residing in the mixing shed, it was in perfectly good working order. The bus fare wasn't expensive and it would certainly cost more in petrol to go by car, but for the sake of a few more pennies spent it wasn't worth the hassle of having to set off much earlier and without the comfort of a door to door service. So I had another cup of tea and came to a decision, I would check to see if the Austin had enough petrol, and if it had I would travel in style to work. I was in luck, the tank was almost full and I set off fifteen minutes later than if I had caught the bus, arriving at the mill car park in time to have a smoke before clocking in, and from then onwards I never caught the bus again. Once I had spoken of my new mode of travel in the canteen the Cogger told me he only lived half a mile from my place and asked if he could come with me. When

I said "yes" he told one of the Swing Grinders, and the Cold Rolling mill's head man, as they lived near him. I became known as the Stocksbridge "pick-up". It was company for me and they took care of the fuel bill plus a little extra.

I have said before how that little car was to be of great service to me and it performed very well, none more so than when the weather turned nasty. With Stocksbridge bordering on the Pennine moors, all the roads leading to it became very bad indeed in the winter snows. The strong winds that usually accompanied the snow swept it into deep drifts making a great many roads impassable, sometimes for two or three days. Our journey took us along the main Barnsley to Sheffield road for a couple of miles and then turned off onto hedge lined narrow country roads with deep ditches either side. To make matters worse there were steep hills up and down. As I had experience of this kind of travel I knew that keeping the car in as high a gear as possible would help to keep us going, so maybe I kept up a little too much speed on occasions, enough to cause my passengers a few heart stopping moments.

It had snowed quite a bit during one night when we were on the day shift but we had no problems getting to work. It was a different kettle of fish however when we were on our way home. It had continued to snow all that morning and had altered the driving conditions considerably, so much so that we had extreme difficulty negotiating the early part of the journey, then we rounded a bend almost on the brow of the final hill and came up behind a bus that had given it's all and decided it had had enough, and stopped. We were going fine but I couldn't get round it, so we stopped as well. I knew the driver of the bus and he allowed it to slither back just enough to enable us to get past, but as we had stopped on a rather steep incline all efforts to get going again were proving to be hopeless, that is until the driver of the bus asked his passengers to lend a hand, then we literally flew over the top of that hill. We were all slightly damp after paddling in the deep snow, but we were on our way home.

We were fortunate in many ways to get the twenty odd miles or so there and back without serious mishap during the winter months, but one night shift we had to admit defeat. It was all down to snow again. We had made it as far as the last hill on the Barnsley side but the drifts were so high they threatened to cave in the radiator, and there was nothing else for it but to manhandle the car round and set off back. As we travelled towards the main Barnsley-Sheffield road I was going through the road patterns for the area and fathomed out that if we turned right when we arrived at that road there was another route that might allow us to still make it. I told my passengers, and as we were not relishing the thought of having to admit defeat we agreed to try it. So when we arrived at the main road, instead of turning left towards Barnsley and the comforts of sitting in front of a blazing coal fire, we turned right, and headed towards Sheffield. Then, one mile along that road we turned right again and out into the unknown. The road was a bit wider and still lined with low hedges but fairly wide open to the elements. It wasn't snowing, but still blowing. The wind was howling and piling the snow into ever higher drifts as we made our way painstakingly towards what we thought would be a left turn that would bring us back onto our original route. We had probably done a mile, when we came face to face with what could only be described as a solid wall of snow from one side of the road to the other. We turned tail, and went home.

A completely different situation was to arise when we were working an afternoon shift. It had been snowing on and off for the past few days and during that shift it began to get worse. By the time we were ready to leave I considered it safer not to attempt it. The wind was very strong, the snow deep, and many drifts would have formed on the roads we had to travel. I didn't fancy spending a cold unpleasant night snowbound on one of those roads, but just as we couldn't get home neither could any men on the next shift who had to travel get home. So, we had a short break and then got on with doing the night shift. Things were even worse at six-o-clock the next morning; no day shift would be able to come, so we had a short rest and then walked to the other end of the works where there was a large canteen staffed by cooks whose job it was to prepare man sized meals at any time of the day or night. It wasn't pleasant staggering through the deep snow but we had to eat, and one good thing, the management were aware of the situation and we were allowed to have anything we wanted, on the house. We were probably away from the mill for a couple of hours but when we got back we did the job again, and that meant we had worked three full shifts, apart from the trip to the canteen. At two-o-clock, it was time for 'our' afternoon shift and things hadn't improved weatherwise. The foreman told us to go to the rest room and try to get a few hours sleep. The benches in the room were very hard and sleep didn't come easy but at least we rested and managed a further trip to the canteen for a solid meal and then worked the night shift. We had more time off next morning but still worked the day shift and at two o'clock the roads were passable, but we were now back to our shift and we couldn't leave the men coming on without a Cogger, or the Cold Rolling mill without the boss. Hopefully we would be on our way home at the end of the shift so we agreed to stay. As everything had been upside down on the past few shifts the foreman was very lenient with us and we had quite a long break, which was just as well because we were "rather tired". The firm was very appreciative of what we had done and paid us for all the time we had been there. It made for a fat pay packet the following week.

When the boys; Michael, Phillip, and Robert, were growing up, probably aged six, seven, and eight, and off school, I would arrive home from the night shift and find them sitting on their fishing baskets waiting for me to take them to the reservoir for a day's fishing. I would make sure they had taken some food and drinks and see them safely deposited on the reservoir bank about seven, and I arranged to pick them up around five after I had been to bed. They had all got a full compliment of tackle and spent many happy hours sitting on that bank watching a float dancing on top of the water. I saw nothing in it at all, but I wouldn't do or say anything to prevent them from enjoying themselves.

Every year the mill closed for two weeks and I was looking forward to the time off, there were plenty of things to do at home and as the children had a school holiday at the same time we would be making a few day trips. I think it was the second year I had worked there and the Cogger had been on at me for weeks to go with him and quite a few of the other men to a horse race meeting at York during the first week of the holiday. I did have a flutter on the football pools, and I liked a game of cards occasionally, but backing horses was something I had never been interested in. Some of the other fellows we worked with were also going and I thought it could be a nice day out. The Shearer took a great interest in horse racing, and knowing I was an absolute rookie he gave me the benefit of his many years spent studying form. He wasn't going but suggested that I should buy a "Handicap" book and study it carefully, he explained what I should look for, and that I should not bet with the bookies, but to use the Tote instead.

I arranged to meet the Cogger, and walked with him into Barnsley where we boarded a specially laid on coach for the journey, calling at a newsagents on the way to buy a handicap book and a daily paper containing all the runners and riders at York. When we had got on the coach I had to withstand some cheerful, friendly ribbing about the book. They were well aware of the fact that I was no racing enthusiast and suitable comments were made as to my reasons for wasting my brass on such a useless thing as that book. There were plenty of empty seats on the coach and our lot were all congregated at the back, so I made my apologies to my companion saying I was going to study the book, and sat down in a seat on my own. The comments were still coming thick and fast but I ignored the lot.

The Shearer had explained how to use the book and I followed his instructions to the letter. It meant looking at each of the named horses for each race in the paper and using the index in the book to find out when and where it had last ran, and how it had done. It was a marathon task but I stuck to it until I had selected one horse in each of the six races to be run that day. The coach stopped at a pub and everyone disappeared through it's doors, everyone that is except me. I had done my share of going into pubs during my time in the army and the only time I entered them nowadays was to avail myself of their facilities or buy a packet of fags. I stayed in the coach with my nose stuck in the book and by the time we arrived at the course the sports page of the newspaper was suitably marked with my selections. I followed the rest into an enclosure, ready to do battle.

It was a warm sunny day and there were a lot of people milling around. I wandered off on my own to familiarise myself with what was taking place. I had decided upon a strategy whereby if I was unfortunate enough not to have selected even one winner the total cost of my day out would not have exceeded two pounds. It was my intention to place half a crown (two shillings and sixpence) on each selection to either win or come second or third, which meant five shillings for each race. I got out my two half crowns, went to a window at the Tote and got a ticket, then stood near the rails to watch the race. I strained my eyes trying to see where they were and just managed to catch a glimpse of them as they flashed past. I didn't see much, then I heard an announcement and blow me down it was mine! I collected my winnings and put five bob on the second race, but my calculations were a fraction out as the horse could only manage third place, but at least I still collected more than I had put on. When I went to a window to put my half crowns on for the third race I did notice there was a lot of activity taking place at each of the eight or so windows. I had no idea why at the time but I was to have it drummed into me when we were going home on the coach. Apparently that race was the first "leg" of what was known as the Tote Double, and the second "leg" would be the next but one race after that. As there were a large number of people attending the meeting, if you were lucky enough to have picked the winners of both these races, you could expect to receive a large amount of money. I didn't know anything about this so I just put the usual stake on mine. I do remember that horse very well, it was a strikingly handsome dappled grey and went by the name of "Expensive Luxury", and as I checked it's odd's on a bookmaker's board I thought, "there goes my five bob, it hasn't a chance", because written in bold white chalk were the figures, 33/1. I took a steady stroll down to the rails and heard the creaking and breathing as they flashed past, and awaited the result. I had no qualms about what that would be having already resigned myself to the fact that I had just lost five bob, and when the winning number was announced I glanced casually down at the sports page to see what it's name was and received a very pleasant surprise, "Expensive Luxury". The bookies had quoted thirty three to one but when I collected my winnings the Tote had paid far in excess of that and twelve pounds and a few shillings were pocketed with glee. The fourth race choice came third, the fifth won at a reasonable price and the sixth also won. I had picked four winners and two thirds, and collected and shown a profit on all of them. I hadn't made a fortune as I had stuck to the five shilling stake but I was some eighteen pounds or so better off after all deductions had been made and I was feeling quite pleased with myself. On the way to the window to collect for the sixth time I bought a large tin of toffees and some other things from a stall to take home for the children. It was the end of the proceedings for that day and the enclosure emptied quickly but I had to wait to be paid out and consequently I had kept them all waiting for me on the coach and got an earful. Worse was to come when I told them how I had done, as they'd had a disastrous day and the fact that I had managed to choose the winners of the Tote double, and hadn't done it, didn't go down well at all. The irony of it all was that I had studied that book, taking everything into consideration for each individual horse in every race, with regard to weight's carried, distances of previous races, what type of ground it was, soft or hard, which jockey, etc. I had given the task my full attention but, at the end of it all I had been no wiser than before I had started, so I had gone through each race and simply selected the name I liked in each one! Although I didn't tell my coach companions that,, let them think I was a genius if they wished. The conclusion I reached however was that it was just "Beginner's Luck", and I could live with that.

The menagerie was now so depleted it could no longer be described as such. Although I did have a job at present which would allow me plenty of time to look after them, and I had enjoyed every minute of the work it had entailed, I considered it was now time to concentrate on another use for the main building. The main cow shed was now completely empty and it was quite large enough to house the battery cages I now wanted to make use of. There were two blocks of sixty cages in each block with water troughs running the full length of each side of each block, fitted so that they went across the middle of the front of each cage. Every cage had a separate food trough attached and a separate droppings tray. We had about one hundred laying hens in the run at the top end of the garden and these were introduced to the cages, along with a few more to fill them up. After a settling in period of a few days the eggs started to roll. The lighting in the building was from our generator and the lights were left on quite late every night to give the impression it was still daylight, this also increased production. There were some small problems with the hens living in such close proximity to each other as some of them began to peck at their next door neighbours, it didn't do any harm, but their appearance was not very pretty with almost all their feathers being removed from around their necks. When they were in full production it was the norm for each one to lay two eggs each day and some of them three. Sometimes, despite being liberally supplied with grit in the food tray to ensure strong shells, there were a number without any shells. These were used in the house as they were perfectly good.

The more I saw of this method of egg production the more I disliked it, but the information I had obtained from the various sources lead me to believe it had great potential as a money earner. The government had set up an egg marketing board, I contacted them, and they sent me three large special wooden packing cases, with trays inside for the eggs, every week by truck. I would fill them and they were collected. It did pay for the amount of work and time put into it but the feed costs rose inexorably, and I found the ways of the egg marketing board to be not to my liking. I did, however, keep those batteries in operation for quite a few years. The mill work didn't get any easier, with all too many aching muscles, and yet I found it necessary to work the odd weekends overtime now and again. I suppose it was a nice change from the usual hard slog and I did enjoy using the high flyer crane, doing jobs that required skill and precision. However, now the animals had gone I could go home at the end of the normal shifts and take it easier. The greenhouses received more attention, the garden was extended to take in the hen run which was now obsolete, and all in all there was a much more relaxed atmosphere about the place.

There are bound to have been some instances in everyone's life that have stuck in the memory for one reason or another, and I have probably had more than my fair share of things that I have found impossible to forget. One such instance occurred when I took all four children with me for a car ride one afternoon. I had someone to see whose home was about two miles on the other side of Barnsley and I had decided to give the Lanchester a run out for a change. It was about ten miles there and back and they didn't waste any time climbing aboard when I asked if they wanted to go. Laurice would have been about three years old and Michael ten. We drove through Barnsley and out towards Wakefield, down Eldon Street North, which was quite a steep hill. About halfway down another road, Old Mill Lane, joined it and where they joined the road became exceptionally wide. I saw the man and was on my way back home when the Lanchester spluttered and stopped just about where those two roads merged. It had run out of petrol again, the nearest garage was at the bottom of the hill around a sharp bend, and there was nothing for it but to collect the petrol can from the boot and walk back to the garage and fill it. I told all four of them to stay in the car, and that I wouldn't be long. Michael was left in charge and told not to let them lark about. A tall order for one so young I know but I felt sure he was quite capable of keeping them under control for the short time I was expecting to be away. I filled the can and was soon on my way back. I rounded the bend on my way back, and the sight I saw will remain with me for as long as I live. The car was where I had left it but not so the children, they were playing in the middle of the road chasing each other all over the place. Laurice wasn't anywhere near the others she was just skipping about moving from one side of the road to the other. That three hundred yards was the most heart stopping distance I have ever travelled in my life. I could see what they were doing and couldn't do anything about it, trying to shout to them from that distance could have made them panic, even if they could

Phillip, Michael, Robert, Laurice taken at West Street, Worsborough Bridge 1956 where they lived.
Left Phillip age 8, Michael aged 9, Robert 7, Laurice aged 3.

have heard me. I started to run and was almost on top of them when one of them saw me, he shouted to the others and they all ran to the car and scrambled in. I couldn't stop shaking as I tried to empty the petrol into the tank. Not one word was spoken during the rest of the journey. I parked the car, took all four into the house, and went straight to the stack yard where I sat in a greenhouse and had a cigarette before I could trust myself to go into the house and face them. It was only by the grace of God that the outcome of that afternoon didn't turn out to be catastrophic!

The days of the "petrol guzzling" Lanchester were numbered. I took it to a chap who specialised in that class of car, he stripped it down and worked on the engine but the petrol consumption was only slightly better when it came back. A workmate of mine asked if he could borrow it to take his family on holiday touring Cornwall and when he came back he offered to buy the car for what I considered to be a fair price, so the "guzzler" changed hands. I wasn't sorry to see the back of it.

The type of work we were doing on the rolling mill was very hard and no-one could be expected to work like that continuously for any length of time, so there was always a break after a complete furnace of slabs had been rolled to allow the next lot of slabs to get hot enough to roll. These breaks could sometimes be as long as fifteen minutes and probably three or four of them before snap time and another three or four after. They were very welcome and just enough time to have a smoke, a nice rest, and a good old fashioned chin-wag, when views were expressed on any subject. From the day I had started working on the hot rolling mill I seemed to get on very well with everyone, with two exceptions, one was the younger brother of a man my uncle Harold knew, he was a Backer and Hooker. His parents lived just along the street from the farm but apparently he didn't live with them so consequently I had never seen him before. I soon got to know him though, and his hanger-on who worked on the Finishing end mill. They were both tall and well built and well known for their loud mouths and the incessant arguments they provoked about anything at all. I had very little to do with the Finishing mill chap but when I started the Backing and Hooking jobs I worked alongside the other one and he began to come out with some very personal details of my life with Anna. The things he said could only have come from his brother, which lead me to believe that my home life was being discussed when he and his brother got together. He delighted in trying to belittle me in the eyes of the others, who never seemed to take any notice of a word he said. I didn't want any trouble, nor could I afford to have any, so I did my best to ignore him.

The other fellows kept telling me to ignore him, but once we were on the night shift and everything was going well. He was working on the right hand hook and I was backing between him and another chap. The slabs we were working on were very heavy and there should have been two backers on the job but our fourth man was not experienced enough to do it so I was having to manage on my own. The finished sheets were about three feet wide and ten feet long: not easy things to handle by any means. We had done about six sheets and as the seventh one reached it's required size I dragged it away from the rolls and pulled it on top of the six already there, where it would be stamped. This dragging across, and on top of, the other sheets was awkward. As the sheet came out of the rolls it was propelled forward and that had to be maintained in order to drag it over the ends of the sheets already there. I had just got the sheet in it's correct position and let go of it when I heard a bang and looked up at the mill housing where I saw the right hand hook swinging wildly from side to side on it's chain from being slammed hard against the housing. Out of the corner of my eye I saw the bloke responsible heading towards me with his right fist raised, intending to strike me. I dropped my tongs and put two straight lefts, one after the other, into his face and then followed up with a perfectly timed right uppercut to his chin. He staggered backwards on top of the now black but still dangerously hot sheets, how he managed to keep his feet I shall never know, but he did. As he cleared them he dropped down just in front of the rolls covered with the electric blankets and stayed there. Then the foreman appeared, he walked straight over to me and told me to go and get my jacket on as I was going to be sent home. I didn't say anything and was on my way to the locker room when the union man caught up with me. He said that if I went home the mill would stop as they would all go on strike, then he started laying the law down to the foreman. I just stood there, I had done enough. I was aware that any kind of fighting in workings of that sort was a sacking offence, but what option had I had? There was no way I was going to just stand there and let him have a go. After some time the foreman came over to me and said he hadn't known the facts when he had told me to go home, and would I go back and carry on working on the mill. My aggressor recovered and was sent home and I did wonder how two straight lefts could have caused all the damage they had done. His eyes were badly bruised, his nose swollen and bleeding, and both cheeks puffed and discoloured. He was off work for two weeks and when he came back tried to make it appear he had been unlucky and that any future combat would be quite different. I am of the opinion now that I should have never allowed him to get away with the things he had said about me previously. I feel sure that he thought I would not stand up to him and so could behave how he wished.

I was a confirmed Pools fanatic and firmly believed that one day all the studying I was doing would pay off and I could then retire in comparative luxury. I formed a syndicate of men in the mill, and after almost three years during which time we had not received one penny in return (and consequently the numbers in the syndicate had reduced considerably to seven), we hit the jackpot. Our excitement was tempered by the knowledge that many other people had also won that week. Then I received the cheque for £1,765, which in those days was a great deal of money. I took pleasure in writing out the six cheques, and if I remember correctly it worked out at around two hundred and fifty pounds each. We didn't have another substantial win, just the odd few pounds, but at least we had made it pay and that was good enough. Needless to say those that had left the syndicate were green with envy.

In a way I was reasonably settled in the steelworks but I was still looking for something in which to settle down with better prospects at the end of it. In the end I opted for doing something that I hoped would offer me a future as it was something I had already experienced. I applied for a return to the Army, in the Intelligence Corps. I sat an exam and had an interview with a high ranking officer in the War Office in London, where my previous experience was discussed along with the time spent in Palestine and my ability to speak Arabic. The officer I saw held a conversation with me in Arabic, and slipped in the odd phrase or two in French or Italian, some of the latter two I understood but insufficient to hold a conversation.

Anyway the information obtained from the interview must have been to their satisfaction as I was despatched to an Intelligence Corps depot in the south of England. I left the steelworks with the understanding that if things did not work out I could return there and resume my employment with them. I did find it strange at first going over things I had done all those years ago but soon got the hang of it. All the time I was thinking and asking what my prospects

Barnsley

Subject:- **Enlistments**

Tel. No. 2485.

Mr. J.L.WOOD

Reference No. SRO/72/1/50

68 West Street, Worsboro, Bridge, Nr.Barnsley.

Dear Sir,

With reference to your application for ~~enlistment~~/re-enlistment into Her Majesty's Army.

You have been allotted a vacancy in the Intelligence Corps the rank of Private.

Would you please therefore arrange to attend at this Centre by 9.30a.m. on Wednesday, 4th April,1956 for attestation.

After your attestation you will be despatched to join your Unit situated at The Commandant, Intelligence Corps immediately or on one of the following dates Centre, Maresfield Camp, UCKFIELD,Sussex 16-4-56 or 30-4-1956.

When you attend for enlistment will you please bring references from any of the persons shown on the attached slip.

If you do not elect to join immediately, you will be placed on "Unpaid Leave" until the date specified for joining, during which time you will not be entitled to any pay or allowances, until you join for service.

The following documents should be brought with you when you report for enlistment and when you join your Unit.

Army Release or other Discharge Documents, Health Insurance Card (and Number) Army Form X.202B (Ex-Soldiers only), Panel Doctor's Card, Birth and Marriage or Family Certificates (for Documentation purposes) Towel and Soap, Brush and Comb and a clean change of underclothing.

You should not dispose of your civilian clothing after receiving your Uniform for at least the first month after service.

Yours faithfully,

Lieut.Colonel,

Major,
Officer i/c No. 72 Army Recruiting Centre

Ministry of Labour & National Service,
York Street,
BARNSLEY.

DL 16233/2

Letter confirming re-enlistment into Her Majesty's Army 1956

were. The main problem was my being away from the children. My efforts to find some sort of accommodation were not fruitful. The kind of work I was doing was just up my street and I did find it much less stressful than being at home in the midst of one long argument after another, but the fact that I was not able to obtain a satisfactory answer to my enquiries about accommodation, with which it would have been possible to resume life as a family left me with no alternative but to resign. The commanding officer understood my reason for doing so and we parted company on good terms, he gave me an excellent reference and I returned to the steelworks back on my old job.

INTELLIGENCE CORPS CENTRE,
MARESFIELD,
NR. UCKFIELD,
SUSSEX.

TEL. UCKFIELD 534.

To whom it may concern

J. L. Wood

For the past nine weeks the above named has been under my immediate command. Within that period I have formulated a very high opinion of his worth. He has integrity, he is loyal, intelligent and hard working. I have found him to be honest and thoroughly conscientious in everything that he tackles. He is a good family man with strong ties and it was in

Reference from the Intelligence Corps Centre

Upon my return, Anna came up with a suggestion which I considered to have great potential. She knew everything there was to know about them, her mainstay being the actual making of the dresses. But she also knew which material was suitable for what, and taking this into account, what could be more sensible than for her to buy and sell those materials. We had no premises in which to do this but we made enquiries and found that we could rent a stall on Barnsley market. The main place in the area to purchase the material was Manchester, and would mean having to go there. I came off one night shift and Anna and I made the journey in the Austin to see what we could do. Anna had clearly done her homework and it came as no surprise to me when I was introduced to an obviously high class Arab businessman. We entered a large, imposing, building and travelled three or four floors up on a lift and came out into a luxuriously furnished office apartment where we were effusively greeted by this distinguished looking gentleman. From what I could gather he was a well known and highly respected figure in Palestinian circles and knew many of Anna's friends. Anna "lapsed" into Arabic in an obvious attempt to conduct things in that language, not because English held any difficulties for either of them but she was well aware that if they were to converse at the speed at which Arabic is normally spoken then I would not be able to understand the finer points of the conversation. Nevertheless we spent quite a long time there having coffee and biscuits during which he told us where to go to obtain the materials we required

Our next port of call was to one of the wholesalers we had been told about. He was an Arab and specialised in certain types of materials, some of which Anna decided we could sell, so we made our first purchase from him and we were to make frequent visits to his showroom each time we went to Manchester. The next warehouse was owned by Jews, they made us very welcome and were also to provide us with really good quality stuff at a reasonable price and they were to become our main source for obtaining the stock we required.

We were given a stall to rent on Saturdays in what was known as the Fish market in Barnsley, and although it did take a few weeks to become known we soon became established and it wasn't long before we had many regular customers. We made many trips across the Pennines, usually once every two or three weeks, to replenish the stock. It soon became clear that we would have to find another way to do things as we were having to make two trips to the market on the Saturday mornings and two trips to bring the unsold stuff back home in the evenings where it took up almost all of one room in the house. I made a number of requests to the market's inspector for a box and eventually we were allocated one which made things much easier, all we had to do was to bring the box out from the warehouse, which was only some fifteen yards from the stall, put the rolls in, lock it and push it back into the warehouse, and vice versa when setting up. As custom increased we were able to take out stalls on Fridays and on Wednesdays. When the weather was nice it was a pleasant job meeting all the different people and of course in the knowledge we were making a bob or two. It was hard to tell, but I do believe Anna enjoyed what we were doing.

We appeared to be moving along on an even keel when something happened which was to turn everything upside down and completely change our lifestyle. I was at home one morning when our landlord, Mr. William Elmhirst, paid us a call. He told me it had been decided that they would sell our property, the house, the buildings, and all the land, but not including the field opposite. As I was the tenant I would be given the first opportunity to buy for the sum of £500. After a first initial payment the rest could be arranged by mutual agreement and spread over a period of time to suit me. It was an exceptional offer and one which anyone would have jumped at the chance to own such a property. The land alone was worth much more than that and I was fully aware of the potential of the place. It was situated in an area that would soon be required for the re-developement of the whole district and I knew our days there were numbered no matter what I did. It would have been no problem at all to buy it but the situation in my home life was desperate, so desperate in fact that nothing else seemed to matter. I had become convinced that Anna was determined to force me to do something which would contravene the court order hanging over me. It was for this reason I declined the offer. A few weeks later a man came and told me he had bought the place and gave me notice to quit.

The Worsbrough Council housing department were sympathetic to our cause and allocated us a house in a nice area. It was a very depressing time for me having to leave everything I had worked for behind. Packing was a nightmare and there was much we were unable to take with us. The council house we were allocated had been built in a field at the top end of Worsbrough Bridge where the cows had grazed when I worked for my uncle. We were going to find it strange having to live in such a small cramped space. It consisted of three bedrooms, a bathroom, a living room and kitchen. Each room was only a fraction of the size of the equivalent room in the house we were leaving. Outside there was a tiny front garden, and a rear garden the size of ten rows of my vegetables. Instead of the large buildings there was a very small brick built outhouse in which I was going to have to store all my tools, and built into the house was a small toilet with access only from the outside.

One evening I had been working on the afternoon shift and came home to be confronted by an over excited Anna. I had hardly got through the door when she started babbling on about something which didn't make any sense to me as I removed my jacket and boots. To be quite honest I wasn't really taking in what she was saying as my only concern at the time was to go upstairs, have a good wash, change out of my working clothes, and sit down to a long awaited meal. She must have realised that what she had to say was going to have to wait until I was in a more receptive mood and I did manage to reach the bathroom without any further comment. The children were in bed so as soon as I came down and sat at the table, knife and fork in hand, suitably clean and tidy, the words came tumbling out of her mouth thick and fast. As I ate I listened intently.

She informed me that she had been contacted by a member of the Iraqi Royal Family, and they wanted to speak with me. I had switched off but suddenly sat up and took notice. The first thing I wanted to know was how this "contact" had been made. We had no telephone, and if the postal service had been responsible I am sure Anna would have taken great pleasure in waving the letter under my nose; this she hadn't done. I was then informed that it was going to be a great opportunity for me and all the family to make something of ourselves and that I must not miss it. My brain came up with a multitude of questions which needed answers but I got none, so, frustrated and tired I went to bed.

Two days later I was working as a Backer and about three o'clock in the afternoon the foreman came and told me a clerk from head office was waiting for me at the mill doors. I went to meet him and he told me I was wanted on the telephone by someone who said he was a member of the Iraqi royal family. We arrived at the office, the phone was off the hook, so I picked it up and gave my name. A voice at the other end said he was Aide to the Emir Abdullilah, the Prince Regent of Iraq, and acting upon his instructions he was authorised to invite me to take up the prestigious position of personal bodyguard to the young King Feisal and his family. He went on to say, with the usual flamboyant Arab way of speaking, that my service and duties in the Palestine Police force had been brought to their attention along with other recommendations as to my suitability for such a position. There were three or four members of staff in the office at the time which made it difficult for me to converse freely. I cut the conversation short after he had gone into a little more detail and had explained that there was no need for me to give an answer at that precise moment as the King, the Emir, and their entourage were staying in England for a further two weeks, but if I did decide to take the post it would be necessary for me, and my family, to be in London on the Thursday of that week in readiness to leave with them on the Friday. He asked if I would phone him at the Iraqi Embassy as soon as I had reached a decision but no later than the morning of that Thursday as there would be a considerable amount of paper work and organising to be done if we were to leave with them. That conversation, even though I had been forewarned, took me by surprise. One thing for sure was there must have been a very good reason for this unorthodox method of recruitment.

During the remainder of that shift I found it extremely difficult to concentrate on the work in hand with so many things on my mind determined to distract me, but fortunately I completed it without causing any problems for my workmates or myself. Questions were asked as to why I had been called to the office and avoiding the issue had been uncomfortable. When I got home that evening I went through the events of the afternoon with Anna, who showed no surprise whatsoever. Her only comment was, "good, we must phone the Emir straight away". Her enthusiasm was overwhelming but I was hungry and it was very late. I doubted the Emir would still be taking calls at 11.30pm. Anna did condescend to tell me that she was a friend of his and other members of the Royal family, saying she felt sure he wouldn't mind speaking to her no matter what the time was. In any case it wasn't practical to go to a phone box and leave the children alone (Anna would have to come too) so a decision was finally reached that we would speak to the Emir in the morning. Laurice had reached the age of five and was going to school so Anna took her that morning and then we went to a phone box. On the way there I made it plain that I would need time to consider what I intended to do, and that she must not commit me to anything at present. It didn't go down very well as she had already made her mind up as to the outcome. The call was made, with Anna doing all the talking. I was able to follow the more important aspects, and I managed to prompt her on one or two points getting her to ask what sort of accommodation we would have, where our children would be educated, and was it important for all the family to leave here at the same time. I gathered that the answer to the first one was that we would all be living in the palace in Baghdad, the second and third interpretations would have to wait until we got home but at the time she seemed satisfied with the answers. There was one thing worrying me though and that was the way the phone was gobbling coins, so no final decision was made, only that I would phone as previously arranged.

On the way back home we dealt with the two questions to which I had not been able to decipher the answers, there was to be no problem with the children's education as a school of the highest standard was situated in the grounds of the palace, and apparently it was regarded as being very important that all the family leave at the same time as they considered we would most certainly find it easier to settle down if we were all together in the same place. I couldn't disagree with that but when we arrived home Anna set to work trying to convince me by saying I was going to be an important person very soon, it was an excellent job, and I should jump at the chance. That may well have been the case and I could understand why Anna showed such enthusiasm, but I had always found that to take things at their face value was paramount to courting disaster. I used the time I had away from work during the next eleven days to put things into their proper perspective.

The way things stood at that time in the country known as the Kingdom of Iraq left very little cause for complacency. The Prince Regent was in charge until the young King came of age, and it's population consisted mainly of Arabs whose religion was Islam. I knew from first hand experience how volatile some such people could be. Our family came first in everything and I wasn't prepared to subject them to any of the situations I had found myself in during the years I was in their midst. That was one thing solidly in favour of turning the offer down but something else was important and that was the actual job I would be expected to do. I had never shirked responsibility when I knew exactly what was required of me and had the experience to carry it out, but this was entirely different. I had no experience as a bodyguard, and the responsibilities were enormous. After giving the matter my most careful consideration I decided it was not something I wished to do.

I had agreed to inform the Iraqi embassy of my decision on the Thursday but I saw no reason why I should keep them waiting. I went to a phone box on my way home from work and spoke with the chap I had spoken to. I gave some reason for my turning down the offer and accepted his apology for asking for a decision at such short notice. He said they would be returning to England in three months time when my wife and I would be contacted in the hope that we had changed our minds.

The sequel to the previous few paragraphs can only be described as being horrendous and very tragic. The Iraqi Royal party did leave, and arrived home on the Friday evening. I had wangled some overtime on the Saturday morning and in the afternoon had gone to help on the market stall and then brought Anna home around six thirty, after a meal I settled down and listened to the radio news. I shall never forget what I heard that night. "There is chaos in the capital of Iraq, where during the early hours of this morning rebels attacked the King's palace in Baghdad and murdered everyone inside, men, women, and children. The bodies of the royal family were attached by ropes to horses and dragged through the streets of the city amidst large cheering crowds". The days that followed were full of ifs, and buts, but I felt vindicated in my decision.

The boys; Michael, Phillip, and Robert, were now old enough to be allowed to do certain things on their own and when they suggested taking a camping holiday together I gave the matter careful consideration for a couple of days before agreeing to their request. I had given them the benefit of my "camping" experiences with the scouts, the school and the army and preparations were made. One Saturday morning I took them to "Primrose Valley" camping area near Filey. It consisted of one large grass field and a building which served as a general store.

This particular field had fond memories for me, it was perched at the top of the cliffs and sloped downwards towards a one hundred foot drop to the beach and was where my Father had put the wind up my Mother when he bump started that Ford Prefect car to within, what I imagined to be at the time, a few inches from that steep drop. The boys remembered it as well because it was here where their masculinity had been questioned when they had played and built sand castles, wearing their creamy white short trouser suits. It was a nice, clean, quiet place to take a camping holiday, there were other tents dotted around and one or two caravans. They were sensible lads and despite a few arguments and differences of opinion that were bound to develop I knew they would stick together when necessary. I helped them put up the tent, saw them settled in, made sure they had sufficient money to last out the week, gave Michael a telephone number where I could be contacted in case of emergency and left them to their own devices.

On the following Tuesday morning I received an unexpected visitor, a chap I had worked with on the buses, and he gave me some disturbing news. There had been an awful thunderstorm at the camping site during Monday night. He had been staying in a caravan he owned for the weekend and almost all of the tents had been affected. He had seen our boys looking at the remains of their tent with despair and had spoken to them. During the conversation he realised they were my boys and took them and all their belongings to his caravan. He and his family had returned home that morning leaving the boys to continue their holiday in the caravan, where he said they would be quite comfortable and that I had nothing to worry about, all I needed to do was pick them up on the Saturday as previously arranged. I knew him to be a very kind and considerate person, but the only way I could be certain the boys were all right was to go and see them for myself. I was on the night shift and that meant having to leave home around nine fifteen that evening, but I managed to do the round trip to the camp and back with at least half an hour to spare. I was very relieved to see they were all in good health and cheerful enough after the upheaval of the previous night and were enjoying themselves. The weather had improved considerably, the caravan was clean and well furnished, so I returned home and made my report to Anna while I was having a quick bite to eat in between getting ready to leave for work. She said she thought I had been stupid letting them go in the first place but I felt sure the boys would have obtained real benefit from their experience. I picked them up on the Saturday morning and it was quite obvious they had enjoyed themselves and were feeling pleased that I had trusted them to manage on their own. I was quite proud of them.

An exceptionally large building was being constructed a couple of hundred yards further up the road from the mill. It was even larger than the building which housed the mill and all it's subsidiaries, and very soon we found out It was going to contain all the equipment necessary to be able to perform the work we were doing at present but in an automated form. It was going to affect the Roughing end, the Finishing end, and the Cold Rolling mill. Apart from a few labourers only the real professionals amongst them would be required, like the Coggers, the Rollers, and Furnacemen. It wasn't going to take effect immediately, probably in about three months time, but I suspected my services would not be required as there were a number of local men who had worked there for far more years than myself.

For reasons best known to myself I had bought a Piano Accordion. The shop keeper from whom I acquired the instrument was a real nice chap. At that particular stage of the rock and roll era anyone with a modicum of talent, or who thought they had talent, were prepared to put themselves into debt to get hold of a guitar hoping they would soon be famous. Very few of them were to reach the dizzy heights of fame and consequently experienced great difficulty paying off the debt. There were the odd one or two who simply ignored any request for payment. When I made return visits to his shop the shop keeper expressed the difficulties he was having with so many non-payers. I had thought at the time it would be a good job for someone to go and find these people and apply a little pressure. Unfortunately I now found myself in need of a job, one which would allow me to choose the hours in which to work, so I paid him a visit, and after some discussion an agreement was reached. Consequently my years at the steelworks came to an end, and I took on the task of trying to relieve his heavy backlog of debt.

Most of the defaulters were young men who had formed themselves into groups and were doing low paid work in clubs and pubs. One group I contacted consisted of five fairly young lads who went under the name The Syndicate Five. Times had been hard for them and each one owed a considerable amount on their instruments; guitars, drums, and amplifying equipment. They were genuinely concerned about the debt and explained that work was hard to come by. After giving me details of their forthcoming appointments and paying me a reasonable amount, I agreed to their suggestion that they be allowed to pay off a certain amount each time I saw them. I used to go to their engagements fairly regularly and liked their music, especially their signature tune "You've got your troubles and I've got mine". This seemed very appropriate to my way of thinking! I decided to ask around and managed to obtain more appointments for them. This was appreciated and their debt diminished fairly rapidly until it was finally cleared. I continued getting them some work, but after a while they began to get a bad reputation for playing well during the first half of the evening's entertainment but turning into a shambles later due to drinking in the interval. I pointed this out a couple of times but it made no difference, so I gave up on them.

Most of the people I had to deal with were individuals who were trying their hand at playing an instrument, and as it was a phase at that time the instruments were usually guitars. Finding and making contact with them did prove to be difficult. It meant calling at their homes, sometimes having travelled a fairly long distance, only to find they had changed their place of residence, and in some cases had moved out of the area altogether. Sometimes it was necessary to make very long journeys to meet someone at a particular venue, one such journey took me to Cardiff in South Wales. I learned that an entertainer, who was one of the top names in show business, was appearing as the star attraction at a popular night club, he owed a considerable amount and had resisted all attempts to obtain payment by not replying to letters or keeping prearranged appointments. I turned up at this club and after waiting for more than an hour for him to come off stage I spoke with him. He was very apologetic, put forward a number of feasible excuses, and said he would see me and completely settle his account after he had done one more session that evening and collected his appearance fee from the manager. I waited in the hall expecting to see him come on stage, he didn't. After a while the manager came and asked me if I had seen him. Apparently he had already been paid for that evening's show and had been seen driving away shortly after speaking to me. Unfortunately I didn't catch up with him again and he went on to become a nationally famous star making large numbers of recordings.

The shop owner must have had faith in my endeavours as he recommended me to a firm in Doncaster which required a representative for work of a similar nature in the Barnsley area. They got in touch and were to give me quite a lot of work, so much so in fact that I deemed it necessary to rent an office with a phone and an answering machine. The office was conveniently situated in the centre of town, quite large, and really much too big for what I needed, but it didn't cost an arm and a leg in rent and served my purpose well. I could go out and when I returned there were nearly always messages awaiting me. I decided to canvas the local businesses for more work and I was pleasantly surprised to find there were many who could use my services. There were shops dealing in furniture, domestic appliances, electrical goods, and surprisingly the more expensive clothing stores; all had outstanding and long overdue accounts on their books. Some repossessions had to be made but if I could see that things like washing machines or televisions were in daily use I only did so as a last resort. It soon became a busy time for me and before I realised it almost all the work I was doing required attention in the evenings; the number of calls to be made during the daytime had reduced dramatically, and so had the cash flow.

On my travels around the different districts I had bought a bun or two from one certain chap doing a bread and confectionery round. I liked his attitude and his humorous outlook on life. He told me he owned a grocery store and had three vans doing bread rounds but he was operating one of them because he couldn't find anyone he could trust to take it on. It appeared to be just what I was looking for, working in the daytime and free in the evenings, and as I knew where this shop was I called round to see him one evening. After he had explained what the job entailed I thought it would fit in nicely with the collection work, so I arranged to meet him at the unearthly hour of four thirty a.m., in a plot of ground where the vans were kept and loaded up for that day's deliveries. I hadn't been used to getting out of bed so early for the past couple of years but I arrived at the place in good time.

I went with the boss on his round for the next three days, each van had an established round which meant calling at houses, delivering what was requested and collecting payment. At the end of those four days I was well versed in what was required and was ready to take over and organise things so that I could fit in the other work, some of it in the late afternoons and every evening. It was a bit awkward at times and I found more and more of the non-payers either unable or unwilling to pay and the number of repossessions increased accordingly. It soon became obvious that my little car was unsuitable. I had taken a look around and had seen a small van that would do the job very nicely. Although it went very much against the grain I sold the Austin, and bought it. Apart from the repossessions, it would be handier for those trips to Manchester.

Everything carried on in a reasonable sort of way for the next two or three years although the domestic side of things left much to be desired. The house was so small it meant we were practically living in each other's pockets, and this brought about the type of continuous arguments it was in my best interests to avoid. It was at these times when I would have disappeared into the garden or the greenhouses but here the little bit of garden only took an hour or so to keep it in good trim. However, I was out during the daytime on the bread round six days each week and out every evening on the enquiry and collections work so this helped matters considerably. There were times when we managed the odd day trip to the seaside or visiting some place of interest, and even had one whole week in Rhyl, North Wales, but somehow there was always the feeling of emptiness at a job not very well done. Despite very adverse conditions our children were growing up nicely.

In the August of 1963 Michael left school and immediately found employment in a well known jewellers retail shop and appeared to settle down quickly. He looked very smart serving behind an imposing glass counter. One of the first things he did was to buy me a very good cigarette lighter, a chromium plated "Ronson Viking", and had my initials J.L.W. engraved on the front. With the work came a desire for more independence, but I was still of the opinion that the hour of ten thirty p.m., was a reasonable time for someone of his age to be at home. I was quite flexible in my demands and did make it later if he was attending a cinema where the show didn't end early enough for him to comply with my wishes, but I insisted upon being informed that he may be late because of this circumstance beforehand. Despite all my efforts to alleviate the situation he continued to come home late and it soon became a high source of contention. Then something occurred that has given me cause for uncomfortable thoughts ever since.

One night I had waited patiently until one thirty a.m., knowing I had to leave the house at four to go to work, and consequently I was not in the best of moods when he did arrive, accompanied by four of his friends, all of whom proceeded to give me a garbled account of the previous evening's events. Unfortunately I allowed my annoyance to get the better of me and ordered the lot of them, Michael included, to go away, saying I wasn't interested in hearing their excuses. Apparently the four did go to their homes but Michael took refuge from the biting cold winds in the outside toilet. I went to work having no idea he was sheltering there, and it wasn't until the rest of the family came down around eight that he came out from his hiding place, cold and very miserable. I returned home around three in the afternoon and for the next half hour I was given, a well deserved, rollicking, together with the reason why Michael had been so late. He and his friends had been in one of their homes where they foolishly played around with a Samurai sword. Michael had decided to try and grab the sword by the blade and in so doing he received a six inch cut in the palm of his right hand which required stitches. The reason why he was so late was because of the long wait he had to endure in the casualty department of the hospital.

I was fervently hoping that he would have learned from that experience, but not a bit of it, he was at it again long before his hand had healed and things went from bad to worse in a very short time. We weren't to know then but he had found himself a young lady friend, and a few weeks later he brought her to see us. The impression she gave was of being well mannered, elegant, and highly intelligent. Just the sort of person to bring out the best in Michael. However, after another very late night the arguments again got out of hand and he said he was going to live with her at her grandmother's house. Although it was not what we would have wished it didn't worry us unduly. As it happened we had no need to worry at all as they were to get married eventually, and after the initial upset had died down somewhat they came to visit us regularly.

Another year later Phillip left school and had a job working with cars, it was something he had always been interested in and had always been quick to lend a hand helping me when I was working on one of ours. Meanwhile I had seen fit to change my early morning job, even though I was quite content with the actual work, having to be up and about so early six days a week, rather took the pleasure out of things. I had given it a fair crack of the whip but when I was offered a job with a sewing machine company I considered it for a while and then decided it would probably be better all round if I took it on. They had a shop in Barnsley which sold and repaired sewing machines which required a manager. What appealed to me most were the hours, nine to five, six days a week. I had never worked such hours before. I became very interested in the repairing side, and with the help of a chap from head office who came to the shop at regular intervals, I soon picked it up and could sort out all but the more complicated machines.

I didn't know it but another phase in my life was about to begin. Home life had deteriorated to such a degree that it was fast becoming impossible for me to think straight about anything. My main aim was to make a good life for my family so I decided, after many uncomfortable hours of soul searching, to do something about it. What I had in mind was so drastic I had to be sure I was about to do the right thing. A few days before one Christmas something happened to strengthen my resolve to act.

I had managed to be home early one evening and during the course of it a full scale argument developed, the consequences of which forced me to seek refuge in the office. Phillip, who had been present throughout the episode took it upon himself to accompany me. The two chairs and one desk in the office were no substitute for a bed so I went back home the next morning, knowing that Anna would be otherwise engaged on the market, and picked up a bed, some bedding and a couple of pillows. The office was large and it had an adjoining room alongside the working area which proved to be quite adequate for use as a sleeping quarter. Our situation wasn't ideal but tolerable. I did some work for the next three days leading up to the holiday and Phillip went to his job at the garage. Evening meals were at the Chinese restaurant, and a small cafe close by kept the pangs of hunger at bay at other times. We were all right until Christmas day arrived, then things changed dramatically. The Chinese restaurant and the little cafe closed on Christmas eve and remained closed until the 27th. We spent hours walking around looking for somewhere to obtain food without success. It was pretty miserable, and although he didn't say so, Phillip couldn't have been very happy. We stayed there for the following two weeks and then went home, cap in hand.

For the previous twenty years I had been hoping that somehow life would cease to be one long bitter battle but my hopes were in vain. Instead of getting better as the years went by they became progressively worse. I was now firmly convinced that in order for the children to have any chance of leading a normal life I would have to leave home.

The children were growing up; Michael had already left the nest, Laurice was the youngest at eleven. Robert was midway through his final exams and had to stay to complete them. On the other hand Phillip made no bones about his preferring to stay with me whatever I decided to do. It was my intention to leave everything except my own personal items and the van. The market business was a source of income which could quite easily support them all for a considerable length of time. The material box in the market lock-up was full to capacity. Later there would have to be another appraisal of the situation and steps taken to deal satisfactorily with the outcome. I knew that my actions would be very upsetting for Laurice and Robert, but after much consideration I put my plans into operation by leaving the sewing machine job, informing the firms I was doing collection work for and giving notice to end my tenancy of the office. During the next few days I managed to pack a few clothes and personal items into a small case and put all my tools in a wooden box, both of which I secreted in the back of the van. I told Laurice, Robert and Phillip what I intended to do. I had to dissuade Phillip from leaving at the same time as myself, explaining that I would have to find somewhere to stay. I would also have to obtain some means of supporting myself. I said I would come back to see them before too long. I made no mention of my intended destination as it would have been difficult for them if they had known and had to disclaim all knowledge of it.

The next morning when Phillip had gone to work and Laurice and Robert had gone to school I made my intentions known to Anna. I made it plain that I regarded our future together to be non-existent. With that I made my way to the van, got in, started it up, and drove off, Anna still shouting in my wake.

CHAPTER 13

It was with very mixed feelings that I negotiated the roads to the outskirts of the south of London where I brought the little van to a halt at the rear of a transport cafe lorry park, had a wash and a meal before settling down for the night in the back of the van. I awoke to a beautiful day with clear blue skies and feeling very much warmer than the place I had left. It seemed to be a different country altogether. I had a wash and some breakfast before beginning my search for accommodation. This I completed by the afternoon.

I had obtained a one room flat which would would suffice for the moment. It was situated in a long downward sloping street with large houses, mostly converted into bed sits in South Norwood. There were no parking spaces but plenty of cars lined the street from top to bottom. I checked the contents of the room and placed the case containing all my worldly goods and the box of tools underneath the bed. I then took a walk up to the top of the street where I bought an evening paper and had a cup of tea and a bun in a cafe while perusing the situations vacant. I came to the conclusion I should have no trouble obtaining suitable employment as the columns were full of jobs I could do. I found a phone box and made an appointment to see the manager of a security firm at 4-30 p.m. the next day. Once my thoughts subsided that night, I slept pretty well.

The firm in Doncaster, for whom I had been carrying out collection work, had given me work on behalf of a finance company from London. So early the next morning I drove across London to their head office, which was on the northern outskirts of the city, and obtained an interview with their credit controller. I explained who I was and after consulting their records he confirmed that they did require a representative to cover the area south of the Thames and I agreed to start at 9 am the following day. My first week was to be spent working in head office, before starting in my area.

I only just made it to my second interview of the day at the security firm. The interview went well and two hours later I had been issued with a uniform and found myself in the company of a man with whom I was to spend the next twelve hours doing security checks in and around an area on the south side of the Thames. This was where I would be working, on what was known as the night shift, six p.m. to seven a.m. I now had two full time jobs! My mind wandered involuntarily, attempting to see just how it was going to be possible to do both. At first I thought it to be impossible and was trying to decide which one to relinquish, but as they were both well paid jobs I visualised the many pound notes which would be forthcoming from doing both and I allowed greed to overcome common sense. We were back at the depot before seven and I was able to have a quick wash and a tidy up and be on my way to the finance company's offices. To my relief the journey took less time than I had envisaged and I was in

255

the office well before nine. I had to put my foot down on the return trip to clock on for six at the security firm and I only just made it. It was more of the same on the Friday, but on the Saturday morning there was no need to go north as my presence was not required at the office on Saturday or Sunday. I drove to the flat where, after stopping at the cafe for breakfast, I had a good scrub and slept all day, only waking up to do the night shift and then back into bed all day Sunday until I had to leave to clock on again at six. Not very exciting for my first "liberated" weekend but sleep was what I needed and I took full advantage of the time off.

Those first days in the office, Thursday, Friday, and the following Monday, Tuesday, and Wednesday, I spent going through the records of all the accounts in arrears and being advised as to the best way to approach each one. I was pleased when on the Wednesday afternoon I was given the keys to a brand new van which was to be my means of transport to do the job from the following morning. It would no longer be necessary to make my way through the city traffic twice each day and I should get more sleep. I was ready, and had learned all that was necessary and couldn't wait to be working on my own once more. At leaving time I arranged with the gate man for me to leave my van in the car park until the weekend, when I would come and fetch it.

At the end of each night shift I returned to the flat and prepared for a day working in an area somewhere south of the Thames. It was only necessary for me to go to the office once each week to collect the work sheets and discuss any problems. The job was almost the same as what I had been doing before in Barnsley, except for the fact that most calls were made to fairly large firms.

The security job was easy once I had got used to the things I had to do. I had a van, stored in the depot when off shift, and It was fitted with a short wave radio which I used to notify the controller of my whereabouts. There was a mixed bag of buildings and places to be called at during the night. Some of these visited three times, others four, including a number of warehouses, disused factories, and one large hospital. All of them had a special type of clock strategically fixed somewhere on the property and I had been issued with a large bunch of keys and somewhere amongst these keys was the one which fitted the clock at each individual place. There was nothing to it really as it was simply a case of find the key for that particular clock, insert it and turn. This registered the time at which this was done, therefore obtaining a record of a visit having been made. During the hours of darkness some were very foreboding places. I had been in situations before where it had been necessary to walk about with extreme care anticipating the unexpected, but then I was carrying a gun and a heavy truncheon, now I had the heavy bunch of keys and a large rubber coated torch which were a very poor and inadequate substitute! This situation had the effect of making me even more vigilant as I entered and patrolled these properties. I did utilise one aspect of the "town patrols", that of varying the times at which I visited places. Sometimes this had me returning to some place I had been to only half an hour before. At that time there were many gangs of unscrupulous villains operating in and around London. They wouldn't think twice about forcibly removing anyone who impeded their approach to their objective, drugs being high on their agenda. As far as I was concerned "fear" didn't come into it, but common sense, vigilance, care, and self preservation did.

Those first few days, and nights, when I had to fit in the two jobs meant being on the go for practically twenty four hours each day. This was difficult and tiring. The thing I disliked most was not having the time to eat properly as I lived on sandwiches alone. This all changed once I was out on the road, doing the collections. There was still the matter of insufficient sleep. I utilised the weekends recharging the batteries in bed. It is only possible to deprive one's self of sleep for a limited period of time, then it is not only bad for your health but dangerous. So after putting myself under great strain for one month I allowed common sense to take precedence over greed and worked the required one week's notice at the security firm. With that satisfactorily completed I returned to something akin to a normal life.

The first full weekend off I went up to Barnsley to see Laurice, Robert, and Phillip. My situation down south was now suitable for Phillip to come and stay with me but he had to work one weeks notice at his place of employment. Arrangements were made and I went up again for the weekend and brought him back with me on the Sunday night. During the first visit I had been permitted to enter the house and I had thought it would have been an opportunity for Anna and I to discuss various things but she wasn't in any mood to talk to me.

The flat was only one fairly large room but it proved to be adequate for Phillip and I. There were all the necessary utensils and a small free standing electric hob with two rings suitable for boiling a couple of eggs or putting the frying pan to good use. Extreme care had to be taken when using this, the lights, or the kettle, as the "landlord installed electric meter" was very hungry. For the few weeks Phillip and I were there we found it cheaper and more practical to eat out. The little cafe at the top of the street became our watering hole for breakfast and if we were back in time, for dinner there as well. The kettle and tea pot came in handy for a drink late at night. He seemed to settle down and accompanied me on my calls for a couple of days and then decided to get a job. This proved to be no problem, and Phillip was shortly installed in a garage at Streatham as odd job man. It wasn't a good job but at least it kept him occupied and allowed him to drive from time to time. The flat on the whole was only used for sleeping. We made a trip into London on a couple of Sundays to have a look round. It may seem out of the question now but we did actually park in Oxford street and once opposite Hyde Park, outside Grosvenor House. We went to Brixton quite a few times, it was an interesting and different kind of place with an extremely noisy colourful market and some parts of it reminded me of the Souk. Fish and chip shops were in an abundance along with shops selling Kebab's, Halawi, and Baclava. Phillip had acquired a taste for these things when he was in Transjordan on holiday with Laurice and his Mother. They weren't exactly the same but we both had our fair share. There was a large swimming pool in Streatham and we made good use of it. Alongside it was an ice rink and this is where we spent most of our time. Neither of us had ever been ice skating and consequently the first session was spent holding onto the side barriers, but I was surprised at the way Phillip adapted himself to it.

Two or three weeks before Phillip joined me in the flat I was faced with a dilemma when I started receiving daily letters telling me I was causing overcrowding in the street. This was because I had both my work van and my own van. I didn't much like the anonymous complaint, but was sympathetic to it's concerns. Finding a solution made it inevitable that one had to go. The firm's van was part of the job so I sold mine to a garage. Without somewhere secure to park it I felt I had no option, but when Phillip moved down I realised it had been short sighted. Although the principal cause of my instability and stress was now left far behind, I was still not focusing properly on the job in hand.

The evening newspaper was still very much in evidence and Phillip went through the situations vacant columns with a fine tooth comb every night. He was happy with the garage work but knew there were very little prospects of his bettering himself there. One evening he saw an advert for a trainee chef and said it was something he thought would suit him so the next day he phoned and made an appointment. In the afternoon I took him to the "Le Petit Montemar" restaurant in Wigmore street, just off Oxford street in the centre of London. He was offered, and took, the job and on the way back to the flat he told me what the position entailed. The hours would be long and he would start with the menial duties. A normal day would start around four thirty in the morning with a break of a few hours, then resume in the late afternoon until the early hours of the next day. The pay would be poor to begin with as he would have a long period of learning, but he would have no expenses as far as food or living accommodation were concerned. All his working day meals would be taken in the restaurant and he would live in. Listening to him going over what had been said his obvious enthusiasm knew no bounds but I thought it sounded like a lot of hard work for a pitifully small remuneration. He assured me the long term prospects were very good and said it was what he wanted. The following Sunday evening I took him, suitcase and all, to his new place of residence and returned to the flat alone.

CHAPTER 14

A new phase in anyone's life warrants a new Chapter and none more so than in my case as I was about to embark upon something which was to alter my lifestyle completely. Fortunately the giant step I was about to make proved to be something I had got exactly right, as the next thirty five years or so were to prove.

For the next few weekends I picked Phillip up from his workplace and we swam and skated as the mood took us, and spent time in various places of interest before he had to return on the Sunday evening. Then one weekend we went to see Laurice and Robert and took them out with us on the Saturday. Phillip, surprisingly, was still welcome to stay with them overnight and I went off to see someone I hadn't seen for months. When I had been doing the bread round, some two years before, I had become friendly with one of my customers: a married woman, a young lady of tender years according to my age, but we got on well together right from our first meeting. On that Saturday evening I told her of all that had transpired since the last time I had seen her about two months previously, and asked her if she would be prepared to come and live with me. This was no spur of the moment request and it came as no surprise to her as we had discussed the probability more than once during the time we had been spending together over the past twelve months prior to my leaving Barnsley. She had repeatedly stated that she was unhappy in her marriage, and despite the obvious difficulties we did see each other on a fairly regular basis. Inevitably the friendship became more than just platonic, and in this context I do hold up my hands to be counted. I have said before that I was accused of infidelity from the very early months of my marriage, even during our time in Palestine. When the accusations were made immediately prior to my leaving Barnsley and the times after I had left some of the things Anna said were true, but only up to a point. That point being that there had been no grounds for all the accusations directed at me before that final twelve months.

The thought of making such a move and leaving everything behind that she knew, not knowing how things would turn out, must have been very difficult for the young lady (her name being Valerie) but the answer she gave to my request was positive. Neither of us had a telephone at home so in order for us to be able to keep in touch a date and time were fixed when I would make a call to a phone box which was a short distance away from her home. Over a period of a few weeks a number of calls were made culminating in a decision being reached that I would pick her up at the same phone box at a certain time on one particular day. When I had known for sure that the wheels were about to be set in motion I had made preparations by obtaining a fully furnished first floor maisonette close to a large area of common woodland in a delightful part of Surrey (almost back to my place of birth).

It would not have been in Valerie's best interests to have informed anyone of her intentions and consequently it would have been difficult for her to have brought all her clothes with her, so I made provision for some to be available for when she arrived, and two days before I went up I paid a visit to the local Tesco supermarket and bought enough food, including some for a seven month old baby which Valerie would be bringing with her. She did have two children, the baby Christine, and another girl, Julie, who was the apple of her Father's eye, and she was almost four. Although Valerie was very upset at having to do so she had to leave Julie at her Mother-in-law's, where her husband would be able to pick her up when he came home from work. She had left him a note informing him of her intentions, although nothing specific. In a situation like this people were going to be hurt and there was no easy way to soften the blow unless both parties concerned could sit down first and discuss the matter in a sensible manner. Valerie thought this would have not been possible under the circumstances. Cruel, Heartless, Selfish, Inconsiderate, all these come to mind and could rightly apply. It had been heartbreaking for Valerie having to reach the decision to leave Julie but she finally had to concede that it would be altogether wrong to deprive her husband of both children and as he was so attached to Julie it would be best if she stayed with him.

I arrived at the phone box much earlier than arranged, but just as I got there I saw her walking up the small road towards the box with Christine in her arms and carrying a small suit case. I was very relieved and by the look on her face so was she, and were soon on our way to start a new life together. It was a beautiful day, warm and sunny, and we made the journey in good time, arriving at the maisonette in the early evening. It didn't take long for Valerie to settle in.

The maisonette was very nice in almost all aspects. It was the upper floor of a recently built detached property with gardens at the front, one side, and rear, and a driveway leading into the rear garden on the other side. There was a door on this side which provided access and opened into a very small hallway and quite a few stairs which travelled upwards at a rather steep angle. It was situated almost at the end of a quiet tree lined avenue where at the very end was a large area of woodland interwoven with earth footpaths which were well trodden by the public. The maisonette itself was well appointed and modern. The stairs were a bit of a problem though as they were narrow and very steep; Christine would have been better suited with a pram rather than the carry cot we bought, but negotiating those stairs with a pram would have been extremely difficult even for the two of us. Overall though it was a really nice place.

The first weekend we were there I picked Phillip up from the restaurant at lunch time on the Saturday, and during the journey down I told him of the change in my circumstances. He was surprised and quite naturally a little shocked. We spent the weekend together, Valerie, Phillip, and I, and when I took him back on the Sunday evening he appeared to accept the changes but it was difficult to know just what he was thinking. However, he came down almost every weekend and seemed quite happy to do so. On a number of ocassions he was adamant that he was not going to go back to continue with his training. I sympathised with him as he was being treated like a general "dogsbody" and doing very little in the way of training and the head chef was proving to be a bit of a tyrant. I did my best to explain how I thought things would change after he had been there a while. We continued to make that journey back to the restaurant on Sunday evenings and both of us are now exceptionally pleased we did so.

Those first few months seemed to pass very quickly. I was away doing my job from early morning to late evening Monday to Friday. We made good use of most weekends when Phillip came down by going swimming and ice skating, two things in which Valerie was quite content to be a spectator, and a trip to Brighton gave Christine her first taste of the seaside.

The whole district where we lived had an abundance of fresh air as the roads and streets were clean, light and airy. In the evenings, when it had cooled down a bit, it was very pleasant to stroll through the trees and shrubs in the common woodland. There were also quite a few evenings when we ventured into the small town a couple of miles away to do a bit of shopping at the supermarket, and ocassionally followed that up by calling at a Chinese restaurant where they served a really good mixed grill.

Our first few years together seemed to pass very quickly. We made one or two trips up to Barnsley for Valerie to see her friends and for me to see Robert and Laurice and on one occasion I paid a visit to my Father. He had remarried, and he and his wife were living with her parents in a very nice bungalow on the outskirts of Barnsley. He appeared to be happy enough and was pleased to see me.

One or two incidents of note took place during those first few months, which I shall recall later, but first I will relate how things were to change dramatically during that time owing to the fact that I was summoned to appear at the local magistrates court where I was informed that Anna was obtaining a Social Security Benefit on behalf of the "Four" children which she claimed were living with her, and that it was my duty to pay maintenance for these children. After I had explained that there were only two children at present living in the family home as Michael had left home long before I did and that Phillip was living at his place of work in London it was decided that the case would be adjourned until the correct number of dependants was ascertained. It was extremely annoying that things had reached this stage as it had been my intention to sort something out with Anna before the Social Services had any reason to become involved but on the one occasion I had tried to discuss the matter with Anna, on the first return visit I had made, it was a disaster.

I thought it very unfair that I should pay back money she was obtaining under false pretences, and to that end I decided to do something about it, at least for the immediate future. Valerie and I discussed the matter and I changed jobs and we moved house. It was an unwanted upheaval and one which we didn't really wish to make but it had to be done. The new job included repossessing cars where their owners had not kept up with the payments on their hire purchase agreements, it was to prove interesting if nothing else.

We didn't find accommodation immediately and before we did a couple of things of interest were to take place. Valerie had informed me that we were about to have an increase in our family and that according to her reckoning this would occur sometime in February. Pauline, having shown complete disregard for her Mother's prediction, arrived on the scene at approximately eleven o'clock on the evening of December 9th 1966, two months premature. Around ten thirty Valerie said she didn't feel very well and went for a lie down on the bed. As I had an early start the next morning I did the same. It was obvious that Valerie was in pain and finding it hard to settle down, but I was totally unprepared when she said "I think the baby is coming". My first reaction was one of disbelief and I suggested I phone the doctor, but she said it was too late for that. I have done many things in my life but none so frightening as what transpired during the next few minutes, not knowing what to do but sincerely hoping that what I was doing was correct. It seemed to take a long time before the tiny bundle was safely wrapped in a small sheet and handed over to Valerie to cradle in her arms but in fact the whole procedure took less than five minutes. After I had regained control of my nerves and stopped shaking, I phoned a hospital. Within fifteen minutes an ambulance came, bringing with it a midwife, and both Valerie and the baby were taken to the hospital. Christine was fast asleep and didn't take kindly to being woken up but I quickly dressed her and the two of us followed a short while later. It was decided that Valerie would stay in for a couple of days to recuperate from her unexpected ordeal but as Pauline was exceptionally underweight she was placed in an incubator in the baby intensive care unit and she was to stay there for almost two months. The following two months were a trying time. We were concerned about Pauline, Valerie was having to visit her and look after Christine at home, I was having to work odd hours to be there when Valerie was at the hospital. We were all relieved when, in early February, Pauline was allowed home.

Repossessing cars was a thankless job and one which I took no pleasure in doing at all. The cars had to be collected and then delivered to a garage where a receipt had to be obtained. The one good thing about it was that it allowed me to have flexible hours. There was also a downside though as I was using public transport to get to where I wanted to be there was no need for me to have a vehicle for my own use.

There were two ways in which a repossession could be made and the one I favoured most was to approach the owner and obtain permission to take it. The other was to just take it wherever and whenever it was possible to do so.

One chap I went to see was unusually obliging and extremely helpful. He handed over the keys gracefully, checked the oil and water and waved as I drove the car down his driveway and out into the road, which gave me the impression he was pleased to see it go. Early that day I had taken the train to Torquay in Devon to repossess the vehicle, a Triumph soft top sports car. When I arrived it was cold, very windy, and raining heavily and it continued to do so as I set off to make the return journey. The petrol gauge was showing empty so I put quite a few gallons in at the first petrol station I came to but on checking the gauge again I noticed it still showed empty which meant it wasn't working, at the time it didn't worry me as I considered the amount I had put in would be sufficient to get me home. What did worry me was that the soft top was ripped in a number of places and that the plastic side window had no press studs with which to secure it to the door frame as they had been torn off. As it flapped in the wind a lot of rain entered the car. I was travelling for the most part along narrow country lanes and the weather was getting progressively worse. I don't know what it was about me but if ever it became my lot to drive a car with a dodgy fuel gauge, no matter how I tried to calculate fuel economy it seemed inevitable that at some stage it would run out of petrol, and never within easy reach of a garage. The Triumph spluttered a bit, coughed a few times, and rolled gently to a stop. The ensuing trudge through blustery winds and relentless rain to a garage and back was unpleasant to say the least. I borrowed a can from the owner of the garage, filled it and upon arriving back at the car poured the contents into it's tank and drove to the garage where I put a few more gallons in, hoping it would be enough to see me all the way home this time. It was now dark, the dipped headlamps didn't work, and sidelight driving is not a nice way to travel along poorly lit country roads. The wipers became more and more sluggish making it even more difficult to see. I was soaked to the skin and very disgruntled and sat and shivered for the next forty odd miles. Nevertheless I got it home and took it to it's designated garage the following morning where I handed it over and heaved a great sigh of relief as I did so. Of one thing I am certain, my tried and tested "Gut Feeling" had proved true to form once again. I had known something was not quite right about the ease with which the car was so willingly handed over, he was obviously just as happy as I was to see the back of it!

A few weeks after Pauline had been allowed home, I had arranged things so that I had a reliable repossession at my disposal for the weekend and we went up to Barnsley. I dropped Valerie and the two girls off at her parents' home in Worsbrough Bridge. This was the first visit she had made to them since leaving Barnsley. At this point in time I was regarded as being responsible for breaking up their daughter's marriage and so was not welcome in their home. I expected this and waited in the car until Valerie came out and assured me she would be all right and then made my way to Thurgoland, a small village a short distance from the Pennine moors to see my Father in the country cottage he and his wife had moved to a few months earlier. They were both in good health and appeared to be enjoying life. I stayed with them for about two hours with Dad and I discussing many things, but his wife didn't sit down with us and join in the conversation. My Dad told me he was looking forward to making a move in the next week or so to another cottage about four miles away which had a large garden and a greenhouse where he would be able to grow his own vegetables and flowers. I was to have the opportunity to call in and see him there about six weeks later. This came about when I had to make a somewhat different kind of repossession on the outskirts of Liverpool.

The owner of the vehicle in question had reached an agreement with the hire purchase company to hand it over to their representative at 10 o'clock of an evening. Apparently the owner worked long hours, and so I wasn't surprised when he was very late. I duly took possession of the car and started back looking forward to a pleasant drive. It had been my intention to make a slight detour and call at my Father's new home and so it was that I found myself standing outside the door to the cottage at two thirty in the morning. Not the best of times to pay someone a visit but I knew Dad wouldn't mind so I gave the door a couple of hefty knocks. They didn't have the desired effect so I scrambled around and collected a handful of very small stones and slung them up a few at a time to a bedroom window. I had almost got down to the last of them when he appeared at the window and seeing who it was disturbing his sleep he came down and let me in. I explained how it came about that I was there and almost before I had finished speaking he must have worked out that I hadn't eaten for quite some time and the frying pan was soon on the go. At a very early stage in the proceedings his wife appeared on a small balcony at the top of the stairs and as soon as she saw me she said, "How can you justify waking people up at this unearthly hour?" I couldn't, and made no attempt to explain, but my Dad said something to the effect that she should go back to bed. We had a long chat and then I left to resume my journey.

I was to see him on three occasions after that. When we were at the cottage-this time in daylight-he had taken great pleasure in showing me the large vegetable patch he had created and a colourful flower garden containing his favourite plants. His enthusiasm knew no bounds when he proudly presented the well stocked greenhouse. It was very obvious the garden was keeping him fully occupied and enabling him to enjoy life to the full. I thought that all the exercise and the fresh country air he was getting would go a long way towards ensuring he remained in good health for a considerable length of time, but it was not to be.

The next time I went to the cottage, a good six months later, I took Laurice and Robert with me and we were met at the door by his wife. She invited us in, and when we were all seated comfortably I enquired as to her health and she said "I'm all right". When I asked if Dad was around, she replied in a very matter of fact tone of voice saying, "No, he died last month". To be given that kind of unpleasant and totally unexpected news was bad enough but to have it delivered in such a manner without any feeling in her voice whatsoever was beyond belief. A conversation of sorts followed and it emerged that Dad had died in his sleep. It was plain to see our presence was not appreciated, so having mumbled some measure of condolence and made a none-too convincing enquiry as to there being anything I could do, we left.

The reason for our reception with it's underlying feeling of hostility can be laid quite firmly at my door. I had given my step-Mother a number of very valid reasons to act in the way she did, and should have apologised to her on that last visit I made for my thoughtless and inconsiderate behaviour towards my Father. I think it would be fair to say that I had made no more than six visits to see him over a period of fourteen years. All my life from the time I was old enough to understand I looked up to my Father and thought of him as the type of person I wanted to be when I became a man. The very special kind of soldier he had been as a Coldstream Guardsman was something which fascinated me. Although he had been very strict, which sometimes could have reached standards akin to ruling with a rod of iron, I am absolutely certain that kind of upbringing stood me in very good stead in later life. There were hiccups, yes, but on the whole I am very grateful for the influence he had upon me in practically everything. Even though I have had a rather mixed up life and for many years I had no permanent address there was nothing to stop me from writing to him. With a little organisation I could have gone to see him on a fairly regular basis. Regrets? Yes, a thousand and one.

Our time at the maisonette finally came to an end. We had been happy there but a move was necessary. I obtained a fairly decent flat which was still in Surrey but more to the west of London, but before we moved I did one more repossession which as it proved could have well been the last thing I ever did. It appeared to be nothing out of the ordinary so I made a short bus journey and arrived at the address, which was a semi-detached house in a nice clean looking estate of obviously fairly well to do residents. The house itself had an open plan grassed front garden and a downhill sloping driveway. On this driveway was a beautiful grey coloured Saab which looked almost new. I walked past it to the front door and rang the bell, it was answered by a woman and when I asked if this was Mr. Frazer's house she said it was. I told her I had come about the car and did he want to pay the arrears because if not I would have to take it away. While I was speaking another woman came and popped her head round the door listening to what I was saying. When I had said my piece they both stood there with looks of amazement on their faces. I repeated the question as to whether Mr. Frazer wanted to pay me the arrears, with that one of the women turned away from the door and went back into the house only to return a few minutes later and whisper to the other woman, "They are on their way". I decided to take a closer look at the Saab. As I was doing so a large truck drove up the road and stopped at the top of the driveway. The driver and his passenger got out and at the same time four exceptionally beefy looking individuals jumped off the back and all six approached me. As they did so one of them said, "What do you want mate ?, if it's this car you're after forget it. You aren't going to take it ". I have always believed in the saying "There is safety in numbers". I made some lame excuse and walking straight across the immaculate lawn I departed. I made my report on the afternoon's events to the office manager, and he then enlightened me as to exactly where I had been. It turned out that I been to the home of a certain Frank Frazer and told his wife that I intended to take away his beloved Saab. He was best known by his nickname, "Mad Frankie Frazer", and his close association with the infamous Krays left very little cause for speculation as to the kind of person he was. My reception committee would have consisted of some of his devoted gang members. I consider myself extremely lucky to have been allowed to even "walk" away.

That was the last job I "nearly did?" for that firm. I left, and we moved to the flat, which was to be the first of many moves we were to make during the next five years, all of them in and around the outskirts of north London. This made it possible for Phillip to come and see us regularly. He was well on the way towards completing his apprenticeship at the Le Petit Montmatre restaurant and appeared to be satisfied with the progress he was making but he couldn't disguise the fact that he was looking forward to the time when after a few more years he would become a qualified Chef. I, on the other hand, had many jobs, brought about by the number of moves we were making. There was never any problem obtaining work of some kind even though some were things I never imagined I would do, like Taxi driving, and the door to door selling of electric fires or vibrating beds and chairs. The most depressing job I did was repossessing television sets in an obviously deprived district. This kind of work brought in enough money to keep the "wolf from the door" and one good thing about it was that it wasn't full time employment, therefore my address was not required by the firms for whom I worked, thus ensuring there wouldn't be any brown envelopes pushed through the letter box informing me that my presence was required at some specific court in relation to maintenance.

Following yet another move I decided to take a steady job as a bus driver with London Transport on the famous double decker Route Masters with automatic gear boxes. I had a few days driving an empty bus around accompanied by an inspector during which time I had the dubious "pleasure" of driving it through the awesome specially prepared skid patch, in the grounds of Chiswick depot. That part of the proceedings completed satisfactorily I was deemed to have passed my test and despatched to Uxbridge depot where I worked the route from there to Shepherds Bush. At that time a large number of bus companies had progressed to one man operated buses where the entrance was at the front and the driver took the fares as each passenger got on, but this particular route made that an impossibility as there were always large queues of people at almost every stop. During the rush hours the traffic was so bad with queues forming at so many bottlenecks there were times when we had taken two hours to reach the halfway stage, rather than completed the journey as the timetable said.

It was whilst doing this job that the powers that be had me in court again, and this time I had to travel to Barnsley. This meant having to take a day off work, but it wasn't a waste of a journey altogether as Valerie and the children went along for the ride. I deposited them at her parents' home while I went to face the music. After a rather lengthy wait I was called into the courtroom. Once there I was questioned about 'disappearing', and it was stressed to me that if I didn't comply with the court order I would go to prison. I was then asked if I had anything to say. My attempts to put forward my point of view didn't appear to have any effect and proceeded to order me to pay one half of my weekly wage into court. The first few weeks I complied, but as it wasn't leaving enough for me to pay the rent it became time to move. It was a pity really because I could have settled down driving the buses but had I done so and not complied with the court order I would have been sent to prison so we moved.

During this period of moving from one place to another we made many trips to Barnsley, leaving Valerie at her Mother's and then me tootling off somewhere to spend some time with Laurice and Robert, see my Dad, and call on Jacqueline and Harry in Wombwell, but it wasn't really a satisfactory state of affairs and we were to make probably four or five trips before I was finally accepted into the fold. Then these visits had to be curtailed for a while as our family was to increase. Early one morning in February I drove Valerie to the maternity department in Charing Cross hospital where a very short while later Catherine was born. Thankfully baby and mother were doing fine and both were allowed home after a couple of days.

Our place of residence changed twice over the next three years and it was when we were living in Hayes, Middlesex, that Valerie found it necessary to enter the maternity department of Hillingdon hospital, where, on another day, also in February, Eileen was born. We now had a fairly large family, six in all, and so, after a reasonable time had elapsed, probably a couple of months, we obtained the tenancy of a beautiful house in the countryside. When we were settled in we invited Valerie's elder sister Janet and her Mother to come and stay with us for a few days where they enjoyed the delights of the lovely house and it's surroundings. It made a nice change for Valerie as this was the first time any member of her family had been able to stay with or even visit us.

Throughout the many moves we made, Phillip always found time to come and see us and stay when he had a few days holiday but the outcome of one of his shorter visits was to give me big problems. There weren't many job opportunities close to where we were living so I had obtained a fairly good one further afield. It was only labouring in a factory but it was well paid. I was doing my bit to keep those gorgeous "Avon" ladies in full employment. There was a pleasant side to the job whereby everywhere you went in the factory your nose was assailed by scents of every description. It was a good firm to work for, I liked it immensely, and was extremely disappointed when through no wish of my own I had to leave. This was brought about by that short visit Phillip made one winter's day. It had been snowing on and off for the past couple of days and although the roads were passable they were not ideal. He had arrived on the Saturday around midday and it appeared that he had met a young lady whose home was off the beaten track where buses were few and far between, and so in order for him to call on her he requested the use of my car. He had driven it a number of times before in my company and he had handled it reasonably well so I agreed to let him have it, after obtaining his profound assurances that he would take very good care of it. He left after lunch and sometime around midnight we received a phone call from him explaining how he had managed to turn the car over without injuring himself or his lady friend. The car had sustained some damage and it was in a garage near her home and would be repaired in the next day or two. That left me with no transport to get me to work. I wrote a letter to the firm apologising and saying I wouldn't be able to get in for a week at least. Unfortunately that estimation was way out because it was more than one month before finally Phillip brought it back. I was horrified when I took it for a run to find the steering was positively dangerous. It was obvious the underbody was twisted and both front and rear axles were badly out of line. There was no way I would use that car again.

I ended up selling it to a garage who claimed they could do something with it. So, that ended my employment with "Avon" as I had no way of getting there. Over the next few days Valerie and I discussed what we should do, there weren't too many options open to us but it was agreed that I should go to the city of Lincoln and find suitable accommodation for us. I knew Valerie wanted to live much nearer her family without actually returning to Yorkshire and that could have had something to do with it. Later that week I found myself trudging around Lincoln calling at estate agents in an effort to find somewhere to rent. I had almost given up hope when finally one of them came up trumps, and three weeks later we took possession of a house not far from the city centre.

Chapter 15

Although it was in the middle of a row of terraced houses, very small and without a bathroom, our new house did have two rooms and a kitchen downstairs and two decent sized bedrooms. One blot on the landscape was the position of the toilet; outside at the bottom of a small yard. Even though it was 1971, when man had two years earlier walked on the Moon, we had to purchase a couple of beautifully decorated "Guzunder's" (Chamber Pots). In our new abode we were certainly lucky as we couldn't have wished for better neighbours. There were some very nice people in the street and Valerie soon made friends with the family who lived next door but one to us. We didn't know it at the time but they were to become very close friends of our's for many years, and they came round offering to help when we were still in the process of unloading the furniture van. At that time there were three members in their family one was a teenage girl named Janet, her mum, Jean, and her father, Allan. Our next door neighbour was a dear old lady named Mabel. She was kind hearted and very caring, and with our girls being of tender years, Christine five, Pauline four, Catherine three, and Eileen the baby at four or five months, Valerie was to find her very helpful at times.

A few hectic days of moving furniture around, saw things more or less organised enough for me to apply for a job bus driving for the Lincolnshire Roadcar Company Ltd. I was accepted, but first had to learn to drive a bus with a manual gearbox and, as the buses were one man operated, I had to get the hang of the cash machines.

The county of Lincolnshire has the reputation of being flat open countryside and apart from a few well populated towns and three very well known seaside resorts it consists mainly of farms, with many villages dotted around here and there. It is possible to travel many miles along country roads without seeing anything except for a small hamlet or the odd house standing back in the fields or surrounded by trees. It really is beautiful. The majority of the county is flat but there are one or two exceptions to the rule and one of them is the city itself as it is almost split in two, one part being low down, the other high up and the dominating factors of the high part are the very imposing cathedral, and an ancient castle surrounded by a high stone wall. It is said, and rightly so, that on a reasonably clear day the cathedral can be seen from a distance of eleven miles from whichever direction you approach the city. Other exceptions are when negotiating the roads through an area known as the Lincolnshire Wolds. Here in places it is similar to being on a rollercoaster with the many frequent switchbacks up and down, all of which can create screams of laughter from children even when the "rises and falls" are taken at a very steady speed. Overall it was a lovely part of the country to be in and a change for the better from the places we had previously lived. Our accommodation was cosy and comfortable even though it was on the small side and when we had been here a few months and after some deliberation we decided to settle down, but we would soon need a larger house so we had our name entered on the waiting list for a council property.

As the months went by things began to pan out nicely. For far too long it had seemed to be an uphill struggle for all of us, coping with all the accommodation and job changes we had made since 1966. I had contented myself by coming to terms with the fact that the drastic decision Valerie and I had made then was bound to have some problems, but I considered these problems to be a very small price to pay. The children were growing nicely and seemed to be happy enough and after a couple of weeks in her new home Christine started school. She had spent a few days at a school in the last place we had lived but she was quick to point out that the one here was much better. One year later Pauline was raring to go, but all the wonderful things said about it did not convince Catherine. When, after another year, it was her turn to sample the delights she took a leaf out of my book by giving her Mother and her teacher a difficult time getting her to stay. She fought and struggled and voiced her opinions. I had capitulated after about six months but she continued to raise the roof every single day for more than three years. At some time during those years she, together with Christine and Pauline, had changed schools as we had moved into a council house in another area. It was at this new school when Eileen began her education and in order to avoid her having to witness those daily tantrums, Valerie and Catherine's teacher concocted a method whereby she would be held a virtual prisoner in the classroom until Eileen had been safely deposited in her's.

We had been in the small house about twelve months when we made one of our trips to Barnsley and I was able to see Laurice and Robert for a few hours. Laurice had left school a few weeks earlier and expressed her desire to come and live with me. Robert was carrying on with his studies and so had to stay.

When things appear to be going well for me it is always the case that something comes along to put a damper on them. It came in the shape of the usual official looking small brown envelope. The first time I went to the court in Lincoln I was in full employment on the buses and an order was made accordingly for half the wages I earned every week to be deducted by the bus company. My average wage was usually about £32, a little above average as I was able to put in some overtime, but when the deductions were made this £32 was at the top of the payslip and underneath was the deduction of £16, then the national insurance, union dues, other bits and bobs, and at the bottom the amount I had to take home, a measly £14 plus, and I had a family of six to take care of out of that. There was nothing that could be done about it as I had no wish to be on the move again, so that was the state of affairs all the time I worked on those buses. We managed, but only just.

That was when I pawned my war medals to help matters. For quite some time I had been looking back over the preceding years and had reached the conclusion I had been dealt a very poor hand by some government departments, especially the Judicial system, the War office and the Ministry of Defence, and the Foreign and Colonial offices. I had always put my faith in these establishments but had become disillusioned with them. I felt the judicial system had let me down in my dealings with Anna. At no point were investigations made into her potential culpability in anything that happened between us. There seemed to exist an unwritten assumption that it was probably all my fault. My "beef" with the Foreign and Colonial offices was with the issue of my Certificate of Discharge. It is regarded by some as being a person's reference, and the one I received was a disgrace, given the innaccuracies it contained.

Despite the problems arising from the meagre take home pay we were all happy and contented. Janet, the girl from next door, and her mum were always dropping in to lend a hand, and Mabel was a regular visitor doing anything she could and making a fuss of the children. Laurice had arrived and was fitting in nicely, helping Valerie to look after us all. I was doing work I thoroughly enjoyed. Phillip had completed his apprenticeship, and was now a fully qualified Chef. He had left the restaurant and was working in the galley of one of the P&O liners, experiencing life on the ocean waves. Robert was still studying hard but I saw him only occasionally now as I had to work on Sundays which was the usual day when he was at home. Things were completely different as far as Michael was concerned as I hadn't seen him for years, but that was to change soon after we had moved into the council house. One Christmas, he and his wife and daughter turned up out of the blue and kept us company over the holiday and again during the following Easter, although I wasn't to see him again for many years.

Our finances hadn't changed, but things were now on a more stable footing. We had the time and the opportunity to go out in search of some form of entertainment suitable for a young family, and as one of my favourite pastimes was stripping off and taking a plunge, what better way to start than seek out a swimming pool? So it was that one Saturday morning saw us all suitably equipped with swimming costumes and relevant arm bands, having the time of our lives splashing around in a pool attached to a nearby school. It was great fun, and accompanied by lots of screams, shouts, and protests. The swimming lessons began, and from that day we made it a regular item on the agenda. You cannot imagine how pleased I was when I realised that along with my instruction and the lessons they had at school each one of the girls turned out to be a natural born swimmer.

When I heard of a ballroom dancing school in the centre of Lincoln, where the lessons took priority but were integrated with a large amount of social dancing it sounded to be an ideal place for all of us to spend a few relaxing hours. Valerie took to dancing like a duck does to water and after only a few lessons she was more than capable of keeping her feet out or harm's way. I wasn't sure what the girls thought about the instruction side of things and they must have found everything rather awkward as they were young. Christine would have been nine, Pauline eight, Catherine seven, and Eileen four, but the instructor's were good, taking each one of them in turn, making it all appear to be great fun and any mistakes were greeted with giggles or roars of laughter. I did my bit of course, I would take one of them and hold her hands, leaving plenty of space between us to avoid the prospect of our feet becoming entangled, and guide both of us through the different steps. The social dances were where they all excelled and really let their hair down, especially the ones where everyone arranged themselves in lines across the width of the floor, all doing the same steps in time to the music. Laurice came with us but wasn't too happy with the instruction and after a few weeks she went somewhere else, where after a while she met a young fellow and brought him home to see us. He seemed a nice enough chap and when I knew he was the son of a driver I worked with on the buses, who was also a decent friendly fellow, I raised no objection when after a month or two they requested my permission to marry. They did so and went to live with his parents until some time later when they obtained a house of their own at the lower end of the High street. They appeared to be very happy, especially when their son, Matthew, arrived on the scene.

For about three years Pauline had made steady progress after the initial problems of her arrival but then she refused to eat. She would sit at the table with furrowed brow and a scowl on her face picking at the food with her fork. Occasionally, she would fill her mouth and simply sit there making no attempt to chew whatsoever. It didn't make any difference what kind of food was prepared for her, it all received the same treatment. I am sure many parents will recognise the symptoms and have had first hand knowledge of how frustrating it can be, but there are many reasons why some children go through this stage. When Valerie took Pauline to see the doctor he said that she had tonsillitis and this was making it painful and difficult for her to swallow. He went on to explain that she would need an operation but that this couldn't be done until she was at least seven years old. With her being barely four at the time it meant she was going to have to suffer for more than three years. She did have soups and milk puddings, and things that could be mashed to a pulp, but everything was a struggle and knowing how she must have felt every time she tried to swallow the least little thing made it all the more difficult trying to persuade her to have something. It was a very trying time for everyone, especially Valerie. She tried everything but nothing changed and all the time Pauline seemed to be getting thinner and thinner even though she appeared to be healthy enough. Shortly after her seventh birthday she had the tonsils removed. As soon as things settled down she came home and from then on she began to eat like any other normal person. Well like a little horse would be more to the point. In a very short while she could no longer be called skinny and meal times were once more pleasant for all concerned.

We had been in Lincoln for almost three years and things were going well until an incident at work interferred with all that. Some of the single deckers had dodgy gear boxes. There was one where the gear lever had to be thumped in on every gear change. One day I thumped it and my hand slipped off the top of it. My fist went forward with some force and struck the bodywork in front of the dashboard. My hand swelled up immediately and the doctor put me on the sick list. I was off for more then a month and awarded four hundred pounds compensation as it was deemed to have been caused by a faulty gear box. The hand returned to what I thought to be something like normal and I resumed my duties only to find that it was still giving me trouble, so I followed up a suggestion which had been put to me during the time I had been off. Apparently there was a driving school in the city requiring suitable drivers they could train to become instructors. I had my doubts as to whether it was what I wanted as I had turned down a similar opportunity many, many years ago in Barnsley, but the hand appeared to be a problem which wasn't likely to go away in the very near future. Regrettably I ended my service on the buses and signed up to become a driving instructor.

It was with some trepidation that I made the short walk to the offices of the driving school one Monday morning. That first day I was given the lowdown on what I was about to do and filled in a number of forms to enable the school to apply for the appropriate licence which would allow me to give instruction on their behalf. This would not entitle me to give any lessons which were not allocated to me by the school and I would not be fully qualified until I had completed a certain number of hours training and instruction and then taken and passed an instructor's examination. This would take approximately five months. Meanwhile I would be taught by them and after a few days out on the road with another instructor, I would then be considered capable to take out certain pupils on my own, for which I would be paid an instructor's wage. It was reasonable pay, and better than the buses as I had once again dodged the issue of paying that maintenance.

When I went to that school on that Monday morning I fully expected to be given some sort of training in the art of teaching someone how to drive. Those expectations were not fulfilled in any way and it was left to me to ask questions on the subject. It is one thing being able to drive but it is a totally different kettle of fish teaching someone else. Apart from the couple of days I went out with an instructor during a lesson, I was taught absolutely nothing. I took a paying pupil out on my own after being on their books for only three days! I did learn, but it only came about through practical experience.

My worst fears of having made another "cock-up" of a job change were to be pleasantly unfounded as during the following five months I was to work with some exceptionally good people. There was a friendly environment in which to work when we were all in the office awaiting our orders for the day and during the changeover periods between lessons. It hadn't taken me very long to realise that this was a job I could get my teeth into and make a success of it.

I did lessons every day, including weekends, and passed the instructors test at the end of the five months. Shortly afterwards the office manageress left and the man who replaced her had his own ideas which led to the school beginning to go downhill. The instructor's started to trickle away one by one. I contacted a lease hire firm and took possession of my own car, a Mini, as I saw no reason to change to anything else even though they were a bit on the small side. They were ideal for the job and I knew that the learners appreciated their easy manoeuvrability. I was lucky in that the pupils I had been teaching through the school all expressed their wish to continue with me so I unashamedly took them all and I was in business. In the years that followed I was to find myself in the pleasant situation whereby it was a case of one out (having passed their test), and one waiting to come in. This came about solely through word of mouth recommendations. Nevertheless I couldn't say in all honesty that I felt full of confidence during those first few months but I operated in what I considered to be the best way to overcome my deficiencies in that I put myself in the pupil's shoes and taught them to do what I myself would have done in the varying circumstances. It seemed to work. As far as I was concerned it was soon to develop into a routine and I adopted a method which gave me the satisfaction of feeling the pupil was gradually gaining in confidence and making good progress towards what I considered to be the correct way to drive. Although I had developed this routine it was not in any way a "conveyor belt system". Every person was an individual and they were all different in some way. Those first few minutes in their company on the first lesson were very important to me. It was then I used to make my assessment and decide the manner in which to approach the forthcoming lessons.

One pupil I taught in those early days was to test my ability to deal with whatever was thrown at me to the limit. A young fellow I taught had failed his first test. He was a quiet chap, very polite, and always listened to what I was telling him, but he had an erratic streak. This had been his downfall on that test because he had done something wrong, knew it, and promptly went to pieces. He explained to me later that after that he had mistake after mistake right up to the end of the test. I spent the next six weeks prior to his next test trying to rid him of this tendency to panic. He thought he had cured it but I wasn't so sure. He had a lesson on the evening before his test. It was dark and had been raining heavily for most of the day which didn't make things any easier for him but he seemed to feel comfortable in everything we did. After we had completed all the usual things we set off for home. On the way we had to cross Pelham bridge, an extra large span over a road and quite a few railway lines leading out from the nearby station. It was fairly wide, with two lanes in both directions, footpaths on each side, and was well lit. It had a steady incline up and then down. It was in a 30mph zone but as we approached we were well within that limit as the rain was bucketing it down. We were about halfway across this bridge when I noticed a large black dog on the opposite side footpath to us, with it's nose to the floor sniffing at everything around it. It began to wheel round in circles moving backwards and forwards gradually making it's way across the road, then it picked up speed and crossed, well in front of the car, leapt onto the footpath on our side and trotted off. It must have been at sometime during this manoeuvre when my companion must have seen this dog out of the corner of his eye and, forgetting everything we had done in the last six weeks, slammed both his feet forward onto brake and clutch simultaneously. The car span completely round a couple of times before eventually coming to rest facing the oncoming traffic. Fortunately we were able to do a quick shuffle round and complete the journey. The next day he took his test-and passed!

Another time, I received a phone call from a man asking me to take his son out in their car.

The boy was, in the opinion of his father, ready to take a test. He had taught him but wanted me to give him a few lessons to polish him up. I had by this time been instructing for a few years and I had always said I wouldn't do any lessons without dual controls so I managed to put him off at first, but he made more calls and in the end I agreed as he seemed so certain his son was absolutely safe and there would be no need for dual controls. I went to their home to pick the boy up and to my surprise and annoyance the car was a 2CV, which I I disliked intensely. After a short conversation we set off to make a short tour of the city to give me some idea of his capabilities; I was not impressed. Every time we had to stop it was always done suddenly. I pointed this out to the young chap, who was a quiet unassuming fellow, and he did try to alter what he was doing but he had been allowed to drive this way for a long time and it had become a habit. The rest of his driving was nothing to write home about and he was going to require a lot more instruction than his Father had anticipated. When we got back I spoke to the Father who seemed surprised that I thought this way. I outlined one or two things, especially the sudden stopping, and he agreed to work on those things each time he took him out. He had another lesson, his second, and still the sudden stop was being used more often than not. On the third we had negotiated a steep hill coming down from the Cathedral area, about five minutes into the lesson, and we came up to a pelican crossing, the lights of which were green. The front wheels of the car had passed the middle of the crossing when the lights changed to amber. His right foot went hard down on the brake pedal and we stopped dead. The car, and it's occupants shuddered momentarily and then we were on the move again. This time courtesy of a whacking great lorry which had caved our backend in and shoved us for all of ten yards before stopping. Neither of us were hurt in any way and the lorry driver only had his pride dented. The 2CV was a complete write off. I thought it only right that I should apologise to the truck driver even though he must have been running too close, and there was no need to call the police as there was only material damage. We exchanged particulars and after helping us to push our car into the side of the road he drove off. The young fellow phoned his Father and he came down and inspected the damage and said he would soon get another car for his son and I could carry on with the lessons. I made no comment and thankfully never heard from either of them again!

I had been recommended by someone to a middle aged chap who had been having lessons with another school, and he took his first lesson with me in the Mini. It became obvious in the first few minutes that we were destined to have fun and games. His driving was awful, but that didn't worry me too much, but something that did worry me was his tendency to stop for no logical reason. I could put the brakes on but I couldn't take them off and the same thing applied to the clutch so I could only tell him that what he was doing was wrong and potentially dangerous. Every time when he moved off from somewhere he would start the car moving and then stop suddenly, shuffle about in his seat, and set off again. His excuse was that he didn't feel comfortable so he stopped to settle himself. I had no qualms about putting him into situations where if he did it wrong I could put him right, in that way he would soon get the hang of things and his confidence would grow. On his second lesson we travelled along a road to a "T" junction, with no right turn. It was an exceptionally busy junction and visibility was no more than fifteen yards to a sharp corner on the right. It was a case of look right, left, and right again and again to make sure there was nothing coming round the bend, and then move out in a positive manner before something did come. Once the observations had been made and it was all clear then that positive move had to be made immediately. We arrived at the junction, stopped and he did everything perfectly. As soon as it was safe to go he set off, then almost immediately he stood on the brake, and we stopped dead. There was still no sign of anything coming from our right but something had been following behind, it was a sports car and had set off when we did, crumpling as it ran into the back of us. Both cars had sustained some damage but they were driveable and after exchanging the relevant particulars we both drove off. Mine wasn't too bad but it had to be off the road for a day to be repaired. I lost lessons and the chap who had bumped us would have to pay for those and the repairs. I felt sorry for him because it was our fault. I dropped my chap off at his home having had to listen to his profound apologies all the way there and his vehement vow not to do anything of a similar nature when next he took a lesson. I made very little comment as I had no wish to offend him but I had already reached a decision he would have no future lessons with me. Neither I nor the car could stand it.

Once, I had been teaching a young woman for about eight weeks and she was making good progress in most aspects. We had worked around the Cathedral area which has many undulating roads and streets. There was one street in particular which was exceptionally steep and so far she had not negotiated it. It could only be approached from the top as it was a one way street downhill, with a kind of hump at the top and a sudden drop. It was my usual practice to leave this to near the end of all their training when they were almost ready to take a test, but I considered her to be quite capable of taking it in her stride. She had not had the experience of actually going over a brow of a hill before so we spent a few minutes stationery discussing what she was about to do before we got to the street, then we made a steady approach to it at a comfortable speed. When we rolled gently over the hump she had a wistful smile on her face but it was to disappear as if by magic when the steep drop came into view. She immediately exclaimed "My God", still keeping her foot firmly placed on the accelerator pedal, and as she had pushed herself hard back against the seat, that foot went flat to the floor. At the same time she took her hands off the wheel and clamped them firmly over both eyes. The little mini took off, ably assisted by the steepness of the hill. It is not easy trying to speak calmly when asking someone to take their foot off the gas pedal when hairing downhill towards a busy junction at the bottom, but for a few seconds I did try, without any response and the junction was approaching fast. I used the duals, then we came to a stop with adequate room to spare. At that point my young companion condescended to release the gas pedal and the noise subsided. She passed her test first time and became a reasonable driver, I saw her fairly often when walking round the shops and we usually had a quick word and a laugh about the time she nearly killed us both!

Now to something which came as a big surprise and one which brought home to me that good health and the ability to perform even the simplest of tasks in life is so very precious. I had been instructing for about seven years when I received a letter from the Department of Transport to the effect that they wanted me to teach totally disabled people in their own Invalid vehicles and get them through a driving test. To be asked to do this was indeed an honour as it could only mean that they must have had knowledge of, and confidence in, my overall instructing capabilities before they would have even considered me for this type of work. I replied, saying I would be pleased to do as they asked but at the same time informing them that I was extremely busy. They sent me the relevant paperwork telling me how the instruction needed to be carried out. It was an entirely different type of teaching as the cars were only made to accommodate one person, the driver. It is one thing being able to handle and drive a car but things of equal importance are knowing the correct road positions and how to deal with the varying situations as they arise. These situations could not be made to order so I had to describe them to the pupils from a theoretical standpoint. In order to do this I took them around the area in my school car, taking up, and pointing out, the differing road positions, and incorporating where and when various situations could occur and how they should be dealt with. I knew it couldn't have been easy for the pupils as there was such a lot they would have to remember so we did many areas and many routes until I was satisfied they had got the hang of the more important things. The first lesson in the invalid car was taken up with controls, steering, starting and stopping, and although all of them had varying disabilities they showed a great aptitude when actually handling the car. I cannot find any suitable words to aptly describe the feelings I had when they started the engine and began to move forward for the first time. I walked alongside offering encouragement but knowing I could give no practical help at all if anything started to go wrong. It must have been nerve racking for them as well as for me and I couldn't help but admire them for the way they handled themselves. They were all very appreciative people and a pleasure to teach, despite the difficulties. Once they had become reasonably proficient I drove my car and they followed, and after a few days of this they went in front and I followed, which all finally lead to the test where everything went according to plan with not one hiccup.

I had left the buses where those deductions from my pay had been made every week and did have a few months respite from paying anything but I hadn't changed my address, and in due course I was summoned to appear in the Lincoln court where I was ordered to pay, into court, another ridiculous amount each week. I complied for a while and then allowed the payments to lapse even though I had been warned that I faced a prison sentence if I didn't comply fully with the order, so when I received another letter informing me that they required the pleasure of my company once more I feared the worst. I had been forced to explain so many things in this particular court and none had been accepted by them before, so I had no reason to think anything would change this time around, however, I put in an appearance and noticed that it was the same clerk of the court who had dealt with the matter on those previous occasions, he therefore knew all about the case and the difficulties any form of payment had previously caused me. The proceedings this time didn't follow the usual pattern, I wasn't made to answer any questions, and the first five minutes or so were taken up by the clerk and the magistrate holding a very close conversation, there was nothing heated about their discussion it was as if they were trying to reach a decision. I just stood there slightly bemused and feeling rather awkward but when the clerk returned to his place in the well of the court I was totally unprepared for what he was about to say, I can almost remember his exact words, they were, "I think this case has gone on long enough and no matter what anyone may think to the contrary this man will not be brought before this, or any other court again, and that is the end of the matter". I couldn't believe it, this was the first time anyone had taken my side throughout the whole sordid business, and it did take me by surprise as I fully expected a repeat performance whereby I would be threatened again with a session inside one of her majesty's prison's. I knew there was no-one living with Anna now as Robert had also left home and this could be the reason why I wasn't to be held responsible any more. When I left the court that day I felt

Family holiday at Butlins in Filey, September 1979 and September 1978
(Above) Jack, Pauline, Christine, Catherine, Valerie with Eileen taking the photo

Valerie, Pauline, Christine, Catherine and Eileen with Jack taking the photograph

as if a large weight had been lifted off my shoulders, I would no longer have to approach the letter box wondering if it contained an official looking brown envelope, not knowing what the outcome would be from another appearance in court, and I could rid myself of the feeling's that I was defying the authorities as I hadn't taken any pleasure out of what I had been forced to do despite everything I have previously said on the subject. Nevertheless I was firmly convinced that the family I had left were financially secure without any contributions from me, but failing to comply with the court orders had given me cause for concern even though I knew my doing so would have no adverse effect upon the family. I am still of the opinion I was right to do what I did but that still didn't alter the fact that it had made me feel guilty for some reason or another. In the summer of that year we spent a week at a Butlins holiday camp in Filey. It was a clean, well maintained camp and there were plenty of entertainments for young and old. We preferred to go to the beach during the daytime but made good use of them in the evenings. The girls sampled the rides on the fun fair or go to other places in the camp where entertainments were specially laid on for them. Valerie and I would put on our best bib and tucker and sally forth to the dance hall to do a spot of ballroom dancing. It was good fun, sedate, and we really enjoyed ourselves. It was a good holiday and we went again the following year, and I am sure the girls will always remember the two we had there with fond memories, I know Valerie and I do. On one of the weeks we went out of the camp and travelled a few miles towards Bridlington and paid a visit to that large field overlooking a beach where in 1932 my Father had used the Ford Prefect (with my Mother, Jacqueline, him, and me, sitting inside it) in such a manner as to bring it to the point where it came close to depositing us all on the beach below. The field was also the one where I had left the boys, Michael, Phillip, and Robert, to spend a week fending for themselves in that small tent which succumbed to the strong winds. I had told Valerie and the girls all about these two instances, and this visit was to have been my opportunity to point out exactly where they had taken place. I hadn't reckoned with the rapidly ongoing need for progress. We drove up the short lane leading to the entrance to the field that day and instead of a wide open grass tufted sandy entrance we came face to face with a gaudily painted barrier and a man in a sentry box type hut who informed us we had arrived at the Primrose Valley Commercial Caravan Site and if we weren't booked in he had no alternative but to turn us away. Well we did come away and found a place to park and walked back to the beach. As we started our descent we had a good view of the site with it's dozens of caravans, all neatly parked alongside constructed roadways. A few yards inside from the barrier was a large brick building containing an open fronted shop, a cafe and offices. Overall it looked to be neat and well organised but was not the unspoilt landscape of all those previous visits. I had visited that place in the previous phases of my life and was disappointed that it was now not as I remembered it.

When Valerie and I had chosen to end our previous marriages the law at that time required both parties to wait a full seven years before a divorce could be granted, and so it was that after those stipulated seven years had elapsed we were free to marry again. There were no wedding bells, no white dress and veil, no church service or reception. If I remember correctly my suit had been ironed and all four present were sporting white carnations. Our vows were made in the dignified atmosphere of the Lincoln register office, with a bus driver friend of mine and his wife as witnesses.

Meanwhile the girls were growing up and when Eileen was five it was agreed they should all be christened in the local church. The date was fixed and for the next month the house was turned upside down as the four dresses were painstakingly made. The girls had agreed to be christened together and being dressed from head to toe in matching outfits, with the same two Godmothers and one Godfather having the honour of representing each one of them in turn. Jean was one of the Godmothers and the other was a middle aged woman I had the privilege of teaching to drive. She was a tall, well spoken, refined person, and became a close friend of the family. The Godfather was the husband of another woman I had taught, and they were also our friends. Almost all our relatives were in attendance along with many friends. It was quite a gathering and an exceptionally pleasant occasion. The vicar who performed the ceremony was an elderly gentleman and held in high esteem by all his parishioners. He spoke in a quiet, understanding tone of voice which calmed the proceedings, especially when he used the water from the font very sparingly, thereby avoiding the possibility of even the tiniest drop falling onto those beautiful dresses. It was a great day and one which will be remembered by all those who had the pleasure of being present.

The christening ceremony must have prompted Valerie to do something she had thought about but never got round to, and that was to take the necessary Bible lessons in prearranged Confirmation classes before attending a Church of England ceremony in Lincoln Cathedral and be Confirmed. When she made this decision Christine asked if she could do it at the same time, and they both attended the classes, one every week for six weeks. Two weeks before the Confirmation took place Christine was running in the snow, fell, and broke her leg. She was given a pair of crutches and for the next ten days she practiced using them. On the day we went to the Cathedral and while Valerie and Christine went into the rooms to prepare, I escorted Pauline, Catherine, and Eileen, into the Cathedral and found a suitable position where we would all have a good view of the proceedings. By the time we had settled down the place was almost full. It was a spectacular ceremony, with the Cathedral Choir walking down the aisle at the head of the procession, followed by the Bishop and his retinue in all their regalia. The ones to be Confirmed walking at the rear, and last of all was Christine, trying very hard to keep up. It was necessary for all the participants to kneel before the altar and this caused more problems for Christine, but a steadying hand from the Bishop ensured she did not sustain further damage.

Something else occurred about this time which didn't result in any broken bones but which has given me cause for thought and great concern ever since because of what was to transpire a few years later. The girls had pestered me to let them all have bicycles but my years spent acquiring knowledge of the roads left me convinced that cycling wasn't a safe thing to do, so I refused point blank. Not to be deterred, Catherine decided to borrow a friend's bike. She had managed to reach a roundabout some 200 yards from where she had set off when a car knocked her over, the driver of the car took her to the hospital where she was examined and found to be suffering from nothing more than a few small bruises. Then he brought her home. I was working and only found out about it when I came home late that night. Catherine was in bed and the story I got from Valerie told me very little so I decided to go and see the fellow the next morning. He was very apologetic but said she had ridden out across him at the roundabout. I thought she was lucky not to have been seriously injured and told her so in very forcible terms. Whether it made any difference I don't know, but I never heard of her or the other three doing any more bike riding.

279

The driving school was taking up most of my time but I arranged things so that we all went out together for various forms of entertainment on a fairly regular basis, swimming was usually first and top of the list, with dancing a close second. Our places for dancing were varied and so was the style of dancing. We added sequence dancing to our repertoire. The girls went with us to begin with, but as the participants were of the older generation, it must have been rather boring for them and gradually it was left to Valerie and myself to continue.

The driving school was still buzzing which meant I was up to my eyes in work and had been for quite some time. It seemed to come as a big surprise to me when I suddenly realised the girls were no longer children but were now young ladies. This was brought home to me, and Valerie, when one day Christine brought a young man home who, unknown to me, she had been seeing for quite some time. He had been brought to what he may have considered to be "The Lion's Den" in order for him to be given the once over. She did bring him to see us regularly after that first time and the more I saw of him the more I liked him. Nevertheless, at that time they seemed happy enough just to be in each other's company, but sometime later they said it was their intention to live together, and after making several unsuccessful appeals to the local authority they were finally allocated a small council house in an avenue not too far away from us.

There are lots of good things to be said for owning a driving school but there are also some which can prove to be not so good. One in particular I never gave a thought to until I began to feel under the weather. To make a success of anything you have to be prepared to work hard, sometimes both physically and mentally, but in the case of a driving school there is nothing of a physical nature. I became so involved with doing as many lessons as it was humanly possible that in order to save time I never broke off to have any meals. I had breakfast in the mornings but nothing else until late at night. The truth of the matter was that after nearly twelve years of operating in this fashion it was bound to catch up with me sooner or later. I was thoroughly washed out and not only did I feel sluggish and unable to concentrate I had more aches and pains than I care to remember, so I visited the doctor, he gave me a few pills, the car was parked in the driveway and I took it easy for a while.

For the past twelve years I had been self employed and "Should" have sent off yearly tax returns. I didn't, so when the tax man demanded an astronomical sum, thousands of pounds, for those twelve years it shouldn't have come as a great surprise to me. It didn't, but the amount did, and it wasn't until there had been a large number of argumentative meetings and one court appearance that a compromise was reached. The amount was reduced but I still thought it was far in excess of what it should have been. Nevertheless there was no-one to blame but myself, and I paid, but it was only made possible by the sale of the car, a deep delve into the coffers, and the consequential winding up of the driving school. This wasn't to be half as traumatic as I had envisaged it would be, maybe because of the period of self inflicted idleness I had only recently been forced to endure. For the next month or so I was unemployed and not relishing the fact one little bit.

Pauline left school at the age of sixteen and immediately found herself a steady job in a factory making aerosol sprays. She purchased an Austin Allegro Estate, badly in need of repair and refurbishment, and asked me if I would do the honours of bringing it back to something like it's old self. This gave me something to do and I set to work with a will. Repairs were made to the engine, the bodywork had a complete face lift, and although I say it myself, that car looked a picture when it was finished.

When Catherine reached school leaving age I do believe she heaved a great sigh of relief. Even though she had obviously taken a great interest in the subject of maths, her exam results proved that. She never spoke of any plans she might have for the future and she was to drop a bombshell one day when she brought home the brother of Christine's boyfriend and said she wanted to emulate Christine and take up residence in his rented caravan on a registered caravan park in the south of the city. I did run the rule over the place and it didn't seem too bad. Valerie and I were not impressed with what had taken place but we had to go along with it and help in any way we could. Some time later they were allocated a council house, again not far from us. It was then that Catherine went one step further than Christine and got married.

We had been in Lincoln almost fifteen years and I had thought we may have settled there for good but things had quickly deteriorated in the previous couple of months. I moped about, doing nothing in particular. Then after an evening discussing what we should do it was decided that we would take the bull by the horns and make positive enquiries about a move. We found someone prepared to take our house in exchange for their's in Hemel Hempstead. It took a few weeks before everything was organised and there were many tears shed at the thought of leaving all our friends, and our two girls Christine and Catherine, but finally one morning the removal van was loaded. Just before it set off on the long journey to Hemel, Valerie returned from the test centre, where she had been taking her driving test, with the good news that she had passed. There was no time to break open the "bubbly" as the Austin was straining at the leash to be on the move. We piled in, and except for an unexpected stop when the engine overheated, we arrived at our new residence without any problems. It was a semi-detached four bedroomed house in a very pleasant area and we soon settled in. We weren't to know it at the time but many things of great importance were to take place here.

Chapter 16

I had recuperated sufficiently to feel that I was now able to work again, and so after making a few phone calls and having an interview I found a driving school in need of someone to perform some part-time work for them. Pauline found herself a job in a newsagents in the centre of the town, where she stayed for a few years and was eventually to become the manageress. Eileen went to a school in an adjoining district not too far away but it meant she had to be taken there by car. This is where Valerie's new found freedom of being able to drive the car came into operation. Eileen's grumbles about the school and it's unfamiliar curriculum made me realise just what we had done. She had made all the preparations for the forthcoming GCSE exams in the school in Lincoln, and I do believe she had thought she would have done well, but because of the move and the change in the way in which things were done she was finding it very difficult indeed. She decided not to take the exams and left school after six months to take a job in a factory assembling micro chip boards. It was rather boring and exacting but she stuck it out for quite some time. I didn't know that she had also been very friendly with a young fellow in Lincoln. He came to see her in Hemel once or twice on his motorbike and after a few months he came to stay with us and found work.

Valerie and I had plenty of time to spare during the evenings as Pauline Eileen and Simon went into Hemel town very often. There were a number of entertainments suitable for young people, but it wasn't our cup of tea so when we were told there was a dance hall only a couple of miles away we paid it a visit and found it to be just what we wanted. It was a large church hall and the people were very friendly. They told us that most of them went to another hall a few miles away on a different evening, so we started to go there as well.

It is a well known fact that "Time waits for no man" and it was certainly true for us in Hemel, it seemed to fly, and it was also the case for those we had left behind in Lincoln. Christine was blessed with a baby boy (Nathan) Catherine a girl (Katie) and Janet a boy (Paul). Janet had married when we were in Lincoln. After we had been in Hemel a few months Janet, her Mum, and Paul, came down in her car and stayed with us for a couple of weeks. This brightened up Valerie's life considerably as they went out touring the area sightseeing, into town shopping, and the odd full day out visiting Theme Parks and Safari Parks. They were to come down to stay with us quite a few times.

Christine, Nathan, Catherine, and Katie came many times, sometimes we would go up to Lincoln and bring Christine and Nathan back to stay with us for a week or so, at other times we would collect Catherine and Katie, and occasionally either one of them would decide to come down on the train. Catherine liked nothing better than to explore the surrounding countryside with Valerie to keep her company and Katie in her pram.

One evening Pauline came home from work as usual but she seemed in a hurry eating her dinner and then disappeared upstairs. This wasn't like her as she would normally sit and discuss the day's happenings, but about seven-o-clock a sports car drew up and out stepped the reason for all the haste. He rang the front door bell and asked to see her, whereupon she invited him in and we were introduced. His name was Andrew, better known as Andy, and he was very smartly dressed and spoke politely in a rather quiet voice. It was then that the story began to unfold that they had first met in one of the local night clubs and had been seeing each other on a fairly regular basis ever since. Pauline had thought it was time for him to meet her Mum and Dad. His parents lived in Hemel but he had his own flat about half a mile from where we were living. It had never been difficult for me to reach a conclusion fairly quickly as to whether I liked someone or not, and this young fellow I did like. He had all the hallmarks of a real gentleman and his overall demeanour led me to believe that he and Pauline were well suited as they were both quiet, unassuming, and sensible. After that he came calling frequently. After a few months Pauline asked if she could move out and go and stay with Andy in the flat. By this time we had seen more of him and as we liked what we saw we raised no objections.

We had been at Hemel about eighteen months when Valerie and I went on our own to St. Neots, in Cambridgeshire, to see my brother Peter and his wife Rosie. They were on their own as all their family had by this time left home. It was a lovely day, nice and warm, and we spent most of the day in their beautiful garden. After promising not to leave it so long before we came to see them again we returned home. About two months later I was surprised when the two of them paid us a very short visit, so short in fact that they didn't even stay for a meal. I sensed something was not quite right. Then one morning, about two weeks later, I got a phone call from Ben (Peter's son). He said his Father had been rushed into hospital with a suspected heart attack. He was obviously very upset and the way he spoke was as if he didn't hold out much hope for Peter. I tried to reassure him by telling him that many people survived heart attacks these days. He said he would phone me as soon as he had any further information and about half an hour later he did, with the devastating news, that

His brother Peter and wife Rosie (taken in Hong Kong)

283

Peter had died. There are no adequate words to describe just how I felt, I couldn't understand it, he had appeared to be strong and perfectly healthy. Apparently I had been told that he had been in hospital with a heart problem three years before this happened and that he had been having tests periodically ever since.

Shortly after Peter was born I left home and we saw very little of each other during that time. I did see quite a lot of him after my return from abroad, especially when he helped me with some of my short-lived business ventures. When he was fifteen he joined the army as a boy soldier and the next time I saw him was at Mother's funeral, and then a few months afterwards at Jacqueline's wedding. He served in many countries, one being Malta, and it was there he met, and later married Rosie. When we were established in Lincoln we had taken the girls to see Peter and his family in St. Neots. It was the first time Valerie and the girls had met any of them. Their family of one girl and two boys; Susan, Ben, and Raymond, were quite grown up. He was only fifty three when he died. With such a big difference in our ages, some fourteen years, and my being absent for almost all of the first ten years of his life there was really very little contact between us. What little we did have I shall always remember fondly.

And now on to something entirely different where smiles and laughter were to be the order of the day. After a number of years Phillip had grown tired of cruising around the world in those magnificent P&O liners. He decided to settle down in Australia doing the same kind of job on dry land and he met and married a young Australian lady, called Claire. They set up home together in their own delightful house with a large garden and beautiful landscape. From the letters and photographs we received it was obvious they were very happy and contented, so it came as a bit of a surprise when he wrote to say they were coming to England and could they stay with us for a while until they found a place of their own. That was no problem for us with our large four bedroomed house and so one day they arrived bringing with them another surprise, their first baby daughter Emily, she would have been just a few months old. Preparations were well under way for Eileen and Simon's wedding day. It had been agreed that they would marry in a quaint old church in a sleepy village where Simon's parents lived, a few miles from Lincoln. The weather was unkind and it rained heavily on the way to the church. It was a very nice service and the participant's looked resplendent, Eileen in her white dress and veil with a red and white bouquet, Simon, best man Andy, and page boy Nathan, in their top hats and tails. Bridesmaids; Christine in pink dress with white posy, Katie in white dress with white flowered headband. The reception was held in the local village hall and was very lively and entertaining which made everyone reluctant to see it come to an end. Eileen and Simon had arranged to go to Jersey for their honeymoon. Two or three months after their return Simon was promoted but it meant having to work in Rotherham. He and Eileen soon bought a small house on the outskirts of Rotherham and settled down to married life in their own home.

Meanwhile Phillip had obtained an excellent job as an Executive Chef in a high class restaurant in Oxford street, London, and did quite a lot of travelling until he was lucky enough to be given the keys to the top flat in a high rise building in south London. The flat itself was fairly big and comfortable but I didn't like it. I helped them to move in but every time I carried something to the top I swear I could feel the building sway. It did have one benefit though as it was possible to sit in your own armchair and watch a game of first class cricket going on right under your nose as it overlooked the Oval cricket ground, where England played many of their

Test matches.

There must have been something in the air that year because no sooner had we dusted the confetti off our clothing from Eileen's wedding than it was time once more to get out the best bib and tucker for Pauline's. This time we weren't going to have to travel quite so far as it was to be held in a lovely church surrounded by a large area of lawns and trees and almost in the centre of Hemel. It took place on one of the hottest days we had experienced for years.

The church was almost full and it was a grand wedding with everything having been arranged to perfection. The bride looked strikingly beautiful and carried herself in a very composed elegant manner, accompanied by her two suitably attired bridesmaids, one the sister of the groom, Janet, and the other Katie doing the honours for the second time in the space of only a few weeks. The groom and his close friend and best man, Gideon, were exceptionally smart in their top hats and tails, and the page boy, Nathan, also in top hat and tails, sporting once more an eye catching dickie bow tie as he had done a few week's earlier. The reception went well enough, to start with. It was a very large room and all the guests were seated at small round tables, four at each one, in preparation for the sumptuous dinner which was about to be served. The past few weeks had been rather stressful as I had remembered Eileen had said my speech had been too short at her wedding with not enough content. I had spent those weeks studiously working on this one. My theme was to be the many pitfalls that surround a marriage and how best to avoid them, and in order to point out these things I had prepared a few instances which were really short stories, there were five of them, and I had timed the speech. When it was time for me to put in my twopennyworth, the Master of Ceremonies gave the table three or four resounding whacks with his auctioneer's hammer and in a loud resonant voice announced, "Pray silence for the Father of the Bride". I stood, and at the same time withdrew from my inside pocket a fairly large bundle of sheets of writing paper. Only about three sheets contained the speech! The usual niceties were said and then in full view of the expectant audience I painstakingly unfolded the bundle, hesitated, and then made a show of deliberately returning "all" of it to my pocket giving the impression of having decided to "play it by ear". That was mistake number one, even though the sighs of relief were very audible. The first two stories were told with everyone paying attention and some even put their hands together at varying intervals, but about halfway through the third I couldn't hear myself speak and hadn't the faintest idea what I was saying. I looked down at Valerie and mumbled some-thing about, it's gone! I think it must have been the heat but instead of doing the sensible thing of cutting it short I muddled my way into further difficulty by trying to explain what I was intending to say. At this stage I couldn't help but notice the uncomfortable shuffling which was taking place all around the room, but still I persisted. It did come to an end, eventually. The rest of the reception went perfectly and was a resounding success, but for me there was still to come another mistake. The master of ceremonies had dutifully announced, "The bride and her father will now lead off the dancing", but unfortunately the bride was left standing, and waited in vain for someone who was once again noticeable by his absence. I was back at the house supplying cold drinks to enable people to cool off, and had simply forgotten.

Phillip had been in the high rise flat for almost one year when he got a nice house in Watford, the flat had served it's purpose but I know Claire wasn't sorry to leave it. They had been in the new house nearly two weeks when Claire had another baby, Amy. The birth went well enough but the half hour or so leading up to it did give Phillip a problem. The telephone had been cut off as the house had been empty and the phone company had said it couldn't be put back on for at least two weeks. When he needed to call an ambulance to take Claire into Watford hospital in a hurry he had to leave her and Emily while he ran down a long road in search of a phone box. When he found a working one it was being used so he had to kick his heels for almost five minutes before he was able to make the call, and then run back to be there before the ambulance arrived. When we first moved into the crescent in Hemel it had been a nice clean respectable place but it had become decidedly scruffy when an unsavoury crowd had taken up residence in the area. So once again we decided a change of scenery would do us both good and so we moved back to Yorkshire where Eileen and Simon lived, Rotherham.

It was a fairly new council house and it looked good with decent sized rooms both upstairs and down. There was a nice sized front garden but a small corner shaped one at the back. It was only a few miles from Worsbrough Bridge and Valerie's parents came to see us quite often during the time we were to reside there, which wasn't long. Although it did appear fine from the outside it was an absolute nightmare to live in. On the very first night I woke up in a cold sweat after only being in bed half an hour, and each time I managed to drop off the same thing happened. I stuck it for a few nights and then contacted the council who sent someone to inspect it thoroughly. They did a good job but found nothing which could cause any problems. During the next week or two I spoke to some of the neighbours and found out that the house had been on fire and there had been fatalities. Normally I am not supersticious but I was certain of one thing all the time we lived there; I didn't have one decent nights sleep.

The house was about one mile from Eileen's and as it was a pleasant walk through a well cared for park she would place her new daughter Siobhan, in her pram and pop round to see us. We visited each other regularly. Valerie was happy living here although we both missed Pauline because we knew she was finding it very lonely since we left Hemel.

I was doing absolutely nothing because of the way I felt, not sleeping began to have a debilitating affect upon me and I was getting really down in the dumps, although one bright spark was a win on the football polls again, this time for £4785. I received the expected cheque and set to work putting it to good use. We needed a few things, including a new bed, which meant the winnings were depleted somewhat, but we intended to hang on to the remainder for a rainy day. Little did we know that a thunderstorm was about to descend upon us during the next few months.

One day we received a phone call from Catherine saying she was ill and could we go to see her, and if possible take Katie to stay with us for a while. We went to her home in Lincoln where we found her to be in an awful state. She was in bed alone, with only Katie to help her, as her husband had walked out. She looked terrible and complained of having violent headaches. A doctor had been that day and put the pain down to her having a migraine but there looked to be more wrong with her than that so Valerie phoned another doctor. After a short while the doctor came and as soon as he saw her he phoned for an ambulance and she was taken to the hospital in Lincoln. She was examined by a specialist who told us she was going to be transferred the next day to the Hallamshire hospital in Sheffield for a more specific examination. We stayed with her for a while and then went home, taking Katie with us. The next morning we went to Sheffield and saw Catherine. She was still very ill and had undergone many tests and the consultant surgeon said Catherine was very poorly and that she had had a Cerebral Hemorrhage. He was going to have to operate in two days time when she had become more stable. He went on to explain that it was a very dangerous operation. We went to see her again that evening and twice the following day but she had the operation the day after. We weren't able to see her until late that evening but she had recovered enough to be able to talk to us. Valerie, Katie, and I went to see her twice every day until she was well enough to be taken back to the Lincoln hospital for a few days convalescence. The Professor spoke with us again and assured us the operation had been a success and that Catherine would have no further problems and would soon be back to normal.

She appeared to be doing well in Lincoln, but then she began to complain about having severe head pains. When I asked the staff about this they said there was nothing to worry about, it was just the after effects of the operation. I wasn't satisfied and made myself a nuisance, but they all insisted there was nothing wrong. Eventually they said she was well enough to be discharged and could go home. There was no way we were going to let her go home so we took her back to Rotherham with us. After two days she still complained about the pains and said they were getting worse so we sent for our doctor. He said she needed urgent attention and phoned the Hallamshire and was told to bring here there straight away. We took her and she was immediately put to bed in a private room. During the next few hours she had a number of tests, then the same Professor spoke to us and told us that there was a serious problem. Apparently there was an infection in the bone which had been removed, and replaced, during the operation and she would have to undergo another operation which would mean removing that particular piece of bone.

I have vivid painful memories of sitting in that room seeing Catherine sat on the bed with her head swathed in bandages looking very sad and dejected. I knew she must have been very frightened at the prospect of having to undergo another operation, and I tried to offer her some words of comfort and encouragement, which at the time seemed totally inadequate. Despite everything she held herself under control, and along with all the other feelings I had I also felt very proud of her. She had the operation the next day and recovered fairly quickly but that didn't stop her from having to stay in hospital for six weeks. We kept her company by seeing her every day. Katie was a real brick, she had seen her Mum in this awful situation but she had been very understanding for one so young. Catherine was discharged and needed time to convalesce and we insisted she come to stay with us instead of going to the hospital in Lincoln. She stayed with us for a few more weeks and when she said she felt strong enough to look after herself and Katie we took them home to Lincoln and saw them settled in.

We kept in close touch with Catherine by phone and she seemed to be making good progress so it was time to do something about a move. When we had been in Rotherham about seven months we were fortunate enough to get an exchange of houses with someone in Long Eaton, Nottinghamshire. Some urgent repairs to our car and the cost of the very large furniture removals van depleted the winnings still further and were now close to being completely exhausted. We had to concentrate on the job in hand, and that was to thoroughly clean the house from top to bottom as it was unbelievably filthy. Valerie was hard at it for well over a month removing thickly engrained dirt from walls, doors, skirting boards, window frames. One day Robert came to see us and seeing the state the place was in told me to forget about any decorating as he would make all the arrangements for it to be done from top to bottom by a professional. He did and the place was upside down for about two weeks. When it was finished we had a lovely bright house. Valerie and Robert had made this possible so now it was my turn to open my shoulders and put my back into the task of making the garden look presentable. Our predecessor had kept a large dog and we were to be told by the neighbours it was never taken for walks. They said the place always had an awful smell and it was so bad they were unable to sit outside in their own garden. I decided to dig down to a depth of at least one yard and a half and in so doing turn the mess of a so called lawn into the bottom together with all the other surface soil. It was going to be a marathon task but I was determined it would be done properly with no half measures.

I was also "chafing at the bit" to get back into the saddle (front seat, of a driving school car). Old habits die hard and if I could find something to relieve those pangs, even if it were only for two or three lessons a week, my longings would be satisfied. After taking a trip into Derby and showing my credentials to the owner of a large driving school he agreed to phone me to do the odd hour or two here and there, and I was back in business.

Then it was time for the excavations. I started at the bottom end and got stuck in. Slowly I worked my way back towards the house. In my excavations I came across a full sized coiled spring bed and a coiled spring mattress, more then four dozen pint glass bottles in bin bags. There were hundreds of pieces of glass, broken bottles, rusty steel bars, curtain rails, and all manner of rusty bolts, screws, nails, pieces of iron and many hessian bags full of goodness knows what. I came across at least six separate piles of bones, where some animal had been laid to rest, most probably dogs. It took almost six months to complete and had absolutely shattered me, so much so that I looked forward to going to work for those few odd hours each week for a rest.

The really hard work having been done, a design was decided upon and a fence was erected at the end of the garden and a small gate and a five barred gate across the front. The whole of the garden was then dug over and a number of beds constructed down both sides, across the top, along the bottom, and all suitably fertilised. Some shrubs and a variety of herbaceous plants were purchased and planted, and all that was necessary then was to prepare the base for a lawn and lay the turf. The weather was beautiful so we Valerie and I were perspiring and feeling hot and bothered. We couldn't have chosen a much worse day for tearing around as we were expected at Eileen's in the afternoon for Siobhan's birthday party. By the time we had finished it was two o'clock. Despite both of us feeling more than a little up tight during the journey to Rotherham we made it.

We now had a nice home and garden and resigned ourselves to settling down here. I felt sure Valerie would not appreciate another move and I certainly didn't want one. We found two places to go sequence dancing and a leisure centre with a large swimming pool. We availed ourselves of their facilities as often as we could in between visiting our families and friends, or accommodating them when they came to see, and stay, with us. Janet, her son Paul, and her Mum, came frequently, Jacqueline and Harry popped in now and again, as did Robert and his family. The second summer we were there the girls, Christine, Pauline, Catherine, and Eileen, must have thought their Mum and Dad could do with a rest so they arranged for us to go to a holiday camp near Yarmouth for a week. Catherine and Katie accompanied us and we had a reasonable time but it was marred by the awful weather, it rained all the way there and all the time we were there and it was so bad that on the Thursday we returned home. The following year Catherine booked another one, this time in a different camp but still near Yarmouth and it was a great holiday with lovely weather. Christine was having driving lessons and had been doing so for quite a long time and when she phoned to say she had yet another test coming up I decided to give her the benefit of my expertise and went over to Lincoln on two days and put her through the hoop. It must have done some good because she passed the test. Catherine and Katie had been happy in their new house but when we moved to the Nottingham area she expressed a desire to be near us and sought an exchange. She was successful and was now living in a nice house in Lenton Abbey on the outskirts of Nottingham, about three miles from where we were.

The "sands of time " had been ticking on relentlessly, and so it was that I awoke one morning to realise that I had reached the "end of the line" according to the well known adage "the life expectancy of man is three score years and ten". Obviously I had been aware of this milestone in my life but as far as I was concerned it was only a day, like any other day. I had been informed we were going to Catherine's for dinner at twelve noon. We had a lovely meal and a nice chat, and around two thirty I thought it was time we returned home to enable me to do my jobs before it got dark. I kept suggesting we made a move to Valerie but each time she came up with an excuse for us to stay a bit longer. I never thought anything of it because she was always reluctant to leave whenever we were there. Eventually we all piled into the car, Valerie, me, and Catherine and Katie as well, and came home. I do remember thinking at the time why they were coming with us as it would surely

Jacqueline and Harry taken at Lancaster University Hotel where their son Gary was presented with an MBA

make them late getting home that night. Anyway, upon our arrival they all got out of the car, Valerie unlocked the front door and they went inside. I got out of the car and went to lock it up and saw a load of balloons draped around the windows and a large bright red banner fastened across the front of the house proclaiming in white lettering, 70 years old today. I went into the house, took off my shoes, and opened the front room door to be met with the loudest rendering of Happy Birthday I have ever heard. The room was choc-o-block with the girls and all their families. They had taken me completely by surprise and something happened to me which very rarely occurred, I was at a loss for words. The house was decorated with streamers and balloons, and the dining room table was groaning from the amount of food stacked upon it. In it's centre was an exceptionally large and beautifully decorated birthday cake, with seventy

289

candles of different colours. I was to learn that this extravagant party had been arranged a long time ago, each one of them having been allotted a certain task to perform. Some of them had travelled hundreds of miles, other's rather less. It was a well organised plan and one of which I would have been proud.

Valerie and I had settled down and were enjoying a reasonably quiet life here although we didn't travel very far. The garden was now a source of pleasure as all the hard work had been done. The driving lessons were few and far between and those there were came at short notice and interfered with our plans. I decided to end my association with the driving school and do as I should have done quite a few years ago, retire altogether. My intention being to do absolutely nothing and spend all my time with Valerie. We would be able to do exactly what we wanted. When the children had been small I had contributed very little to their upbringing, it had all rested on Valerie's shoulders. I have only myself to blame for that but I could make amends in some small way and that was my intention. So, I had everything organised in my mind and it seemed to be working

Jack's 70th surprise birthday taken at Long Eaton Nottingham in 1992

nicely during those first fourteen days of my retirement. Then, on the fifteenth, exactly two years and nine months after my 70th birthday, I went to bed that evening and woke up the following morning only to find that I was unable to move my left leg or arm.

The doctor paid me a visit and confirmed my fears; I was a victim of the dreaded "stroke" and it had adversely affected my brain in some way. That immediately put paid to almost everything. I couldn't go swimming, dancing, walking, shopping, or do even the smallest of small activities in the garden. For the first week or two I was practically a vegetable. Then I began to gingerly exercise both arm and leg and thankfully they responded, and as each day passed I increased the exercise until finally I could, somewhat hesitantly, walk around the room and use the arm slightly. There was nothing really painful about any of it just a feeling of frustration at the slowness of the progress, until eventually I put the leg through it's paces by taking a slow walk a few yards up the street and back, it was then that it tightened up, refused to go, and hurt like blazes. It took weeks of extending the walk each day and making it perform but gradually I reached a stage whereby I could walk to town and back, about two miles, albeit with quite a number of stops and rests on the way, but I had cracked it, all that was needed now was to keep at it.

During this time I had been to the hospital and had various types of check-up in different departments. One day I was sent to the neurology specialist who put me on a course of Warfarin tablets, and blood pressure tablets. He gave me a barely understandable explanation as to why the stroke had taken place. From what I was able to decipher it had arisen from a burst blood vessel in the right hand side of the brain which consequently affected the left hand parts of the body. The Warfarin was to thin the blood down, and the others to lower the blood pressure. Hopefully both would help to avoid a repetition. For the first month I had to attend the hospital every day for a blood count. I began to feel the effects the Warfarin was having upon me after only a few weeks. I became very weak and listless and I experienced great difficulty walking. I persisted and took both tablets as prescribed but when it got to the eighth month I was feeling so bad that I decided enough was enough and stopped taking the Warfarin. Every muscle in my body either ached or was very painful so I went to see my own doctor.

He was alarmed at the state I was in and told me he thought I had contracted a serious illness called Poly Myalgia which weakens the muscles, and put me on a large dose of steroids, and arranged for me to attend the Rheumatology department in yet another hospital, where the illness was confirmed. Since then I have been attending that hospital on a regular basis, usually once every month, to have the blood count checked. For various reasons more tablets have been added to those I was originally taking, and I swallow such a large number every day that if I were able to jump up and down I would surely rattle. I am now out of all proportion with an exceptionally large girth, and a fat face, the left arm and leg perform sometimes and both ache and hurt regularly. The weakness in the muscles in my back prevent me from standing up for more than a few minutes, I cannot have a bath without someone being in attendance and giving assistance in the washing and drying process, and the simple task of fastening and unfastening shoe laces leaves me breathless. All of this has made a right cock-up of everything I intended to do or practically anything I am ever likely to want to do. To say I am cheesed off would be an understatement and I cannot help thinking that had I been left alone to my own devices things would have been better. I am bitter and I think under the circumstances I have every reason to feel this way.

What about Valerie? Everything we had looked forward to doing together, the dancing, swimming, shopping, walking, gardening, all had now gone by the board. She had brought up the girls and looked after everything and everyone with very little help from me and as soon as it became possible for her to relax a bit and start to enjoy life she was once more tied down in the home, looking after me. She is now required to wait around for hours in hospitals and has to lift and carry things which she should never have to do. All of the above I find hard to come to terms with.

When the initial effects from the stroke had receded somewhat I was able to resume driving because we had an automatic car. During my term of enforced incarceration we had plenty of visitors and we were now able to return the favours by going to see them. Catherine, Katie, Valerie, and myself, had previously booked another caravan holiday in Skegness for later on that year, 1996, and again we had a very nice time. The weather was good, warm and sunny, and we spent more time on the sea front than anything else. We had been there a couple of days when Catherine had a visitor, a young man she had known from the time she lived in

291

Lincoln, and he stayed in the caravan with us for the rest of the week. He seemed to be a decent sort of chap, very friendly and accommodating and he saw Catherine regularly when we returned home. It came as no surprise when Catherine said they were going to be married. It took place in the registrar's office at Caistor in November of that same year and a reception was held in the village hall at Faldingworth, both in Lincolnshire. Thankfully I wasn't called upon to make a speech and it all went off to the satisfaction and pleasure of all concerned.

For the next eighteen months things were to travel on an almost even keel. One day Shirley, Robert's wife, phoned me and asked if I had seen the item on television which stated that a special service for members of the Palestine Police Old Comrades Association, a 50th Anniversary "Stand Down" Memorial Service, was to be held in York Minster. She gave me the phone number of the person to contact for further information. I spoke to a Mr. Reg Saxon, an ex Palestine Policeman and the secretary of the Yorkshire branch of the Palestine Police Old Comrades Association. An association I hadn't known existed. Reg and I discussed many things and apart from his insistence that it would be in my best interests to join his merry band he gave me the details of the forthcoming service in the Minster to which were invited all ex-Palestine Policemen, their families and friends. I spoke to him again a few days later when it had been decided that Jacqueline and Harry, and Robert and Shirley, would accompany Valerie and myself on the day. The service was to take place on Sunday the 17th May at 2pm and it had been arranged that we would form up and parade outside the Minster before the service. It was obligatory for all service medals to be worn, which was something which gave me a problem as I had disposed of mine some eighteen years before. Unbeknownst to me, Eileen decided to give me a pleasant surprise by contacting a numismatist in his shop in Sheffield and arranging for him to make a further set, which he made as a lighter 'dress' set, which I wore on the day.

Reg had sent me all the necessary tickets but about two weeks before the occasion Phillip and his lady friend Hasmik arrived from Australia to stay with Robert for a few weeks. I obtained tickets for them without any problems. On the day we had set off in what we thought was plenty of time but we hadn't reckoned with the volume of traffic we were to meet and consequently we arrived late. There was just enough time to meet up with Jacqueline and Harry and then present ourselves, and our tickets, to the three ex-PPs on duty at the door leading to the Minster Chapel where the service was due to begin. We were each handed a booklet containing the Order of Service (on the front cover of this booklet was a picture of a British Palestine Police Constable in full uniform and wearing a leg holster containing a revolver) and ushered to our seats.

When we had settled down my inquisitive nature prompted me to take a look around and I couldn't help but notice that white or grey hair was very much in evidence! The Canon in Residence, asked the congregation to stand, and the Palestine Police Colours, unfurled, were majestically carried into the Chapel by the standard bearer accompanied by two escorts and presented to the Canon. He placed them reverently upon the altar with the colour itself draped over the front. Then a very poignant service began. The Canon spoke of the British policeman in a foreign country, surrounded by people he didn't know, finding himself in many tricky situations and always exposed to acts of terrorism. How dangerous the work was, knowing he could possibly die there. Towards the end a bugler sounded the 'Last Post'.

Phillip volunteered to collect the car while we waited at the rear entrance to the Minster for him to come and take us to the re-union meeting and the buffet. The streets all around were busy and thronged with people and traffic and once again we were late, and we arrived after everyone else. It was a scorchingly hot day and as my legs weren't up to standard I chose to sit in the grassed quadrangle. Valerie and Jacqueline got hold of a couple of plates each and went along the line of tables which had, contained the buffet, but had been practically exhausted by the time we arrived. Eventually I pushed my way through to where the actual meeting was taking place in another room but when I finally reached the entrance I couldn't get in for people standing two or three deep on the approach to it. I did manage to speak with one or two chaps, none that I knew, but it was a nice day out and I do believe we all thoroughly enjoyed it.

Valerie and I were still adding improvements to our abode and as she had expressed the desire for a patio at the rear of the house at the time when I had completed the garden renovation some three years earlier, I thought it high time she got her wish, and I had one made, and at the same time I had the front drive improved. The garden furniture, chairs, table, and canopy, took their places on the patio, and the car stood majestically in it's neatly designed surroundings.

Valerie appeared to be pleased with our improvements, and as she had been able for the past three years to tootle off to see Catherine, and pop into town whenever she liked, she seemed to be enjoying herself. Even though my requirements were many she never complained. Everything was fine, in spite of all the trouble my problems must have caused her, and we were happy enough.

The 50th Anniversary stand down of the Palestine Police Force at York Minister, 17th May 1998 - Proudly showing off his medals

One day in September of that year '98, I received a call from Robert who told me there was a new car about to be marketed under the name Skoda Octavia. He went on to say that he wanted me to have a look at one, an automatic, in a garage near me to see what I thought to it as someone he knew was interested. The garage in question wasn't far away so Valerie and I popped over to have a look and a chat to the salesman. As we liked what we saw I asked to be taken for a run in it. It was an exceptionally comfortable ride and looked very impressive. I had thought it was a strange request by Robert as he was more than capable of making his own decisions, far more capable than I was, but I had done as he had asked and returned his phone call telling him of my findings. It was then he revealed who the interested party was, ME. He arranged for one to be delivered to me in October. From then on we drove around in style.

I had been taken by surprise at Robert's decision to provide me with a new car but what he did next bowled me over completely.

About two weeks after taking delivery of the car Valerie and I drove up to Yorkshire and we had a nice day with them as Shirley, Victoria, and James, were there. At some time during the conversations he said, quite casually, "I don't think you should be climbing stairs, a bungalow would be much better for you, so decide where you would like to live and find one suitable". Such a startling announcement left me dumbfounded. However, he was serious and there was only one thing for me to do and that was to do as he suggested and find a bungalow. The conversation between Valerie and myself during the journey back to Long Eaton was quite something. I don't think either of us could take it in. Eventually Catherine found one located down a country lane and it was brilliant. It had three bedrooms, a very spacious kitchen diner, a front room and a gorgeous bathroom, complete with shower. The gardens front and rear were big and as they were both lawned they left plenty of room for improvement. There was a ten feet high double iron gate into a driveway which could hold at least seven cars, and a double garage. We liked it, Robert went to see it, and that is where we are now living.

About two months before we left, and before we knew of the move, I had cause to attend the eye clinic at the hospital where it was confirmed that I had cataracts in both eyes and was put on the waiting list to have them operated on. A few weeks after that visit I had reason to go again as one day I felt something like a fly strike the eyeball of my right eye. I rubbed it but the feeling still remained and after a few minutes I couldn't see anything at all out of that eye. Upon my return to the eye clinic some six or seven days later I was told I had suffered a mini stroke and that when things had settled down I would probably be able to see, but only straight ahead. They were correct in their assessment as it did improve but I had very limited vision straight forward, and could see nothing to the right except rolling images of numbers, circles and hexagons.

When the weather picked up a bit in April we made borders and beds in the back lawn but as neither of us were capable of doing any hard digging Catherine and Chris came and did the honours. We have now got things more or less to our liking. I don't have to struggle climbing stairs as there aren't any, the sides of the shower are such that I can lean up against them to get my breath back. I still need assistance for the lower leg and feet but at least I can manage, after a fashion. For the first two or three months here I did some driving but then reached the conclusion that I shouldn't because my eyesight had become worse. Valerie has now taken over the responsibility of chauffeuring me around. Old habit's die hard and it is extremely difficult to sit there and make no comment. Valerie is my wife, my life, the Mother of our children, my right hand man, and looking at it from a selfish point of view without her I would be hard pushed to survive, so even though she takes umbrage, I shall still comment where necessary. During the next couple of years Valerie and I had many visitors and we made quite a few trips around the country seeing our girls and their families. In March 2000 I had the cataract operation on my left eye, and in the December of that same year the right eye was done, both have been reasonably successful but the impaired vision of the right hasn't improved as the mini stroke damaged the optic nerves.

It is now mid-March in the year 2001, my 79th came and went on the eleventh. Owing to circumstances beyond my control there have been times when I was unable to proceed for some reason or another, nevertheless I have finally arrived at the end. I have endeavoured to avoid boring anyone to tears, whether it is with or without success only you can tell, but I do hope you will have gained something in the reading thereof as that has been my whole intention. I am very pleased to have been able to inform you of some of the more interesting aspects of my life and to enlighten you of things and times of which you will have known very little. The story is ended, but not my life, and I do sincerely hope to be allowed to hang around quite a bit longer.

SUMMARY

So many things have happened in my life and I have chosen the ones that I thought would be of most interest to the reader. On the whole they are mostly ones with a touch of humour in them. Some things I have written in a very sombre manner, as there is nothing funny about them at all, but my aim was to recount my life in a light hearted vein, with a twinkle in my eye and a smile playing around my lips. I hope I have succeeded.

I have tried to portray how things were during the early years of my life where almost everything was so different to what it is now. The changes make for a much better way of life, just as the place where I was brought up has changed. It wasn't noted for it's affluence and times were extremely difficult for the majority of the people. Any change is nearly always accompanied by drawbacks and discomforts, and this is the case with our overall change in lifestyle. When I was a child we used to go for pleasant walks in the countryside, unaccompanied, just a few kids together, and spend hours climbing trees and playing hide and seek in the woods, or we would play games in a quiet street with a lamp post as the focal point. Inevitably there were also times when we would indulge in some kind of games which were regarded as being mischievous but they never amounted to much and there was nothing malicious about any of them. These activities and others used to get us out of the house, our parents knew where we were to a certain extent and we had few problems.

The final part of this summary takes on a more personal note. I think it fair to say that for practically everyone a look back in hindsight would inevitably bring about the wish to change something, but in my case it would amount to doing almost everything differently! I have done so many things wrong and made so many mistakes that when I look back it is paramount to finding myself in the "House of Horrors". I won't mention them all again, but here are a few. My first big mistake was joining that particular branch of the Territorial Army in the village of Wentworth. I could and should have been allowed to choose the type of soldiering I wished to do, and that wasn't it.

Joining the Palestine Police Force was definitely the best thing I ever did but it brought about what I consider to be the biggest mistake of my whole life, which can be laid firmly at the door of my being such a big-head and having the mistaken belief that I knew best regardless of what anyone else may say to the contrary. I didn't listen to people I now know had my best interests at heart and consequently went ahead with my marriage. I cannot rid myself of the thought that if I hadn't married and had made a career out of being a Colonial Police Officer my whole life could have been entirely different. When I started this book it had been my intention not to divulge in any kind of detail the problems I had during the years of that first marriage but then it became all too apparent that if I didn't do so it would be impossible to account for the kind of life I was forced to lead. I have still not gone into detail of a lot that took place but I feel enough has been told for you to get the overall picture. But a great deal of good came out of my first marriage in the shape of my three sons and my daughter. I suppose it can be said, without fear of contradiction, that those good things outweigh the bad.

I have been big-headed, self opinionated, and bolshie, with a reluctance to make friends. I have managed to keep alcohol at arms length but have allowed the objectionable habit of cigarette smoking to become my master. It is quite possible that some people have found that I have considerably more faults than I have mentioned! To others I say, having made you aware of my many faults throughout this story it may seem rather inappropriate for me to offer some advice but I think it could be of some help. Children, if you have been able to read this then you are old enough to understand what I am about to say and to act accordingly. I know this may come as a shock to you but your parents do have their problems in more ways than you think; in the majority of cases finance being the usual one, so when something doesn't go exactly as you wish, spare a thought for your parents and see things from their point of view.

To parents I say, don't let work dominate your life to such an extent that you neglect your wife or your family. Make time for relatives and friends, I emphasize this because I have been guilty on both counts. Remember what I have previously said about not leaving things till tomorrow what you could do today. You have no idea what problems can arise from allowing this to happen.

Just a few more words to, "get me off the hook", so to speak. If I haven't written as much about any one particular person as they think I should it doesn't mean that I think any the less of you for not having done so.

Jack's surprise 80th birthday party in March 2002

297

RESUME

Just in case you are wondering what happened to some of the person's I have had cause to mention in my travels, and to bring you up to date with the progress of my two families, the few paragraphs hereunder will enlighten you.

Johnny Love - My partner incrime during my early years in Wombwell with whom I first tasted the delight's of the Tobacco Weed, and who was someone I shall be ever grateful to for being partly responsible for persuading my Father, (the very amateur barber), to discard his decrepit hair cutting shears, as that decision saved me from many painful hours of sitting on a stool while my Father attempted to make my bonce look respectable with those practically toothless shears. When we moved to Barnsley I lost touch with Johnny and haven't seen him since.

Brian Greaves - The young chap with the large appetite for fish cakes and chips which we used to enjoy on our return cycle journey's from the T/A drill hall in Wentworth. He was my constant companion throughout the war until I left the regiment in Italy to go to Palestine. He came to see me at my parents home soon after I returned, and I went to see him three times when he was working in his Mother's shop in Barnsley but when I went again many years later he wasn't around so I am not sure what happened to him.

Patrick Carey - A good pal in so many ways, our trips together to many dance hall up and down the country were memorable to say the least. He was a good boxer and he and I went to great pains trying to show the German prisoners of war in a camp in North Africa that boxing can be a mild and gentle sport! Our friendship very nearly came to an end in a watery grave when that ferocious tide in Swanage Bay did it's best to sweep the pair of us out to sea. He was a Scotsman from Stirling and we haven't seen each other since my departure from the regiment in Italy.

Peter Mills - He of the "exceptionally high" diving skills. We met for the first time on board the liberty ship in Toronto harbour, Italy, bound for Palestine with that short stop-over in Augusta bay, Sicily. The larger part of my time in the Police Force was spent in his company and he proved to be a really good friend eventually performing the duties of Best Man at my wedding to Anna. He remained in the Force until 1948 and in 1949 I went to see him at his parent's home in Penge, South London. Unfortunately I didn't keep in touch and haven't seen him since.

Anna - She didn't re-marry. She was visited at infrequent intervals by Laurice, Phillip, and Michael, but Robert saw her regularly and took care of her. When she died in the mid-nineties I was informed but, rightly or wrongly, I chose not to attend her funeral, I feel that to have done so would have been hypocritical.

Michael - Has kept himself to himself as far as I have been concerned, and I think it fair to say that I haven't seen him more than six times since he walked out on the family to take up residence in his future wife's Mother's home, He has worked exceptionally hard both before and after his divorce and from what I can gather from his very few phone calls he has at last achieved his aim of being a successful businessman. He has re-married and has one daughter, Estelle, they live in a nice house near the south coast and he seems happy enough.

Phillip - Has lead a very interesting but at times turbulent life and now lives permanently in Australia with his new wife, Hasmik, having divorced his first wife, Claire many years ago. He thinks the world of his two daughters, Emily and Amy, from his marriage to Claire and sees them often as he resides close to them in Melbourne. He makes fairly frequent trips to England, usually staying for a few months at a time, which gives us the opportunity to enjoy his company. I think he is happy with his lot even though it hasn't been without its problems.

Robert - has done well for himself having worked exceptionally hard in doing so. He is happily married to Shirley, and their two children, James and Victoria are a credit to them in every way. Shirley is a member of a golf club and spends as much time as possible, weather permitting, teeing off on one golf course or another. We see them often but nowhere near as often as we would like, their home is quite a long way from here and somewhat out in the wilds fairly close to the Pennine range where the weather in wintertime can be quite atrocious. The past few years of my life would have been pretty mediocre without the assistance he has afforded me in so many ways, and both Valerie and I will be ever grateful.

Laurice - Life hasn't been too kind to her for many reasons but she has always faced it with a smile. Her marriage to Frank failed after only a very short period of time but their son Matthew, who will now be in his late twenty's, was happy enough living with the other three children she was to have, Michael now in his mid twenty's, Martin in his early twenty's, and Maxine early twenty's. Martin has three children, Daniel, Stephanie, and Caitlen. Maxine has one boy and one girl, Shannon and Aiden. Matthew had one little boy, Billy Rae, but he was born with all kinds of problems, and after undergoing at least three major operations and putting up a terrific fight to survive it was all in vain and he died, aged two months, poor little chap he tried so hard to stay with us. The Baby Intensive Care Unit at the Queens Medical Centre in Nottingham are to be congratulated for the tender loving care they gave to the so tiny Billy Rae. We used to live close to Laurice when we were in Lincoln and saw all of them every day but since our four moves it hasn't been all that easy, however we do visit them occasionally, not enough by any means, but we do keep in close touch by phone.

Valerie - Is kept very busy looking after home and husband. Nuff said.

Christine - Is a busy little bee, her six children see to that. Nathan, Natalie (not partial to school), Samuel, loves school and has been in the school football team since his days in the junior's and by all accounts is quite some player in his role as a defender. Blake, again loves school and again is also in a school football team as an attacker and left winger, I am aware of his abilities to thump a ball with his left foot having seen them at first hand. Jessica, was a very shy little girl but has now come out of her shell. Emily, cried continuously for the first month or two but has now changed to a very quiet and contented baby, (when fed to her complete satisfaction). For reasons best known to herself Christine has chosen not to get married but she breezes through life as if she hasn't a care in the world with more hearty laughs than scowls. Things cannot be easy but she carries all before her and appears to be happy enough, most of the time. She visits us on a fairly regular basis and we go to see her although not often enough, but things should change now this seemingly endless saga has finally reached it's conclusion.

Pauline - Has been happily married to Andrew. They have three children, Daniel, Kirsty- a very quiet and shy young lady but is gradually being brought out of her shell by the sometimes tom boy qualities of her brother and younger sister, Chloe, she has a mind of her own but very sweet with it. Their home is a long way from here and we don't go very often but they come to see us frequently usually staying for a day or two. Andrew is preparing the photographs I need for this book, it is quite a mammoth task but he is well qualified and says he enjoys doing it.

Catherine - Did have serious health problems as you know but she is happy enough now since her son Ashley arrived on the scene. He is a proper livewire keeping her and Chris on their toes and running rings round his elder sister Katie. They are happy and as they live only three miles away, we see them regularly, Catherine is delighted at our move to be near them and so are we as they have been a great help to us in many ways.

Eileen - We did think she was happy with her husband Simon but somewhere along the line things turned sour and they were divorced. They have two children, Siobhan, she was a delightful child but seems to have taken her parent's problem to heart and is now very moody, but Hannah, appears, I say again, appears, to have coped rather better and has been very understanding for one so young. They are both doing well at school and have made many close friends and it is a shame that their home life has been disrupted in such a manner. Eileen had taken a course at college and after two years qualified as a Nursery Nurse which is a good thing because she is now able to support herself and her two girls doing such work, she has bought a small house in a nice area and making the best of things even though, in my opinion, she seems to be always on the go with very little time for herself. They live about seven miles from here and visit us on a fairly regular basis, we on the other hand are not so regular with our visits to them, they have been very few and far between, except when it has been a necessity for some reason or another. I do feel very sorry for the way things have turned out for Eileen as we couldn't have wished for a more caring and helpful daughter, and we can only hope the future will bring her happiness, she most certainly deserves it.

Jacqueline - My baby sister, who just had to spoil my peaceful day fishing by falling into the canal. She has been married to Harry for umpteen years and they have three boys, Clive, who will soon retire from the police force after completing twenty five years. Timothy, who followed in his Father's footsteps and became a Joiner. Gary, who's head for figures has served him well in the upper echelon's of high finance. Clive and his wife Elizabeth have two children, Joanne, has expressed her desire to become a Veterinary surgeon and is studying towards that end, and Emma, has still to decide what to do but is a sporty type. Timothy and his wife Jayne have six children, Samantha, Laura, doing very well at school and a good all round athlete, Luke, a lively little lad, Thomas, bit of a card, and likes nothing better than to rummage around in his grandfather's workshop, and quite adept at making things in timber by all accounts, Joshua, apparently much quieter than the others- a thinker, Elicia, has no inclinations towards anything at the moment. Gary and his wife Michelle have two children, Naomi and Oliver. Jacqueline and Harry moved from their home of forty years into a bungalow a few miles away on the outskirts of Wombwell and seem to be enjoying the change. They are in reasonable health even though they have both attained the seven score years and ten mark, we don't see them as often as we'd like which is a pity because they are both exceptionally pleasant and we enjoy being in their company.

Peter and Rosie's Family - Susan and her husband Leon are still living in Cambridge and have two children, Stephanie and Sophie. They are both very well mannered young ladies and the distance between our homes prevents us from seeing them very often, but they have been to our new bungalow and we've visited them a couple of times. Ben has no wish to marry but he is a keen gardener and has a lovely garden at the house where he lives on the outskirts of Cambridge. Raymond and his wife Amanda live in Silkstone Fall, a countryside offshoot from Barnsley, and they have two children, Adam and Callum. We have yet to visit them but they did come to Long Eaton to see us.

The members of my Father's side of the family deserted me completely and there is very little I can add to what has already been said on that painful subject, except to say that my life has been very much the poorer because of it. Jacqueline told me she had been in contact with our cousin Mae up to a few years ago and by then she would have been well into her eighties, and I did hear that uncle John had been blind for quite a long time before he died at the age of ninety plus. I hadn't seen any one of them for years except for uncle Harold on those few occasions I have previously mentioned. It was an unfortunate state of affairs but I have only myself to blame. All of which leaves me very sad, very sad indeed.

The members of my Mother's side of the family have all lived within the confines of Norwich during their latter years and except for uncle Ted and his wife Gladys I haven't seen any of them for more than the briefest of visits on the odd occasion. When I attended Ted's funeral I met Mother's elder sister Gladys and her daughter Sheila and son Raymond, and her elder brother Sonny and his two daughters, but the only contact I have had since then has been to speak to Sheila on the phone. They were a fairly close knit family and it is a shame I didn't see them more often as it would have been nice to have known them all better.

The members of Valerie's Family all live in or around Barnsley except for her younger brother Johnny, he has been around a bit and has had more than his fair share of problems but has finally settled in Lancashire. He has been married three times and has two sons, the one to his first wife is named John, a big strapping young fellow who obtained a number of trophies playing football for a local team much to the delight of his Grandfather who followed his career with great enthusiasm. He married but has no children. The other was born to his third wife, and is only a very young boy named Macblain. Janet, the elder of her two sisters has been happily married to Alec for yonks and they have two children, both married, Diane, she has two children, Arron and Alec, young Alec. The other, Stephen, he has two also, Dean, and Dale. Her other sister, Margaret has been happily married to Geoff for ? years, they have three children, Dawn, she has two children, Christopher, a staunch rugby player, and Amee, following in her Grandad's footsteps with her love for playing the piano. Then Geoff, obviously known as Young Geoff, he has also two children, Tara, hopes to go to college, and Darcy. Their youngest, Karen, a career woman, has one boy, Thomas. Valerie's father, John, worked down the mine all his life and died a few years ago aged eighty six, her Mother, Mary, only recently passed away from a heart attack, also aged eighty six. When Valerie and I left Barnsley together in 1966 quite understandably it gave rise to many worries for her parents, those worries should have been allayed much sooner than they were, but under the circumstances we thought it best not to inform them of our whereabouts straight away, we were wrong, and I, not Valerie, accept full responsibility for that wrong as it was entirely my misguided decision, regretfully.

I bring this resumé to a very sad conclusion by relating a set of events which are beyond all understanding. Ever since the time when we had moved into that tiny house our neighbours, Janet, and her mum Jean, had been very much a part of our lives, during those first few years there they were a great help to Valerie when the girls were little and after Janet had passed her driving test she took Valerie and the girls all over the country, sometimes to places of entertainment long distances away. Janet got married and had a son, Paul, unfortunately the marriage didn't last and she returned home to live with her Mum and Dad, but her Dad died shortly afterwards. They were frequent visitors to the various houses we had and stayed with us for a week or so in Hemel a few times. It was when we were living in Long Eaton that Jean became ill and was taken into hospital, we knew she hadn't been well for a long time but were totally unprepared for what happened, after only a few days she died. Five years later Janet became ill and went into hospital with some kind of breathing problem, she had been visiting her doctor regularly but nothing specific had been diagnosed although she said she had been feeling really ill for quite some time. When Paul phoned to say she had been admitted to hospital it was only a couple of days after I suffered the stroke and Valerie was reluctant to leave me unattended so she phoned Catherine, she went to the hospital that same evening and phoned us that night to say Janet didn't appear to be too bad and that she was hoping to leave hospital in a few days. Three days after she had been admitted Paul was sitting with her and she was holding his hand and talking to him quite normally, then suddenly she stopped breathing. He was a young fellow about nineteen but his Grandmother and his Mum had kept him very much under their wing and he had only recently come out of his shell enough to find himself a very nice young lady, but the awful experience of the manner in which his Mum had died, so abruptly and so unexpectedly, caused him to suffer greatly from a nervous disorder. It was put down to many things, the loss of his Grandma whom he adored, and the tragic circumstances of his Mother's death, and he was treated accordingly by his doctor, nothing specific really but more a case of trying to settle him down but he never got over the trauma, and when we had been here in the bungalow about eighteen months we received a phone call from his young lady saying he had been taken into Lincoln hospital. Valerie and Catherine went to see him in the Hallamshire hospital in Sheffield as he had been transferred to there the day before, and although it was never made clear what excatly was wrong with him he died a few days later. However it was eventually confirmed that his death was due to a brain hemorrhage. Jean had died unexpectedly, Janet had died suddenly, and for no apparent reason at the time Paul also died suddenly, all within the space of a few years, and had brought about the untimely end of a family in who's company we had all obtained great pleasure in so many ways.